# WEEDS OF THE
# PACIFIC NORTHWEST

MARK TURNER AND SAMI GRAY

PHOTOGRAPHY BY MARK TURNER

# WEEDS

## *of the*

## PACIFIC

## NORTHWEST

────────────

### 368 UNWANTED PLANTS
### AND HOW TO CONTROL THEM

TIMBER PRESS

PORTLAND, OREGON

Endpapers by Kerry Cesen

Photo credits appear on page 434.

The information in this book is true and complete to the best of our knowledge.
All recommendations are made without guarantee on the part of the authors or
Timber Press. The authors and publisher disclaim any liability in connection with
the use of this information. In particular, eating wild plants or using them medicinally is inherently risky. Plants can be easily mistaken and individuals vary in their
physiological reactions to plants that are touched or consumed. Although we
have included information about potential edibility, medicinal use, and toxicity
for most species, this book is primarily a guide to identification and is explicitly
*not* a foraging guide.

Published in 2024 by Timber Press, Inc., a subsidiary of
Workman Publishing Co., Inc., a subsidiary of Hachette Book Group, Inc.

1290 Avenue of the Americas
New York, New York 10104

timberpress.com

The publisher is not responsible for websites (or their content) that are not owned
by the publisher. The Hachette Speakers Bureau provides a wide range of authors
for speaking events. To find out more, go to hachettespeakersbureau.com or
email HachetteSpeakers@hbgusa.com.

Printed in China on responsibly sourced paper

Text and cover design by Kelley Galbreath

ISBN 978-1-64326-108-9

A catalog record for this book is available from
the Library of Congress.

We dedicate this book to
Sami's father, Lysle Benton Gray
(8 November 1926–4 November 2020),
who always wanted her
to write a book.

# Contents

# Preface

Weeds are everywhere. They crowd out valuable agricultural crops, compete with the tomatoes and beans in your vegetable garden, spread rampantly along roads big and small, and pop up from the tiniest cracks in urban sidewalks. Some are so well established, and have been part of our environment for so long, that many people think they're native. And some fine native plants have a weedy character that leads them to become unwanted in certain circumstances.

When we first started planning this book, we proposed calling it *Kill This Plant!* Our editor graciously disagreed with the title, but for many who are doing battle with unwanted and invasive plants, killing them is what we set out to do. However, other gardeners have decided to learn to live with their weeds, or at least to not get too fastidious about removing them all. Except for officially listed noxious weeds that state and provincial laws require you to control, the choice to kill or tolerate is up to you. However, your neighbors may not appreciate you letting your weeds go to seed, spreading them across their property as well as yours.

We were driven by curiosity. We wondered about the plants crowding our roadsides, sneaking into our gardens seemingly overnight, and shooting up at the edges of farm fields. While we were already familiar with many of the plants in this book, we were somewhat surprised to find that there were a significant number of non-native and potentially invasive plants that were new to us. The territory we cover is large, with many different habitats and environments. Plants that are terrible scourges west of the Cascades may not show up on the dry east side at all.

Much of the planning and thinking that went into this volume took place while wielding weeding tools in our home gardens. Mark gardens on five acres on the edge of Bellingham and composts wheelbarrow loads of creeping buttercup, shotweed, purslane, sow-thistles, ground-ivy, and other assertive weeds from his flower and vegetable beds. He's dug masses of ivy and blackberries and removed English holly from his woods. Sami gardens in containers in Port Angeles and pulls buckets of dog violets. Digging weeds can be strangely meditative, the repetitive action giving the mind plenty of time to wander.

While some of our weeds have been with us for centuries, brought to North America intentionally by European settlers as food or medicinal crops, others are new introductions to our region. We've included the great majority of both groups, so you'll find your common nemesis as well as weeds that are just starting to invade our space. Many of those newcomers are officially classed as noxious, requiring their removal before they can become widespread and well established.

First and foremost, this is an identification guide. Most entries have multiple photos so you can see key features. The subject is serious, yet we tried to keep the tone light and friendly. You might even find a bit of weird botanist humor here and there. Since weeds are by definition unwanted plants, we also suggest ways to control their growth and spread.

We relied on the much larger, and much heavier, regional floras to identify specimens in the field and as primary sources for our descriptions. Books like *Flora of the Pacific Northwest*, its big brother *Vascular Plants of the Pacific Northwest*, and both the 1993 and 2011 editions of *The Jepson Manual: Vascular Plants of California* are well-thumbed references, in some cases held together by duct tape.

In addition to printed references, we made extensive use of online resources. Herbarium and iNaturalist records guided Mark to locations to find many of the species at the right time to catch them in bloom. Websites like the Burke Herbarium Image Collection and Calflora aided in identifying plants in the field.

Botany has undergone many changes in recent years. Taxonomists have challenged old relationships and discovered new ones, often based on DNA research rather than the morphological observations of old. We used the most up-to-date names at time of writing as the primary entry and listed one or more older names as synonyms. For our older readers, many of whom learned plant names from Hitchcock and Cronquist, join us in learning the newer names as well.

We live in a complex world, full of both native and non-native plants. While learning that the pretty little yellow flowers invading your lawn are creeping buttercups and the similar-looking ones painting your pasture yellow in the spring are tall buttercups won't make either of them any less of a pest, learning the difference between poison hemlock and Queen Anne's lace could save your kid's life.

We doubt that many readers will take this book along and deliberately seek out new weeds to identify on their hikes or road trips. However, we hope you'll use it to learn about the plants that pop up in your garden or along the path you take every day when walking your dog.

# Acknowledgments

*Weeds of the Pacific Northwest* would not have been possible without the help of the many people who generously lent their time, expertise, and patience.

First, thanks to Grace Hensley for connecting the two of us.

Mark's family put up with his long road trips to find and photograph weeds. His husband, Brian, served as model for many of the photos in the control chapter. He also wrote bits of computer code that made the transition from database to final manuscript significantly faster and easier. And gardener-in-chief Natalie McClendon accepted that weeds in our home garden needed to grow big enough to photograph rather than being grubbed out while still tiny.

Chandra, Sami's dog, must have wondered why she was spending so much time at the computer rather than engaging in fun activities with her.

In the early stages of preparing this volume we received support and suggestions from the noxious weed professionals in many Washington and Oregon counties, as well as from Master Gardener coordinators. Laurel Baldwin, with the Whatcom County Noxious Weed Control Board, was particularly helpful. She revealed locations of several noxious weeds, often just in time for Mark to photograph them before her crew went to work knocking them down. Laurel also provided important feedback on the noxious weeds and control chapters, particularly on wetland weeds and herbicide regulations. Cathy Lucero, with the Clallam County Noxious Weed Control Board, shared generously, particularly on the details of weed management.

We had advice, suggestions, and help from numerous members of the Weeds of the Northwest, Whatcom County Gardeners, and PNW Plant Geeks groups on Facebook. Richard Hoffman, moderator of the weeds group, was particularly helpful, providing locations for some Oregon weeds.

Mark made significant use of herbarium records, available online through the Consortium of Pacific Northwest Herbaria web portal, as well as iNaturalist records, to locate weed patches across our region. David Giblin, curator of the University of Washington Herbarium, gave us good advice and suggestions, particularly related to nomenclature.

Jane Abel took Mark to several Tri-Cities area sites to photograph weeds in that part of our region. She went so far as to collect specimens of some aquatic weeds along the Columbia River so they were ready to photograph when Mark arrived. Michael Taylor welcomed Mark to his property to photograph false brome. Mark Johnson pointed out a patch of goatsrue down the road from his place and also invited Mark to photograph a veronica in his garden.

Thanks to Barbara L. Wilson, of the Carex Working Group and Sami's longtime friend and trusted botanical resource, for her usual patience and generous sharing of expertise, and help with the grasses particularly. Barbara also shared numerous plant locations with Mark. Thanks to Linda Chalker-Scott at Washington State University for her encouragement, generous help with fact-checking and editorial suggestions on the control chapter, and in general for her influential work on related horticultural subjects. Thanks to Susan Stuart, friend and knowledgeable native plant enthusiast, for support, encouragement, and practical help.

T. Abe Lloyd and Ellen Zachos, both experienced and knowledgeable foragers, made suggestions and reviewed the information our research revealed about edibility and medicinal uses of many of our weeds. However, any errors are ours and not theirs.

This book has been a big part of our lives for over two years. Thank you to each and every one of you who touched upon it during that time. Thank you, too, dear reader, for choosing our book as your companion as you learn about the often beautiful, but mostly unwanted, weeds around you.

# Who Cares about Weeds?

Weeds are seemingly everywhere. They pop up overnight among our vegetables and prized perennials, emerge from sidewalk cracks, form riotous swaths of color on our roadsides, invade valuable agricultural crops, and crowd out native species in wild lands. Nearly everywhere you look you'll see these plants we've come to call weeds. Some we've learned to live with, just as we tolerate a common cold. Others are a much more serious problem, like a cancer that spreads throughout the body and eventually kills its host.

Botanists and gardeners share a love of plants (and many botanists are also gardeners). But some of their assumptions and priorities are different. It took us some years to realize that there are competing definitions of the word "weed" in the overlapping worlds of home gardening and field botany or plant conservation.

In your garden, you may call anything you didn't plant and don't want there a weed. Seedlings from last year's heirloom tomatoes may be unwelcome guests when they pop up right where you want your new lilies to flourish unharassed. The oft-repeated axiom says, "A weed is any plant that shows up where it isn't wanted." While most weeds are introduced from other parts of the world, native plants like stinging nettle, fireweed, and bracken fern can all be weedy and unwanted in a garden where space is at a premium and tidiness is valued.

Oxeye daisies and smooth hawksbeard grow luxuriantly on a western Washington roadside.

**BELOW, FROM LEFT**
Perennial sow-thistle and purple loosestrife cover a large area near the Columbia River in eastern Washington.

A bigleaf maple seedling, while a fine native tree when mature, is an unwanted weed in a flower bed.

Cape jewelweed is native to moist places in eastern North America. It's a relatively recent introduction to the Pacific Northwest, where it is beginning to crowd out native species.

Traveler's joy clambers over butterfly bush. Both are garden escapes that crowd out native vegetation.

Botanically and environmentally speaking, however, a weed is a widely disseminated non-native plant that outcompetes other plants. In the wild landscape, weeds are competing with the native flora—plants that are known to have evolved here and were present on the continent before the arrival of European settlers. This competition is a major threat to native plant species and the ecosystem in general; native species can disappear from large tracts due to weedy invasions, and biodiversity suffers.

Many weeds on our continent were brought here by European settlers who grew the plants in their gardens for ornamental, culinary, medicinal, or other purposes. Other weeds arrived as stowaways, in feed and in bedding for livestock, or in a ship's ballast.

A plant that's native and well behaved in one part of the continent where climate, soil, or plant competitors keep it in check may prove so aggressive and successful in another region that it's classified there as a noxious weed. Cape jewelweed (*Impatiens capensis*) is native to eastern North America but is rapidly invading moist habitats in the Pacific Northwest (and is already a listed noxious weed in Washington). Tree lupine (*Lupinus arboreus*) is native to coastal southern and central California but is considered an invasive non-native weed farther north on the west coast.

Horticultural invasives, or garden escapes, are a plant group of increasing environmental impact and concern. English holly and English ivy were introduced to North America as respectable garden plants but have muscled out everything in their path over wide swaths of the western landscape. Butterfly bush (*Buddleja davidii*), a popular garden shrub, has been invading woodland edges, highway medians, and riparian zones throughout the coastal northwest. Pampas grass (*Cortaderia selloana*), bachelor's buttons (*Centaurea cyanus*), yellow archangel (*Lamium galeobdolon*), common tansy (*Tanacetum vulgare*), and periwinkle (*Vinca* spp.) are other aggressive ornamentals causing environmental consternation in our region.

You may be able to control these assertive plants in your own yard, but you need to be cognizant of their potential impact on neighbors and on surrounding wild landscapes. For instance, butterfly bush produces thousands of tiny seeds that can be carried on the wind and plant themselves far from the mother plant. Birds eat the fruit of holly and ivy, depositing the seeds with a little packet of fertilizer in woodlands.

A troublesome weed may spread widely because, like perennial sow-thistle (*Sonchus arvensis*), it has many wind-borne or bird-carried seeds. Many weeds can grow in poor

**LEFT TO RIGHT** English ivy climbs trees, weighing them down, and covers the ground, preventing native species from growing.

A honey bee nectars on the flower of short-fringed knapweed, a noxious weed.

Poison hemlock and Scotch thistle at the edge of a fallow farm field in eastern Washington.

soils daunting to other species, grow rapidly and proliferate before other species get established, or grow easily on disturbed ground, such as roadsides and agricultural areas. Some weeds, English ivy among them, also have ground-smothering foliage that keeps seeds of other plants from sprouting. When a diversity of native plants is replaced by many acres of a single non-native species, the natives are increasingly squeezed into smaller and smaller remnants of their former range. The associated diversity of native animal life, including pollinators, may also be reduced or lost.

There is currently a great deal of interest in the subject of pollinators, but the public conversation is often rife with confusion and misinformation. One repeated refrain is that various weeds are essential to pollinators. We're curious: are people envisioning the pre-colonial North American continent as a wasteland void of pollinators, awaiting the arrival of Europeans with their dandelions, oxeye daisies, and honeybees? While pollinators will use weedy species if those are all that's available, in the long view pollinators are not benefitted by the reduction in native plant diversity inflicted by weedy invasions.

Weeds are a big issue in agriculture, as well as plaguing home gardeners. They cost farmers money for both herbicides and non-chemical controls. Several weed species,

including tansy ragwort, Scotch broom, poison hemlock, and yellow starthistle, have been responsible for livestock sickness, mortality, miscarriages, or birth defects.

When a non-native invasive plant becomes a threat to native vegetation, agriculture, livestock, or the economy, your state or province's weed agency may list it as a noxious weed. The federal government maintains a list of widespread noxious weeds, but more local regional lists have priority, and control is determined by state or provincial laws. Control may mean prohibiting the sale, transport, or growing of certain plants. Counties and municipalities may also maintain their own noxious weed lists and enact ordinances regarding their control.

In this book, we provide a primer for the home gardener and others interested in the plants around them to assist in identifying and knowing what to do about most of the weeds found in the Pacific Northwest. It can also help the budding naturalist sort out native vs. introduced plants and understand the significance of the latter. While we cover 368 species, beginners should take heart in knowing that in the average garden one will usually find only about a dozen of the "usual suspects."

# How to
# Use This
# Book

Weeds of the Pacific Northwest will help you identify the weeds in your lawn and garden, on your farm, and along roads and trails. It includes color photographs and descriptions for 368 species of plants considered to be weeds from southern British Columbia to northern California. Most of these were introduced to our region from other parts of the world, but a few weedy native plants are also included.

Our goal in selecting plants was to include as many of the weeds you are likely to find in our large territory as possible. Nearly all the plants on the official noxious weeds lists for the states and province we cover are here. So are many others that aren't on the noxious lists but are generally unwelcome on the land.

## How to Identify a Plant

It is very easy to miss a critical detail about a plant you are identifying if you don't adopt a systematic way of looking. While we're usually attracted first to the flowers and their shape and color, the rest of the plant is also important.

Start by getting an overall impression of the plant. Is it woody, like a tree or shrub? How big is it? Does it grow like a vine, form a mat on the ground, make a clump of stems, or have a single stem that stands by itself? Are the stems stiff and strong or are they weak? Are there any spines, prickles, or hairs?

Queen Anne's lace and red clover among grasses on a western Washington roadside in mid-September.

## EXAMINE THE LEAVES

Are they mostly right at the ground (basal) or do they grow along the stem? Some plants have both basal and stem leaves. Typically, the basal and lowest stem leaves are longest, the stem leaves becoming gradually reduced in length higher on the stem, with simpler outlines and shorter petioles. Measurements are given first for basal leaves, followed by the arrangement (alternate/opposite/whorled) for stem leaves and their length.

What shape are the leaves? Leaf shapes are pictured inside the back cover. Stem leaves can be opposite each other or arranged alternately. Leaves can be basal, growing at ground level, or cauline, along the stem. They can be attached to the stem with a long petiole, clasp the stem, have little appendages (stipules) at the attachment point, or appear to have the stem growing through the leaf (perfoliate). Many plants have compound leaves with several leaflets. You may need to count the leaflets and note how they're arranged. Leaf texture is another clue. Are they soft, leathery, hairy on one or both sides, or spiny?

## STUDY THE FLOWERS

Identification often requires a close look at the color, arrangement, and number of the flowering parts. Color is obvious, but it may change as the flowers age, following pollination, or among individuals of the same species. Flower colors can vary; plants don't read field guides to learn what color they're supposed to be. Most species whose flowers are normally colored pink or purple will have occasional individuals that are white.

Sometimes petals have spots or blotches of a second color. Count the petals, if there are any. Some flowers don't have any petals, or they are very small and inconspicuous. The number or description of the sepals (or calyx, as a group), located at the base of the flower, may be clues.

Flowers are described with the most common color(s) first, then the number of petals or lobes, then a measurement. For most flowers, the measurement is the maximum width of the corolla; for tubular flowers, the length may be given. Within the sunflower family, though, the rules are a little different. What we often think of as a "flower" in this family is actually a "head" or inflorescence of many tiny florets. So for this family, the measurement will typically be the width of the head. The head will often be described as daisy-like (with countable "petals" or ray flowers around a central disk) or dandelion-like (all "petals"). The visual glossary inside the front and back covers and the more extensive glossary can help you with any technical terms you haven't yet learned.

Wild mustard and giant horsetail blanket a western Washington hillside in May.

Grasses have their own specialized technical language and specific characteristics to observe. Even experts find them challenging to identify. Examine the inflorescence (the flowers, and later the seeds). Is it open and airy or packed more tightly? You may need to look carefully at the ligule (the joint where one piece of stem emerges from the one below) to determine its length and hairiness. For some grasses, such as quackgrass, the way the roots grow is an important characteristic. In other books, you will encounter some pretty challenging terms for tiny parts within the inflorescence that often require magnification to see. We'll stick mostly to describing what you can see easily in the inflorescence.

# Organization

This book is organized into sections for trees and shrubs, forbs/herbs and vines (herbaceous plants), grasses and grass-like plants, and aquatic weeds. Within each section, they're sorted by family, genus, and species. That keeps related plants together.

The fastest way to look up an unknown plant is to turn to the appropriate section and then leaf through the pages until you come to the flowers with the same shape or number of petals as the plant you're trying to identify. Then start studying the photographs and reading the descriptions until you find a match. Once you have a preliminary identification, you may want to reread the description as you study the plant carefully a second time.

Some plants are easier to recognize than others. Large families like the sunflowers and grasses are especially challenging and may require consulting a technical manual for additional information if you need positive identification. Remember that there may be native plants, not included in this book, that resemble the weeds covered here.

# Photographs

In most cases there are two or more photographs for each plant. They were selected to show as many of the important identifying characteristics as possible. Flowers receive more emphasis than foliage, which may appear somewhat soft-focus or in the background. Use the photographs to get a general feel for what the plant looks like, then read the description. Unfortunately, it is sometimes impossible to show all the characteristics of a flowering plant in a photograph.

# Plant Names

Each plant has a unique scientific name, which has two parts—the genus and the species. In some cases there are also subspecies and varieties, but for the most part this book discusses those under the currently accepted name of the main species. Because plant names can change over time, generally due to additional botanical research, we've given parenthetical synonyms for some plants. We generally follow the names in the Washington Flora Checklist, the Oregon Flora Project, Calflora, or e-Flora BC.

Each plant also has one or more common names. The same plant may be called by different names in different places, or the same name may refer to different plants in the same location. The plant known as salsify, oyster plant, and goatsbeard is one example, with goatsbeard also referring to a completely different species. Some plants have so many common names we couldn't list them all.

The index includes the common and scientific names for the plants described in the book. If you know a plant's name but aren't sure what it looks like, turn to the index to find it quickly.

## Descriptions

The descriptions begin with parenthetical synonyms (if any) and notes about where the plant is found; its origin is often included. That's followed by a general overview of the plant's habit, its stems and leaves, and flowers. There's information about the environment where the plant grows, such as soil preferences and moisture and why the weed is a problem. If a weed is noxious, it is noted. Reproductive strategies—such as seed production and vegetative reproduction from rhizomes, stolons, or bits of broken root—suggest timing and techniques to control the weed's spread. Recommended control strategies conclude each description.

Each plant entry also includes the plant's size, growth cycle (annual, biennial, or perennial), bloom season, and whether it is native or introduced.

### HEIGHT

Plant heights are given in inches or feet and are an approximate figure for the high end for mature plants under normal growing conditions. The measurement given is typically for the length of the main stem, but for lazy/recumbent or crawling plants or vines, the length may be much longer than the actual height from the ground up. You may find individuals that are taller or shorter than the figures given, but if you're looking at a plant that is only 4 in. tall and the description says "to 24 in.," there's a good chance that you need to reconsider your identification.

### GROWTH CYCLE

Plants have one of three growth cycles. Annuals come up from seed, flower, produce seeds, and die in one growing season. Biennials take two years to produce seeds. In the first year the seed germinates and the plant puts down roots and grows leaves. The second year it blooms, produces seed, and dies. You'll find both flowering and nonflowering individuals of biennials every year. Perennials live three or more years and most flower every year, although some may only bloom occasionally or lay dormant for many years between blooms. You can often identify a perennial by looking for the previous year's dried leaves, flower stalks, or seedheads. Some plants can exhibit more than one of these growth cycles.

## BLOOM TIME

While most wildflowers bloom only for a fairly short time each year, some of our weeds bloom over an extended period. We've subdivided spring and summer into early, middle, and late. Few of our flowers bloom in autumn and even fewer in winter or year-round. The bloom times should be used with caution. They're more related to weather conditions and local microclimates than calendar dates.

In general, early spring begins in mid-March at low elevations, although you may find flowers as early as February in warm exposed locations such as the Washington side of the Columbia Gorge and sun-baked sites along Puget Sound or warmer urban areas. Mid-spring comes with the leafing out of bigleaf maples. Late spring arrives as Oregon white oak leaves get to full size.

Early summer runs up through the solstice. Midsummer is July and a week or so on either side. Late summer is from the middle of August into late September. Autumn is short, as seeds mature and foliage dies back.

## EDIBILITY/TOXICITY

Many weeds have edible or medicinal parts, but others are poisonous to varying degrees. Some are also toxic or otherwise injurious to pets and livestock. We've included this information for each plant for which we could find anything in the literature. Be sure to read the next chapter for details about this aspect of the plants.

## CONTROL TECHNIQUES

Since the plants in this book are weeds, you probably want to know how to get rid of them (or at least keep them under control) on your property. Each entry includes suggestions for controlling or eradicating the plant. A separate chapter gives more information about these control techniques.

# Edible or Deadly?

"Can I eat it?" is a question many people ask about their weeds, as well as the more desirable native plants in their environment. We're not sure why the idea of eating your weeds is so important to those who raise the question. Perhaps it involves the desire to take revenge on the plants competing with their prized tomatoes or lilies. Maybe it's just curiosity. For others, it's wanting to live more lightly on the land and make use of what would otherwise end up in the compost pile. Regardless of the reason, more and more people want to eat "wild food."

Neither of us are big-time foragers. We'll occasionally nibble wild greens while hiking or cook up a batch of nettle pesto. We're not going to encourage you to eat your weeds, nor to harvest them to use medicinally. That's a choice we'll leave to you. This book is definitely *not* about foraging. However, we think we ought to let you know where reputable foragers and other experts place a plant on the scale of edibility to poisonous. For each plant covered, we have included a few words about edibility and/or medicinal uses:

**Parts edible.** At least some part of the plant is widely regarded as safe to eat, tasty, and nutritious. No part of the plant is likely to harm you if eaten in small to modest quantities.

**Parts edible with caution.** One or more parts of the plant are edible. However, some people may be sensitive to it; consuming large quantities can cause problems; it's edible only at some points in its life; one or more parts are edible but other parts are poisonous; or it should be avoided during pregnancy. The plant may cause skin irritation when handled, but cooking destroys that property.

Dandelions have several edible parts, as long as they're collected at the right time and prepared properly.

**Parts medicinal.** One or more parts of the plant are widely regarded as having medicinal properties, and it is generally regarded as safe to consume.

**Parts medicinal with caution.** One or more parts of the plant have medicinal properties. However, some people may be sensitive to it; consuming large quantities can cause problems; it has medicinal value only at some points in its life; one or more parts are usable medicinally, but other parts are poisonous; or it should be avoided during pregnancy. The plant may cause skin irritation when handled, but cooking or other processing destroys that property.

**Unpalatable.** The dictionary definition of unpalatable is "unpleasant to the taste." However, we use the term more broadly to also include plants that won't necessarily hurt you if you eat them, but their texture, taste, or lack of food or medicinal value says "don't bother."

**Poisonous.** Consuming the plant can make you very sick or kill you. Poisonous plants also include those that cause serious skin irritation, like poison-oak or poison-ivy.

## Identify Positively

If you're going to eat some of your weeds, it is imperative that you are absolutely positive about identifying them. This book is designed to help you with that. However, many edible wild plants, including weeds, are best while they're growing rapidly and before they flower. That means you have to learn to identify them by foliage, growth habit, and

Note the finely divided foliage of these poison hemlock seedlings. This plant is quite poisonous to both humans and other animals. No part of the plant has prominent hairs, and the foliage is a bright yellow-green.

This seedling is Queen Anne's lace, which has edible parts. While the foliage is somewhat similar to poison hemlock, Queen Anne's lace leaves are a softer blue-green, and the petioles are covered with soft hairs.

environment alone. Since the descriptions and photographs in this book emphasize mature plants with flowers, you may need to do some additional work before you munch.

Learn to recognize the plants around you when they're in bloom. Study their foliage and growth habit. Note where they're growing. Then watch your seedlings as they develop and grow into full-blown plants the following year. It may take you a couple of years or more to feel comfortable distinguishing similar-looking plants when they're still young and tasty. The young leaves of oxeye daisy (*Leucanthemum vulgare*) resemble those of common groundsel (*Senecio vulgaris*). You can eat the daisy leaves, but common groundsel is poisonous. Queen Anne's lace (*Daucus carota*) resembles poison hemlock (*Conium maculatum*), especially when young. They aren't really that hard to tell apart, but you do have to pay attention to all the details. Mistaken identity can have serious consequences, from an upset stomach to death. If in doubt, leave it out of your body.

## All Plants Have Chemicals

Some people think that eating wild foods, including weeds, is a way to avoid chemicals in their diet. That's only partly true. While weeds and other wild foods generally aren't fed manufactured fertilizers or treated with agricultural pesticides, all plants contain chemicals. Most plants, since they are immobile, practice self-defense through the chemicals in their tissues. Toxicity in plants is not rare and not a fluke. It's a common and effective evolutionary adaptation whereby a species protects itself against herbivores, including humans. The quantities are generally small enough that our bodies tolerate them. Apple seeds contain cyanide, a deadly poison, but ingesting an occasional seed usually doesn't hurt you because there's not much poison in each seed. Toxicity depends both on how much you consume and how potent the poison is.

Speaking of chemicals, think about where a plant is growing before collecting it for the table. Frank Zappa's immortal line, "Watch out where the huskies go / And don't you eat that yellow snow," reminds us that if you have pets that pee outside, you don't want to harvest the weeds there. We wouldn't harvest plants from a cow pasture, either. The edible weeds in your vegetable garden are probably safe, especially if you don't use herbicides, fungicides, insecticides, or other chemicals. Roadside weeds are questionable. You really don't know whether your local weed board or road department came through with their spray truck a day or two before you were ready to harvest. Roadside plants can also absorb toxic heavy metal-laden exhaust from cars and trucks.

## Only Some Parts May Be Edible

Many times, only part of a plant is edible. Consider a few common fruits and vegetables. We eat the roots of potatoes, but the fruits of tomatoes. We eat lettuce leaves, broccoli flower buds, the swollen stem of kohlrabi, and the fruit of a cherry tree. The same principle applies to weeds and other wild plants. Just because we've noted that a plant is edible doesn't mean you can eat all parts of it. We love a rhubarb pie, made with just the petiole of the leaf. We don't eat the leaves or roots because they're poisonous to humans. The young, freshly emerged shoots of American pokeweed (*Phytolacca americana*) can be eaten, but mature leaves, stems, roots, and especially the seeds are quite poisonous. Before you eat any of the plants in this book, consult a reputable foraging book or two and learn which parts are edible, when to harvest, and how to prepare the good parts. We like the ones by Euell Gibbons, Sam Thayer, Ellen Zachos, and Douglas Deur listed in the bibliography.

Some foragers consider purslane a delicious potherb or raw as an addition to a salad; others don't care for the okra-like mucilaginous texture when it's cooked.

The mushroom forager's adage—"There's no such thing as an old, bold mushroomer"—applies equally well to eating wild plants. Even those listed as edible may not agree with everyone. It's a bit like peanuts. Most people can eat them, but others have a severe allergic reaction that can be deadly. Start small, perhaps with just a little nibble, and see how your body reacts. A day later, have a bigger nibble. Slowly build up to a meal.

You may also find that you just don't like the taste or texture of the weeds you encounter. Purslane (*Portulaca oleracea*) is a good edible, but it is also mucilaginous, like okra. A lot of edible greens have a bitter taste. Many people like some degree of bitterness, such as that imparted by hops to a good IPA. However, bitterness is an acquired taste. Garden lettuce is bitter when the plants get old and begin to bolt. In *Stalking the Wild Asparagus* famed forager Euell Gibbons wrote, "There are many wild plants reported in the literature to be edible that I don't like at all. In research for this book, I tried several hundred different kinds of plants, and disliked most of them." Another author repeatedly writes that a plant "tastes like spinach," with the note that he doesn't care for spinach.

## Medicinal Plants

Many of our weeds have a long history of being used medicinally. In fact, that's how some of them got introduced to North America in the first place, brought here by European settlers. Just as you should be cautious when gathering weeds for the table, you should be careful using plants medicinally. In some cases, the difference between the useful dose and the toxic dose is small. Reading through the literature on plant toxicity, you'll find that quite a few of our weeds were once used as abortifacients. That means that if you're pregnant or thinking of becoming pregnant, you should be extra cautious.

Even if you're a healthy male who can never get pregnant, be careful. The drugs in plants can interact with other drugs you might be taking. It's a good idea to have a conversation with your doctor before using potentially medicinal plants to treat yourself.

A big challenge in gathering plants from the wild to use medicinally, including weeds, is that it is nearly impossible to determine how much of an active chemical is in any given plant; often it depends on the genetics of the population, the growing conditions, and the stage of growth (juvenile vs. mature or senescing). Different parts of a plant can contain widely varying amounts of active chemicals. Caution is advised, and "a little bit is good" does not translate to "a lot is even better."

As you browse through the plant descriptions in this book, you'll find that only a relatively small number are poisonous to humans. The great majority have some edible part, or at least won't hurt you if you sample them in small quantities. That's good news, especially for those with children who are prone to put almost anything in their mouth.

# Danger to Animals

Cats and dogs, horses, cattle, sheep, pigs, goats, and chickens can all experience problems when they eat too much of some plants or consume them under certain conditions. We've noted for each plant in this book whether the scientific literature indicates that the species may be toxic to one or more of these common domestic animals. In a few cases the amount that causes a toxic effect is quite small, but for most plants the effect is evident only when the animal consumes a large quantity of the species in a short period of time, or when the plant makes up a large part of the animal's diet.

Even plants that are grown as livestock feed may under some circumstances be toxic. According to Cornell University's Department of Animal Science, "Alfalfa and clovers continue to be fine forages when properly grown, harvested, carefully preserved and fed to the appropriate species in appropriate amounts." However, "Fresh legume forage (alfalfa, red and white clovers mostly) is notorious for causing bloat in ruminants, even to the point of threatening life in some cases." According to the US Department of Agriculture,

Common burdock burrs readily detach and stick to animals, becoming an irritant as well as a means by which the seeds are spread around.

"Under normal conditions, some poisonous plants form an important part of livestock diets without negative effects on the animals. Poisoning occurs only when these animals are enticed by hunger or other stress conditions to eat too much too fast."

If you raise livestock or have pets, learn the plants that can cause problems for your animals and take action to keep them from indulging and getting ill. Backyard chicken keepers should avoid tossing problem weeds to their hens. Livestock owners will want to minimize the presence of potentially toxic weeds in their pastures and paddocks.

Other steps you can take to keep your animals healthy, according to the USDA Agricultural Research Service, include avoiding exposing them to poisonous plants when they're stressed, such as when they are driven, branded, otherwise handled, or unloaded from trucks because animals graze less discriminately at these times. Make sure your animals have plenty of water and food so they aren't as likely to eat problem plants because they're hungry.

Prevention is the key, because in most cases there is no treatment for animals poisoned by plants. Sometimes the animals will recover on their own once they're removed from exposure to the toxic plants, but there's no guarantee.

In addition to toxicity, some plants can cause mechanical damage to animals. Grasses with long awns and plants with burrs are particularly problematic and can affect both household pets (particularly dogs) and livestock.

This book makes no attempt to quantify how much of a plant it takes to be a problem, nor the specific effects on each livestock species or pet. Use the notes on animal toxicity as a starting point to ask questions of your veterinarian or to do additional research in other books and/or online resources. It's also important to note, as does the Canadian Poisonous Plants Information System, that "much literature on poisonous plants is anecdotal and therefore of limited reliability." There is much we don't know, and rigorous research on the topic is somewhat limited.

## Final Thoughts

Our weeds run the gamut from tasty and nutritious to deadly poisonous, with most somewhere in between. A few, like poison hemlock (*Conium maculatum*) and Douglas's water-hemlock (*Cicuta douglasii*), can be deadly when eaten, and contact with the foliage can cause serious problems. Keep your hands off poison-ivy, poison-oak, and giant hogweed. Yet there's no need to panic. Poisonous plants aren't going to jump out and grab you. Be aware of the plants around you, and give the toxic ones the respect they deserve. As with many subjects, knowledge is power.

If you're going to explore putting weeds in your salad or cook up a mess of wild greens, make the effort to learn to positively identify what you plan to eat. If you're not sure, don't eat it. Ultimately, the responsibility is yours.

Common St. John's wort causes photosensitization in many animals when eaten and may cause vomiting, diarrhea, or other problems in dogs, other pets, and humans. It may also have medicinal value for humans when used with caution.

# What Makes a Weed Noxious?

**W**hile nearly any plant growing where it's not wanted can be considered a weed, not all weeds are ranked noxious. Each state and province in our region defines and lists noxious weeds a little differently. The plants on, or off, these noxious weed lists can be a little surprising. English holly (*Ilex aquifolium*), prickly lettuce (*Lactuca serriola*), prickly sow-thistle (*Sonchus asper*), common dandelion (*Taraxacum officinale*), and wild mustard (*Brassica rapa*) are all common weeds that are not yet on any official noxious weed lists in our region. You might wonder why not. It all comes down to how noxious weeds are defined.

In broad terms, noxious weeds have a significant impact on agriculture. That's understandable since ag is big business in all parts of the Northwest. The first weed to be regulated in Washington was Canada thistle, way back in 1881, before Washington became a state. Farmers were concerned that thistles on neighboring property could spread to theirs and affect their crops, and they got an act passed. Current noxious weed law in Washington dates to 1969, with regular updates to the list of species. We're still fighting Canada thistle and other weeds that affect crops and rangeland.

Beginning in the late 1980s, the Washington noxious weed board began to adopt weeds that impacted natural resources (other than crops and livestock), including local ecosystems, wildlife and fish habitat, etc. Since then, additions to the noxious weed list have largely been weeds that affect ecosystems, particularly ornamental plants introduced through the horticultural industry that have escaped into the wild.

Canada thistle was Washington's first official noxious weed in 1881. Gardeners, farmers, and land managers are still trying to control it.

From an environmental perspective, one would think that a plant like English holly (*Ilex aquifolium*) that invades forested areas and crowds out native plants would be on the noxious weed lists, but it's not. That's because holly doesn't much affect agricultural lands and is itself an agricultural product; commercial holly growers argued against the species being listed.

Some weeds are more difficult to get rid of than others, but it's not only the challenge of killing them that puts them on the noxious weed list. Some species are added while they're still rare in a jurisdiction but considered a serious pest elsewhere. The idea is to prevent them from getting established and spreading farther.

Complementing noxious weed lists are lists of species that are prohibited for sale or introduction as either seeds or plants.

## Noxious Weed Laws

According to the Washington State Noxious Weed Control Board, "'Noxious weed' is the traditional, legal term for invasive, non-native plants that are so aggressive they harm our local ecosystems or disrupt agricultural production. These plants crowd out the native species that fish and wildlife depend on. They also cost farmers, orchardists, and ranchers millions of dollars in control efforts and lost production—and that can make the food we buy more expensive." That last part is particularly important because the economic impact of a weed plays heavily into the decision to list it as noxious.

**ABOVE, FROM TOP**
Road signs, like this one outside Leavenworth, Washington, remind everyone to control noxious weeds.

Whitetop, listed as noxious in BC, Washington, Oregon, and California, is shown growing along a farm road in eastern Washington.

Depending on where you live, weed laws may require you to control some of the officially noxious weeds on your property. Just which weeds you're required to control or eradicate depends on the weed's classification in your state or province. It's a little complicated because the weed laws vary from place to place, and there may be more than one weed list in a jurisdiction.

For each of the plants in this book we've noted whether they're included on the noxious weed list for Washington, Oregon, California, or British Columbia as of the time we finalized the text. State noxious weed lists are generally updated annually, and no doubt new plants will be added to the lists. It's less common for a plant to be removed from a noxious weed list.

For the most up-to-date information in Washington, visit the Washington State Noxious Weed Control Board (nwcb.wa.gov).

In Oregon, noxious weed laws are managed by the Oregon Department of Agriculture's Noxious Weed Control Program (oregon.gov/oda/programs/weeds/oregonnoxiousweeds/pages/aboutoregonweeds.aspx).

The California Noxious Weeds program is administered by the California Department of Food and Agriculture (cdfa.ca.gov/plant/ipc/encycloweedia/encycloweedia_hp.html).

In British Columbia, invasive plant priorities and management is often led by regional invasive species organizations, with guidance from the provincial government. To find the regional organization priorities within BC, visit Invasive Species Council of BC (bcinvasives.ca).

# What Does It Mean for Home Gardeners?

Home gardeners in the United States must control or eradicate some classes of noxious weeds on their property. North of the border there's no legal requirement that you eradicate designated noxious weeds on your property, but it is good citizenship to do so.

Noxious weed classifications can be confusing, with cryptic letter codes that vary from one jurisdiction to another. In general, weeds that are just beginning to show up are the highest priority to eradicate, to prevent them from getting a foothold. Other officially noxious weeds may be so established and widespread that eradicating them is unlikely to be possible so the goal is containment.

Individual counties may further regulate weeds, so a weed that must be controlled in one county may not be regulated in the adjacent one. Consult your local weed board for the most current information. A web search for the name of your county plus "noxious weed board" will usually get you to the right place.

Officially noxious weeds are only part of the picture, although a big one. Of the 368 weed species covered here, 164 of them are on a noxious weed list in one form or another. You're legally required to control some of them, but that doesn't mean you should just ignore the rest of the weeds in your garden or landscape.

On a practical basis, most home gardeners want to keep their weeds under control or eliminate them. While eradicating a problem weed, whether or not it's officially noxious, can be challenging, you can hope that by putting in the effort once, you won't have to do it again. But for others, and especially those listed as noxious, repeated efforts may be required to keep them under control and prevent their spread to previously unaffected areas.

Garden yellow loosestrife is a Class B noxious weed in Washington and a targeted Class A weed in Oregon.

# Out, Damned Weed

In the home garden, the prime motivation for diligent weeding is usually aesthetic. Standards vary greatly according to the setting, from formal display garden to casual backyard vegetable patch, and the temperament of the gardener.

Some people work tirelessly to achieve their vision of perfect control and tidiness. Others are a bit lazier or more permissive. The happy gardener is one whose standards align well with what they are willing and able to do, whether formal and tidy or wild and unkempt.

You can weed on a daily or weekly schedule, on a casual basis, or with intermittent marathons punctuating periods of laissez-faire. For some people it's an energetic workout, for others a relaxed and meditative quiet time. Of course, it's easier to be meditative while plucking shallow-rooted annuals from among your tomatoes on a pleasant summer day than when doing battle with a large patch of Himalayan blackberries or reed canary grass.

One person may be merciless in clearing out even the seedlings of their chosen garden plants when they volunteer anywhere outside of the planned design. Another may enjoy a natural look and the serendipity of nature, delighted to see seedlings of desirable plants filling in available spaces: free plants!

A tolerance for occasional uninvited green guests can sometimes yield surprises. Last year, a small seedling didn't look like any weed Sami had encountered, so she opted to keep it a while. Behold: *Eupatorium cannabinum*, a fine ornamental she'd never grown before.

A wheelbarrow full of weeds, ready for the compost pile.

**LEFT TO RIGHT** Lesser celandine, brought to North America as an ornamental, has taken over this perennial and shrub garden.

The parsnips have been cleared of weeds, but plantain, cudweed, spotted lady's-thumb, and redroot pigweed still crowd a nearby vegetable garden path.

Purslane and redroot pigweed blanket the ground under young eggplants in a vegetable garden.

Apart from issues of aesthetics or tidiness, larger weed infestations can also impact the health of garden plants. Too many weeds can smother small, desirable plants, shade them out, cause disease problems due to lack of ventilation, and provide habitat for insect pests. Weeds inevitably compete with your garden plants for space, water, and soil nutrients.

The responsible and environmentally educated gardener also knows that no garden is an island, and weedy plants may spread to the surrounding landscape, in some cases even miles away, via wind-borne or bird-carried seeds.

Conversely, no garden is safe from sources of weeds beyond its boundaries. Stoloniferous weeds like creeping buttercup and English ivy can sneak in from less well-kept neighboring yards; weed seeds can float in on the wind. But at least you can avoid bringing in the weeds yourself. Beware of the potential of uncertified compost, purchased bulk soils, and animal manures to contain weed seeds. Avoid planting aggressive horticultural plants you may soon regret. That likelihood depends somewhat upon gardener preferences, site characteristics (sunny or shady, well watered or not), and region, but some popular

ornamentals belong to genera known for their pushy ways: *Lysimachia*, *Euphorbia*, *Mentha*, *Houttuynia*, *Verbena*, *Vinca*, and *Cotoneaster*, among many others.

    Whatever your gardening style, you're sure to encounter weeds that you'll want to remove or keep under tight control. But what techniques work best for each species? It depends greatly upon the plant's growth habit, size, and how big the weed patch has become. For each plant in this book, we suggest ways to control it. Most of the time, it's some form of getting the weed out of the ground, whether by pulling, scraping with a hoe, or digging. Sometimes mowing repeatedly is effective, but often it merely spreads seeds and rhizomes around, or stimulates branching and sprouting. For large woody plants, cutting to the ground and painting the stump with herbicide is often the only practical solution, although girdling may work in a few cases. For a very small number of weed species, you may need to bring in a backhoe or just decide to move. While herbicides are effective on many weeds, we think they should be the choice of last resort, used only when there are no other practical options. Bare soil invites weeds, which makes mulch an effective way to prevent their appearance or recurrence.

Hand-pulling weeds, like the shotweed here, is easiest when the soil is moist and workable.

# Pulling, Scraping, Digging

Pulling by hand is often the best bet for smaller areas, particularly where weeds are closely interspersed among plants we want to save. It's easiest when the soil is soft and moist (but not saturated, as your activity will compact the soil), or when lightly rooted weeds are growing on surfaces like gravelly or compacted soil that don't allow them much of a foothold.

Annuals, first-year biennials, and all young seedlings are easily hand-pulled and can often be killed by a mere scraping with the side of one's foot or a hoe. For these wimpy weeds, nothing more is needed, and measures like herbicide or propane torches are simply a waste of time and money. You'll want to control annual weeds early, before they set seed. Some germinate in the fall, then burst into bloom in late winter or early spring before much else is growing.

With perennial weeds, it's usually necessary to extract the root, as plants that lose only their upper portions will often come right back from the roots. Taprooted or rhizomatous perennials will require more diligence. Some of these plants, like thistle, tansy ragwort, dandelion, periwinkle, ivy, and horsetails, will quickly regenerate from any severed portions left underground. Other perennials can be killed simply by cutting a little below the crown. Blackberries, knotweed, and reed canary grass may come back for years after the first attempt to remove them. Deep excavation with a digging fork, shovel, or backhoe may be required, sometimes multiple times over a period of years. Linda Chalker-Scott adds the caveat that repeated excavation will damage soil structure, destroy underground networks, and increase compaction and erosion. After digging, add a layer of coarse woody mulch to protect the soil and allow it to regenerate.

# Weeding Tools

Weeding tools come in many designs and variations. Each is known by a few different names, and some names are shared by multiple styles of tools. Most gardeners have a preferred tool that they've found to be effective and suited for the soil conditions and weeds they encounter.

Long-handled tools designed for use while standing include the basic hoe (with a squarish, fixed blade); the loop hoe (with a stirrup-shaped, fixed blade); the action or hula hoe or stirrup hoe (similar to the loops, but movable); and the diamond scuffle hoe (a pointed, triangular or diamond-shaped blade for cutting weeds just below the soil surface). Long-handled digging forks may be simple three-pronged tools resembling narrow pitchforks. Others are designed with a punching action to extract deep-rooted weeds, sometimes with a foot-operated lever. Some weed warriors use a spading fork, shovel, or mattock to get at deep-rooted invaders or to clear large weed patches.

A weed wrench or broom puller is a long-handled tool with a hefty wrench-like device at the lower end designed to grip the lower part of a shrubby weed like Scotch broom to

CLOCKWISE FROM TOP LEFT A stand-up weed puller grabs the roots of a bull thistle to pull it from the ground.

An Uprooter weed wrench works well to pull shrubby weeds, like Scotch broom, from the ground by the roots.

Short-handled weeding tools: hori-hori, notched dandelion weeder, CobraHead weeder.

Long-handled weeding tools: diamond scuffle hoe, loop hoe, and basic hoe.

facilitate uprooting the plant. These work best when the soil is moist in the spring. In some areas they can be borrowed or rented from your weed-control agency.

Short-handled tools are used while kneeling or squatting. They include the notched dandelion weeder, which is like an awl with a flattened, notched end; it's a favorite of Sami's for extracting taprooted weeds like dandelion and dock. Mark can't imagine weeding without his CobraHead, a curved tool with a sharp point that can be wielded vigorously but precisely to get under the roots, even when they're close to desirable plants. Many gardeners are religious about their hori-hori—a Japanese gardening knife with one serrated side and one smooth side. Weeding forks with two or three tines are good for extracting fibrous-rooted weeds. Even a narrow, sharp-edged trowel may be useful for some weeding tasks.

# Burning

Careful torching with a propane weed burner can be a labor-saving method in some situations and is often favored by people wishing to avoid poisons. While it may be touted as an environmentally friendly choice by people who mistrust herbicides, it uses fossil fuel. A propane burner can be immediately effective for seedlings and annuals but will not get to the deeper roots of established perennials, and so may need to be applied repeatedly. The job of a weed burner is to desiccate plants, not set them on fire. It's safest to target weeds in otherwise nonflammable surroundings like rocky landscaping, gravel or stonework paths, and driveways. Nearby desirable plants can be damaged by the heat of the burner, even without direct contact with flames. It's a fire hazard near anything dry and flammable; never use near combustible vegetation like dry grass or during hot, dry weather. Burners should never be used on poison-oak or other toxic plants whose smoke would be dangerous to inhale.

# Conventional Herbicides

For tough and labor-intensive weeds, or for infestations over large areas, the beleaguered gardener may choose to use herbicides. As with any garden or household chemical, the key to safe and effective use is to choose the right product, read and follow the label directions, handle and store them carefully, and wear appropriate protective clothing to avoid damaging your skin, eyes, and lungs. You need to be careful and thoughtful when using herbicides. If in doubt, consult an expert or avoid using them.

The right choice of herbicide depends upon the kind of weed, the site, and timing. Selective herbicides like 2,4-D target broadleaf plants and are less harmful to grasses and related plants. Nonselective or broad-spectrum herbicides like glyphosate are effective against grasses as well as broadleaf plants. There are many herbicides on the market,

A propane weed burner in use on annual weeds in a gravel patio.

containing several different chemical compounds that act to inhibit plant growth. It's important to choose the correct one; herbicides are definitely not a "one size fits all" product. That's among the reasons some gardeners prefer to avoid them altogether. All herbicides are chemicals designed to kill plants, but they vary significantly in how long they persist in the soil, how fast they act, and how toxic they are to humans and other animals.

In general, herbicides are low in toxicity to non-plant organisms. To be on the safe side, always wear gloves, shoes, long pants, a long-sleeved shirt, and eye protection if the label recommends it. Riskier products are often regulated and cannot be purchased or legally used by anyone other than licensed applicators.

## CONTACT HERBICIDES

Contact herbicides kill only the plant tissues they come directly in contact with; they are most effective when plants are small. They are very fast-acting, but when only top growth is killed, underground portions may survive and regrow, necessitating repeat applications. Examples of contact herbicides include Goal, Sharpen, Treevix, and Gramoxone, along with glufosinate ammonium, which is the active ingredient in Liberty and Rely. Contact herbicides are generally nonselective and can affect nearly any plant tissue they come in contact with.

## SYSTEMIC HERBICIDES

Systemic herbicides like glyphosate are transported through the plant's vascular system into the roots, killing the whole plant. They're generally slower-acting than contact herbicides, and it may take several days after application to see any result. Some systemic formulations include a contact herbicide as well, so the user sees foliage dying back faster. Different systemic herbicides work in several ways, although most affect the biochemical balance within the plant. For instance, some inhibit growth and starve the plant; others interrupt photosynthesis.

## PRE-EMERGENT HERBICIDES

Pre-emergent herbicides, typically applied in fall or winter, kill weeds before shoots from newly germinating seeds emerge from the soil. They are useful only when weed seeds are already present in the soil. They work by limiting the root growth of freshly germinated seeds, killing the plant before it gets big enough to emerge from the soil.

## TREATING SHRUBS AND TREES

Shrubs and trees start their lives as tiny as any herbaceous plant. As trees get larger, the digging effort to remove them can become formidable. Some young invasive trees can be removed by girdling, removing the bark in a band all the way around the trunk, or simply cutting them to the ground, but some will resprout from the stump. Many trees, and even woody vines like ivy, can be prevented from resprouting by painting herbicide directly on the fresh cut.

Painting concentrated herbicide directly on the cut stump of an English holly is an effective treatment for this and other weedy trees and shrubs, although it may need to be repeated the following year if shoots continue to emerge from the roots.

## HERBICIDES AND THE ENVIRONMENT

Herbicides and pesticides all carry some risk of environmental damage, which can be limited by choosing the appropriate chemical and using it correctly. The alternative of letting invasives have their way can be extremely damaging to the entire landscape, not only by displacing natives and desired non-natives, but in some instances changing soils, hydrology, vegetational structure, and wildlife habitat in wild landscapes. Agricultural managers, environmental agencies, the Forest Service, noxious weed agencies—all are faced with sometimes thousands of acres of aggressive and unkillable invasives, so their choices are limited. The average home gardener has more latitude to invest the time and muscle required to dispense with herbicides, but sometimes it's just not practical to do so.

We are not taking positions with respect to herbicide use in general or in any given instance; we are providing general information about types of herbicides available and reporting on the experiences of the experts in combatting some specific weeds we cover in this book. It's up to you to decide for yourself whether to include herbicides in your weed control toolbox. If you do choose to use herbicides, you'll want to do additional research to select the right one for the job and to learn the regulations regarding its use. Don't just grab the first one you see on the garden center shelf and spray it willy-nilly on every weed you see. Detailed information about herbicides is available online and should be provided by garden centers selling these products.

# Alternative Herbicides

A few products and homemade concoctions have been promoted as "natural" alternatives to herbicides.

## HORTICULTURAL VINEGAR

Horticultural vinegar is acetic acid in a concentration of 10–30% (household vinegar is 5%). In some formulations, citric acid, clove oil, and other ingredients may be added. It's a contact herbicide (sometimes mixed with a "sticker," a viscous substance like yucca extract to facilitate sticking to target plants) and applied as a spray. Unless it is sunny and the plant is young, vinegar will do little more than burn some leaves. It works best on very small, young plants, killing foliage almost immediately but having no effect on roots. Repeat applications can be more effective. It may be most useful for weed seedlings in gravel. Caveats include potential harm to small animals that may inadvertently be sprayed, and damage to metal and wooden objects like furniture, fences, and trellises that may be present in your garden. And this vinegar is not for salads. At the strength needed for herbicidal action, it is quite toxic and must be handled with care. Protective clothing is needed to avoid contact that can cause skin and eye damage, and prolonged use can cause other health problems. Horticultural vinegar is also quite expensive.

## VINEGAR, DETERGENT, AND EPSOM SALTS

One homemade weed-killing recipe circulating online has received viral PR. This is the herbicidal mixture of household vinegar, Dawn detergent, and epsom salts. Containing much weaker acetic acid, it is even less effective than horticultural vinegar. Its fans proclaim it to be "natural" and "chemical-free," though there is nothing natural about any of these ingredients in the outdoor environment, and they are definitely composed of chemicals: vinegar is acetic acid, epsom salts are magnesium sulfate, and the detergent (read the label!) is hardly organic, but at least it's cheap.

## TABLE SALT

Table salt is another "natural" weed killer that may be used on surfaces like gravel, where no plants are intended to grow but weeds often find their happy place. It's so familiar, seemingly benign, yet sodium chloride is by no means environmentally harmless. Most of what is known about salt toxicity to the environment is based on the effects of road salt,

**BELOW, FROM LEFT**
This horticultural vinegar is 20% acetic acid, much stronger than the vinegar you put on your salad.

The ingredients label on a bottle of Dawn dish soap lists several nearly unpronounceable chemicals.

Common table salt can leach into the environment when used to control weeds.

but the same caveats apply to the use of salt as a weed killer. Runoff from salted, nonporous surfaces like gravel roadways will find its way to bodies of water and to underground water supplies. It is toxic to aquatic plants and animals and to soil organisms.

### CORN GLUTEN MEAL

Corn gluten meal has been promoted as a natural pre-emergent herbicide that works in part by desiccating the soil, so that germination and root development of some species of weed seeds are inhibited under some conditions. An inevitable limitation to its efficacy is that it does not harm existing weeds but actually provides them with nitrogen, which can result in a net increase in weeds on a plot that has not been completely cleared beforehand. While corn gluten meal seemed to perform well as an herbicide in the Midwest, where it was first patented for this purpose, according to Linda Chalker-Scott, results in field trials in the Pacific Northwest have been disappointing. Weed control was limited, perhaps in part due to the moist climate here. There may be a slight gain from the added soil fertility that may sometimes help intentional crops to outcompete weeds, but such gains are better achieved with less expensive fertilizers.

## Ruminants

When a large area needs to be cleared of brush prior to garden installation, an increasingly popular option is to bring in goats. Goats are famously open-minded about what they'll eat, an attitude that will extend to your desired garden plants and the siding on your house. But with guidance and containment, goats can make short work of formidable thickets of herbaceous and even large shrubby weeds like blackberry, though roots will then need to be killed or removed by other means. There are businesses that will bring in goats to do this work, leaving in their wake the bonus of extra-strong fertilizer. Not all goats are equally open-minded about what they'll eat; they learn to eat what their mothers teach them to eat.

## Withdrawals from the Seed Bank

One trait of successful weeds is producing mass quantities of viable seeds. Any site that has had weeds setting seed, possibly for several years, will have acquired a seed bank—an accumulation of often thousands of viable seeds in the soil. Some of the activities involved in weed removal and replanting—digging, watering—will inevitably bring more seeds to the surface and provide them with moisture for germinating.

Below-surface drip irrigation systems can be labor-intensive to install and maintain, but they get water to the roots of the plants you want to grow and they conserve water, while not providing moisture for weed seeds at the surface to germinate. Otherwise, a thick layer of coarse, woody mulch (not compost, bark, or fine-textured mulch) will prevent most weed seeds from sprouting.

Be aware of cycles of bloom and seed production. In the Northwest, many plants germinate in fall and grow all winter, blooming in late winter or early spring. If you remove weeds before they can go to seed, you save yourself labor for years to come. Low-growing groundcovers that hug the soil prevent weed seeds from germinating, functioning as living mulch.

# Mulch

Mulching is the most effective, easiest, and least expensive strategy for long-term weed prevention in the garden. Do it right and do it early, and you'll save yourself a huge amount of time weeding.

Mulching between desired plants in an established garden will prevent germination of weed seeds from the existing seed bank, as well as any that happen to drift in on the wind. A thick mulch (4–6 in. deep for ornamentals, 8–10 in. for restoration sites) applied long before planting can eliminate many perennial weeds by starving them of light.

## COARSE WOOD CHIPS

More and more people are discovering the utility of a coarse wood-chip mulch, which has proven more effective than other materials for weed suppression and soil health. It breaks down more slowly and doesn't compact as much as many other mulches because the pieces vary in size. It absorbs water, which is then released slowly to the soil. Best of all, it's sometimes available free from arborists and tree service companies, or if you have a chipper you can make your own.

Wood chips (aka arborist chips) are available from arborists' tree-trimming and felling activities. A popular service, ChipDrop, connects arborists with gardeners seeking chips. Alternatively, you can contact tree services in your area and ask them if they have chips. Businesses selling bulk landscape materials (soil, rocks, etc.) also often carry wood chips. Prices vary from nothing to not very much.

**ABOVE, FROM LEFT**
Wood chips are a coarse mulch that breaks down slowly.

Bark mulch, a timber-industry byproduct, is attractive but breaks down faster than wood chips.

## BARK MULCH

Bark mulch, which is darker and much finer-textured, has been widely used for aesthetic reasons and as a matter of habit and established expectations. And the sale of this otherwise unusable material is a profitable sideline for the timber industry. However, it is much less effective than wood chips in suppressing weed-seed germination and less useful for moisture retention because it does not hold water: bark is waxy and thus hydrophobic; water just slides across it. Due to its uniform and fine-grained texture, it is also prone to compaction.

# Things Not to Do

## ROTOTILLING

Faced with a large patch of blackberries or broom, some gardeners might be tempted to use rototillers to take the monsters down, and this is occasionally advised by rototiller purveyors. It's a bad idea. Many weedy perennials will come back more numerous, sprouting new plants from each broken piece underground. The tilling brings weed seeds to the surface, where they can germinate, and also damages soil structure.

## SOLARIZATION

In solarization, a large sheet of clear (usually) or black plastic is laid on the ground to use solar energy to heat the soil, killing weeds, pests, and pathogens. It is sometimes favored as a cheap, fast, chemical-free way to clear garden areas prior to planting. This may be most useful in commercial agriculture, but in the home garden, its drawbacks may outweigh the benefits. It kills absolutely everything in the soil, including beneficial insects and microorganisms. The plastic becomes brittle over time, breaking into thousands of pieces that are hard to find and remove.

Alternative approaches like mulching may require more time but can also be very inexpensive and more sustainable.

## LANDSCAPE FABRIC

Landscape fabric has enjoyed widespread popularity in home and commercial landscaping where neatness was desired. This product is often called "weed barrier," but that is an awful misnomer. Tough perennial weeds like thistles and blackberries will punch right through the fabric to find light. Other weeds love the fabric as a substrate for seedlings and rhizomatous spread. Meanwhile, the fabric makes installation of new garden plants difficult, can interfere with existing plants as they grow, and creates a permanent source of environmental pollution. As it photodegrades and becomes tattered, the fabric is an eyesore and a maintenance issue. It's synthetic, meaning that its half-life is basically forever, and as it breaks down into scraps, it will eventually end up where all plastic does, in the ocean, choking an albatross. Trust us: if you install this stuff, years from now some landscaper or gardener will be cursing you. Just don't. Don't lay down plastic and cover it with mulch to make it pretty, either.

Landscape fabric breaks down, weeds may grow on top, and it can be challenging to plant through or remove.

51

A bowl of Himalayan blackberries, one of our tastiest weeds.

# Forgiven Weeds and Foraging

Some plants are what a friend has called "forgiven weeds." They're the weedy species we love for their beauty, pollinator appeal, or edibility. Scrupulous deadheading or fruit removal can be a compromise to preserve plants we want to keep but don't want to allow to take over the garden or spread to the surrounding landscape. Weeds treated this way by some gardeners include English holly; the ubiquitous purple foxglove; the invasive butterfly bush; the edible and pretty yellow and purple salsifies; the tall, pretty, rambunctious terror of native fireweed; and various other cherished green hooligans.

Foragers have long advocated harvesting wild plants for food or medicine, some of them native and many of them non-native weeds. Now, some environmentalists promote this notion, with events designed to educate the public in a fun way by focusing on edible weeds.

It's not that we can eat our way out of the environmental impact of invasive plant and animal species, but uprooting or de-fruiting some invasives for dinner sure can't hurt. The Institute for Applied Ecology, a Corvallis, Oregon–based nonprofit, hosts an annual fundraising event, the Invasive Species Cook-off. Contestants offer original recipes featuring invasive plants and animals.

# Set Your Priorities

Not all weeds are equally troublesome. You probably have limited time and energy to devote to creating a weed-free environment. Unless you're one of those extremely fastidious gardeners who wants everything looking perfect and weed-free all the time, you're going to have to prioritize.

If you've been cursed to have Class A noxious weeds on your property, the ones you're required by law to remove, then they are your highest priority. Remove them promptly if and when they appear.

For everything else, decide which ones bother you most. Mark, for example, lives with lots of weeds (nearly 15% of the photos in this book were made without stepping off his property). He successfully eradicated a patch of Bohemian knotweed before it got too large to control. He spends several days each year in late winter cutting and digging Himalayan blackberries from his woodland, an ongoing task. He has dug out small English hollies and treated the cut stumps of larger ones with herbicide, repeating as needed for several years so his woods are now mostly holly-free. He lets his mind wander while extracting creeping buttercups, quackgrass, and shotweed from his perennial and vegetable beds but doesn't worry so much about them in the lawn, where he encourages nitrogen-fixing clover to coexist with turf grasses. He mulches extensively to keep the weeds out of his vegetable patch and perennial beds. Prevention is preferable to marathon weeding sessions on hands and knees. And if a few weeds survive, it's not the end of the world.

# Trees and Shrubs

Trees and shrubs are the woody plants; the differences between them can be unclear or subjective, and some species may take the form of either a large shrub or a small tree.

Shrubs are typically multi-stemmed and much-branched from close to the bottom, not much taller than 12 ft., and with main trunks not thicker than a couple of inches. Trees are typically taller at maturity and have one main stem, but may have several. Their mature trunks are typically thicker than 3 in. at human-chest height; branching is usually higher from the ground.

Russian olive (*Elaeagnus angustifolia*) was introduced as a windbreak. It thrives in moist zones east of the Cascades, where it crowds out native species.

# Rhus glabra

SMOOTH SUMAC, SCARLET SUMAC, WESTERN SUMAC

Native perennial, to 10 ft. Flowers yellow, 5-lobed, to 0.25 in.; midspring–midsummer. Leaves alternate, to 18 in., leaflets to 4.5 in. Parts edible/medicinal with caution.

*Rhus glabra* is a native shrub or small tree common in dry habitats on the east side of the Cascades in the PNW, with a range over most of North America. The shrubs are found on woodland edges, roadsides, railroad embankments, and other disturbed sites. Related to poison-oak and poison-ivy, also natives, smooth sumac belongs to a genus of attractive shrubs often sold in nurseries.

*Rhus glabra* usually has a single trunk to begin with but spreads rapidly via aggressive rhizomes. The plant typically has a few branches, with many long, odd-pinnate compound leaves. A single leaf may have up to 31 sessile leaflets, which are lanceolate with serrated margins and pinnate venation. The leaves are deciduous and turn red in autumn.

Upright clusters of small flowers are borne at the ends of the upper branches. The species is dioecious. In the fall, the female flowers give way to erect, tight clusters of small, fuzzy, bright red berries, which often persist through winter.

Though native, smooth sumac is considered invasive in many wild habitats where it spreads aggressively and suppresses other natives. Many gardeners are fond of the colorful berries, attractive leaves, and interesting branch structures but may become less fond of the rampant suckering and generous self-seeding. Environmental agencies tackling large invasions have tried many strategies, most with limited success. *Rhus glabra* recovers quickly from mowing, burning, grazing, and cutting, and the rhizomes may even be stimulated to increased growth by incorrect application of any of these. Foliar and stump applications of herbicide have been effective.

Small invasions in home gardens may be suppressed by persistent and repeated pulling, digging, or cutting.

# *Toxicodendron diversilobum*

## POISON-OAK

Native perennial, to 40 ft. Flowers yellow, 5-lobed, to 0.06 in.; midspring–midsummer. Leaves alternate, trifoliate, leaflets to 4 in. Poisonous.

*Toxicodendron diversilobum* (syn. *Rhus diversiloba*) is found along the west coast from BC to California, and in the PNW is mostly on the east side of the Cascades. It typically grows in moderately dry, open woodland and hillsides at low elevations. Though native, it can be invasive and, because of its severe dermal toxicity, is widely considered a pest in yards and parks where humans may encounter it. It invades wood lots, tree farms, rangeland, cropland, and recreational areas. Urushiol, found in all *Toxicodendron* species, is the compound that causes the painful and itchy rash; it is contained in every part of the plant except its pollen.

Poison-oak grows as a large, erect shrub in sun and as a vine in shade. As a vine, it can wind through trees and shrubs to 100 ft. long. Its root system can cover an area of several square feet. The leaves of this and several closely related species are trifoliate: each leaf is composed of 3 leaflets (except for some populations with 5). The leaves are rounded, either entire or wavy-margined to lobed; they can be hairless and glossy, dull, or slightly fuzzy. Small flowers are borne in the leaf axils, with male and female flowers separate on the same plant. These are followed by loose clusters of small berries that begin greenish-white and mature to tan. In fall, the leaves, which are deciduous, may turn orange and red.

Poison-oak spreads via stolons, which will resprout when broken off, and via the berries, which are foraged and deposited far and wide by birds.

Control efforts on agricultural or public lands have included mowing and plowing (with limited success) and assorted herbicide application methods. Grazing animals can harmlessly munch the young foliage. Burning is a giant no-no: inhaling the smoke could do great harm.

For small infestations, pulling can be effective: control efforts should always be undertaken with protective clothing and never by individuals with known sensitivity. Pull and dig when the soil is moist, removing as much of the roots and stolons as possible. Vines growing up trees should be cut at the base; it may be impossible to remove all the vining material from a tree. Bag and carry away all uprooted or detached plant material.

# Toxicodendron radicans var. rydbergii
## WESTERN POISON-IVY

Native perennial, to 6 ft. Flowers white, 5-lobed, to 0.2 in.; midspring–early summer. Leaves alternate, leaflets to 4 in. Poisonous.

*Toxicodendron radicans* var. *rydbergii* (syn. *T. rydbergii*, *Rhus radicans*) is very closely related to poison-oak, with a different and only slightly overlapping range, from the east side of the Cascades eastward across much of North America. The plant inhabits woodland edges, riparian zones, prairies, and hillsides.

This is a large, upright shrub of varying height, spreading by runners and often forming colonies. Unlike its close cousin poison-oak, western poison-ivy does not have a vining form and does not bear aerial roots on the stems. The leaves are deciduous and trifoliate but otherwise distinctly different from those of *Toxicodendron diversilobum*, with the leaflets being ovate and sharply pointed at their tips. The leaves may turn yellow or orange to red in the fall. The flowers of western poison-ivy are similar to those of poison-oak, with branched clusters of up to 25 small, stalked flowers in a mix of male and female, borne in the leaf axils. The flowers are followed by clusters of small, greenish- or yellowish-white berries.

Western poison-ivy, like poison-oak, contains the toxic compound urushiol in all plant parts except pollen and can cause potentially severe dermatitis in most people. People who spend a lot of time in the outdoors for recreation or work are most often exposed to this.

Western poison-ivy can be removed by hand—carefully, with full coverage of protective clothing. Pulling and digging is most effective when the soil is moist, facilitating removal of the roots and stolons. Mowing does not work: it leaves the roots and stolons or rhizomes intact, and they will resprout readily. It's also somewhat hazardous, in that sap is released when the plants are cut.

Small seedlings can be pulled easily enough (with gloves!), but more tenacious roots are formed by the time young plants are 2 months old. Home gardeners with persistent or large patches, and those who are particularly sensitive to urushiol, may be better off using basal, foliar, or stump applications of herbicide.

# Ilex aquifolium

### ENGLISH HOLLY

Non-native perennial, to 50 ft. Flowers white, 4-petaled, to 0.2 in.; mid–late spring. Leaves alternate, to 3 in. Poisonous. Toxic to cats, dogs, livestock.

*Ilex aquifolium* is the most widely known member of a monotypic (single genus) family of 480 species. Like most species in the holly family, English holly is dioecious, and to get the showy red berries on female plants, it is necessary to have a male plant nearby. The leaves are evergreen, glossy, and spiny. As a tree, it can reach 50 ft. high and 15 wide but is usually smaller.

Many plant ID newcomers are confused by English holly's resemblance to native Oregon-grape species, particularly holly-leaved Oregon-grape. A simple trick for distinguishing these: holly's simple leaves are attached alternately along the stem, while the similar-looking leaflets of Oregon-grape's compound leaves are opposite each other along the leaf rachis.

English holly has been a staple of Christmas decorations for centuries. Native to Eurasia and Africa, it has been present in PNW landscaping and then as a widely grown agricultural product since the 1870s. It has found a particularly comfortable home in the PNW climate. Due to its cultural and economic importance, it is not yet listed as noxious, but it is widely considered invasive and environmentally harmful. The berries, though toxic to mammals, are eaten by birds and subsequently "planted" far and wide, particularly in woodlands.

Plants are very easy to pull or dig when young. Large, established plants may require herbicide. The glossy leaves do not absorb readily, so cut-stump treatments must be used and repeated applications may be needed.

# *Lonicera tatarica*

## TATARIAN HONEYSUCKLE

Non-native perennial, to 10 ft. Flowers pink, red, tubular, to 1 in.; midspring–midsummer. Leaves opposite, to 2.5 in. Poisonous.

This Asian shrub is found throughout North America, having been introduced in the 1700s as an ornamental. It is listed as invasive in numerous states, particularly in New England and the upper Midwest. Thus far, it is found only in a few scattered sites in the PNW. It grows in sun or part shade and often forms dense thickets in open woods, woodland edges, fields, and on roadsides. It can crowd out native plants and competes with them for pollinators, thus reducing their seed set.

This multi-stemmed deciduous shrub, as tall as wide, grows from shallow, fibrous roots. It is very similar to several other weedy, introduced shrub honeysuckles. Young plants have hairy, brownish stems; mature stems are hollow, and the bark is light gray, often peeling. The fragrant flowers are borne in pairs along the stems at the axils. Like other honeysuckles, the flowers are 2-lipped (bilaterally symmetric) and tubular; they are pink or red (sometimes white). Flowers are followed by many orange to red berries, which are loved by assorted birds and wildlife, which then become agents of dispersal.

Invasions of this and other shrub honeysuckles can be combatted by grubbing out or pulling seedlings, digging mature shrubs, or repeatedly cutting them low. An invaded site may require repeated efforts over a period of several years.

If you long for a shrub honeysuckle, the PNW has several nice native species that are less rambunctious, particularly *Lonicera involucrata*, which is not fragrant but is attractive and a hit with hummingbirds.

# Elaeagnus angustifolia

RUSSIAN OLIVE

Non-native perennial, to 25 ft. Flowers yellow, 4-lobed, to 0.4 in.; late spring–early summer. Leaves alternate, to 2.75 in. Parts edible/medicinal. Noxious in WA.

Russian olive is widespread throughout most of North America, and in the PNW is found on the drier east side. It's an invasive escape from cultivation, having been planted widely in the US beginning in the early 1900s. In the PNW, it was often planted as a windbreak. It invades moist zones within warm, dry regions, particularly riparian areas and irrigation canals. An aggressive self-seeder that is hard to eradicate once established, Russian olive displaces important native flora. It is a listed noxious weed in several states.

*Elaeagnus angustifolia* is a large shrub or multi-stemmed tree with often thorny branches. Its root system is deep and travels laterally for many feet; it is sometimes associated with nitrogen-fixing organisms in the soil. Its deciduous leaves are simple, narrow, and silvery. It has fragrant yellow flowers in small clusters in the leaf axils. They lack true petals but have sepals that are petal-like. The grayish, olive-like fruit are widely dispersed by birds and other animals.

Mature Russian olives, particularly in larger numbers, are famously difficult to impossible to eradicate: the roots survive all kinds of assaults and resprout. So the best cure is prevention: if you're in an area where these might show up, be on the lookout for seedlings and saplings and any stray seeds. Pull and dig when the soil is moist, and be sure to get all the roots. Roots that remain and can't be removed should be cut below the soil level and buried. Mature plants can be killed by cutting to the ground and treating the stump with herbicide. Foliar sprays of herbicides have also proven effective.

61

# Acacia dealbata

## SILVER WATTLE

**Non-native perennial, to 30+ ft. Flowers yellow, heads to 0.2 in.; late winter–early spring. Leaves alternate, to 6.5 in. Parts edible. Toxic to horses.**

Silver wattle is native to Australia and has become invasive on several other continents. It has long been planted as a landscape ornamental in California and is now a widespread garden escape there and in Oregon, invading prairies, woodlands, and riparian zones. The plant spreads aggressively, crowding out natives. Like many members of the pea family, its roots have nitrogen-fixing associations that can result in detrimental changes in soil chemistry on sites where it becomes dominant.

The common name refers to a whitish coating on young branches and the tips of juvenile foliage and the often silvery to blue-green color of the mature foliage, which is also densely hairy. The leaves are borne on short, hairy stalks and are bipinnate: the rachis of a leaf bears up to 30 pairs of opposite branchlets, each of these in turn bearing as many as 60+ pairs of small, linear leaflets.

The minute flowers, borne in small spherical heads on short stalks, look fluffy due to their many stamens. Each head contains up to 40 small flowers, and these heads are then arranged alternately along the stalk of a larger, elongated, compound cluster. The flowers are followed by typical pea-type pods to 4.5 in. long, each containing several seeds, which are long-lived in the environment and dispersed by wind and water.

Control of established *Acacia dealbata* is challenging because it resprouts and suckers after being cut. Herbicides have been used with limited success. Young plants can be dug out; larger plants can be girdled or treated with cut-stump herbicide application. Remove all seedpods from the site, mulch heavily, and monitor for re-emergence.

# *Alhagi maurorum*
## CAMELTHORN

Non-native perennial, to 4 ft. Flowers red-purple, pea-like, to 0.4 in.; midsummer. Leaves alternate, to 1.25 in. Parts edible/medicinal with caution. Noxious in BC, WA, OR, CA.

*Alhagi maurorum* (syn. *A. pseudalhagi*), an Asian species, was accidentally introduced to the western US in the early 1900s and has since spread from Texas to the PNW, invading arid regions of multiple states and provinces and listed as noxious in several. It invades pastures and rangeland, riparian areas, and irrigation ditches. It is particularly a problem when it competes with more suitable forage on rangeland.

Camelthorn grows from a robust root system, with vertical roots to 6 ft. or more deep. Like many plants in the pea family, it has root nodules associated with nitrogen-fixing bacteria. The deep and horizontal rhizomes can give rise to new plants as far as 25 ft. from the mother plant. The stems are green and multi-branched, bearing spines to 2 in. long. Leaves are oval to lanceolate, with a rough upper surface and somewhat hairy, grayish underside.

The small pea-like flowers are purple to maroon, borne in small axillary clusters of 1–6, arranged alternately along spine-tipped axillary branchlets on the upper stems. Flowers are followed by inch-long brown pods that are constricted between individual seeds. A single plant may produce as many as 6,000 seeds in a season, and these are dispersed by wind, water, and animals that consume them. Seeds may also be dispersed in arid and windy regions where upper portions of a plant may break off and become tumbleweeds. Agricultural machinery may spread seeds as well as rhizome fragments. Despite the considerable seed output, most reproduction is vegetative, by sprouting from rhizomes and rhizome fragments.

Camelthorn has proven extremely resistant to control efforts by land managers and weed agencies. Most standard methods (burning, tillage, mowing) only stimulated more reproduction from rhizomes and roots. Herbicides have been the only recourse in dealing with large invasions. Small invasions, particularly if caught early, can be tackled by pulling and digging when the soil is moist, with continued monitoring and repeated yearly efforts.

# Amorpha fruticosa

## WESTERN FALSE INDIGO, DESERT FALSE INDIGO

Non-native perennial, to 12 ft. Flowers blue, violet, purple, to 0.25 in.; late spring–midsummer. Leaves alternate, to 12 in., leaflets to 2 in. Parts medicinal. Noxious in WA, OR.

*Amorpha fruticosa* (syn. *A. dewinkeleri*, *A. occidentalis*), native to eastern North America, is present in most western states and invasive in many of them. In the PNW, it's found primarily on the east side, as well as in the Columbia River Gorge. It invades areas with sandy soil particularly, on roadsides, vacant lots, meadows, dunes, wetlands, and riparian areas. An aggressive colonizer, it changes plant community structures, outcompeting locally native flora. It's attractive and has often been introduced to new territory as an ornamental.

Like many genera in the Fabaceae, *Amorpha* ("without form," a reference to the unusual structure of its flowers) has associations with nitrogen-fixing bacteria and nodules on its roots. In this species, multiple stems arise from a deep root system. They are green and hairy when young, aging to woody, and branched at the top. The upper portions of the stems bear deciduous leaves that are odd-pinnate with up to 31 leaflets. The leaves are whitish and fuzzy underneath, nearly hairless and gray-green above. The flowers are borne in many upright terminal and near-terminal racemes to 6 in. long. Unlike typical pea flowers, each consists of a single petal. Flowers are followed by dark brown, curved pods to 0.25 in. long, each containing 1–2 seeds. The pods float and may be dispersed by water; seeds are also dispersed by birds and other animals. In addition to self-sowing, *A. fruticosa* produces new plants from buds on lateral roots and may form dense colonies.

Efforts to control large infestations have included repeated mowing or cutting to modest effect, grazing, and herbicides. Cutting and mowing can stimulate growth by resprouting of stems but if done repeatedly can delay seed production. For small invasions, young plants can be dug or pulled, preferably when soil is moist; remove any seedpods that have formed from the site. Effective digging may not be possible for more mature plants, due to the root system, so persistent cutting may be the only option to slow the plant down, unless herbicides are used.

# Caragana arborescens

## SIBERIAN PEA-SHRUB

Non-native perennial, to 18 ft. Flowers yellow, to 0.75 in.; mid–late spring. Leaves alternate, to 5 in., leaflets to 1 in. Parts edible/medicinal.

Siberian pea-shrub, native to parts of Asia, is a fast-growing woody shrub or small tree once common in landscaping and now a widespread garden escape over much of North America, excluding the southeastern US. It invades woodlands and grasslands and can be seen on roadsides and in vacant lots. In natural areas, it displaces native vegetation and damages ecosystems: its nitrogen-fixing function alters soil chemistry.

This shrub develops a deep root system, which may have nitrogen-fixing nodules, like many members of the pea family. A single plant produces multiple erect, branched stems. The deciduous leaves are pinnately compound, each with up to 12 narrow leaflets, and no terminal leaflet. The foliage is hairy when young, hairless and smooth as it matures. Clusters of 1–5 stalked, tubular flowers are borne in the axils of lateral branchlets. The yellow flowers are followed by pods to 2 in. long, each containing about 6 seeds.

Small plants can be pulled or dug. Larger plants or multiple plants can be controlled by repeated burning, cutting or mowing; they will resprout from the root crown, but will eventually succumb.

# Cytisus scoparius

## SCOTCH BROOM, SCOT'S BROOM

Non-native perennial, to 10 ft. Flowers yellow, pea-like, to 0.75 in.; late spring–early summer. Leaves alternate, to 1 in. Parts edible with caution. Toxic to horses, cattle, sheep. Noxious in BC, WA, OR, CA.

Scotch broom, arguably the most problematic noxious weed in the PNW, was introduced to Victoria, BC, in 1850. By the 1860s, it was being used in California as a garden plant and was later widely used in many states as a soil-stabilizing plant along highways. It rapidly escaped and became established in the wild from Canada to California. It now covers millions of acres throughout the west. In addition to environmental impacts, it is toxic to livestock. It's a listed noxious weed in several western states; in the PNW, it is particularly widespread west of the Cascades.

Scotch broom favors open areas, including pastures, roadsides, waste areas, and native meadows and prairies. It rapidly forms extensive, dense colonies, crowding out other vegetation.

The shrub is a formidable invader: it's large, long-lived, deep-rooted, and tolerant of poor soil and drought. A single plant will produce thousands of seeds in its lifetime, and the hard-coated seeds can persist in the environment for several decades. The seeds are dispersed by animals, by wind, and by lodging in the tread of vehicle tires.

The twigs of broom are largely green. The leaves are simple on the upper stems, trifoliate on the lower stems. The flowers are stalked, bright yellow (occasionally yellow/red bicolor), and borne singly or in pairs in the leaf axils. The cup-shaped flowers are bilabiate, with 2 petals forming the upper lip and 3 forming the lower.

Eradication of Scotch broom from any site can take years: the seed bank is large and long-lived, and the resupply of seedlings from nearby infested landscapes is often constant. Pulling and digging can be effective for small infestations. You can rent a weed wrench to facilitate pulling out the shrubs by the roots.

As a less labor-intensive strategy, cut plants when in bloom to discourage resprouting, or cut to about a foot high and peel the bark down to dry out the crown. Large areas may require repeated mowing, digging, and herbicide.

# Genista monspessulana

## FRENCH BROOM

Non-native perennial, to 10 ft. Flowers yellow, to 0.4 in.; midspring–midsummer. Leaves trifoliate, to 1 in. Poisonous. Toxic to horses, cattle, sheep. Noxious in WA, OR, CA.

Similarly to *Cytisus scoparius* and during the same period, *Genista monspessulana* (syn. *C. monspessulanus*) began its west coast career as a horticultural introduction but rapidly escaped cultivation. Like Scotch broom, French broom spreads via copious self-seeding and forms dense thickets that contribute to fire hazards and displace native flora and fauna. It also displaces forage crops used by livestock, and is toxic to cattle and horses.

The flowers and foliage look similar to *Cytisus*, except that the flowers are a little smaller and are typically clustered in groups of 3–10 at the ends of branches. Leaves are trifoliate in both. The stems of *Genista* are covered with silvery hairs, as are the pods; the stems of *Cytisus* are smooth and green.

The distribution of *Genista monspessulana* is much more limited than for *C. scoparius*. It is less cold-hardy than *Cytisus* and so occurs more frequently at lower elevations and lower latitudes. *Genista monspessulana* covers hundreds of thousands of acres in the west, predominantly in California. In Washington and Oregon, it is found in scattered sites primarily on the west side of the Cascades.

Once established on a site, French broom is difficult to eradicate due to the long-lived seed bank. Control options and concerns are similar to those for Scotch broom: pull when small, dig when larger, cut when much larger, repeat over time.

# Laburnum anagyroides

## GOLDEN CHAIN TREE

Non-native perennial, to 30 ft. Flowers yellow, pea-like, 5-petaled, to 0.75 in.; midspring. Leaves alternate, trifoliate, to 3 in. Poisonous. Toxic to cats, dogs, horses, cattle, pigs, chickens.

Golden chain tree is a popular landscaping plant that has "jumped the fence" as a garden escape along the west coast from California to BC and in Utah. In the PNW, it prospers mostly on the more moist and mild west side of the Cascades, where it invades woodland edges and other disturbed areas near residential property.

The leaves and flowers of *Laburnum anagyroides* are very recognizably pea-like. The deciduous leaves are trifoliate, with the leaflets narrowly ovate to elliptical, and the bright yellow flowers are borne in terminal racemes to 10 in. long. Each flower has delicate reddish-brown lines etched on the insides of the upper petals. The flowers are followed by seedpods to 2.5 in. long, containing hard-coated black seeds.

All parts of this plant are highly poisonous, particularly the seedpods and seeds. For this reason, the tree is not recommended for homes with small children or grazing pets, and if a mature tree is present, precautions are recommended. To prevent garden domination or escape and to reduce poisoning risks, deadhead thoroughly. This is an easy task when the tree is young but will soon be impractical.

Watch for seeds and seedpods, bag and remove. Pull seedlings, dig out saplings, cut more mature trees to the ground and uproot or use herbicide.

# *Lupinus arboreus*

## TREE LUPINE, YELLOW BUSH LUPINE

Perennial, both native and introduced, to 6 ft. Flowers yellow, to 0.7 in.; midspring–autumn. Leaves alternate, leaflets to 2.5 in. Poisonous. Toxic to horses, cattle, sheep, goats, chickens.

Tree lupine is a California native but is considered non-native and invasive north of the Bay Area. It was introduced to northern California in the early 1900s, when land managers and agencies planted it as a dune and slope stabilizer. It has since invaded coastal beaches from northern California to BC and is of great concern for its environmental impact. The large, robust species forms broad monocultures, crowding out more diverse native dune flora. As a nitrogen-fixer, it alters the dune ecosystem, facilitating increased invasion.

Growing from deep roots, this tall, well-branched plant is clothed in finely hairy compound leaves, each composed of 5–11 elliptical leaflets, palmately arranged. The flowers are borne in many loose racemes to 12 in. long, held more or less upward. The mostly yellow, bilabiate flowers often have a purplish tint on the banner (the uppermost of the 5 lobes), and some purplish plants are thought to be hybrids. Flowers are followed by fuzzy, grayish pods, to 2.5 in. long and 0.4 in. wide, each bearing up to 12 long-lived seeds. The large numbers of seeds are dispersed by wind and rodents, and when plants break off and tumble across the dunes.

Small invasions of tree lupine can be removed by pulling, digging, or deployment of a weed wrench—depending on size and maturity of the plant. The entire root mass should be removed if possible to prevent resprouting. When this proves impractical, the plant may be cut at its base and the trunk split. Eradication is best attempted before bloom, and the resulting debris can be dried and burned, or bagged

and removed. Established populations will likely have a seed bank, so the site will require repeated monitoring and weed-wrangling for a few years.

# *Robinia pseudoacacia*
## BLACK LOCUST

Non-native perennial, to 90 ft. Flowers white, 5-lobed, pea-like, to 1 in.; early summer. Leaves alternate, to 14 in., leaflets to 2 in. Parts edible/medicinal with caution. Toxic to cats, horses, cattle, sheep, goats, chickens.

Black locust is native to the eastern US but has often been planted as an ornamental and is widely introduced in the west and in parts of Canada, where it can be seen in riparian zones, on woodland edges, in meadows, and in residential areas. It suckers aggressively, rapidly forming broad, dense thickets that crowd out natives.

*Robinia pseudoacacia* grows from very wide-spreading roots that may be deep or shallow. Its compound leaves are deciduous and typical for the pea family; each has up to 21 odd-pinnately arranged leaflets, hairless and bright green on top, lighter on the undersides. Sharp thorns to 0.5 in. long are often found at the bases of the petioles, particularly when the trees are younger; other trees are thornless. The flowers are showy and fragrant, white with a yellow blotch, borne in drooping racemes to 5 in. long containing as many as 70 flowers. These are followed by typical pea family seedpods, to 4 in., each with up to 8 seeds.

The first rule of management is to notice black locust immediately and act quickly. If there's a tree in the vicinity, beware: suckers and seedlings may soon pop up. Small plants can be pulled or dug up; take care to remove all roots, because they can easily resprout. Repeatedly cutting the tree to the ground may deplete its resources and ultimately kill it. While herbicide has often been the strategy for land managers faced with large invasions, this has not always yielded victory, because herbicided trees may eventually come back.

# Sesbania punicea

## RATTLEBOX

Non-native perennial, to 15 ft. Flowers orange, red, pea-like, to 1.2 in.; late spring–summer. Leaves alternate, to 8 in.; pinnate leaflets to 1 in. Poisonous. Toxic to horses, cattle, sheep, chickens, livestock. Noxious in CA.

This South American native was introduced in California as an ornamental by the early 1900s. It has since escaped and become a weed of concern, particularly in the Central Valley of northern California. It is also present as an invasive plant of riparian areas in the southern US from Texas to Florida to Virginia. The plant is still widely available in the nursery trade and may be passed around among gardeners even where illegal, because it's undeniably showy. However, its aggressive seed reproduction enables it to colonize riparian sites, blocking access to the water, crowding out native plants, and degrading habitat. It is also poisonous to humans and toxic to wildlife and livestock when eaten. Modest quantities have caused death in livestock and poultry consuming them.

This woody, deciduous, large shrub or small tree has pinnately compound leaves typical of the family, each bearing up to 20 pairs of opposite, elliptical leaflets. The flowers are borne in axillary racemes to 10 in. long, each composed of up to 30 flowers. These are followed by distinctive, oblong pods to 3 in. long and 0.4 in. wide, in clusters of up to 10, each containing up to 10 seeds. They begin yellowish-green, maturing to dark brown, and can persist on the plant through winter. A single plant may produce as many as 1,000 such pods annually, or potentially 10,000 seeds. The pods are buoyant, readily dispersed by water, and may thus travel long distances, eventually beginning new populations.

Small plants can be pulled out by hand or with weed wrenches fairly easily. Larger plants may be cut down and dug out, or a cut-stump herbicide treatment applied, but if the plant is near water or in a designated wetland, check with your noxious weed agency for guidance. When digging disturbs the soil, it can facilitate germination of additional seeds, so follow-up monitoring is recommended.

# Spartium junceum

## SPANISH BROOM

Non-native perennial, to 10 ft. Flowers yellow, pea-like, to 1 in.; midspring–autumn. Leaves alternate, to 1.2 in. Poisonous. Toxic to horses, cattle, sheep. Noxious in WA, OR, CA.

Native to Africa, this very drought-tolerant broom was formerly planted along highways in southern California and sold by nurseries as an ornamental. It proved very aggressively invasive and is now found all along

the coast of California and in scattered sites in western Oregon and Washington. It can be seen on roadsides, vacant lots, woodland edges, in parks, and in pastures. It crowds out natives and displaces desirable forage for livestock and wildlife. Being a legume with nitrogen-fixing nodules, it alters soil chemistry and vegetation structure. With vast dry, mature biomass, it has proven a fire hazard in parts of California. The entire plant is toxic, particularly the seeds.

Spanish broom can be confused from a distance with several related, invasive leguminous shrubs, particularly Scotch broom (*Cytisus scoparius*). However, there are several distinct differences: *Spartium* has round, thick, waxy stems (vs. the more ridged and wiry stems of *Cytisus*). The fragrant flowers of *Spartium* are borne in long, loose, terminal racemes to 18 in. (vs. the less fragrant to musky, single axillary flowers of *Cytisus*). The leaves of *Spartium* are present only from February to June and are single and linear to lanceolate (vs. the trifoliate leaves of *Cytisus*).

The bright yellow flowers of *Spartium junceum* are followed by flat, linear, hairy seedpods to 3 in. A single plant may produce as many as 10,000 seeds in a season, and these can remain viable for up to 80 years.

Management approaches are the same as for Scotch broom: pull and dig smaller plants, being careful to remove all roots and seedpods. Larger plants may call for a weed wrench. Alternatively, cut to the ground and treat the stump with herbicide. Mulch well and watch for new seedlings.

# Ulex europaeus

## GORSE

Non-native perennial, to 10 ft. Flowers yellow, pea-like, to 0.75 in.; midspring–autumn. Leaves to 2.6 in. Parts edible with caution. Noxious in BC, WA, OR, CA.

Gorse is a massive and thorny shrub introduced in Oregon and elsewhere as an ornamental and "living fence." It proved aggressive, fast-spreading, and very difficult to remove, and is now found all along the west coast from BC to California, as well as in the northeastern US. It invades roadsides, riparian zones, fields, parks, and pastures, crowding out natives and other desired vegetation. A single plant can form a thicket to 30 ft. in diameter, often with a dead center. With the dry, dead centers and the high oil content of the leaves, the plant has proven a fire hazard. After introduction to the Bandon, Oregon, area in the 1890s, gorse was identified as the cause of a wildfire that burned the town to the ground in 1936. Despite intensive efforts to control it, gorse has infested over 55,000 acres in Oregon alone. (Beware, a close relative, Spanish broom, is sometimes also called gorse. You will know this one by its spines.)

Growing from a woody crown, the shrub has mostly green stems, with prominent spines at their tips. The stems are covered in thin, trifoliate evergreen leaves that mature into spines. The yellow flowers are borne in terminal clusters. Bloom season is predominantly as stated, but plants can bloom at any time throughout the year. Flowers are followed by seedpods to 0.75 in. long. The pods open explosively when ripe, shooting seeds several feet from the parent plant; seeds can remain viable for 30 years.

Always wear thick gloves and other protective gear when doing battle with this monster. Small invasions of gorse can be pulled or dug up; take care to remove all the roots and the crown. Repeat-mowing a few times yearly for several years may eventually deplete the plant's stored reserves. After mowing or cutting mature plants to the ground, the crowns can be treated with herbicide. Follow with thick mulch and monitor for seedlings and resproutings.

# Morus alba

## WHITE MULBERRY

Non-native perennial, to 50 ft. Flowers yellow-green, to 0.07 in.; midspring–early summer. Leaves alternate, to 4 in. Parts edible/medicinal with caution.

White mulberry is a Chinese species that was introduced widely in the US beginning in the 1600s, and then with renewed enthusiasm in the 1800s. The hope was to develop a silk industry, but the trees soon succumbed to cold winters in the north and diseases in the south. A prodigious self-seeder, the tree escaped cultivation and is present in nearly all US states, as well as in BC, Ontario, and Quebec. In the PNW, it's found primarily east of the Cascades. It invades roadsides, fields, and woodland edges, particularly in riparian zones, and displaces native vegetation.

*Morus alba* grows from a wide root system with a taproot to 10 ft. deep and shallower lateral roots that can spread horizontally as far as 40 ft. at maturity. The leaves are variable in shape, basically oval and coarsely serrate to deeply lobed. They are glossy above and may be glabrous to slightly pubescent below. Male and female flowers are borne in separate catkins, usually on separate trees (dioecious) but occasionally on the same tree (monoecious). The small male flowers are on catkins to 2 in. long; the smaller female flowers are compressed on short spikes. The female flowers are followed by multi-seeded berries that resemble blackberries, only more cylindrical; these may be black, purple, or white. White mulberry trees have been estimated to produce as many as 20 million seeds in a season! These are widely dispersed by wildlife that consume them and then deposit them elsewhere.

Pull, hoe, and dig seedlings and saplings as soon as they appear. More established trees can be cut to the ground or girdled. Stumps, which resprout readily, can be removed with a stump grinder, or the stump can be treated with herbicide.

# *Eucalyptus globulus*

## TASMANIAN BLUE GUM

Non-native perennial, to 180 ft. Flowers white, to 2 in.; winter–early spring. Leaves opposite, alternate, to 9 in. Parts edible/medicinal with caution.

One of several *Eucalyptus* species introduced to the US in the mid-1800s, *Eucalyptus globulus* has since escaped cultivation widely in Hawaii and along the coast of California from Humboldt County to San Diego. The large, robust tree self-seeds abundantly, crowds out native plants, and has allelopathic properties that suppress nearby vegetation.

Tasmanian blue gum grows from an aggressive root system; lateral roots may have a spread to 100 ft. and go as deep as 40 ft. Mature trees can reach a diameter of 7 ft., remaining mostly straight for two-thirds of their height, branching out into a high, well-developed crown. The leaves are deciduous and aromatic. On older branches they are narrowly lanceolate and somewhat curved, hanging vertically and attached alternately. On younger shoots they are opposite, oval, sessile, and horizontal, often with a glaucous bloom, particularly on the undersides.

Flowers are borne singly from the leaf axils. The floral structure of *Eucalyptus* is unique, with no typically recognizable petals; the petals and sepals are rigid when in bud, green or glaucous, forming a cap over the rest of the flower. In *E. globulus*, the bud is shaped like a toy top or a cone. In bloom, the cap falls off to reveal numerous stamens, which surround a single pistil and make an attractive, fluffy-looking flower. The seedpods are woody and circular, opening at maturity to release many small seeds that are wind-dispersed.

Seedlings and saplings can be pulled or grubbed out. Burning can be effective in killing young trees, particularly in late summer, before the rains start. Trees can regenerate vegetatively from boles, stumps, and roots, so once the root system is too large to dig out, other strategies become necessary. The trees can be cut to the ground repeatedly, and the stumps removed with a stump grinder or treated with herbicide. When a small invasion has been successfully removed from a garden, follow with mulch.

# Ligustrum vulgare

## COMMON PRIVET, EUROPEAN PRIVET

Non-native perennial, to 12 ft. Flowers white, lavender, 4-petaled, to 0.25 in.; midspring–early summer. Leaves opposite, to 2.5 in. Poisonous. Toxic to horses.

*Ligustrum vulgare* is an attractive shrub widely planted as an ornamental in the past. It has proven to be an aggressive invader in many areas of the world. It has escaped cultivation from BC to western Oregon, in Montana, and across much of the eastern and southern US, as well as Ontario. Common privet invades riparian zones, roadsides, prairies, open woodland, and forest edges. Its tolerance for shade and for a wide range of environmental conditions gives it competitive advantages, and it can form thickets that crowd out native vegetation. All parts of the plant, including the berries, are mildly toxic.

Common privet grows as a multi-stemmed large shrub to small tree, with upright to spreading or relaxed habit. New stems are hairy and green, later hairless and aging to gray. The semi-deciduous leaves are lanceolate with smooth margins. Clusters of small, tubular flowers are borne at the branch tips. The flowers are strongly scented in a way many people find unpleasant. They are followed by clusters of black berries that ripen in fall, each about 0.3 in. in diameter and containing 1–4 seeds. A single plant may produce as many as 10,000 berries in a season. The berries are dispersed by birds and other animals.

Small plants can be pulled or dug out. As they mature, digging becomes more labor-intensive, as all roots must be removed to prevent resprouting. Cutting all stems to the ground repeatedly during the growing season is a temporary measure to forestall spreading, but the stumps can resprout. Larger invasions are often combatted with foliar or cut-stump herbicide applications.

# Paulownia tomentosa

PRINCESS TREE, EMPRESS TREE, ROYAL PAULOWNIA

Non-native perennial, to 60 ft. Flowers pink, purple, violet, to 2 in.; late spring–early summer. Leaves opposite, to 12 in. Parts edible with caution.

Princess tree is a weedy garden escape found in scattered areas of western Washington and in much of the eastern US, where some states have declared it a noxious weed. It was introduced to the US as a garden plant in the 1800s; it continues to be grown horticulturally as well as being produced commercially for its wood.

The leaves are deciduous, broad and fuzzy, oval to heart-shaped. The fragrant flowers are borne in upright terminal clusters as long as 14 in. Individual flowers are foxglove-like, having tubular, 5-lobed corollas with interior spots. The woody, oval seed capsules split open in fall to release many small, winged seeds: as many as 2,000 per capsule, or 2 million for a single tree. The seeds are dispersed great distances by wind and water. Princess tree aggressively self-seeds, colonizing open, disturbed ground including woodlands and riparian areas.

This is an admittedly showy tree and can be seen in yards and gardens throughout the region. If it shows up uninvited, it's easy enough to pull or dig when young. Take care to remove the entire root, to forestall resprouting of fragments left behind. More mature trees that are unwanted can be cut to ground level repeatedly, girdled, and/or treated with herbicide. A compromise move that retains the plant but prevents its self-seeding is to coppice or pollard it yearly. Many gardeners favor this as a way to keep plants small, promoting their attractive leaves while forfeiting the flowers.

# Fallopia ×bohemica

## BOHEMIAN KNOTWEED, HYBRID KNOTWEED

Non-native perennial, to 10 ft. Flowers white, to 0.25 in.; midsummer–autumn. Leaves alternate, to 10 in. Parts edible. Noxious in BC, WA, OR, CA.

*Fallopia ×bohemica* (syn. *Polygonum ×bohemicum*) is a hybrid of *F. japonica* (Japanese or itadori knotweed) and *F. sachalinensis* (giant knotweed), both non-native invasives. It is intermediate between its parent species in several traits, which poses challenges to identification as well as disagreements among authorities. According to the University of Washington's Burke Museum Herbarium, it is present along the west coast from Alaska to Oregon and in scattered areas over much of the northern US, as well as northeastern and northwestern Canada. Like its parent species, this very large and showy, shrubby herbaceous perennial favors moist ground in riparian areas, fields, vacant lots, and roadsides.

Bohemian knotweed forms dense colonies that crowd out native vegetation and alter plant community structure, particularly damaging riparian zones. Its rhizomes can extend 6 ft. deep into the soil and 20 ft. horizontally. Most of our plants are male and produce no seeds, so most reproduction is vegetative, by rhizomes and stem or rhizome fragments.

The stems are bamboo-like, being stout and jointed at the nodes, hollow between the nodes, unbranched or sparingly branched. They are upright and sometimes arching toward the top, brown at maturity. The leaves are roughly oval, more spade-shaped on the upper stem, more heart-shaped on the lower. They are about 7 in. wide and leathery, with hairs along the midveins. The leaves and stems are deciduous, and most of the plant dies to the ground at the end of the growing season, though the dead canes may persist through winter. The small flowers are borne in branched panicles to 14 in., from the upper leaf axils.

Eradication often takes several years of monitoring and repeated efforts. Small invasions can be dug up, though this is labor-intensive, as all rhizomes must be removed. All plant material should be bagged and either disposed of or burned, to avoid leaving behind fragments that can resprout. Cutting or mowing the plants low to the ground frequently during the growing season, annually for several years, can eventually deplete and kill Bohemian knotweed. Herbicide is used by noxious weed agencies and others, but this is typically regulated if in a wetland setting. Contact your local weed agency for guidance.

# *Persicaria wallichii*

## HIMALAYAN KNOTWEED, GARDEN KNOTWEED

Non-native perennial, to 6 ft. Flowers white, 5-lobed, to 0.2 in.; midsummer–autumn. Leaves alternate, to 12 in. Parts edible with caution. Noxious in BC, WA, OR, CA.

*Persicaria wallichii* (syn. *Polygonum polystachyum*), found along the west coast from BC to California, in Idaho, and in eastern North America, is one of several very closely related and very similar-looking invasive plants in the PNW, all introduced as ornamentals. The names for this species and the others have changed several times, and authorities do not agree on identity or range of some of them. This species has the narrowest leaves and is the least common in the PNW but often forms dense clonal patches that exclude other vegetation and alter ecosystem structure, particularly in riparian zones.

Himalayan knotweed grows from underground rhizomes and can spread from any small fragments of stem or rhizome. It also spreads by seed, but this is limited, as it may be fully or partially sterile in some parts of the range. It sends up numerous tall, erect, leafy, reddish-brown stems. The twigs are characteristically slightly zigzag from node to node. Lower leaves are stalked, becoming shorter-stalked to nearly sessile upward on the stem. The leaves are oblong to lanceolate, with tips drawn abruptly to a point. Leaf bases may be somewhat flat, or heart-shaped. As in most members of the buckwheat family, there are ocreas at the bases of leaf petioles. The fragrant flowers are borne in showy terminal panicles.

Like all invasive knotweeds, this one is very difficult to eradicate once established. Pull or dig young plants promptly, excavating roots and rhizomes as much as possible and removing all plant parts, including stem fragments, from the site. They may be dried and then burned to prevent resprouting. For larger invasions or more established plants, frequent yearly cutting for several years may eventually kill the plants. Where it is feasible, you can also cut plants to the ground and then cover firmly with thick landscape cloth for several years. Herbicides are often used but are tightly regulated near wetlands. Check with your local weed agency for ID confirmation and management guidelines.

# Cotoneaster lacteus

## MILKFLOWER COTONEASTER, LATE COTONEASTER, PARNEY'S COTONEASTER

Non-native perennial, to 10 ft. Flowers white, to 0.3 in.; late spring–midsummer. Leaves alternate, to 3 in. Poisonous. Toxic to cats, dogs, horses.

*Cotoneaster* is a genus of widely planted non-native shrubs that can be aggressive in conquest of space in gardens or when escaping into wild landscapes—as milkflower cotoneaster, a garden shrub from China, has done from BC to California. A couple of species, including *C. lacteus*, have in recent years become worrisome invaders along the Oregon and California coasts, where they can be seen near residential areas and in coastal scrub, woodlands, and meadows.

The leaves of *Cotoneaster* are evergreen and dark green, with conspicuous veining and smooth margins. In *C. lacteus*, the leaves are elliptic to oval in shape, and leaf undersides are beige and woolly. The shrub can spread to as wide as 12 ft. The small white flowers (sometimes pale pink in bud) are borne in showy clusters of up to 150. Developing in fall, the bright red berries are about 0.25 in. in diameter; they are mildly toxic to humans and other mammals but not to songbirds. A single shrub will produce thousands of berries annually. These are dispersed by birds, small mammals, and water.

Pull, hoe, or dig seedlings when the soil is moist. Established plants develop root systems that can be difficult to dig out, and the plant will readily resprout when cut down. Large infestations may be handled with cut-stump herbicide treatments; they may still come back, so follow-up monitoring is recommended to intercept resprouting and seedlings.

# *Crataegus monogyna*

## ENGLISH HAWTHORN, ONE-SEEDED HAWTHORN, COMMON HAWTHORN

Non-native perennial, to 30 ft. Flowers white, pink, 5-petaled, to 0.6 in.; midspring–midsummer. Leaves alternate, to 2 in. Parts edible/medicinal with caution. Noxious in WA, OR.

English hawthorn is a small tree or large shrub introduced to North America in the 1800s as an ornamental. By the early 1900s, it had escaped cultivation and is now widely naturalized, found along the west coast from Alaska to California, eastward to Montana, and in much of the northeastern US. In the PNW, it occurs mostly on the west side, invading fields, pastures, meadows, riparian zones, and woodland edges. It can form dense, thorny, impenetrable thickets that crowd out native vegetation, alter vegetative structure, and impede the movement of humans and animals. In the PNW, we have over a dozen *Crataegus* species, two-thirds of them native, most with similar flowers and other features, so attention should be paid to ID characteristics when deciding on a course of action. To make matters more complicated, English hawthorn can hybridize with other *Crataegus* species, with the resulting progeny intermediate in character.

The leaves of English hawthorn are deciduous, 3- to 7-lobed, nearly as broad as long, roughly oval to triangular in outline but lobed in a way suggesting mittens. They are leathery in texture, may be hairless or somewhat hairy, and are toothed near the tips of the lobes. The showy flowers are typically white maturing to pink but may be pink to begin with. They are short-stalked and borne in flat-topped clusters of up to 25. Flowers are followed by round, red berries that ripen in fall and may persist into winter. Each berry has 1–2 seeds, and a tree can produce as many as 2,000 berries in a season. The berries attract birds and other animals, thus dispersing the seeds.

English hawthorn saplings can be pulled or dug when the soil is moist, but even small plants may soon develop deep roots and sharp thorns. Wear gloves and protective clothing when doing battle with these thorny plants. Mature trees can have large root systems, so digging is tough and removal is labor-intensive. Remove all roots if possible, or at least the crown and upper portions of roots. Weed wrenches can be helpful. Merely cutting to the ground will not kill the plants, as stump-sprouting and suckering are common. Cut surfaces can be burned or treated with herbicide to prevent sprouting. Monitor for new seedlings, and intervene quickly to prevent recurrence.

# Rosa canina

## DOG ROSE

Non-native perennial, to 9 ft. Flowers pink, white, 5-petaled, to 2.5 in.; late spring–early summer. Leaves alternate, leaflets to 1.6 in. Parts edible/medicinal.

Dog rose is a Eurasian species that has escaped cultivation and is found invading roadsides, fields, and woodland edges in scattered locations from BC to California, plus Montana, Idaho, Utah, and much of the eastern US. It's a large and thorny plant that spreads by suckering and seeds, forming thickets that crowd out native vegetation and desirable forage plants, as well as impeding the movement of animals, people, and vehicles. Any stems coming in contact with the ground may also root at the nodes.

The tall, multi-stemmed shrub bears deciduous, compound leaves typical of the genus, with 5–7 leaflets in odd-pinnate arrangement. The leaflets are oblong, pointed, about half as wide as long, hairless and smooth, with margins sharply serrated. Prickles on dog rose are random in distribution, thick, flattened, and downward-curved. Flowers are pink to white with yellow centers, borne singly or in small terminal clusters. The sepals, which sometimes have multiple slender lobes, become reflexed at the time of pollination and then drop off before the hips ripen. The hips are bright red, round to oval, to 0.8 in. long, ripening in early fall and then persisting some months and turning black.

With its size, prickles, and suckering, dog rose can be a monster when established. Wear gloves, and be prepared for several years of battle. Small plants can be pulled or dug. More mature plants or larger populations may require the use of weed wrenches, brush mowers, and/or herbicide.

# *Rosa multiflora*

## MULTIFLORA ROSE, RAMBLER ROSE

Non-native perennial, to 12 ft. Flowers white, 5-petaled, to 1 in.; midspring–midsummer. Leaves alternate, leaflets to 1 in. Parts edible/medicinal.

Multiflora rose is an Asian species, introduced to the US in the 1860s as rootstock for ornamental roses. It was widely used in landscaping and promoted by government agencies for slope stabilization, hedging, and highway plantings. It proved an aggressive invader and is now found as an escape from BC to California and over much of eastern North America. It invades roadsides, wetlands, woodland edges, riparian zones, and pastures, often forming vast, dense thickets that crowd out native flora and negatively impact wildlife. In pastures, it impedes livestock movement and displaces desirable forage.

*Rosa multiflora* can be either a multi-stem shrub or a vine, climbing as far as 10 ft. into trees. The stems may be armed with curved thorns, or thornless. The leaves are compound, as is typical for the genus, pinnately divided with up to 11 leaflets, elliptical to oval, with sharply toothed margins. There are pairs of fringed stipules at the base of each petiole.

The shrub bears large terminal and axillary clusters of fragrant flowers. The showy flowers are stalked and usually white (sometimes pink), with notched petals. They are followed by clusters of yellow-orange to red hips, forming in summer, turning leathery and persisting through winter. The hips are attractive to birds, which eat them and thus disperse the seeds, estimated at a million per plant annually. The seeds remain viable for decades in the soil. Multiflora rose also spreads vegetatively, by rooting of canes that bend down and come in contact with soil.

Wear thick gloves and protective clothing when working with mature multiflora roses. Small seedlings can be pulled or grubbed out with a hoe. Dig out larger plants, taking care to remove all the roots. For larger patches, cutting or mowing to the ground several times yearly for several years will at least slow them down and may eventually kill them. Alternatively, cut to the ground and treat the stumps with herbicide. Monitor for seedlings, which may reappear for several years.

# Rosa rubiginosa

## SWEETBRIER ROSE

**Non-native perennial, 3–10 ft. Flowers pink, 5-petaled, to 1.6 in.; late spring–early summer. Leaves alternate, leaflets to 1 in. Parts edible/medicinal.**

*Rosa rubiginosa* (syn. *R. eglanteria*) is a Eurasian/African species widely present as a garden escape from BC to California and across most of the US, plus Ontario and Quebec. It inhabits roadsides, fields, woodland edges, and riparian zones.

This shrub may have as many as 100 stems from a single rootstock. The stems are branched and erect or scrambling; they are covered with prickles that are flattened and curved or hooked. The leaves are deciduous and aromatic, their stalks and rachis finely pubescent, with small prickles. They are odd-pinnately compound, typically with 5–7 leaflets that are oval to round, with lower surfaces glandular and hairy. The margins are doubly serrate: the teeth have teeth. The bright pink flowers are borne singly or in clusters of 2–7, on short, stout, bristly stalks. The hips are round or oval, yellow-orange to red, to 0.8 in. long.

Wear gloves and protective clothing when doing battle with this thorny plant. Small plants can be pulled or dug. Larger ones may be pulled with a weed wrench or tractor, and/or treated with herbicide.

# *Rubus bifrons*

## HIMALAYAN BLACKBERRY

Non-native perennial, 3–9 ft. Flowers white, 5-petaled, to 1 in.; early summer. Leaves alternate, leaflets to 4.75 in. Parts edible/medicinal. Noxious in BC, WA, OR.

*Rubus bifrons* (syn. *R. discolor, R. armeniacus*) was introduced from Europe for fruit production. Although it can be found all across North America, it is eminently comfortable in the PNW in particular and is now very familiar to residents of the west coast from Alaska to California, where it forms endless thickets on woodland edges, wetland edges, margins of farmland and gardens, and riparian zones. It's an aggressive spreader, crowding out natives and making areas impassable for humans and livestock.

This robust, multi-stemmed shrub grows from hefty, deep, woody rootballs. The stout canes, erect to trailing or scrambling, can reach as far as 30 ft., rooting where they touch the ground. They are amply armed with formidable thorns. The leaves are deciduous to semi-evergreen, white-hairy below and hairless above. They are palmately compound with typically 5 leaflets, which are oval to oblong and pointed at the ends, with sharply serrated margins. The inflorescence is a flat-topped panicle of up to 20 flowers, usually terminal but sometimes axillary. Ripening in August, the berries are black and multi-seeded, to 0.75 in. in diameter, and much sought after by grazing humans and wildlife.

Blackberry is a delight for foragers and a bane for gardeners. The thickets can be huge, the thorns mean, the root masses very difficult to extract. Wear thick gloves and protective clothing to avoid injury by thorns. Small invasions and young plants can be dug out. With larger plants, cut the top growth away and then dig out the root crown, an endeavor that may require the use of a mattock.

Larger patches may be mowed or grazed to the ground regularly every year for several years, and eventually subdued. Goats are champs at taking tall and broad thickets to the ground, with no ill effect upon the animal. Faced with large expanses of blackberry, desperate people often resort to herbicide, or call in businesses that specialize in blackberry removal, sometimes using machinery. Blackberry can resprout from root or stem fragments, so take care to remove all plant material and burn or otherwise dispose of it, and monitor the site for subsequent resproutings or seedlings.

# *Rubus laciniatus*

## CUTLEAF BLACKBERRY, EVERGREEN BLACKBERRY

Non-native perennial, to 13 ft. Flowers white, pink, 5-petaled, to 1 in.; midsummer. Leaves alternate, leaflets to 2.5 in. Parts edible. Noxious in WA.

Cutleaf blackberry is a robust, invasive shrub similar in most ways to Himalayan blackberry but with a distinctive leaf shape and a less widespread distribution. It's found from BC to California, plus Idaho, Montana, Wyoming, Colorado, and much of the northeastern US. It inhabits woodland understories and edges, fields, riparian zones, wetland edges, and roadsides. The shrub crowds out natives and blocks access to lakes and streams.

Growing from a large rootball, the several stems are tall, stout, erect to clambering, and covered with sharp, curved thorns. Canes may extend to 30 ft. The leaves are hairless above and hairy below, compound, with 5 angular, pointy leaflets or multiple deeply incised, narrow lobes with sharply serrated margins. The inflorescence is a leafy raceme of numerous flowers, with petals 3-lobed at the tips. These are followed in August and September by oval berries to 0.75 in., black at maturity.

Control options are exactly the same as for Himalayan blackberry: pull, grub, or dig small plants. For larger or more established patches, mow or cut to the ground, or let goats or pigs do the job, a few times yearly for several years. After cutting a plant to the ground, thoroughly digging out the root crown may be mostly sufficient to eradicate it, but watch for resprouts. Alternatively, cut down and treat the crown with herbicide.

# Sorbus aucuparia
## EUROPEAN MOUNTAIN-ASH

Non-native perennial, to 40 ft. Flowers white, 5-petaled, to 0.2 in.; late spring–early summer. Leaves alternate, to 8 in., leaflets to 2 in. Parts edible/medicinal with caution.

*Sorbus aucuparia* is a widespread garden escape found across much of the northern US and southern Canada. It invades woodlands and is considered a threat to native flora in several states, including Oregon and Washington. It looks very similar to *S. scopulina* and *S. sitchensis*, both PNW natives. There are differences in details of leaf structure, and both of the natives grow more as large shrubs, while *S. aucuparia* is a tree. Their range is also different: the natives are more montane; *S. aucuparia* is found in the Puget Sound lowlands.

European mountain-ash leaves are pinnately divided, with each leaf bearing 11–15 narrow, pointed leaflets with serrated margins. The plant is deciduous, and in fall the leaves may turn gold or red. Large, flat-topped panicles of many small white flowers are followed by pendent clusters of small orange to red berries. A single tree may produce thousands of seeds in a season, with high germinability. Birds like the berries and are the major vector of dispersal.

Young plants are easy to pull up or dig out. More mature trees may be cut to the ground, but will require herbicide treatment to prevent resprouting. In areas where native species ranges might overlap with that of *Sorbus aucuparia*, gardeners who wish to preserve the natives may need to consult ID guides or request professional ID assistance before deciding on their course of action.

# *Populus alba*

## WHITE POPLAR, SILVER POPLAR

Non-native perennial, to 80 ft. Flowers yellow-green, tiny; midspring–early summer. Leaves alternate, to 4 in. Parts edible/medicinal.

Present in North America for over a century, this prolific Eurasian species has escaped cultivation and is present in most of the US, plus BC and eastern Canada. It's a fast-growing but short-lived tree that may reach 50 ft. wide, growing from deep fibrous roots. It may send out lateral suckers as far as 100 ft., sometimes forming dense colonies that can crowd out natives. In addition to its aggressive proliferation, the tree causes problems with its brittle branches that break easily due to weather stresses. The species is dioecious, but most *Populus alba* trees in the US are female, so many of their offspring are hybrids with any of the several other *Populus* species present, both native and introduced.

The leaves of *Populus alba* are shallowly palmate and 3- to 5-lobed, somewhat resembling maple but alternate (maple is opposite). The upper surfaces are glossy and dark green, the undersides densely white-hairy (hence *alba*). The reddish male catkins are about 3 in. long. The female catkins lengthen to 4 in. long, after pollination developing small pods that split when ripe and release tiny seeds attached to cottony puffs that aid in wind dispersal.

Pull, grub out, and dig young seedlings and saplings of white poplar. Girdling of young trees and suckers may be successful, but stumps and suckers will readily resprout, so repeated cuttings are usually necessary. Foliar or cut-stump herbicide applications are recommended for those dealing with established trees or larger invasions.

# Salix ×fragilis

## CRACK WILLOW

Non-native perennial, to 65 ft. Flowers yellow-green, tiny; midspring–midsummer. Leaves alternate, to 7 in. Parts edible/medicinal with caution.

This hybrid willow occurs from BC to Oregon, east of the Cascades, and eastward to Idaho and Montana. It's found in riparian zones and on wetland edges, streambanks, and edges of irrigated farmland. It competes with native vegetation and can also interfere with stream movement.

The trunks may be single or in clumps of several, and erect to nearly prostrate. Mature trunks may reach a diameter of as much as 40 in. New leaves are green to reddish and hairy, more densely so on the undersides, becoming hairless as they mature. The leaves are about 1 in. wide, narrowly lanceolate or elliptic, tapering to a point, with finely dentate margins. Small oval stipules are attached at the petiole bases of new leaves but soon drop away. The tiny flowers are borne on slender catkins, appearing in spring with the emerging leaves. Male catkins to 2.5 in. long and female catkins to 3.5 in. are borne at the tips of short branches on separate plants. *Salix ×fragilis* produces little viable seed, and most reproduction is through suckering and sprouting of broken stems or roots.

Small saplings can be pulled or dug up; take care to remove all roots. Grazing and burning can be stopgaps but will not kill the trees. For permanent eradication, cut-stump herbicide applications are recommended, but if in wetland settings will be subject to regulation. Contact your local weed agency for guidance.

# Salix ×sepulcralis

## WEEPING WILLOW

**Non-native perennial, to 80 ft. Flowers yellow, tiny; spring. Leaves alternate, to 6 in.**

*Salix ×sepulcralis*, native to Asia, has been popular in landscaping worldwide for centuries and is still widely sold by nurseries. It is present as a garden escape in a few scattered sites in western Oregon, along the California coast, in Arizona, and in the eastern US. It is particularly invasive in wetlands and riparian zones, impacting hydrology and crowding out native vegetation. It can also thrive on relatively dry soils. Several botanical names have been associated with this hybrid willow.

Though the tree seems old-fashioned and majestic, the ones we see are not likely to be of venerable age. Growing as rapidly as 10 ft. yearly, the tree's lifespan is usually no more than 20–30 years. The root system can reach as far as 100 ft. laterally but is very shallow, often visible at the soil surface and potentially causing problems with sidewalks and buildings. The bark is gray to brown (golden in the popular golden willow, *Salix ×sepulcralis* var.

*chrysocoma*). Branches are long, slender, and pendulous, many touching the ground. The leaves are deciduous, long and narrow, to 0.75 in. wide, lanceolate or elliptic, with finely serrated margins. Appearing with the leaves or soon after, the flowers are tiny, apetalous, and borne in cylindrical catkins to 2 in. long. Male and female catkins may be separate on the same plant, or on separate plants. The flowers are followed by tiny brown seed capsules, which burst when ripe, releasing the seeds in masses of cottony fluff, to be dispersed on the wind.

Pull or grub out seedlings, dig out saplings. Machinery may be used to remove roots of larger trees in dry soil. Mature trees may be girdled or cut to the ground with a chainsaw, followed by use of a stump grinder or treatment with herbicide; stumps will otherwise readily resprout. Herbicide use in wetland settings is subject to regulation; contact your local weed agency for guidance.

# *Acer negundo*

## BOXELDER MAPLE, ASH MAPLE

Non-native perennial, to 75 ft. Flowers yellow-green, to 0.2 in.; early–midspring. Leaves opposite, to 4 in. Parts edible. Toxic to horses, chickens, livestock.

More people may be familiar with the infamous stinky boxelder bug than with its host, boxelder maple. In spring and summer the bug depends primarily on female boxelder maples, feeding on the seeds and newly developing leaves, and laying eggs in bark crevices, branch surfaces, and leaves.

*Acer negundo*, a tall, deciduous, often multi-stemmed tree, is among the minority of maples that are fully dioecious, with separate male and female plants. It has flowers and samaras typical for maples but is distinctive in other ways. Leaves are pinnately compound, with 3–7 leaflets, in contrast with the simple leaves of most maples. Flowers are borne in drooping racemes to 8 in. long, followed by samaras, 1.5–2 in. long, in pendent clusters.

*Acer negundo* is native to eastern North America and considered invasive in many parts of the world as a weed or garden escape. It is not yet listed as noxious in the PNW, but it can show up uninvited and is beginning to invade some riparian areas. It's a fast-growing, short-lived, primarily riparian species, but it's drought-tolerant and can be found in varied settings. *Acer negundo* is an environmental problem when it competes with native tree species, reducing their populations. It's also an agricultural problem when livestock graze on the tree. The seeds and young shoots contain high concentrations of a toxin that causes a potentially fatal muscle disease, particularly in horses.

Gardeners in rural areas may thus wish to be particularly diligent in controlling the spread of this profusely self-seeding tree. Small infestations are easily controlled by early removal of seedlings. Saplings can be removed by digging, or killed by cutting or girdling.

# Acer platanoides

## NORWAY MAPLE

Non-native perennial, to 90 ft. Flowers yellow-green, to 0.33 in.; early–midspring. Leaves opposite, simple, 5- to 7-lobed, to 8 in. Parts edible.

*Acer platanoides* is potentially very long-lived in its native range, but here may live only 60 years. Although the specific epithet means "resembling *Platanus*," that resemblance is slight. It is often confused with sugar maple (*A. saccharum*). The bark of young trees is smooth and gray, forming ridges and furrows as it matures. The flowers bloom in panicles of 30–40, followed by greenish-yellow samaras.

Originally imported from Europe for landscaping, *Acer platanoides* has become invasive in the eastern US and in the PNW. Like many maples, it is an extravagant self-seeder, and can be weedy. In native landscapes, it displaces trees, shrubs, and other native plants by crowding them out and then shading them out.

Norway maple has often been valued for its tolerance of urban conditions, but it has several characteristics and vulnerabilities that lead to problems. It is prone to root-girdling and a few diseases. The roots are broad and shallow, with potential for damage to urban structures like sidewalks, and breakage of the tree.

Control considerations are similar to those for boxelder maple: mulch, monitor for seedlings; pull, dig, or girdle saplings.

# *Buddleja davidii*
## BUTTERFLY BUSH

Non-native perennial, to 15 ft. Flowers blue, violet, purple, 4-petaled, to 0.2 in.; late spring–autumn. Leaves opposite, to 10 in. Unpalatable. Noxious in WA, OR.

*Buddleja davidii* (*Buddleia davidii*) is by far the most well-known member of a genus of approximately 140 species. It has been widely cultivated in North America and, as a widespread garden escape, has been a subject of concern about invasiveness and environmental impact for decades, particularly along the west coast from BC to California.

Butterfly bush is a large, multi-branched, fast-growing but often short-lived shrub with pithy stems. The leaves are deciduous, gray-green, thin, simple, lanceolate, and fuzzy on the undersides. The inflorescences are dense terminal clusters of small tubular flowers with purple (sometimes white or pink) petals. A mature shrub will have many flower clusters and rebloom repeatedly during the long flowering season. The flowers are sweet-scented, like grape juice perhaps, and their nectar attracts butterflies. Adult butterflies can use the nectar as a food source, but their larvae can't eat it, so this is not a host plant: it does not ultimately support butterfly populations as well as many other plants would do.

*Buddleja davidii* is extravagantly reproductive—tens of thousands of seeds have been counted on a single flower cluster. The seeds are tiny and dust-like, dispersed far and wide by the wind and creating groves far from the nearest garden, in wild woodlands and riparian areas, on coastal bluffs, roadsides, and vacant lots.

Fans of butterfly bush should be happy to hear that multiple sterile cultivars are available in the nursery trade, though sterility may not be complete. You may also want to explore other species in the genus.

Because *Buddleja* seeds are so tiny and given to traveling, if you have the shrub in your yard you may never see a seedling from it, but you can be assured it has progeny elsewhere. You may also discover volunteers in your yard, without a butterfly bush in sight. The plants are very easy to pull or hoe when small, and later dig up. Mulch to prevent more seedlings, and plant something else.

93

# *Ailanthus altissima*

## TREE-OF-HEAVEN, STINKING QUASSIA

Non-native perennial, to 80 ft. Flowers green, brown, 5- or 6-petaled, to 0.3 in.; midspring–midsummer. Leaves pinnate, leaflets to 6 in. Parts medicinal with caution. Noxious in WA, OR, CA.

Introduced as an ornamental in the late 1700s, *Ailanthus altissima* has spread throughout North America. In the PNW, it is found primarily on the east side but also in scattered westside locations. It's a large, fast-growing, long-lived tree, aggressively self-seeding and suckering, and its allelopathic properties prevent other plants from growing nearby. It invades woodlands, roadsides, urban parks, and vacant lots, forming dense thickets and outcompeting native vegetation. In urban or residential areas, it can cause structural damage.

*Ailanthus altissima* is polygamodioecious. Foliage and particularly the male flowers exude a rank, peanut butter–like odor. The leaves are very large and pinnately compound, with as many as 41 leaflets. These are lanceolate with smooth margins, typically with 1–2 shallowly indented lobes or teeth near the base. The terminal leaflet is sometimes missing and often smaller, with 1–2 irregular lobes.

Numerous radially symmetric flowers are borne in large terminal panicles, to 12 in. wide. Flowers are followed by samaras. The single-seeded samaras are up to 2 in. long, and twisted. A single tree may produce as many as 350,000 seeds in a season.

Sensitive people may get contact blisters from handling tree-of-heaven, so gloves and protective clothing should be worn when working with the tree. The ideal is to pull seedlings and saplings as early as possible, before more mature root development can occur. More robust saplings can be dug out or extracted using a weed wrench; take care to remove the roots. Never leave severed branches or trunks on the ground, as they can root when in contact with moist soil. Larger trees can be cut to the ground or girdled, but these can resprout or sucker, so monitor and consider herbicide application. Herbicides can be applied by injection, cut-stump treatments, and similar methods. Trees so treated can still resprout, so monitor several times yearly for several years.

# Tamarix parviflora

## SMALLFLOWER TAMARISK

Non-native perennial, to 14 ft. Flowers pink, white, 4-petaled, to 0.03 in.; early summer. Leaves to 0.12 in. Unpalatable. Noxious in CA.

Introduced to the US in the 1800s as an ornamental, *Tamarix parviflora* is now widely distributed through much of the western US and in scattered areas in the east. In the PNW, it is found mostly east of the Cascades; it is considered the less invasive of the *Tamarix* species found here, but it is still problematic when found as an escape, invading riparian zones, ditches, and other moist places in arid regions. It is on noxious weed lists for several states.

*Tamarix* changes hydrology by pulling up available water, dries up wetlands, crowds out natives, and increases fire risk due to high flammability of the wood. *Tamarix* draws up salt from soils then deposits it on the soil surface with dead foliage, increasing salinity and inhibiting other vegetation. The woody root systems of these shrubs go deep into the soil and branch profusely in moist zones.

The bark of *Tamarix parviflora* is smooth and reddish in younger plants, aging to brown. The deciduous leaves are lanceolate, scale-like and sessile, overlapping along the stem. The tiny flowers are borne in long, dense, narrow racemes, arranged in branched terminal inflorescences. Flowers are followed by small seed capsules carrying many tiny seeds—tens of thousands for mature plants. Each minute seed is attached at one end to a little parasol-shaped pappus that aids in wind dispersal. In addition to this prodigious reproductive capacity by seed, *Tamarix* also sprouts readily from severed crowns, roots, or stem fragments.

*Tamarix parviflora* is easily distinguished from the most common *Tamarix* species in our region, *T. ramosissima*. *Tamarix parviflora* has floral parts (petals, stamens, etc.) in 4s; *T. ramosissima* has them in 5s. *Tamarix parviflora* is a somewhat shorter plant, and its racemes are shorter and denser; the inflorescence of *T. ramosissima* is a much larger, more open and freely branched panicle.

Small invasions of *Tamarix parviflora* can be pulled or dug up. Mowing, cutting, burning, and grazing can slow the plant down temporarily, but it resprouts readily, so experts recommend following any of these treatments with herbicide. Herbicide use is tightly regulated near wetlands; contact your local weed agency for guidance. Heavy machinery is sometimes used to remove mature plants, but this is expensive, hard on the soil and on nearby plants, and not likely practicable for most home gardeners.

# *Tamarix ramosissima*

## SALTCEDAR

Non-native perennial, to 20 ft. Flowers pink, red, 5-petaled, to 0.13 in.; late spring–midsummer. Leaves alternate, to 0.16 in. Unpalatable. Noxious in WA, OR, CA.

Introduced as an ornamental and for use as a wind-block in landscaping, this showy plant is the most aggressive *Tamarix* species in the PNW. It is found mostly on the eastern side of our region and is wide-spread across much of the western half of the US, as well as in scattered areas in the eastern US. Like others of its genus, it primarily takes advantage of moist spots in arid regions, crowding out natives. *Tamarix* hogs available soil moisture to the point of drying up wetlands and also draws up salt and then redeposits it at the soil surface, suppressing other vegetation.

Saltcedar's root system is multi-branched and very deep. Stems and trunks are freely branched. The small, deciduous leaves are blue-green and scale-like, reminding people of cedar foliage, thus the common name for this species and sometimes others in the group. The tiny flowers are held in narrow racemes to 5 in. long that are arranged in open, multi-branched, plume-like terminal panicles. Flowers are followed by small capsules that break open when ripe to release many minute seeds, each attached to a delicate pappus that aids in wind dispersal. Seed production per plant has been estimated in the hundreds of thousands. In addition to this extravagant seed output, broken stems, roots, or root crowns resprout with alacrity.

As with *Tamarix parviflora*, early intervention is ideal. Small plants that have not yet rooted too deeply can be pulled or dug out. Deeper roots may be removed by mechanical means (weed wrench or machinery). Cutting, mowing, burning, and grazing remove upper plant portions temporarily, but the plant will respond with enthusiastic resprouting, so herbicide is often recommended. Herbicide use is tightly regulated near wetlands; contact your local weed agency for guidance.

# Daphne laureola

## SPURGE-LAUREL

Non-native perennial, to 5 ft. Flowers yellow-green, 4-petaled, to 0.15 in.; late spring–early summer. Leaves alternate, to 5 in. Poisonous. Toxic to cats, dogs, livestock. Noxious in BC, WA, OR.

Spurge-laurel is neither laurel (*Prunus*) nor spurge (*Euphorbia*), but parts of the plant remind people of both those genera. This is an aggressive weed found from BC to Oregon, primarily on the west side of the Cascades and east along the Columbia River Gorge. It invades yards, vacant lots, roadsides, and particularly moist, shady woodland. It can rapidly spread by seed and suckering to form dense stands that crowd out native species. It is also highly poisonous to people and toxic to animals.

This shrub is often low-growing, with woody stems that may be upright or more horizontal at the base, spreading outward and upward. The leaves are simple with smooth margins, glossy and deep green on top, lighter green beneath. The clusters of up to 20 small, fragrant flowers are borne at the bases of the leaves and partly hidden by them. Many very toxic, small, single-seeded, black berries follow, up to 600 per plant.

When doing battle with spurge-laurel, wear protective clothing to avoid contact with toxic compounds contained in all plant parts. Young plants can be pulled or simply cut to the ground; larger ones can be cut below the soil line or dug out. Take as much of the root as possible. Repeated attacks may be necessary due to resprouting.

# Ulmus procera

## ENGLISH ELM, FIELD ELM

Non-native perennial, to 130 ft. Flowers pink, red, in clusters to 1 in.; early spring. Leaves alternate, to 5 in. Parts edible/medicinal.

A Eurasian species widely planted in landscaping, *Ulmus procera* (syn. *U. minor*) occurs as a garden escape infrequently in the PNW, mostly on the west side. It is more widely introduced in southern California, Nevada, a few midwestern and northeastern states, and Ontario. It is often seen in riparian zones. It has an aggressive root system and propensity for suckering, making it potentially invasive.

The bark of English elm is brownish-gray and when mature is rough and furrowed. The leaves are oval to almost round, drawn to an abrupt point at the tip, with an asymmetric leaf base (typical for elms). They are pinnately veined with doubly serrate margins, somewhat rough to the touch on the upper sides and fuzzy underneath.

The small flowers bloom before the leaves appear; they are borne in round, tassel-like clusters of 15–20, held close to short branchlets. Seeds are held in oval, papery samaras.

As for other enthusiastically reproductive and well-rooted trees, early intervention is desirable. Pull or dig when plants are young, removing all roots. Cutting has not proven effective in controlling *Ulmus procera*, due to its resprouting.

# Ulmus pumila

SIBERIAN ELM

Non-native perennial, to 70 ft. Flowers greenish, in tiny clusters to 0.5 in.; late winter–spring. Leaves alternate, to 2.75 in. Parts edible/medicinal.

Often planted in landscaping, this Asian species has escaped cultivation, particularly in dry regions, all over North America. It is a problematic invasive in the Southwest. In the PNW, it occurs primarily on the east side, where it can be seen on roadsides and fields, pastures and rangeland. It spreads rapidly by seed and suckering, displacing native vegetation and forage plants.

*Ulmus pumila* is an attractive tree, with a spreading and rounded crown to 50 ft. wide. It is fairly short-lived and deciduous in cool temperate climates. The leaves are oval to lanceolate, with sharply pointed tips and single-serrated margins (which distinguishes it from *U. procera*). The leaf base is often symmetrical, different from most other elms, including *U. procera*. The tiny apetalous flowers, borne on branchlets in round, pendent clusters, are followed by inch-wide, circular samaras. The seeds are numerous and readily wind-dispersed.

For small invasions of younger plants, pull, grub out with a hoe, or use a weed wrench. More mature trees can be removed by girdling, a vigorous program of repeated cutting, cut-stump treatment with herbicide, or with heavy machinery. If roots are left behind, monitor for resprouting.

# Forbs/Herbs and Vines

Forbs (excluding the graminoids) are herbaceous plants and may be annual, biennial, or perennial. An annual typically germinates, blooms, sets seed, and then dies, all in the same year. A biennial is one that typically spends its first growing season as a rosette of basal leaves, then blooms, sets seed, and dies in its second year. A perennial may also begin as a basal rosette, blooms for the first time in either its first or second year, and may or may not die back in winter—but survives 3 years or more. These life cycles are important to identification but are often not completely consistent or clear-cut.

Vines are typically herbaceous, but among perennials may be semi-woody, particularly at the base. They sprawl, clamber, and trail over other plants or objects like fences. Some have tendrils that help them cling to their supports; others twine around stems or other projections for support. Plants may take the form of either a long woody vine or a shrub.

Russian knapweed (*Rhaponticum repens*) can quickly form dense stands that are difficult to eradicate, as here along Sand Dune Road, Moses Lake, WA.

101

# Carpobrotus edulis

## ICE PLANT, HOTTENTOT FIG

**Non-native perennial, prostrate. Flowers yellow, daisy-like, to 6 in.; year-round. Leaves opposite, to 6 in. Parts edible.**

*Carpobrotus edulis* (syn. *Mesembryanthemum edule*) was introduced in the early 1900s and continued to be widely planted into the 1970s for stabilizing dunes

and banks along railroad tracks and freeways. One can easily understand its original appeal—an attractive, low-growing, succulent evergreen that spreads rapidly and blooms nearly all year in California. It is now widespread along the California coast from Baja to northern California and has begun to invade the southern coast of Oregon. The most widespread form of this species has yellow flowers that fade to pink, but closely related *C. acinaciformis*, which is also invasive, has pink-purple blossoms.

Ice plant proved all too happy in sandy coastal soils and now poses a significant environmental problem. It is long-lived and fast-growing; a single plant can reach 150 ft. across. It reproduces vegetatively, with long-trailing stems that can root at the nodes, and by seed. Though promoted for stabilization, it actually exacerbates erosion; it is shallow-rooted, and its foliage holds a lot of water. Mature stands can form dense mats as thick as 20 in., covering large areas and displacing native plants. *Carpobrotus* is blamed for threats to several rare coastal species in California.

Small infestations are easily removed by hand, but take care to remove every bit of the plant, because any roots or stem fragments left behind can regrow. Larger infestations are very tough to control, and herbicides may be the only effective weapon, but these are tightly regulated near water. Contact your local weed agency for guidance.

# Amaranthus retroflexus
## REDROOT PIGWEED

Non-native annual, to 9 ft. Flowers yellow-green, to 0.1 in.; summer–autumn. Leaves alternate, simple, to 4 in. Parts edible. Toxic to horses, cattle, pigs, sheep, goats.

The native range of *Amaranthus retroflexus* is a matter of dispute, but it is widely distributed around the world, including a scattered distribution in the PNW, where it is more common east of the Cascades. It is a common weed of fields, gardens, roadsides, and other disturbed sites in open, sunny areas. It's a problem in agriculture, where it competes with and causes yield losses in several key grain, legume, and vegetable crops. Parts of the plant have been used as food, but it can contain excessive amounts of nitrates, causing significant livestock poisoning risk if grazed in quantity.

Redroot pigweed bears many tiny flowers on dense terminal spikes to 4 in. long. It is monoecious and can produce multiple generations in one season. A single plant may produce at least 35,000 seeds, or sometimes seeds in the hundreds of thousands. Seeds are wind-blown, dispersed by animals, or present as contaminants in harvested crops. Simply mowing plants early in the season can help to reduce seed dispersal, and small infestations are easy to remove by hoeing or pulling.

# *Atriplex patula*

## SPEAR SALTBUSH, HALBERDLEAF ORACHE

**Non-native annual, to 3 ft. Flowers white, 5-lobed, 0.12 in.; midsummer–autumn. Leaves lowest opposite, upper alternate, to 3.5 in. Parts edible with caution.**

*Atriplex patula* is a Eurasian weed scattered over much of North America. It frequents yards, gardens, cropland, woodland edges, dumps, and other disturbed sites.

Growing from a branching taproot, the green to whitish stems may be erect but are often multi-branched and sprawling. Leaves are opposite low on the stem, then alternate. Leaves are variable in shape, from linear to lanceolate to oval, and these differences are reflected in the several subspecies. Leaf margins may be smooth or wavy; the upper surfaces are shiny, the lower may be whitish and mealy.

*Atriplex patula* is monoecious. Both male and female flowers are tiny, apetalous, and sessile, borne in spikes, mostly on the ends of upper stems. After pollination, the bracts of the female flowers enlarge and become flattened, arrowhead-shaped pods enclosing the seeds as they develop. A single plant may produce thousands of seeds, and some of the seeds remain viable in the soil for decades. The seeds are dispersed by birds and livestock that consume them, and by wind and water.

In agricultural settings, spear saltbush has been successfully controlled by early spring cultivation, cycles of fallow, livestock grazing, and herbicide. In the home garden, hoeing and pulling should suffice to control this weed, followed by mulch and monitoring for new seedlings.

# Bassia hyssopifolia

## FIVEHOOK BASSIA, FIVEHORN SMOTHERWEED

Non-native annual, to 6 ft. Flowers white, 5-lobed, to 0.07 in.; midsummer–autumn. Leaves alternate, to 2.5 in. Toxic to horses, sheep.

Fivehook bassia is found east of the Cascades in the PNW and in dry areas throughout much of western North America, as well as in a few eastern and midwestern states. Probably introduced accidentally as a seed contaminant in the early 1900s, it now invades farmland, riparian areas, coastal dunes, salt marshes, and other wetlands. *Bassia hyssopifolia* can form dense stands that exclude native flora and impact natural areas by changing the vegetation structure and threatening some endangered plants and animals.

This annual grows as an erect, branched or unbranched plant covered densely with short, silky hairs. The leaves are simple and sessile, linear to narrowly lanceolate. The tiny, membranous flowers are borne in terminal spikes and smaller axillary clusters. The very numerous seeds produced are dispersed by animals and benefit from human activities that move soil and seeds around on vehicle tires.

Small invasions can be easily removed by pulling or hoeing, best done when the soil is moist and plants are young, before seed production. Larger patches can be tackled with mowers or weed whackers.

# Bassia scoparia

## KOCHIA, MOCK CYPRESS

**Non-native annual, to 6 ft. Flowers greenish, tiny, 5-lobed; late summer–autumn. Leaves alternate, to 2 in. Parts edible/medicinal with caution. Toxic to horses, cattle, sheep. Noxious in BC, WA, OR.**

*Bassia scoparia* (syn. *Kochia scoparia*) is a Eurasian weed present in many countries worldwide and throughout much of North America, where it was introduced as an ornamental and forage crop in the 1800s. In the PNW, it is found primarily on the east side of the Cascades, where it dominates many thousands of acres.

Kochia is a significant nuisance for growers of several economically important crops. It invades rangeland, pastures, cropland, riparian zones, roadsides, and ecologically damaged land such as strip-mined areas. With high tolerance for arid, alkaline, and salty soils, it can quickly dominate harsh environments.

Kochia has a taproot that can go 8 ft. deep and horizontal roots extending up to 8 ft. from the crown. The green stems are upright and multi-branched, forming a rounded, bushy shape. In fall, they turn red or purplish. The leaves are short-stalked to sessile, green to blue-grayish-green, and linear to lanceolate, with smooth margins lined with hairs.

The tiny flowers are sessile and apetalous, borne in small clusters in the upper axils and in terminal spikes. The flowers develop into round, bladder-like pods, each containing a single seed. A plant may produce as many as 14,000 seeds, which are dispersed when mature plants break off and form tumbleweeds, scattering seeds over distances as they travel on the wind.

For small invasions of kochia, pulling or digging before bloom is effective. Break or chop the roots below the crown. For larger infestations, mowing or chopping the plants will prevent seed production. This will need to be done repeatedly during the growing season. Herbicides are commonly used on larger patches, but this option is complicated by herbicide resistance and by the waxy surface of the leaves, which prevents herbicides from sticking.

# *Chenopodium album*

## LAMBSQUARTERS, PIGWEED, FAT HEN

Non-native annual, to 40 in. Flowers green, brown, to 0.1 in.; late spring–midsummer. Leaves alternate, to 4 in. Parts edible/medicinal with caution. Toxic to horses, cattle, pigs, sheep, goats, chickens.

Lambsquarters is a well-known European weed widely distributed across the PNW and most of North America. It's a frequent uninvited guest of gardens, cropland, orchards, pastures, vacant lots, roadsides, and stream margins.

Growing from a short, thick taproot, the plant is erect and multi-branched. It tends to be highly visible in contrast to its surroundings, with its green-gray leaves covered with a mealy, white coating. The leaves are firm and oval to diamond-shaped, often with wavy-toothed margins and slender, short petioles. Upper leaves may be sessile and reduced, with lanceolate or linear outlines. Upper surfaces of the lower leaves are green or blue-green and hairless; their undersides may be more whitish and pubescent.

The flowers are sessile, tiny, and barely visible, looking like little nubs in dense terminal spike-like panicles 4–8 in. long. Seed output is huge: diligent seed counters find up to 20,000 seeds per plant, and some champion plants produce as many as 70,000 seeds. The seeds can remain viable in the soil for decades.

Owing to this extravagant fecundity, *Chenopodium album* is an agricultural weed of concern affecting many important crops in many countries. In addition, it can cause problems when grazed because of high nitrate and oxalic acid content, which can be toxic to livestock. Despite the potential for toxicity, leaves and seeds of the plant have been used for food and medicinal purposes in Asia and Europe.

Farmers have used numerous strategies to combat lambsquarters invasions, including flaming, manual removal, herbicides, and repeated close mowing. All have been fairly effective, though the species has developed resistance to some herbicides.

For small invasions in gardens, pulling is usually the easiest thing. Pull or hoe when the soil is moist; the taproots are shallow and easy to dislodge. Follow with mulch to prevent new sproutings.

# *Halogeton glomeratus*

## HALOGETON, SALTLOVER

**Non-native annual, to 18 in. Flowers yellow, to 0.1 in.; midsummer–autumn. Leaves alternate, to 0.8 in. Poisonous. Toxic to horses, cattle, sheep. Noxious in BC, OR, CA.**

Halogeton, a weed of Central Asia, has been present in western North America since the 1930s. It has invaded millions of acres of overgrazed rangeland, dry lakebeds, roadsides, and disturbed sites. In the PNW, it is found in dry areas east of the Cascades.

The plant is ferociously invasive and toxic to grazing livestock and to other vegetation, so federal laws were enacted beginning in the 1950s focusing on its control and eradication. It is on noxious weed lists in several states.

Halogeton has a competitive advantage in its high tolerance of salt; its tissues accumulate salts, making the plant toxic to animals, then release the salts into surrounding soil, which suppresses other vegetation. The plant is very drought-tolerant, with a taproot that may be 20 in. deep and lateral roots to 18 in. wide. The stems are purplish and often branched at the base, spreading out across the ground, then turning upward. Typical of halophytes, the blue-green leaves of halogeton are succulent; they are distinctive, being tubular with a conspicuous spine at the end.

The flowers of *Halogeton glomeratus* are tiny, apetalous, and membranous, borne in tight axillary clusters. The flowers develop into papery pods, producing tens of thousands of seeds per plant. At maturity, plants may break off from their roots, becoming tumbleweeds and spreading seed across the landscape. Seeds are also dispersed by wind, water, animals, machines, and human activity.

In the region where it is most invasive, there's a circular relationship between livestock farming and halogeton. Overgrazing creates ideal conditions for the plant. Particularly as it crowds out more desirable forage, it is eaten by cattle and sheep, and consumption of even a modest amount of the plant can kill them.

Prevention on rangeland involves an emphasis on early detection and on cultural strategies, including competitive plantings and measures supporting soil health. Other methods have failed. Burning only encourages halogeton. Herbicide is too expensive for eradication of large populations. For most home gardens, the key will be recognition and removal before plants mature enough to go to seed. Pull plants when the soil is moist. Even dried plant material is toxic, so all uprooted plants should be removed. Follow with heavy mulch.

# Salsola tragus

## RUSSIAN THISTLE, RUSSIAN TUMBLEWEED

Non-native annual, to 4 ft. Flowers pink, red, 5-lobed, to 0.4 in.; late summer. Leaves alternate, to 1 in. Parts edible. Noxious in BC, CA.

*Salsola tragus* (syn. *S. kali*) is one of many plants that may form tumbleweeds. This Eurasian weed was introduced to North America accidentally in the 1870s and has since invaded every state in the US (except Florida) as well as BC and other parts of Canada. It is a listed noxious weed in a few areas. Requiring very little water to germinate and mature, this plant has a competitive advantage in harsh dry environments and is found on roadsides, vacant lots, agricultural land, sandy riparian margins, and desert areas.

Russian thistle is not a true thistle: it doesn't resemble them and is not related to them. Plants grow from a taproot that can extend 6 ft. downward into the soil, with lateral roots to 5 ft. long. The multi-branched stems may be green to reddish or purple. The leaves are linear, fleshy, and spine-tipped. The small flowers, which appear singly in the leaf axils, have no true petals but rather consist of petal-like sepals. Each is subtended by 3 spiny bracts. A small plant can produce thousands of seeds; a large one can make as many as 250,000 seeds.

Rooted plants can form broad, dense patches, competing with native and agricultural plants and serving as hosts to agricultural pests. After it has matured and set seed, Russian thistle can detach from its roots and tumble in the wind, spreading seed as it goes. Tumbleweeds can impede traffic and create fire hazards. On the last day of 2019 on the Hanford Reservation in eastern Washington, tumbleweeds piled up 20 ft. deep in places, covering vehicles and causing closure of State Rte. 240 for a day.

Large-scale efforts to control *Salsola tragus* have tested numerous strategies. Frequently repeated mowing was effective; burning was not. Several herbicides initially worked, but plants have since developed resistance to some of them. Repeated tillage worked well because the seeds of *S. tragus* don't germinate if buried below 3 in. and are short-lived.

Small invasions in the home garden can be eliminated by pulling or grubbing out with a hoe just below the soil surface, before seeds develop.

# *Allium vineale*

## WILD GARLIC, ONION GRASS, HAIR ONION

Non-native perennial, to 3 ft. Flowers white, pink, to 0.16 in.; late spring–early summer. Leaves few, to 2 ft. Parts edible/medicinal. Toxic to cats, dogs, horses, cattle, sheep, goats, chickens. Noxious in CA.

*Allium vineale* is an onion native to Africa and Eurasia, widely naturalized in North America and Australia. While it can be invasive in gardens, disturbed sites, and natural areas, it is primarily a problem in agriculture, contaminating grain crops and pastureland. When cattle graze heavily on *A. vineale*, it confers an unpleasant garlic taste to milk and meat.

Wild garlic is sometimes sold as a quirky ornamental that is also edible, but it mostly invades gardens via hitchhiking in the soil of nursery plants.

Like some other *Allium* species, the predominant aboveground feature is a cluster of miniature bulbs borne at the top of the stem. Most new plants develop from these bulblets as they pop off the stem onto soil.

The leaves of *Allium vineale* are long, narrow, and tubular. The plant does not consistently bloom. When the small spherical inflorescence does appear, it typically bears just a few, very small white or pink florets on stalks in an umbel, rising above the bulblets. The bulblets and florets are initially tightly enclosed in a papery bract that soon drops away. Persistent, green, twisted, filamentous bracts are associated with the bulblets and stick out in all directions, giving rise to selections like 'Hair' and 'Dready'.

Control of *Allium vineale* is difficult in part because the plant grows actively underground fall through spring, escaping detection until May or June, when a few leaves appear and only some plants develop short-lived flowering stems. Herbicide generally is ineffective. In a small garden, persistent monitoring, pulling, and heavy mulching should be effective over time.

# Aegopodium podagraria

## BISHOP'S WEED, GOUTWEED, SNOW-ON-THE-MOUNTAIN

Non-native perennial, to 3 ft. Flowers white, 5-petaled, to 0.13 in.; late spring–midsummer. Leaves alternate, leaflets to 3 in. Parts edible/medicinal.

Bishop's weed is an aggressive horticultural plant that has escaped cultivation; it occurs widely in eastern North America and in scattered areas of the westside PNW. Present as an escape and already identified as invasive by the 1850s, it is now listed as invasive in several eastern and midwestern states. This plant, valued as a groundcover for shade, is more than happy to cover a lot of ground in woodland edges and understory, as well as fields and areas adjacent to old homesites.

*Aegopodium podagraria* produces a lot of foliage—only about 12 in. high but dense. The leaves are triternate: divided into 3 groups of 3 leaflets each, with toothed margins and sometimes irregular lobes. Many gardeners are familiar with 'Variegatum', a selection of the wild species with white to cream variegation, though this will revert to solid green over time. Seedlings will also be green, and the all-green plants are likely to be more vigorous than the variegated ones.

The tiny flowers are borne in flat-topped compound umbels to 5 in. wide on erect stems that can rise to 3 ft. above the foliage. Bloom is usually fairly sparse, particularly in shady sites. Seed production, germination, dispersal, and seed bank longevity are all comparatively modest in this species.

But bishop's weed hardly needs self-seeding to dominate woodland habitats; it is very deep-rooted and spreads rapidly via rhizomes that can extend horizontally several feet. It expands out of areas where it has been planted and can take root in new patches when dumped with yard waste. With its very leafy character, this plant completely crowds out other plants and prevents germination of any seeds, thus outcompeting with native understory plants, suppressing even tree establishment.

Any large invasion of bishop's weed is daunting, and experts recommend either herbicide or a large number of volunteers prepared for repeated efforts. A small patch in the home garden can be removed by pulling or digging; take care to remove all underground parts and follow with thick mulch. Gardeners who somehow must have this plant should consider confining it to a container or to a site bounded by concrete. A less aggressive, very similar-looking relative is the white-variegated *Peucedanum ostruthium* 'Daphnis'.

# Anthriscus caucalis

## BUR CHERVIL

Non-native annual, biennial, or perennial, to 3 ft. Flowers white, 5-petaled, to 0.1 in.; midspring–midsummer. Leaves basal to 6 in., cauline alternate. Parts edible with caution. Noxious in BC.

This rampant carrot relative was introduced to North America as a salad vegetable. It has made its home from BC to California, east through Idaho and several central to midwestern states, to the east coast. It's found on moist, open, often shaded ground of disturbed woodland edges, roadsides, pastures, and riparian areas. It makes its way around thanks to tiny, bur-like seeds that hitch rides on fur or feathers. The plant is a problem because of its aggressive competition with native vegetation.

*Anthriscus caucalis* can grow as an annual, biennial (often), or short-lived perennial. From a taproot that can extend to 6 ft. deep grows a basal rosette of leaves and then an erect, hollow stem that may be branched near its base. The leaves are stalked, pinnately compound and approximately triangular in outline, reduced in size higher on the stem. The tiny, stalked florets are borne in terminal umbellets (umbels within a larger umbel arrangement) with up to 7 flowers each.

In agriculture and conservation management, bur chervil is combatted with mowing (repeated a few times in a season before bloom), repeated tillage, and herbicides. The deep taproots can resprout, which poses a problem for mowing, tillage, and pulling. The plant can cause dermatitis, so gloves and protective clothing are recommended when working with it. For small infestations, the most practical strategy may be to pull and dig when the soil is wet; take care to remove the entire taproot and to bag any seeds that have formed. Follow with mulch and monitor for resprouting taproot sections or germination of remaining seeds.

# *Cicuta douglasii*

## DOUGLAS'S WATER-HEMLOCK, WESTERN WATER-HEMLOCK

Native perennial, to 6 ft. Flowers white, 5-petaled, to 0.1 in.; mid–late summer. Leaves basal to 18 in., cauline alternate. Poisonous. Toxic to cats, dogs, horses, cattle, pigs, sheep, goats, chickens. Noxious in BC.

*Cicuta douglasii* is widespread in western North America, from California to Alaska and northern Canada. It is one of four *Cicuta* species native to this continent. All are wetland plants, found in moist meadows, riparian areas, and marshes, and all are very toxic. In the PNW, we also have *C. maculata* (spotted water-hemlock), distinguished by purple spots at the stem nodes, and *C. bulbifera*, so named due to formation of bulbils in upper leaf axils.

Douglas's water-hemlock produces one or a few stout stems from a thick crown and taproot, with underground tubers and slender fibrous roots. The leaves are pinnately compound and more or less triangular in outline. The leaflets are about 4 in. long, lanceolate with serrated edges. The tiny flowers are borne in compound umbels.

Cicutoxin is a substance with a strong carrot odor, found mostly in the tubers but also in the leaves and stems of young plants, as well as in the seedheads when green. It causes violent convulsions and death rapidly after ingestion of a small amount of any plant part. Animals can be poisoned by very slight contact with the plant, drinking the water around it, etc.

*Cicuta douglasii* usually occurs in small patches in very wet areas, including standing water. It's a large plant, very similar in appearance to many of its carrot family relatives. Keep livestock and pets away from any suspected water-hemlock plants. The water-hemlocks are likely to show up only in very wet gardens or in wetlands. One cultural approach to discouraging these volunteers in the home garden is to reduce available moisture in the area when possible. You can pull or dig up small patches, but be sure to wear protective clothing and gloves. Any plant material removed should be bagged and discarded, not composted or left lying around, as the dead plants retain toxicity for some time. The plant typically grows in wetlands, so herbicide use is subject to regulation; contact your local weed agency for guidance.

# Conium maculatum

## POISON HEMLOCK

Non-native biennial, to 9 ft. Flowers white, to 0.2 in.; midspring–midsummer. Leaves alternate, to 20 in. Poisonous. Toxic to cats, dogs, horses, cattle, pigs, sheep, goats, chickens. Noxious in BC, WA, OR.

This cosmopolitan European native has been famous since antiquity as the poison used to execute the ancient Greek philosopher Socrates. *Conium maculatum* is widely distributed in North America and common in the PNW on both sides of the Cascades. It occurs along roadsides and in fields and vacant lots, typically in sunny, open locations. It spreads by seeds and can be invasive.

Beginners in plant ID often confuse this plant with some of its relatives in the carrot family. Poison hemlock (which has no connection to the hemlock trees of *Tsuga*) can be easily distinguished by its parsley-like leaves; smooth, purple-blotched stems; and towering height, to 6 ft. or more. The only related plants of comparable size are giant hogweed and cow parsnip, which both have broadly palmate (not dissected) leaves.

Typical for a biennial, poison hemlock produces a basal rosette of leaves in its first year, then a branched flowering stem the second year. The main stem is usually purple-spotted (hence *maculatum*, "spotted"). The leaves are pinnately dissected and triangular in outline. The flowers are in compound umbels to 8 in. across.

Poison hemlock is one of the most toxic wild plants in the PNW; eating a few leaves can be fatal. Most toxicity is related to ingestion, but it's possible to have a reaction from skin contact, so gloves and protective clothing are recommended when working it. Never burn the live or dead plant material, as the smoke is hazardous.

A small infestation can be removed by digging, but be sure to extract the entire taproot. After digging, monitor for resprouting of pieces left behind and for seedlings, which can be numerous. The toxicity of the plant is retained when it's dead and dried, so keep pulled-up plants away from livestock, pets, and children. Do not compost, but bag and send to the landfill.

# Daucus carota

## QUEEN ANNE'S LACE, WILD CARROT

**Non-native annual, biennial, or perennial, to 4 ft. Flowers white, to 0.1 in.; late summer–autumn. Leaves basal to 5 in., cauline alternate. Parts edible/medicinal with caution. Toxic to horses. Noxious in WA.**

This is the species from which our domesticated carrots are derived. It's a Eurasian native that is widespread throughout the PNW, often seen in fields and on roadsides, in meadows, and in yards. *Daucus carota* is a listed noxious weed in several states. The plant is sometimes regarded as an ornamental, and some cultivars and very similar species are offered as horticultural plants, but the species is on the quarantine list for Washington, meaning its sale or distribution there is prohibited.

Some gardeners are fond of the plant, and many assume that because it's ubiquitous, it must be native. It can quickly wear out its welcome by self-seeding and becoming invasive. In meadows, it can compete with our many less aggressive native meadow species and make of itself a monoculture. It is also an agricultural pest: slightly toxic, it can adversely affect domestic carrot production through hybridization and the taste of milk from cows grazing it.

The single stem of *Daucus carota* rises from a carrot-like but bitter taproot. Leaves are very finely dissected. It may produce a basal rosette of leaves in its first year, blooming in its second. Like many of its carrot relatives, it has a compound umbel of small white (sometimes yellowish or pink) flowers. The umbel is up to 4 in. across. A distinguishing and charming touch is that the central floret in each umbel is often pink to purple.

The species spreads only by seed, with a single plant producing thousands of seeds. A small Queen Anne's lace invasion is easily quashed by mowing before seed set, followed by removal of plants by pulling, digging, or hoeing.

# *Foeniculum vulgare*

## SWEET FENNEL, FENNEL

**Non-native biennial or perennial, to 7 ft. Flowers yellow, 5-lobed, to 0.1 in.; summer–autumn. Leaves alternate, to 6 in. Parts edible/medicinal with caution. Noxious in BC, WA.**

Long grown in gardens for culinary, medicinal, and ornamental purposes, sweet fennel has escaped cultivation and is present as an invasive plant in landscapes from BC to California and across much of North America. It can be seen on roadsides and in native grasslands, vacant lots, riparian zones, wetland edges, and fields. An exuberant reproducer via self-seeding, it can form dense colonies that crowd out native vegetation. There are several subspecies, varieties, and cultivars, including the ornamental bronze fennel ('Purpureum') and the culinary bulbing fennels, grown primarily as vegetables.

Sweet fennel is a short-lived perennial or biennial, growing from a white taproot that can be thick and deep at maturity. The plant has a single stout, branched stem that is hairless, soft, and hollow. All plant parts exude a strong anise or licorice scent. The leaves are stalked, their petioles swollen and sheathing where they clasp the stem. They are very finely divided, with a triangular outline and feathery appearance.

The inflorescence is a flat-topped terminal compound umbel. The tiny yellow flowers are followed by many oblong, ribbed seeds to 0.15 in. A single mature plant may produce hundreds of thousands of seeds in a season. These are widely dispersed by birds and other animals and by human activities.

An established sweet fennel population can be formidable simply in its sheer abundance, and any mature plant may be somewhat difficult to extract due to its hefty taproot. Pull and dig when the soil is moist,

preferably before bloom. Otherwise, a longer-term strategy is to cut to the ground or mow repeatedly, possibly multiple times a year, for several years, eventually exhausting the plant's stored energy. After clearing the site of sweet fennel, mulch and replant.

# Heracleum mantegazzianum

GIANT HOGWEED

Non-native biennial or perennial, to 10 ft. Flowers white, 5-petaled, to 0.5 in.; late spring–early summer. Leaves alternate, to 8 ft. Poisonous. Toxic to horses, chickens. Noxious in BC, WA, OR, CA.

Giant hogweed, a Eurasian weed, may have been introduced to North America as an ornamental or collector's plant. Certainly, it was present as a garden escape by the early 1900s and is now widely introduced in the northeastern US, eastern Canada, and in the PNW from Oregon to BC. The plant has been increasing its range in the PNW since the 1990s.

It invades meadows, riparian areas, cropland, and woodland openings and edges, and is often found near residential sites. It has achieved noxious weed fame in several states because of its invasiveness and because of its considerable dermal toxicity: contact with the plant or its sap can cause painful burning, blistering, and scarring, exacerbated with sun exposure.

Giant hogweed grows from a stout, branched taproot with vertical and horizontal fibrous roots. The crown of the plant can expand to several inches and become woody with age. From this rises a single stem that is hollow and may be several inches wide. It is purple-blotched, a trait that distinguishes it from cow parsnip (*Heracleum maximum*) but may add to the confusion with poison hemlock, which has purple blotches but much different leaves. The leaves of giant hogweed are 3-lobed, and more or less palmate in outline. They are decidedly more deeply incised, pointier, and coarser in texture than those of cow parsnip. They are huge, the lower ones sometimes measuring up to 10 ft. long. Leaves higher on the stem are smaller.

*Heracleum mantegazzianum* is typically monocarpic, growing without blooming for about 3 years,

then blooming, setting seed, and dying. The flowers are borne in compound umbels that may be larger than 2 ft. across. Flowers on the outer margins of an umbel have outer petals larger and irregularly lobed. Seed production is huge, with estimates of 10,000 to 50,000 or more for a single plant. Dispersal is assisted by wind, water, animals, and human activity.

With 3 years before bloom and seed set, recognition of seedlings can be an important key to stopping the spread of giant hogweed. With thick gloves and other protective clothing, pull or dig out any plants, taking care to extract the taproots. Simple cutting has limited utility, as it must be done below the ground surface and can release sap that is hazardous to humans. For large stands of more mature plants, the labor investment and cumulative health risk may be considerable, and herbicide may be preferred.

# Heracleum maximum

## COW PARSNIP

**Native biennial or perennial, to 8 ft. Flowers white, 5-petaled, to 0.25 in.; late spring–midsummer. Leaves alternate, to 20 in. Parts edible/medicinal with caution.**

*Heracleum maximum* (syn. *H. lanatum*) is native to North America and parts of Asia, common across the PNW, and widely distributed throughout the US and Canada. It's a (very) large plant of moist meadows, forest edges, and wetland margins. Beware: this plant is often confused with *H. mantegazzianum*, its larger and meaner non-native cousin.

Like its cousin, cow parsnip grows from a taproot and cluster of fibrous roots, with a single tall, thick stem. The ternately divided, palmate leaves are a bit smoother and less divided than those of giant hogweed. The largest leaves at the base of the plant are up to 20 in. long and wide; the 3 individual leaflets are up to 12 in. long and each is divided into 3–5 lobes. The large leaves are stalked, with thick petioles to 10 in. long, sheathed at their bases.

In its first year there is only a basal rosette of large leaves; in the second year, the tall, hollow flowering stem appears. The flowers resemble those of giant hogweed and are similarly borne in compound umbels, but the individual flowers are somewhat smaller, as are the inflorescences.

Painful blistering can result from contact with cow parsnip plant parts, and particularly from the sap when the plant is cut or crushed. *Heracleum maximum* can be an interesting and attractive vertical accent in a native garden but may be undesirable in gardens frequented by children or sensitive adults, as well as being a nuisance when it self-sows into places where the gardener has other plans. Wear protective clothing and good gloves, pull and dig when the soil is moist, and remove all taproots as well as aboveground parts and particularly any seeds that have formed. Follow with mulch to discourage additional sprouts.

# *Pastinaca sativa*

## WILD PARSNIP, COMMON PARSNIP

**Non-native biennial, to 5 ft. Flowers yellow, 5-petaled, to 0.2 in.; midspring–midsummer. Leaves basal to 18 in., cauline alternate, leaflets to 3 in. Parts edible with caution. Sap causes phytophotodermatitis in humans and animals. Noxious in BC.**

Wild parsnip is common throughout North America, including the PNW. It's a weed of open, disturbed ground, including vacant lots, roadsides, prairies, meadows, and agricultural fields. This European native, long cultivated for its edible roots, has escaped cultivation, becoming an aggressive weed impacting agriculture and natural environments on several continents. In addition to competing with crops and with native vegetation, the plant is widely considered noxious because of significant toxicity to humans and animals.

As a typical biennial, *Pastinaca sativa* appears as a basal rosette of leaves in its first year. Basal leaves and lower stem leaves are pinnately compound, with up to 15 leaflets that may have toothed margins or divided lobes. From a thick, fleshy taproot, the plant produces an erect, stout, leafy, branched flowering stem in its second year. Higher on the stem, the leaves are shorter and simpler and have fewer leaflets. The many tiny flowers are borne in flat-topped compound umbels, 3–8 in. across, terminal on main and lateral stems; each flower has 5 pale yellow, reflexed petals around a greenish center. Seeds are dispersed by water and wind.

Any skin contact with the plant can cause phytophotodermatitis, resulting in serious burns and blisters. People who work with or near the plant are strongly advised to wear gloves and other protective clothing. Small infestations can be controlled by pulling or digging when the soil is moist. Plants can also be killed by repeated cutting below the root crown, or repeated mowing. Large infestations may be combatted with herbicides.

# *Vinca major*

## GREATER PERIWINKLE

Non-native perennial, to 5 ft. Flowers blue, purple, 5-petaled, to 2 in.; spring–summer. Leaves opposite, to 2.5 in. Poisonous. Toxic to horses, chickens.

*Vinca major* was introduced to the US as an ornamental in the 1700s. It is still widely used in landscape plantings and is present as an escape in much of North America, excluding the north-central US and central Canada. This aggressively spreading groundcover

invades shaded habitats, including woodland edges and understories, vacant lots, roadsides, and areas around old homesites. It spreads by stolons and rhizomes, forming dense mats that exclude all other vegetation and are extremely difficult to dislodge. It is a significant environmental problem particularly in California, where it has become the dominant species in many habitats, suppressing native flora, impacting endangered species, affecting sedimentation of rivers, and altering the stream environment for aquatic organisms. It is also a problem for vineyards, as a host for a pathogen affecting grapevines.

*Vinca major* has deep roots, long horizontal rhizomes, and stolons that root at the nodes. The stems are tough, green, and semi-woody. The semi-evergreen, glossy, dark green leaves are simple and oval or heart-shaped. Attractive blue to purple (sometimes white), long-stalked flowers bloom in the axils. It is very similar in appearance and ecology to *V. minor*. Greater periwinkle can be distinguished by its slightly larger flowers and more rounded vs. narrow leaves. It is also a bit less hardy than *V. minor*.

Once established, greater periwinkle is very difficult to eradicate. For a small patch, repeated pulling and digging may eventually be effective, if care is taken to remove roots and rhizomes. Mowing is ineffective, as the rhizomes resprout quickly. Larger invasions may require herbicide, or deployment of excavators, followed by deep mulch and repeated spot-pulling.

# *Vinca minor*

## LESSER PERIWINKLE

Non-native perennial, to 18 in. Flowers blue, lavender, 5-petaled, to 1 in.; late spring–early summer. Leaves opposite, to 2 in. Poisonous. Toxic to horses, chickens.

*Vinca minor* is a popular horticultural plant that has widely escaped cultivation and is found going wild and weedy in woodland edges and understories, vacant lots, roadsides, and areas around old homesites. It is present in the PNW from Oregon to BC, particularly on the west side of the Cascades. It is very similar to *V. major*, and like *V. major*, it was introduced to the US as an ornamental in the 1700s and is still widely sold in nurseries.

*Vinca minor* is a trailing groundcover valued for its attractive evergreen foliage and pretty flowers, as well as its broad tolerance for a range of conditions. The leaves are glossy, deep green, and lanceolate to elliptic. Some cultivars have variegated leaves and may be less vigorous than the species, but they are likely to revert to solid green over time. The long, slender stems are mostly prostrate and often root at the nodes.

Flowers are blue or lavender (sometimes white or burgundy) and pinwheel-shaped. Seed set is scant; the plant spreads primarily by rhizomes and stolons. It forms dense, broad mats particularly in woodland understories, crowding out natives. One of the principal ways that *Vinca minor*, like *V. major*, acquires new territory is through inappropriate disposal by home gardeners or landscapers: old plants ripped out of yards or from dumped hanging baskets persist and reroot in the soil of shady natural areas.

Once established, whether in a yard or in the wild landscape, *Vinca minor* is extremely hard to eradicate. The first and best method of control is to refrain from planting it in the ground, and be careful with any plants disposed of. If you must have it, grow in a container or bounded by concrete.

For small infestations, pull and dig deeply when soil is moist, being careful to retrieve as many of the roots, rhizomes, and stolons as you can, and remove them from the site. Be prepared to do this repeatedly. Mulch heavily, and watch for recurrence. Faced with a large patch or with a patch that will not give up, the beleaguered home gardener may find that herbicide is the least burdensome strategy.

# Arum italicum

## ITALIAN ARUM, ITALIAN LORDS AND LADIES

Non-native perennial, to 18 in. Flowers yellow, white, spadix to 5 in., spathe to 8 in.; midspring–midsummer. Leaves to 12 in. Poisonous. Toxic to cats, dogs, livestock. Noxious in WA.

*Arum italicum* is an attractive non-native plant that has proven a nightmare as a garden aggressor and garden escape from California to BC and in a few areas in the midwestern and eastern US. In the PNW, this shade- and moisture-loving plant is found mostly west of the Cascades, in or near woodlands, riparian areas, and residential neighborhoods.

Spreading by seeds and by tubers, the plant expands its territory rapidly and can be very difficult to eradicate. It hogs all available space in gardens, and competes with native flora in wild habitats. It is toxic to people and animals, including livestock and pets. The berries are particularly poisonous and can be fatal if consumed by human babies or dogs.

The leaves are stalked, arrowhead-shaped, glossy, and deep green to grayish-green, often with light-colored vein markings. Leaves emerge in fall; they may be evergreen through the winter in mild areas, or may die back and re-emerge in spring, dying back again in summer.

All plants in the arum family have a characteristic inflorescence, in which tiny flowers are borne on a spike-like structure called a spadix, surrounded and partially hidden by a sheath-like bract called a spathe. In *Arum italicum*, the spadix is up to 5 in. long, white to pale yellow, and the spathe is white. The inflorescence has a characteristically foul odor. After blooming, the spathe withers away and the flowers of the spadix are replaced by an upright, columnar cluster of bright reddish-orange berries containing the seeds. The berries scatter and produce new plants nearby, or are carried off by birds and planted elsewhere.

Gardeners who have been beguiled by this plant and allowed it to take over complain that attempting to control it has taken major investments of time and labor for years. Gloves and protective clothing should be worn, because the plant can cause severe skin reactions in some people. By digging deeply around individual plants, the stalwart weeder can follow the roots to the tubers and try to collect them all. Tubers or root portions left behind will make new plants. Remove and bag all plant parts; do not compost. It may be necessary to repeat this chore for several years. Mulch the area heavily, and monitor for any new plants emerging.

# *Hedera helix*

ENGLISH IVY

Non-native perennial vine to 80 ft., shrub to 12 ft. Flowers white, 5-petaled, to 0.1 in.; spring–autumn. Leaves alternate, to 4 in. Poisonous. Toxic to cats, dogs. Noxious in WA, OR.

English ivy is a woody, evergreen vine or large shrub that has been used as a large-area groundcover and as a climber on walls and facades for centuries. In the forests of the moderate-temperature, moist PNW, it has been very happy and is now widespread, covering thousands of acres and invading wild woodlands and parks, particularly west of the Cascades.

When young, English ivy spreads via vines as long as 80 ft., attaching to vertical objects via aerial rootlets. After about 10 years, mature plants become more erect shrubs and bloom, then producing clusters of small whitish flowers, followed by purple-black berries that are dispersed by birds. The berries and particularly the leaves are toxic to humans.

Environmental impacts of *Hedera helix* on woodlands are profound. The tough, evergreen leaves form a nearly continuous cover close to the ground, suppressing all other understory vegetation. English ivy can kill trees by shading them out, or making them vulnerable to storm damage by weighing them down. Its sheer biomass can damage trees and buildings. One group found that vines removed from a single tree in the Olympic National Park weighed in at 2,100 lbs.

Numerous cultivars continue to be offered by nurseries; some of these, particularly the variegated ones, may be less aggressive than the species, but none are entirely benign.

Eradication is complicated by potential for contact dermatitis, which may be severe in some people. Several years may be required to clear a site by intensive digging, cutting, and herbicide application.

# *Achillea millefolium*

YARROW

Native and non-native perennial, to 40 in. Flowers white, daisy-like, to 0.2 in.; spring–autumn. Leaves alternate, to 9 in. Parts edible/medicinal with caution. Toxic to horses.

*Achillea millefolium* is widely distributed throughout the PNW and North America. It is circumboreal and native to several continents, including North America, where it is also a garden escape. Many of the plants in gardens were of non-native origin, and native and introduced populations have hybridized.

In addition to the yards and gardens where it is planted, yarrow finds its way into salt marshes, meadows wet or dry at low to high elevations, vacant lots, woodland edges, riparian areas, pastures, and agricultural fields.

There are about 10 native subspecies with different distributions in North America, as well as one widely introduced European subspecies. There are also many cultivars in a variety of colors, and numerous other *Achillea* species available in the nursery trade. *Achillea millefolium* has a history of medicinal and other uses going back to antiquity, on multiple continents.

An individual plant may have one to several stems rising from the crown. The stems and leaves are often covered with short, fine hairs. The sweetly aromatic leaves are lanceolate in outline and very finely dissected. Leaves lower on the stem are stalked; the upper ones are sessile and reduced in size.

Flowers are borne at the ends of stems much taller than the leaves. The inflorescence is a flat-topped and congested umbel-like cluster 2–4 in. across, composed of tiny daisy-like flowers with white petals (usually, in wild plants) and yellow centers. There may be just a few or up to 100 or more of these florets in a cluster.

Thousands of very small seeds are produced by every plant, and dispersed by wind, by animals, and by human activity. They can remain viable in the soil for several years.

Many gardeners might welcome a volunteer yarrow plant, but whether installed by the gardener or just showing up uninvited, yarrow has potential to become a nuisance. Yarrow spreads readily via deep and wide rhizomes, and even small sections of rhizome, when severed, can sprout and produce new plants. The species can form dense patches that might interfere with the gardener's plans to grow other things. Small seedlings can easily be pulled or hoed out, but more established plants can be tough to remove decisively due to their persistent rhizomes. Dig 12 in. down to retrieve as many of the rhizomes as possible. Follow with mulch and/or competitive plantings, and monitor for recurrences.

# *Ambrosia artemisiifolia*

ANNUAL RAGWEED

---

**Non-native annual, to 4 ft. Flowers yellow-green, heads to 0.1 in.; late summer–autumn. Leaves opposite, alternate, to 4 in. Parts edible/medicinal with caution. Noxious in OR.**

---

Annual ragweed is native to and found throughout most of North America, including the PNW, where the dominant form is an invader from the east. It occupies dry, open areas, including fields, roadsides, riparian zones, vacant lots, rangeland, and cropland. While it's a significant agricultural pest, the species may earn more infamy from its role as a major cause of hay fever, dermatitis, and other allergic reactions.

*Ambrosia artemisiifolia* has a robust root system, from which multiple erect, hairy, branched or unbranched stems arise. The leaves are pinnately lobed, lanceolate in outline, and fuzzy, mostly stalked but more sessile toward the upper stem. Leaves are often opposite toward the base of the plant, alternate toward the top. Plants bear a multitude of tiny flowers in terminal spike-like racemes, with male flowers higher in the spike and female flowers below them. A single plant may produce many thousands of tiny, raspy seeds, well suited to dispersal by wind, water, or animals; seeds are also spread around by agricultural activities. Germination rates may be low, but seeds can live in the soil for decades.

Small invasions of annual ragweed are easily controlled by pulling or hoeing. Larger patches can be conquered by repeated mowing or cutting, which prevents bloom and seed set.

# Ambrosia trifida

## GIANT RAGWEED

**Native annual, to 6 ft. Flowers yellow-green, male in heads to 0.15 in.; midsummer–autumn. Leaves opposite, to 12 in. Parts edible/medicinal with caution. Noxious in CA.**

Giant ragweed, a robust annual native to most of North America, is found in the PNW predominantly on the drier east side. It is considered noxious or invasive in several areas. The species invades various open, disturbed sites on roadsides, woodland edges, riparian habitats, grasslands, and cropland.

*Ambrosia trifida* has a fibrous root system and erect, somewhat hairy green stems. The leaves are opposite, long-stalked (petioles to 5 in.), and oval, with serrated margins. At maturity they are palmately divided into 3 (usually) or 5 lobes. The species is monoecious. The more conspicuous inflorescences are terminal clusters of male flowers. Individual male flowers are tiny and saucer-shaped, held in long, dense spikes, turning yellow to brown as they mature. The tiny, whitish-green female flowers are found below the male flowers, in the leaf axils. Giant ragweed has a prodigious pollen output that is responsible for some allergic reactions.

A single plant can produce over 10,000 seeds; these are tough-coated and can persist in the soil for years. Giant ragweed is an aggressive competitor with native and agricultural plants, forming large stands. It displaces important crops and is considered one of the most problematic weeds for farmers. Mature plants have tough, fibrous roots and stems that can damage farm machines.

On farms, tillage has been effective for control of smaller plants. Repeated mowing reduces seed set but has not helped to eradicate invasions of giant ragweed. Herbicides have been used against large invasions. For small invasions in most home gardens, pulling (ideally before seed set) should be effective.

# *Anthemis cotula*

## STINKING CHAMOMILE, STINKING MAYWEED, DOG FENNEL

Non-native annual, to 24 in. Flowers white, daisy-like, to 1 in.; late spring–autumn. Leaves alternate, to 2.5 in. Parts edible/medicinal with caution. Toxic to cats, dogs, horses, livestock.

Stinking chamomile is a European native with worldwide distribution. It is a very widespread weed in the PNW and across North America, found particularly in disturbed sites with moist, rich soil, including fields, roadside ditches, cultivated landscapes, agricultural fields, and nurseries. Some of its many common names refer to the plant's strong odor, which is unpleasant to most people. Its leaves bear a slight resemblance to those of true fennel (hence dog fennel). It's in the same genus as true chamomile (*Anthemis nobilis*).

This is a small, branched annual with finely dissected foliage and small daisy-like flowers borne singly at the ends of stems. The flower has 10–20 rays (petals) around a yellow disk.

The plant can be toxic to livestock and to pets who nibble it. The foliage can cause contact dermatitis, so gloves are recommended when weeding. It's easy enough to control in the home garden with pulling and hoeing, ideally before seed set, followed by mulch to prevent renewed germination.

127

# *Arctium minus*

## COMMON BURDOCK, WILD RHUBARB, LESSER BURDOCK

Non-native biennial or perennial, to 5 ft. Flowers pink, purple, violet, heads to 0.75 in.; late summer–autumn. Leaves alternate, to 12 in. Parts edible. Toxic to horses. Noxious in BC.

*Arctium minus* is native to Europe and introduced widely on several continents, including most of North America. It occurs on both the east and west sides of the Cascades in the PNW. The plant is widely familiar as a common weed and is sometimes grown for its foot-long, edible taproot.

Common burdock is a big, quirky, bushy garden presence, potentially annoying or amusing. The leaves are simple, coarsely hairy on their undersides, the lower ones 10–12 in. across and heart-shaped to ovate; upper leaves are smaller.

The flowers bloom in spherical heads clustered on branched stems. The flowerheads somewhat resemble thistles, with which common burdock is often confused. Mature flowers are distinct for their hooked bracts, which make the heads unpleasantly raspy and prone to stick persistently to clothing and animals.

A single common burdock plant may produce thousands of seeds. It invades fields, meadows, and other open sites. In addition to competing with agricultural crops and native plants for space, common burdock serves as a host for some fungal pathogens. It's also a problem for wool production, as it gets tangled into sheep's fleeces, and if grazed heavily by cows, it affects the quality of milk.

Best strategies for control of *Arctium minus* include monitoring for seedlings, and removing the plants in their first year when possible, or before second-year plants set seed. Mature plants will require some serious digging and potential battle with the sticky seedheads, but small infestations can be thus removed and their return prevented by heavy mulching.

# *Artemisia absinthium*

ABSINTH WORMWOOD, ABSINTHIUM

Non-native perennial, to 4 ft. Flowers yellow, heads to 0.2 in.; summer. Leaves alternate, whorled, to 5 in. Parts edible/medicinal with caution. Noxious in WA.

*Artemisia absinthium* is grown as an ornamental and as an ingredient in alcoholic beverages. The species is widely distributed in Europe, occurs in parts of Africa and India, and has been used as a medicinal and to flavor beverages since antiquity. In North America, it's a widespread weed or garden escape throughout Canada and in all but the southernmost US states. It competes aggressively with agricultural and native plants. The plant is drought-tolerant and is often seen on the dry ground of roadsides, agricultural fields, and sunny disturbed sites.

This large, sturdy perennial produces several upright, branched stems from a single large taproot.

It bears many small pendent flowerheads, clustered into terminal panicles. But absinth wormwood's most distinctive feature is its handsome, silvery, often deeply lobed foliage. The leaves are strongly aromatic, unpleasant to some people.

*Artemisia absinthium* spreads mostly by seeds, which can remain viable for several years. Thus, in larger infestations, mowing and tillage can help to slow its spread by preventing seed set. In home gardens, control by pulling, digging, monitoring for seedlings, and mulching.

# Artemisia vulgaris

## MUGWORT, LOBED WORMWOOD

Non-native perennial, to 6 ft. Flowers yellow, heads to 0.13 in.; summer. Leaves basal to 4 in., cauline alternate. Parts edible/medicinal.

Mugwort (a name shared with other *Artemisia* species) is a Eurasian weed with a cosmopolitan distribution. Long grown for medicinals and beverage flavoring, it was introduced to North America as a garden plant in the 1600s and subsequently spread throughout the continent. It is widely regarded as invasive and is a listed noxious weed in several states, particularly in the Midwest, but seeds are still sold by many companies to gardeners interested in its medicinal and culinary qualities. Mugwort is found on roadsides and in fields, lawns, and cropland.

*Artemisia vulgaris* is a tall, rhizomatous perennial with aromatic leaves that are woolly on the undersides and mostly green above, sometimes toothed, often deeply cleft. The small flowerheads are borne in dense, narrow clusters arising from the upper axils.

Mugwort spreads via robust rhizomes and through self-seeding. With dense root systems and thousands of seeds per plant, eradication from an established site can be labor-intensive and may require repeated efforts over time. Mowing can slow the blooming and self-seeding, but rhizomes will persist, so digging will be necessary unless the beleaguered gardener resorts to herbicides. After clearing the site, mulch heavily and monitor for new seedlings.

# *Bellis perennis*

## ENGLISH DAISY, LAWN DAISY

**Non-native perennial, to 6 in. Flowers white, daisy-like, to 1 in.; year-round. Leaves basal, to 2 in. Parts edible/medicinal.**

*Bellis perennis* ("beautiful perennial") is an accurate enough name for this charming small daisy. But this European native is a widespread weed in the north-temperate regions of Eurasia and North America. Introduced to this continent as a horticultural plant, it has spread to moist lawns and fields, woodland edges, and streambanks in the northern US and Canada. In the PNW, it's found mostly west of the Cascades.

English daisy is sometimes included in grass seed mixes for lawns; it spreads via short rhizomes and self-seeding, and is short enough to survive lawn mowing. The small white flowers with yellow central disks are borne singly on short stems above rosettes of simple, more or less oval leaves. Those flowers found growing wild often have a pink tinge; cultivars offer double-flowered and pinker or red forms. The flowers are heliotropic: they move to follow the position of the sun.

This is a charming and harmless weed in the context of the non-native monoculture of the typical lawn but could become problematic in a tidy or native-focused garden, and may compete with other small plants in native wild lands. It can be a minor agricultural pest, potentially dominating pastures and competing with other plants.

In the home garden, vigilance and pulling followed by mulch are probably the most effective and economical control strategies.

# Carduus acanthoides

## PLUMELESS THISTLE, SPINY PLUMELESS THISTLE

Non-native biennial, to 7 ft. Flowers purple, heads to 1 in.; midsummer–autumn. Leaves alternate, to 8 in. Parts edible with caution. Noxious in BC, WA, OR, CA.

*Carduus acanthoides* is a Eurasian weed found in much of the US, as well as BC and eastern Canada. In the PNW, it is mostly an eastside plant, invading roadsides, pastures, meadows, agricultural fields, and riparian areas.

Like other biennials, this thistle begins life as a rosette of leaves. It grows from a fleshy taproot that can go several feet deep at maturity. In its second spring, it sends up a tough, very spiny stem, much-branched toward the top, with wings running down its length, formed from the leaf bases. The leaves are deeply lobed or pinnately divided, hairy on their undersides and spiny along their margins. The purple (occasionally white) flowers are subtended by spiny bracts and are borne singly or in clusters of 2–3. A plant may bear as many as 60 flowerheads, producing up to 4,800 seeds. Seeds can remain viable in the soil for several years.

Small infestations of plumeless thistle can be removed by pulling (wear gloves!), digging, or grubbing out with a hoe; take care to remove at least the root crown. For larger patches, mowing before seed set is effective, but timing is important and may need to be repeated, with monitoring for resprouting and new seedlings. Mulch thickly after removing the plants.

# *Carduus nutans*

## MUSK THISTLE, NODDING THISTLE

Non-native biennial or perennial, to 7 ft. Flowers pink, red, heads to 4 in.; midsummer. Leaves basal to 14 in., cauline alternate. Parts edible/medicinal with caution. Noxious in BC, WA, OR, CA.

*Carduus nutans* is a European thistle accidentally introduced to the US in the 1800s or early 1900s, then rapidly spreading throughout North America. It's a listed noxious weed in about 25 states.

*Carduus nutans* inhabits agricultural land, road-sides, meadows, woodlands, and riparian areas. It is an agricultural problem because it is unpalatable to livestock, thus somewhat immune to reduction by grazing, and can crowd out palatable forage, as well as competing with other crops. In native landscapes, it displaces and reduces the cover of native forbs.

Musk thistle is an imposing plant, very tall and branched. Leaves are jaggedly lobed or toothed with spiny margins and vary considerably in shape among several subspecies and varieties. The handsome spheri-cal flowerheads are borne singly at the ends of stems. A single plant may bear 50–100 flowerheads, producing 100,000 seeds or more.

In agricultural settings, tillage may be used to uproot young plants, herbicides are employed to elim-inate large infestations, and dense planting can crowd out seedlings.

For smaller invasions in home gardens, the weed can be dug or grubbed out with a hoe. After the site is cleared, heavy mulching should prevent subsequent seed germination.

# Carduus pycnocephalus

## ITALIAN PLUMELESS THISTLE

Non-native annual, to 7 ft. Flowers pink, purple, heads to 0.75 in.; midspring–midsummer. Leaves basal to 8 in., cauline alternate. Parts edible with caution. Noxious in BC, WA, OR, CA.

This Mediterranean species has invaded many countries on several continents, with impacts primarily on raising livestock. It outcompetes more suitable forage in pastures and rangeland, causes injury to livestock, and reduces the value of wool. It was introduced to North America accidentally in the 1800s and has happily not found much of the continent to its liking. It's present east of the Cascades in the PNW as well as in Idaho, New York, and a few southern states.

Growing from a thick and deep taproot, the stems of Italian plumeless thistle may be branched or unbranched. They are very hairy, with spiny wings running longitudinally. The basal leaves have winged petioles and are sharply incised with pinnate, spine-tipped lobes. The cauline leaves are sessile, simpler in outline, and reduced in size.

Flowerheads are borne singly or in small clusters of 2–5 on the ends of stems or in upper leaf axils. The somewhat cylindrical heads are spiny and bristly, the flowers pink to purple (occasionally white). The relatively few seeds have pappuses, which facilitate wind dispersal. The seeds also get around by sticking to farm machinery or being included in hay bales.

Large infestations on farms have been successfully managed by cultivation and with selective grazing by sheep or goats. Mowing has proven ineffective due to regrowth from taproots. For small patches of Italian plumeless thistle, pull (wear gloves!), dig, or grub out, taking care to sever the root 4 in. below ground level.

# Carduus tenuiflorus

## SLENDER-FLOWERED THISTLE, WINGED PLUMELESS THISTLE

**Non-native annual or biennial, to 6.5 ft. Flowers pink, purple, heads to 0.5 in.; late spring–midsummer. Leaves basal to 10 in., cauline alternate. Parts edible with caution. Noxious in BC, WA, OR, CA.**

*Carduus tenuiflorus* is a European weed with limited distribution in the PNW and Texas and a scattered distribution in eastern and midwestern states. It is a listed noxious weed in several jurisdictions, invading rangeland, roadsides, fields, and vacant lots. It forms dense stands that crowd out forage plants and native vegetation.

The basal leaves of *Carduus tenuiflorus* are woolly, pinnately divided into spine-tipped lobes, and taper to their stalks. Cauline leaves are smaller, unstalked, and less lobed; they are sessile, with spiny bases clasping the stems. The flowering stems may be branched or unbranched and are very woolly, with leaf-like wings formed from the leaf bases running their entire length. The flowerheads are borne in congested terminal clusters of 5–20, each subtended by spiny bracts. Two kinds of seeds are produced, some with a plume-like pappus and some "plumeless"; a single plant may produce up to several hundred seeds, which are dispersed by wind and animals.

This very prickly plant, being annual, can be relatively easily removed by pulling (wear gloves!), digging, or grubbing out with a hoe. Mulch to prevent emergence of more seedlings.

# Centaurea cyanus

## CORNFLOWER, BACHELOR'S BUTTON

Non-native annual, to 3.5 ft. Flowers blue, purple, heads to 1 in.; late spring–autumn. Leaves alternate, to 4 in. Parts edible/medicinal.

Cornflower is a European native with scattered distribution throughout much of North America, spreading as a garden escape into woodlands and grasslands particularly in the coastal states, east and west. This old-fashioned annual is commonly available in the nursery trade as packaged seed. The cheerful blue flowers are loved by many, and many people believe it's a native, a confusion compounded in the US by its misleading inclusion as a cheap filler in many wildflower seed mixes. Like many annuals in the sunflower family, it can be invasive, especially on dry sites (including fields and roads), and it is on the monitor list for Washington.

The showy flowerheads of annual cornflower consist of many small florets. Ray flowers are blue to purple (sometimes pink or white); the central disks are purple or white, with purple stamens. The flowers are borne singly at the tips of branching stems; an individual plant typically has only a single stem rising from the base, but the stem is branched near the top. Leaves are narrow, linear to lanceolate, and usually simple and entire; sometimes the lower ones are shallowly lobed. Leaves and stems are finely hairy.

Many a gardener may be tempted to keep this plant when it shows up unbidden, and there's not much harm to be done, if you can limit dispersal by removing the plants before they set seed. If you choose to exclude them from your garden, they are very easy to remove by pulling or hoeing and digging.

# *Centaurea diffusa*

DIFFUSE KNAPWEED, TUMBLE KNAPWEED, WHITE KNAPWEED

Non-native annual or perennial, to 30 in. Flowers white, heads 0.2 in.; summer. Leaves basal to 8 in., cauline alternate. Noxious in BC, WA, OR, CA.

*Centaurea diffusa* is a Eurasian weed found widely across most of North America and scattered throughout the PNW on both sides of the Cascades. It is found on open ground on a wide variety of sites, including roadsides, vacant lots, fields, rangeland, and riparian zones. It is considered a pest on rangeland, as it is not good forage and crowds out other species. It can produce dense stands that increase erosion and contribute to wildfire hazards.

Diffuse knapweed grows from a long taproot, from which rises a single multi-branched stem that can bear numerous flowerheads. All vegetative plant parts are hairy. The longer basal leaves are often pinnately lobed; the stem leaves are reduced in size and simpler. The basal leaves typically die before the plant blooms.

A single stalk of *Centaurea diffusa* can produce over a thousand seeds, and reproduction is mostly from seed. Small infestations can be combatted by grubbing out with a hoe; take care to remove the plant crowns, which can regenerate if only the stems are cut. Pulling can be effective, but gloves are recommended. Larger infestations may require tillage or herbicide application. Several insect species attacking either the roots or the seeds have been used as biocontrol agents against this weed.

# Centaurea ×gerstlaueri

## MEADOW KNAPWEED, HYBRID KNAPWEED

Non-native perennial, to 40 in. Flowers pink, purple, heads to 0.75 in.; summer–autumn. Leaves basal to 6 in., cauline alternate. Noxious in WA, CA.

*Centaurea ×gerstlaueri* (syn. *C. ×moncktonii, C. pratensis*) is found along the west coast from BC to California, in Idaho and Montana, and in eastern North America. This hybrid of *C. jacea* and *C. nigra* inhabits roadsides, vacant lots, pastures, fields, tree farms, river banks, woodland edges, and industrial property. It crowds out more desirable forage plants in pastures and meadows, and competes with native flora and desired horticultural plantings.

Meadow knapweed has multiple erect, reddish stems. The basal and lower leaves are lobed or have toothed margins and may be 1–1.5 in. wide; those higher on the stem are reduced in length, simpler in shape, and more linear. The flowers are pink to purple (occasionally white). Flowerheads are borne singly at the ends of stems. They are roughly spherical, subtended by tan to brown bracts with papery margins. Seeds are attached to small pappuses.

The best control is prevention, focusing on prevention of seed production and dispersal. Dig or pull the plants, taking care to remove the woody root crowns of the more mature plants. Mulch well, and watch for recurrences.

# Centaurea jacea

BROWN KNAPWEED, BROWNRAY KNAPWEED

Non-native perennial, to 4 ft. Flowers purple, white, heads to 1.5 in.; midsummer–autumn. Leaves alternate, to 10 in. Parts edible/medicinal. Noxious in BC, WA, CA.

Brown knapweed is one of several weedy *Centaurea* species present in the PNW. It is found from BC to northern California and in the northeastern US. The plant can be seen in meadows, riparian zones, vacant lots, ditches, pastures, woodland edges, and roadsides. It is problematic because it displaces native vegetation and quality forage for animals.

Young plants grow from a taproot, which later becomes a cluster of roots below a woody root crown. Stems are single or multiple, upright, hairy, and ridged, branching at their upper ends. The lower leaves may be stalked, with margins that are entire, toothed, or lobed. Higher on the stem, the leaves are reduced in size, simpler in outline, and unstalked. The purple to white flowerheads are borne singly at ends of stems. Overlapping involucral bracts subtending the flowerheads are brownish (thus the common names). A plant may produce as many as 500 seeds, which are without pappus but can be dispersed by water, animals, and agricultural activities.

Brown knapweed can be effectively controlled by pulling and digging, preferably before seed set. Any flowerheads that have formed should be bagged and removed from the site. Mulch well and monitor for recurrences.

# Centaurea melitensis

## MALTESE STARTHISTLE

Non-native annual or biennial, to 3 ft. Flowers yellow, heads to 0.5 in.; summer–autumn. Leaves basal to 6 in., cauline alternate. Unpalatable. Toxic to horses. Noxious in BC, WA, CA.

*Centaurea melitensis* is a Mediterranean species found along the west coast from BC to California, across the Southwest to Texas, and in a few eastern states. It invades roadsides and vacant lots, pastures and range-land, as well as natural areas including meadows and open woods. It displaces native vegetation and quality forage and is suspected of possible serious toxicity to horses. It is one of several yellow *Centaurea* species found in the PNW, some native and some not. The weedy *Centaurea* it most resembles is *C. solstitialis*, which has larger flowerheads.

Maltese starthistle begins as a basal rosette, then sends up one to a few wiry stems, which may be branched or unbranched. Stems and leaves are hairy and gray-green. Basal and lower leaves are stalked and may have margins smooth or toothed, or with deeply cut lobes. Stem leaves are progressively smaller and simpler in outline. The basal and lower leaves may wither away by the time the plant blooms. The small yellow flowerheads are borne 1–3 at a time at the tops of stems. Each head can produce up to 60 seeds, and a plant may have up to 100 flowerheads. The seeds are attached to pappuses that aid in wind dispersal; they are also easily spread by water, or by sticking to animals or people.

The most effective control strategy for *Centaurea melitensis* is early detection and intervention. Pull, hoe, or dig small invasions, taking care to remove taproots. Repeated mowing will prevent seed set and eventually eradicate invasions. Mulch well to prevent subsequent seed germination.

# Centaurea montana

## MOUNTAIN BLUET, PERENNIAL CORNFLOWER

**Non-native perennial, to 2.5 ft. Flowers blue, purple, heads to 2 in.; early summer. Leaves alternate, to 12 in. Parts medicinal. Noxious in BC.**

Mountain bluet is a European native widely sold in the US nursery trade and present as a garden escape in the PNW, northeastern US, and western Canada. It invades roadsides, fields, beaches, desert scrub, and open sunny places on disturbed ground and in woodlands.

This attractive long-lived but short-blooming perennial grows close to the ground with a mounding habit, with flowering stems rising above the handsome, simple, gray-green leaves. A plant may have one to several stems, sometimes branched, with flowerheads borne usually singly at the ends of stems, true-blue with purple centers. As in other *Centaurea* species, the involucre of bracts beneath a flowerhead is imbricate (brick-patterned). *Centaurea montana* spreads by creeping rhizomes and by seed.

While the gardener who likes its look might understandably be happy when *Centaurea montana* shows up without being planted, at least in gardens near wild land it should be discouraged from wandering by deadheading. As an unwanted guest, it can be a bit persistent but can easily enough be removed by digging and grubbing. Left to its own devices, a clump may persist and multiply for years.

# Centaurea nigra

## BLACK KNAPWEED, LESSER KNAPWEED

Non-native perennial, to 5 ft. Flowers blue, violet, heads to 1 in.; midsummer–autumn. Leaves basal to 10 in., cauline alternate. Parts edible/medicinal. Noxious in BC, WA, CA.

Black knapweed is found from California to Washington, through much of the PNW on both sides of the Cascades, and eastward to Montana and Idaho, as well as the northeastern US and eastern Canada. It inhabits roadsides, fields, meadows, and other sites with sunny, disturbed ground. It is an agricultural pest that negatively impacts rangeland by decreasing plant diversity, outcompeting more desirable forage, and increasing erosion and wildfire risks.

An individual plant may have one or many branched stems, with hemispherical flowerheads 0.5 in. long and 1 in. wide, usually borne singly at the branch tips. The hairy leaves may be deeply incised into lobes, or with toothed or smooth margins. The basal leaves have petioles; the stem leaves are more sessile and reduced in size. Black knapweed can be distinguished from some similar-looking *Centaurea* species by its dark-fringed involucral bracts.

Mowing can slow the production of seeds, but plants can regenerate from the crowns or root portions, so effective control requires killing or removing those parts as well. Small infestations can be removed by digging, followed by monitoring and mulching to prevent recurrence. Burning may work where it's safe to do so, and herbicide may be an effective option for larger infestations.

# *Centaurea nigrescens*
## SHORT-FRINGED KNAPWEED, TYROL KNAPWEED

Non-native perennial, to 4 ft. Flowers purple, heads to 1.5 in.; midsummer–autumn. Leaves basal to 10 in., cauline alternate. Noxious in WA, CA.

*Centaurea nigrescens* (syn. *C. dubia*) is a Eurasian weed present in North America since the 1800s. It is not yet common in the PNW, but it occurs from BC to California, east through Idaho and Montana, and in the northeastern US and eastern Canada. It invades woodland edges, pastures, and roadsides, displacing native plants and higher-quality forage for animals. This spread of the species has been boosted by its cultivation as an ornamental.

The plant begins as a basal rosette and may put forth one or multiple stems the first season, or the next spring. The stems are erect and usually multi-branched toward the top. The basal and lower stem leaves are stalked and may be coarsely toothed or shallowly lobed; cauline leaves are reduced, narrower, simpler, and more sessile. Stems and leaves may be slightly hairy or mostly hairless. Purple (occasionally white) flowerheads are borne singly on the many branch tips. They are distinguished from similar-looking *Centaurea* species by their triangular involucral bracts edged with dark, comb-like fringe.

Short-fringed knapweed spreads by self-seeding, by generating new plants rhizomatously, and by sprouting of rhizome fragments. Small invasions can be eradicated by digging, preferably before seed set, with care taken to remove as much of the roots and rhizomes as possible. Repeated mowing and cutting several times a year can eventually reduce the population.

# Centaurea solstitialis

## YELLOW STARTHISTLE, ST. BARNABY'S THISTLE

Non-native annual or biennial, to 3 ft. Flowers yellow, heads to 0.75 in.; midsummer–autumn. Leaves basal to 8 in., cauline alternate. Toxic to horses, chickens. Noxious in BC, WA, OR, CA.

Yellow starthistle was introduced to the US in the early to mid-1800s, probably accidentally, as a contaminant in other seed. It has since invaded nearly every state, particularly in the west, and most of southern Canada. It now occupies millions of acres in California and Idaho and thousands of acres (predominantly east of the Cascades) in Washington and Oregon. Starthistle can be seen on roadsides, in meadows and open woods, on rangeland and cropland, and on other disturbed sites. The species can form large, dense patches that displace native flora and quality forage for wildlife and livestock. The plant is poor-quality (and potentially harmful) forage for cattle. In the PNW we have three other weedy yellow *Centaurea* species: *C. melitensis* and *C. benedicta* have smaller flowerheads and are less common; *C. macrocephala* is a showy garden escape with a larger flowerhead.

*Centaurea solstitialis* sends down a taproot that can extend 4 ft. into the soil, augmenting its drought tolerance and competitiveness for resources. The basal leaves have lyrate to pinnately divided lobes; the stem leaves are more simple and linear in shape. All vegetative plant parts are woolly, and leaves and flower bracts are bristly and spiny.

The yellow flowerheads are borne singly at the ends of stems. The species produces prodigious quantities of seeds, some pappus-plumed and some (those from the outer florets on a head) not. The seeds are dispersed by wind, water, animals, and vehicles, and can persist up to a decade in the soil.

The best management strategy is prevention; spot seedlings and pull or hoe them before they can mature. Larger invasions have been combatted with combinations of repeated mowing, tillage, burning, grazing, and/or herbicide, and replanting with competitive vegetation. For small invasions, identify the problem before seed set and pull, hoe, dig, mow, mulch, and monitor for recurrence. When cutting or hoeing, make sure the root crown is removed. Where it's safe to do so, burning can kill the plants but will not kill the seed bank and may actually improve germination of this pest.

# Centaurea stoebe

## SPOTTED KNAPWEED

Non-native biennial or perennial, to 5 ft. Flowers purple, pink, heads to 0.5 in.; midsummer–autumn. Leaves basal to 6 in., cauline alternate. Noxious in BC, WA, OR, CA.

*Centaurea stoebe* (syn. *C. maculosa, C. biebersteinii*) is one of 16 *Centaurea* species present in the PNW, all introduced and invasive and several with similar coloring, so identification can be challenging. It is found in much of Canada and most US states, dominating millions of acres. In the PNW, this aggressive weed ranges from BC to California and is found on both sides of the Cascades, occupying vacant lots, fields, river banks, woodland edges, and dry meadows. Spotted knapweed crowds out native flora and other desirable plants, including quality forage for livestock and wildlife.

Spotted knapweed grows from a stout, deep taproot. In its first year, it produces a basal rosette of leaves. In its second year, it sends up a single flowering stem, slender, multi-branched, and somewhat hairy. The leaves are light silvery green, and lower on the plant they are deeply incised with pinnately arranged lobes. Higher on the stem, they become reduced in size and simpler in outline. Terminal flowerheads are borne singly on the multiple branches. The heads are oval, light purple to bright pink (occasionally white), atop half-inch-tall involucres. The involucral bracts have short, dark, comb-like tips. A single plant may produce 300 heads in a season, resulting in prolific seed production. The seeds are equipped with a short pappus, aiding in wind dispersal. They also get moved around by sticking to humans, animals, or vehicles. Seeds remain viable in the environment for several years.

For control of this weed, early detection is key. If cut or mowed, spotted knapweed will regrow and bloom quickly. Pull seedlings, or dig them out with their taproots. After removing the weeds, use competitive plantings and mulch to discourage subsequent germinations. Larger infestations may be suppressed by targeted grazing with sheep. Herbicide is often used, and several insects have been used successfully for biocontrol.

# Centromadia pungens

## COMMON SPIKEWEED, COMMON TARWEED

**Both native and introduced, annual, to 4 ft. Flowers yellow, daisy-like, to 0.4 in.; midsummer–autumn. Leaves alternate, to 6 in. Noxious in WA, OR.**

*Centromadia pungens* (syn. *Hemizonia pungens*), native to dry regions of California, Idaho, Nevada, and Arizona, was introduced to the PNW sometime in the past 100 years and has since become a nuisance weed of growing concern here. It's found east of the Cascades in Washington and Oregon and, particularly since the 1980s, is a problem for farmers and ranchers. Common spikeweed colonizes roadsides, prairies, seasonal wetlands, grain fields, and rangeland. It competes with important crops and forage plants, and is not grazed by livestock.

The plant begins as a leaf rosette in fall or spring, then sends up a rigid, well-branched stem. Stems and leaves are covered with stiff hairs, rough and sticky to the touch due to glands secreting a pungent (hence *pungens*) resin. The lower leaves are deeply divided once or twice into narrow segments; upper leaves are reduced, simpler, linear, and bear spines at their tips. The small flowerheads look a bit like tiny sunflowers, each subtended by an involucre of spiny, stiff-hairy bracts; their numbers vary from just a few to 100+ per plant.

Common spikeweed spreads by seed, so the best way to suppress an invasion is to prevent seed set. Pull or dig out plants along with their roots, preferably early in the season, wearing gloves. Large invasions in agricultural settings are often managed with herbicides. All plant material should be bagged and removed from the site to prevent seeding. Mulch thickly to discourage subsequent invasions.

# *Chondrilla juncea*

## RUSH SKELETONWEED, NAKED WEED

---

Non-native perennial, to 5 ft. Flowers yellow, heads to 0.75 in.; midsummer–autumn. Leaves mostly basal to 5 in., cauline alternate. Parts edible with caution. Noxious in BC, WA, OR, CA.

---

This Eurasian species, introduced to the US accidentally in the late 1800s, is now found along the west coast from BC to California, eastward to Idaho, Wyoming, and Montana, and in a few eastern states. It has been present in the PNW at least since the 1930s, primarily on the east side. *Chondrilla juncea* is estimated to infest several million acres in the west, invading dry fields and pastures, high desert, rangeland, cropland, and roadsides. It displaces native plants in natural areas, quality forage plants on rangeland, and grain crops on agricultural land.

*Chondrilla juncea* begins life as a basal rosette of leaves with sharp, backward-pointing lobes. At maturity, the plant may have a taproot reaching downward 7 ft. A single plant may have as many as 6 tall, branched flowering stems, which may appear almost naked of leaves (thus "rush-like"). The few cauline leaves are smaller and simpler than the basal ones, and mostly sessile. The flowerheads, borne in small terminal clusters, resemble small dandelion or hawkweed flowers. A plant may produce up to 20,000 seeds in a season, which are dispersed on the wind with the help of a pappus, as well as being spread about by animals and by human activity. In addition to self-seeding, this plant spreads vegetatively by producing new plants from buds on lateral and vertical roots and also from root fragments.

Control attempts have employed cultural, biological, and chemical modalities, often with modest success. For small areas, the best method is pulling when the soil is moist. This can be complicated by the very long taproot, even on small plants. All parts of the plant are brittle and can generate new plants from broken-off pieces, so repeated efforts may be required a few times a year for several years. Mowing regularly will cut seed production but not eradicate the plants.

# Cichorium intybus

## CHICORY, WILD SUCCORY

**Non-native biennial or perennial, to 6 ft. Flowers blue, daisy-like, to 1.5 in.; midsummer–autumn. Leaves basal to 13 in., cauline alternate. Parts edible. Noxious in BC.**

Chicory is a widespread weed on scattered small sites throughout North America. It has been listed as invasive in a few states, particularly in the Great Plains, where it can invade native prairies. Flowers occur in loose clusters on branched plants 2–6 ft. tall; they are delightfully sky-blue to periwinkle-blue (occasionally pink or white). The leaves are simple, clasping, and coarsely toothed.

*Cichorium intybus* has been widely known as a garden plant for ornament and food for centuries. The large taproots, particularly of *C. intybus* var. *sativum*, are roasted and ground for a caffeine-free coffee substitute. The leaves are a pungent salad herb; assorted cultivars of *C. intybus* var. *foliosum* give us endive, radicchio, and similar vegetables. The very similar *C. endivia* (curly endive, escarole) is also a source of edible leaves.

Chicory prefers poor soils, so it is not so much a garden visitor as it is a roadside ornament or welcome forage for cattle. Unwanted plants are easily forked out and may inspire culinary exploration—or be popped into a vase for a wildflower arrangement.

# Cirsium arvense

## CANADA THISTLE, CREEPING THISTLE

Non-native perennial, to 5 ft. Flowers lavender, pink, heads to 0.75 in.; summer. Leaves basal to 8 in., cauline alternate. Parts edible/medicinal with caution. Noxious in BC, WA, OR, CA.

*Cirsium arvense* is a notoriously invasive Eurasian weed on several continents, including most of North America, where it was accidentally introduced in the 1600s. In the US, it's a listed noxious weed in 43 states, inspiring the unaffectionate moniker "lettuce from hell thistle."

Canada thistle invades both dry and wet habitats, including cropland and pastures as well as prairies, dunes, meadows, riparian areas, and other native landscapes. It is ecologically harmful in competing with native plants and changing plant community composition; it's also an agricultural pest, reducing crop yields.

*Cirsium arvense* grows from a deep taproot, with horizontal roots that can spread as far as 10 ft. in a season, producing large clonal patches. The narrow, spiny leaves are pinnately divided or lobed, with toothed or smooth margins; they are reduced in size higher on the stem. The species is dioecious. Each plant bears many flowerheads, in clusters at the ends of branched stems. A single plant may produce thousands of seeds, with feathery tufts that aid wind dispersal. Seeds can remain viable in the soil for many years.

Canada thistle is not responsive to some herbicides; repeated applications and multiple agents may be required in large infestations. Repeated tillage and mowing have also been used with some success. For small infestations, a combination of repeated digging, close monitoring for new plants, and heavy mulching may be effective.

# Cirsium undulatum

## WAVYLEAF THISTLE

Native perennial, to 4 ft. Flowers lavender, pink, purple, heads to 2 in.; midsummer. Leaves alternate, to 15 in. Parts edible/medicinal with caution. Noxious in CA.

*Cirsium undulatum* is a native thistle found in meadows and woodlands of dry areas throughout much of central and western North America. In the PNW, it is fairly widely distributed on the drier east side.

This short-lived perennial grows from a deep taproot and may produce long lateral rhizomes that give rise to new plants. From the taproot grow one to several branched stems. Stems and leaves are densely woolly and grayish. The leaves may be coarsely toothed or pinnately lobed, the lobes topped with conspicuously long spines. Multiple large, urn-shaped flowerheads are borne in open terminal clusters of 3–10.

Wavyleaf thistle is a native with some aesthetic appeal for lovers of wickedly prickly things. However, gardeners less fond of spines, or wishing to reserve the garden for other things, may be driven to remove them. Thick gloves are highly recommended. Pull or hoe young seedlings; dig out more mature plants, preferably when soil is moist, making efforts to get the rhizomes. Bag and remove any seedheads. Follow with mulch and monitor for sproutings of rhizomes left behind, or new seedlings.

# Cirsium vulgare

## BULL THISTLE, COMMON THISTLE

Non-native biennial, to 6 ft. Flowers red-purple, heads to 2 in.; midsummer–autumn. Leaves basal to 6 in., cauline alternate. Parts edible/medicinal with caution. Noxious in BC, WA, OR, CA.

This robust Eurasian weed is on noxious weed lists throughout North America, including BC and 46 US states. In the PNW, it is common on both sides of the Cascades. Bull thistle inhabits roadsides, pastures, forest edges, grasslands, vacant lots, and disturbed wild lands, such as logged montane areas. It outcompetes native plants on wildlands and as an agricultural pest reduces usable forage for livestock and invades hayfields, reducing their value.

*Cirsium vulgare* is sometimes an annual or a short-lived perennial but typically a biennial, appearing as a basal rosette of leaves the first year and sending up a flowering stem the second. All vegetative parts are hairy, the stem is ridged and spiny, the leaves have sharp spines at the tips of their lobes, and the flowerheads have spiny bracts beneath them. Flowerheads are typically borne singly at the ends of stems but sometimes clustered. Bull thistle produces up to 300 large flowerheads per plant, each with up to 300 seeds.

Pulling or hoeing, best done before seed set, can be effective. Good work gloves are recommended, as these prickly plants can be wicked. Plants that have begun to bloom should be bagged and disposed of, to prevent seeds ripening and spreading on your property. Tillage and repeated mowing can be useful in larger infestations. Horses, sheep, and goats will eat the young plants or flowers.

# Conyza canadensis

## HORSEWEED, CANADIAN FLEABANE

Native annual, to 5 ft. Flowers white, daisy-like, to 0.2 in.; mid–late summer. Leaves basal to 4 in., cauline alternate. Parts edible/medicinal with caution.

*Conyza canadensis* (syn. *Erigeron canadensis*) is widely distributed throughout the PNW and much of North America. Its native status notwithstanding, horseweed's aggressive conquest of territory makes it a problem for agriculture and for wild landscapes, here and in Europe. It's found on open ground along roadsides and in prairies, waste places, cropland, and orchards. It's a pest for ornamental turf and plant nurseries, including those growing trees, perennials, and bulbs. It is also a contaminant of various grain and seed crops.

This tall, fast-growing annual springs from a taproot, from which rises a single (usually) stem that is erect and unbranched except at the top, where numerous flowerheads are borne in open panicles. Leaves are simple, narrow, and somewhat hairy, numerous and closely spaced, appearing whorled along the stem. A plant may produce as many as 250,000 small seeds in a season, and these are assisted in broad dispersal by pappuses.

The species has been the focus of concerted control efforts, particularly in Europe, and has developed resistance to glyphosate and several other herbicides. In large infestations in agricultural settings, regular tillage has been effective. For smaller infestations, pulling works, followed by competitive cover crops, groundcovers, or heavy mulch. When pulling, hoeing, or digging, take care to remove the stem, as decapitated stems left rooted can regrow.

# *Cotula coronopifolia*
## BRASS BUTTONS

Non-native annual or perennial, to 10 in. Flowers yellow, heads to 0.4 in.; early summer–autumn. Leaves alternate, to 2.5 in. Unpalatable.

*Cotula coronopifolia*, a South African native, is a wetland species of marine and freshwater marshes and vernal pools. It is widely introduced on several continents, including North America. Here, it's found particularly in the tidal flats of eastern and western Canada, the west coast states, and Alaska. In the PNW, it is found west of the Cascades, along the shores of the ocean, Puget Sound, and the lower Columbia River.

Brass buttons is a low-growing plant, with glabrous, somewhat succulent vegetative parts. The stems can trail and root at the nodes, allowing the plant to outcompete native vegetation by producing mats. The leaves are simple, narrow, sessile, entire or with coarsely toothed margins. The tiny flowers are clustered in button-like heads, borne singly on stems to 8 in. high. The small seeds are without pappuses; they are dispersed by birds and by moving water.

This weed is considered invasive but is moderate in growth rate. Small invasions can be controlled by pulling, ideally before seeds have been dispersed. Avoid leaving roots or large stem fragments in the soil, as these may form new plants.

# Crepis capillaris

## SMOOTH HAWKSBEARD

Non-native annual or biennial, to 3 ft. Flowers yellow, heads to 0.8 in.; midspring–autumn. Leaves alternate, to 12 in.

This European species is widely distributed over much of North America. In the PNW, it is common west of the Cascades and along the Columbia River Gorge. It's a weed of roadsides, fields, and other open, disturbed sites.

The narrow lower leaves of *Crepis capillaris* are stalked, toothed and/or deeply incised, and pinnately arranged; upper leaves are smaller and more sessile. Flowerheads consisting of all ray flowers (like dandelions) are held in loose clusters at the ends of stems.

*Crepis capillaris* (like other hawksbeards) is likely to be mistaken for *Taraxacum officinale* (common dandelion): its leaves and flowers are that similar. It's distinguished from that familiar weed most easily by its smaller flowerheads, in clusters, and its branched stems (vs. the unbranched, single-flowered *T. officinale*). As with dandelions, *C. capillaris* seeds are aided in wind dispersal by a feathery pappus.

Smooth hawksbeard is easy to remove by pulling or hoeing; mulching should suppress most new seedlings.

# *Cyclachaena xanthiifolia*

CARELESSWEED, BURWEED MARSH ELDER, GIANT SUMPWEED

Non-native annual, to 6 ft. Flowers yellow, heads to 0.12 in.; late summer–autumn. Leaves opposite, to 8 in. Unpalatable.

*Cyclachaena xanthiifolia* (syn. *Iva xanthifolia*) occurs over much of the US and southern Canada. It is considered native in the central US and southern Canada, introduced in the west. In the PNW, it is found east of the Cascades, in moist low places and disturbed areas. The common names hint at the plant's lack of aesthetic appeal—and the lack of affection people have for it. The specific epithet indicates that its leaves resemble those of *Xanthium* (cocklebur).

Carelessweed grows rapidly from a taproot, with tall, erect stems branched only toward the top, in the inflorescence. The somewhat rough-surfaced leaves are generally opposite, sometimes alternate higher on the stem, and often nearly as wide as long. Lower leaves are long-stalked, ovate to triangular to heart-shaped, and sometimes so deeply incised as to appear 3-lobed. Higher on the stem the leaves are reduced in size, narrower, and simpler in outline, with shorter stalks. The leaf margins are doubly dentate: that is, there are large, coarse teeth that bear smaller teeth in turn.

Carelessweed bears an inflorescence of numerous dense, narrow, spike-like, branched racemes from upper leaf axils and ends of stems. The tiny flowers are held in very small, button-like heads on drooping stalks. The plant is a source of strongly allergenic pollen that causes problems for hay fever sufferers.

*Cyclachaena xanthiifolia* reproduces by abundant self-seeding, so the key to controlling it is to identify and remove it before that can occur. Plants can cause dermatitis in sensitive individuals, so gloves

are recommended. Pull, dig, and hoe when the soil is moist, removing taproots and any flower buds. Larger patches can be combated by frequent mowing or cutting, to prevent seed set and exhaust the plants until winter. Mulch well to prevent additional sproutings.

FORBS/HERBS AND VINES

155

# Delairea odorata

## CAPE IVY

Non-native perennial vine, to 30 ft. Flowers yellow, heads to 0.25 in.; winter. Leaves alternate, to 4.5 in. Poisonous. Toxic to livestock, fish. Noxious in OR, CA.

*Delairea odorata* (syn. *Senecio mikanioides*) is a South African vine that has become a problematic invasive in Australia, Hawaii, and California. The northernmost tip of its west coast range is the southernmost Oregon coast, where it was first spotted in the late 1990s. It invades coastal bluffs, riparian zones, woodlands, seasonal wetlands, and roadsides. In natural areas, it can form dense mats that crowd out native vegetation. It is toxic to grazing animals and can kill fish when it gets into waterways.

Cape ivy is still sold in the nursery trade, often as a houseplant. Seeds are produced in abundance but are mostly not viable, so most reproduction is vegetative, from stem fragments, rhizomes, and stolons.

The rootstock typically sends up a single, long, branched stem that scrambles and climbs as a vine. The leaves are shiny and deep green, triangular to rounded and palmately lobed or toothed, with petioles about as long as the leaf blades. Small discoid flowerheads are borne in terminal or axillary clusters of up to 40. Stems are mostly deciduous, those which bloomed the previous winter withering away in fall to be replaced by new growth.

Control cape ivy by pulling and digging; all plant parts must be bagged and removed from the site. Mowing is not effective, because the cut stems will resprout. Agencies coping with large infestations recommend cutting stems to the ground before bloom, multiple times, combined with herbicide application.

# *Erechtites minimus*

AUSTRALIAN BURNWEED, COASTAL BURNWEED

Non-native annual or perennial, to 7 ft. Flowers yellow, heads to 0.25 in.; midsummer–autumn. Leaves alternate, to 8 in. Parts edible with caution.

In North America, *Erechtites minimus* (syn. *Senecio minimus*) is found only in the coastal regions of Washington, Oregon, and California, where it inhabits riparian areas, fields, and roadsides. This Australian native is particularly prone to taking advantage of open areas left unvegetated by recent fires.

Growing from a taproot with branching lateral roots, it produces one to a few tall stems without a basal rosette. The cauline leaves are simple, lanceolate, and slightly fuzzy, with finely toothed margins. They reduce in size and become more sessile higher on the stem. The lowest leaves may wither away before flowering time. The plant is topped by a large, branched inflorescence of 40–200+ dull yellow flowerheads in terminal clusters. The individual flowerheads are button-like, atop cylindrical involucres. The many small seeds are wind-dispersed; each seed is attached to a pappus of numerous comparatively long, fine hairs.

Manual removal has proven effective for control of Australian burnweed. Pull or hoe when the soil is moist and before seed set, making sure to remove taproots and any mature flowers or seedheads. Mulch heavily to discourage additional seed germination.

# Galinsoga quadriradiata

## QUICKWEED, SHAGGY GALINSOGA, CILIATE GALINSOGA

Non-native annual, to 2 ft. Flowers white, daisy-like, to 0.25 in.; summer–autumn. Leaves opposite, to 2.75 in. Parts edible.

*Galinsoga quadriradiata* (syn. *G. ciliata*) is a weed from Central and South America that has become invasive in many countries worldwide. It has found its way to most areas of North America, with the exception of northernmost Canada and Alaska. In the PNW, it inhabits fields, gardens, roadsides, and vacant lots, primarily on the west side of the Cascades. With its rapid proliferation by self-seeding, the plant can be a nuisance in agriculture.

From a fibrous root system rise densely hairy, branched stems, which can be erect or spreading and sprawling. The leaves are hairy and lanceolate to ovate, with coarse teeth along the margins and 3 prominent longitudinal veins. They are stalked lower on the stem, becoming nearly sessile higher up. Flowerheads are borne in both terminal and axillary clusters. Each flowerhead has typically 5 (4–8) white petals, each deeply cleft into 3 lobes. A plant may produce up to 7,500 seeds, each attached to a pappus that assists in wind dispersal.

Where practical, burning can be an effective way of destroying both plants and seeds of quickweed. Otherwise, pull, hoe, and dig when soil is moist, then mulch to prevent new seedlings.

# Gnaphalium uliginosum

## MARSH CUDWEED

Non-native annual, to 6 in. Flowers green, brown, heads to 0.2 in.; summer–autumn. Leaves alternate, to 2 in. Parts medicinal.

Marsh cudweed is a European weed found in much of northern North America, including all of Canada and Alaska. As the common name suggests, it likes moist sites like pond margins, vernal pools, and streambanks, from low to montane elevations. In the PNW, it is most common on the wetter west side of the Cascades. It can be a minor agricultural pest, particularly in grain crops.

This is a very small annual growing from short fibrous roots or a small taproot. It typically is multi-branched and sprawls a bit, spreading laterally. Stems and leaves are usually covered with white-woolly hairs. The light gray-blue-green leaves can vary from barely pubescent to densely woolly. The flowers are very small and nondescript, wispy and cup- or thimble-shaped, in tight clusters in the axils or stem ends.

*Gnaphalium uliginosum* is sometimes confused with seedlings of woolly horticultural plants like lamb's ears or pearly everlasting. There are also several close relatives, including a widespread and somewhat weedy native to our region, *G. palustre* (lowland cudweed); but that one's leaves are shorter and wider, oblong to spoon-shaped, and more conspicuously white-woolly.

Marsh cudweed is easily controlled by hoeing or pulling, followed by mulching to prevent more seedlings.

# Hieracium aurantiacum

## ORANGE HAWKWEED, KING DEVIL, DEVIL'S PAINTBRUSH

**Non-native perennial, to 3 ft. Flowers orange, dandelion-like, to 1 in.; summer. Leaves mostly basal, to 4 in. Noxious in BC, WA, OR, CA.**

Orange hawkweed, a beautiful but "devilish" European weed, has invaded most of North America, with the exception of the Southwest. It is listed as noxious in several states.

It is found in sun to light shade on roadsides, fields, meadows, lawns, agricultural land, vacant lots, and forest edges and understories from low to high elevations. It's an aggressive competitor, displacing preferred forage plants in pastures, and may rapidly crowd out native meadow species. It is sometimes sold in nurseries or in wildflower seed mixes and promoted as an ornamental on online gardening sites, contributing to the problem.

An individual plant sends up a single, generally unbranched stem. The showy flowerheads are held in clusters of 5–30 at the ends of stems, each head producing as many as 30 tiny seeds.

Just after beginning to bloom, a plant sends out fuzzy stolons, up to 12 in. long, to produce the next season's plants. With rapid vegetative spread via rhizomes and stolons, the species can form broad monocultural swaths.

Small infestations may be dug out. Be careful to remove all plant parts, including rhizomes, fibrous roots, and stolons. Mowing will delay seed set but stimulates bloom and disperses stolons. After plants are removed, mulch and monitor closely for seedlings.

# *Hieracium caespitosum*

MEADOW HAWKWEED, YELLOW KING DEVIL, YELLOW HAWKWEED

Non-native perennial, to 3 ft. Flowers yellow, dandelion-like, to 0.75 in.; midspring–midsummer. Leaves mostly basal, to 4 in. Noxious in BC, WA, OR.

*Hieracium* is a large genus with numerous native species in the western US and numerous European invasives. *Hieracium caespitosum* is one of the latter, introduced over much of North America. It is a listed noxious weed in several states. The species is usually found on moist ground, often in disturbed sites including pastures, road-sides, and clearcuts, as well as forest edges and meadows, from low to high elevations. Like some of its relatives, this rhizomatous and stoloniferous perennial rapidly forms dense swaths that crowd out other plants.

From a basal rosette of simple, fuzzy leaves, a single plant may bear 10–30 stems. Each stem may carry as many as 30 dandelion-like flowerheads in terminal clusters. A single plant will produce hundreds of seeds. Each seed is attached to a pappus, which aids in dispersal.

*Hieracium caespitosum* often grows near other *Hieracium* species and particularly resembles the widespread weed *H. piloselloides*. Both species are rampant, sometimes aggressively mat-forming, fibrous-rooted perennials. However, there are some distinguishing characteristics. While *H. caespitosum* has stolons, *H. piloselloides* does not. The latter is mostly hairless, unlike the very hairy *H. caespitosum*. *Hieracium piloselloides* has a similar inflorescence of numerous yellow flowerheads, but the cluster is less compact, with somewhat more numerous heads. Another similar-looking species, *H. flagellare*, has slightly larger (to 1 in. wide) flowerheads, in much smaller inflorescences (2–4 heads to a cluster).

Early detection is the best preventive measure for invasions of *Hieracium caespitosum* and related species.

A small invasion can be thwarted by digging, preferably before seed set; take care to remove all roots, rhizomes, and stolons. Mowing is not recommended, as it can facilitate the plant's dispersal, but annual tillage can eventually eradicate a large population.

# Hieracium ×floribundum

## FLOWERY HAWKWEED

**Non-native perennial, to 3 ft. Flowers yellow, dandelion-like, to 0.3 in.; early–midsummer. Leaves mostly basal, to 5 in. Noxious in BC, WA, OR.**

This hybrid of *Hieracium caespitosum* and *H. lactucella*, both European species, is found in the PNW, Montana, Idaho, and Wyoming, as well as the northeastern US and eastern Canada. Proliferating by seed and by runners, it invades meadows, pastures, roadsides, and gardens. It can form mats of basal rosettes dense enough to prevent germination and establishment of native flora.

Plants grow from rhizomes and send out multiple stolons; a single stem arises from the crown. Most of the leaves are basal, spatula-shaped, and sparsely hairy. The stem branches only at the top, in the terminal inflorescence (a loose cluster of several flowerheads). A single plant can produce as many as 30 small dandelion-like heads. As in dandelion, the seeds are attached to feathery pappuses, which assist in wind dispersal.

The best intervention is prompt removal of the basal rosettes (which will be immediately suspect as belonging to a weedy member of the Asteraceae) before the plant can set seed. Pull, hoe, or dig when the soil is moist, taking care to remove all stolons and rhizomes. Follow with mulch to prevent new seedlings.

# *Hieracium lachenalii*

## COMMON HAWKWEED

Non-native perennial, to 30 in. Flowers yellow, dandelion-like, to 1 in.; late spring–midsummer. Leaves basal to 5 in., cauline alternate. Parts edible/medicinal. Noxious in BC, WA.

*Hieracium lachenalii* is a European weed found mostly on the west side in the PNW. Its range extends from BC to northern Oregon, plus several northeastern states and eastern Canada. The species occupies open woodlands, fields, pastures, clearcuts, and roadsides.

Growing from fibrous roots and a short rhizome, the plant sends up a single stem (typically), which is hairy throughout and sparingly branched. The leaves are mostly basal, grayish, and narrowly lanceolate, with margins that may be smooth or toothed. Cauline leaves are few and reduced in size, unstalked, and often with purple mottling. The inflorescence is a flat-topped, loose cluster of up to 12 small dandelion-like flowerheads. They quickly go to seed, with a fluffy, whitish, dandelion-like seedhead.

Like most invasive hawkweeds, this species spreads only by seed, so the key to successful removal is to get it before it blooms. A small invasion can be removed easily by pulling and digging when the soil is moist. Be careful to remove the crown, as that can resprout if left behind. If flowers have formed, bag the plant material and discard to prevent seeding. Mowing may be a short-term measure to prevent blooming and seeding, but if done when plants have begun to bloom, it has potential to spread seeds, and it must be done repeatedly as the plants will resprout and bloom otherwise. After clearing the site of common hawkweed, mulch well.

FORBS/HERBS AND VINES

# Hieracium murorum

## WALL HAWKWEED

**Non-native perennial, to 2 ft. Flowers yellow, dandelion-like, to 0.6 in.; midspring. Leaves basal to 4 in., cauline alternate. Noxious in BC, WA.**

Wall hawkweed is thankfully rare in our region. It will be difficult to distinguish it from the several other *Hieracium* species it resembles, particularly *H. lachenalii*. Like other weedy hawkweeds, it invades roadsides, woodland edges, and waste ground in scattered sites in the PNW.

Stems and leaves are somewhat hairy. Stems are well branched at the top, in the inflorescence. The leaves are relatively sparse, more or less elliptic, with toothed margins. The plant produces flat-topped, open, terminal clusters of a few small dandelion-like flowerheads.

As with other hawkweeds, early intervention is key. Without rhizomes or stolons, this plant depends upon seeds for reproduction, so remove it before it flowers. Pull or dig when the soil is moist, being certain to remove the root crown. Follow with mulch.

# *Hieracium sabaudum*

SAVOY HAWKWEED

Non-native perennial, to 4 ft. Flowers yellow, dandelion-like, to 0.8 in.; midsummer. Leaves basal to 7 in., cauline alternate. Noxious in BC, WA.

*Hieracium sabaudum* (syn. *Hieracium laevigatum*) is a European species found in southern BC and western Washington, as well as in Quebec and a few northeastern US states. Invading dry fields and roadsides, it competes with desirable forage plants in pastures and rangeland, and may displace native vegetation. It spreads only by seed but is such an aggressive self-sower that it can rapidly dominate a site.

This hawkweed grows from fibrous roots with no rhizomes or stolons. Multiple tall, erect, and very leafy stems rise from a single crown. The leaves have strongly toothed margins and vary somewhat in shape, from lanceolate to oblong to oval, tapering to a long stalk. Leaf undersides are densely hairy, as are the lower stems. Basal leaves may be absent or may wither away by bloom time. Each plant bears many small, dandelion-like heads in loose, branched terminal clusters. Seeds are equipped with a tan to whitish pappus, aiding in wind dispersal.

Control savoy hawkweed by catching it early, preferably before flowering. Pull or dig when the soil is moist, taking care to remove the root crown. If flowering has begun, bag and dispose of the plants. Follow with thick mulch.

# Hypochaeris radicata

## ROUGH CAT'S-EAR, HAIRY CAT'S-EAR, FALSE DANDELION

**Non-native perennial, to 2 ft. Flowers yellow, dandelion-like, to 1.5 in.; spring–summer. Leaves basal to 14 in. Parts edible. Toxic to horses, livestock. Noxious in WA.**

This Eurasian weed, one of many dandelion looka-likes, is very widespread throughout North America. In the PNW, it's found mostly on the west side. Rough cat's-ear is common in lawns and gardens, parks, agricultural fields and pastures, woodland edges and meadows, and waste places like roadsides and vacant lots. It's an annoyance in lawns, where its ground-hugging basal leaves suppress grass; it competes with agricultural or forage crops and with native plants in wild landscapes. A principal concern is its toxicity to horses (particularly) and other livestock.

The most "common" common name, rough cat's-ear, can be confusing for those who encounter *Calochortus*, the large genus of western native lilies, several of which are called cat's-ears. As for false dandelion, *Hypochaeris radicata* differs from true dandelion (*Taraxacum officinale*) in having smaller flowerheads, stems that may be branched, and hairy leaves that hug the ground.

*Hypochaeris radicata* grows from a thick root, with a rosette of basal leaves and one to several upright, generally leafless, somewhat branched stems. Leaf margins are wavy to toothed to lobed. Flowers are single at the ends of branches, sometimes 2–3 on a main stem. Seeds are dispersed with the help of a pappus.

Rough cat's-ear reproduces by seed, as well as vegetative sprouting of crowns and root sections. Small infestations in lawns and gardens can be grubbed out with a hoe in spring; take care to remove the plant's crown. Repeated machine cultivation may be required for larger areas.

# Jacobaea vulgaris

## TANSY RAGWORT, TANSY BUTTERWEED, STINKING WILLIE

**Non-native biennial or perennial, to 4 ft. Flowers yellow, daisy-like, to 1 in.; summer. Leaves basal to 8 in., cauline alternate. Poisonous. Toxic to horses, cattle, sheep, goats, chickens. Noxious in BC, WA, OR, CA.**

*Jacobaea vulgaris* (syn. *Senecio jacobaea*), a Eurasian weed, is widely introduced in the PNW (particularly on the west side) and in northeastern North America. It is listed as noxious, prohibited, and/or quarantined in several states.

Confusion sometimes arises when this plant's common name, tansy ragwort, is mistakenly shortened to "tansy," the partial name of a different noxious weed, *Tanacetum vulgare* (common tansy), which has button-like flowers with no petals.

Tansy ragwort is a weed of roadsides, fields, forest edges, clearcuts, and other disturbed sites. Its noxious weed status is due to its considerable toxicity to livestock. The plant contains alkaloids that cause cumulative and potentially fatal liver damage. Its foul taste mitigates the tendency of animals to graze it, but dead plants are more palatable—and still toxic. It is sometimes present as a contaminant in hay, causing livestock poisoning. Milk from cattle and honey from bees feeding on *Jacobaea vulgaris* can contain toxic alkaloids.

In its first year, the plant consists of a taprooted basal rosette of ruffled leaves. The following year, one or more flowering stems rise above the mature leaves, which are twice pinnately divided, with deeply incised lobes. Numerous flowerheads are borne in a cluster at the top of each stem; typically a head has 13 ray flowers and 13 involucral bracts. A single plant can produce as many as 150,000 seeds, each attached to a feathery pappus, aiding wind dispersal.

Small patches are easily removed by pulling and grubbing out with a hoe; take care to remove the roots, which can otherwise resprout. Gloves are recommended for working with tansy ragwort. Uprooted plants should be bagged and put in the trash.

# *Lactuca serriola*

## PRICKLY LETTUCE

Non-native annual or biennial, to 6 ft. Flowers yellow, daisy-like, to 0.5 in.; spring–summer. Leaves basal to 12 in., cauline alternate. Parts edible with caution.

This plant, native to Eurasia and Africa, has become widely introduced in many countries. It was an accidental introduction in North America beginning in the late 1800s and is now present through most of the continent. Prickly lettuce is common on roadsides, in vacant lots, yards, gardens, pastures, agricultural fields, and woodland edges. It is a problematic weed of grain crops in the PNW.

Typical for a biennial, prickly lettuce produces a basal rosette of leaves in its first year and develops a taproot. In its second year, it sends up a single stem, sometimes branched, with a terminal branched inflorescence of several small pale yellow flowers.

The leaves are thin, with a prominent white central vein on the upper side. Lower leaves are usually coarsely lobed, with a row of prominent stiff prickles on the midrib of the underside. Leaves higher on the stem are reduced in size, unlobed, and without prickles.

*Lactuca serriola* can hybridize with domestic lettuce, *L. sativa*. Prickly lettuce can be confused with several related plants having similar flowers and leaves, including sow-thistle (*Sonchus*) and other *Lactuca* species, but the prickles on the midribs of *L. serriola* are distinctive.

Prickly lettuce is easy to grub out with a hoe or pull when the soil is moist. It can be a little rough on the hands, so gloves are recommended.

# *Lapsana communis*

NIPPLEWORT

Non-native annual, to 5 ft. Flowers yellow, dandelion-like, to 0.5 in.; midsummer. Leaves basal to 6 in., cauline alternate. Parts edible/medicinal.

*Lapsana communis* is a Eurasian weed found throughout most of North America. It's very common west of the Cascades in the PNW, occurring on disturbed ground in sun or part shade in vacant lots, fields, yards, gardens, open woods, and woodland edges. In spring it seems to pop up all over, overnight, along with wall lettuce, a similar-looking weed with which it is often confused. The common name derives from a 17th-century belief that the plant was useful in healing sores on that part of a woman's anatomy.

The leaves are thin and roughly oval, slightly toothed or pinnately lobed; the lower ones are stalked, while leaves higher on the stem are smaller and more sessile. The small yellow dandelion-like flowerheads are held in an open, branched cluster of up to 15. A plant can produce as many as 800 seeds.

Nipplewort appears suddenly and, if left to its own devices in favorable conditions, can quickly fill available ground. However, it's an annual and a lightweight as weeds go—easy to pull or scrape away, preferably before it sets seed—and it should be easy enough to discourage in the future by a thick layer of mulch.

# Leucanthemum vulgare

## OXEYE DAISY

**Non-native perennial, to 3 ft. Flowers white, daisy-like, to 2 in.; late spring–autumn. Leaves alternate, to 6 in. Parts edible/medicinal. Noxious in BC, WA.**

*Leucanthemum vulgare* (syn. *Chrysanthemum leucanthemum*) is considered invasive and problematic in many countries. This Eurasian weed was introduced to the US as an ornamental and has spread as a weed throughout North America. It is listed as noxious or invasive in several states. Oxeye daisy is one of the most invasive non-natives in the PNW. Unfortunately, it is still included in some misleadingly labeled wildflower seed mixes sold in the US.

Oxeye daisy is found on roadsides and often in broad, dense swaths in meadows and pastures. These incursions on agricultural land decrease crop yields. In wild landscapes, the plant frequently forms dense monocultures over acres. It displaces many natives, particularly meadow species, some of which are increasingly rare.

The leaves are simple, lanceolate, the basal ones stalked, with teeth or lobes. Leaves on the flower stem are smaller, more sessile, and may have few to no teeth. Stems are unbranched or may be slightly branched near the top. The flowers are borne singly on the ends of stems, on leafless stalks. This weed is often confused with its close relative, the Shasta daisy (*L. maximum*), but the latter has larger flowers and leaves.

Oxeye daisy spreads via rhizomes and seeds. The rhizomes and root systems are shallow, so tilling can effectively disrupt larger invasions. Small infestations can be removed by pulling and digging, but haste is advised, as this plant spreads rapidly.

# *Matricaria discoidea*

## PINEAPPLE WEED, FALSE CHAMOMILE

Native annual, to 18 in. Flowers yellow, heads to 0.4 in.; spring–summer. Leaves alternate, to 2 in. Parts edible/medicinal with caution.

*Matricaria discoidea* (syn. *M. matricarioides, Chamomilla suaveolens*) is a weedy native widely distributed throughout most of North America. This small, fast-growing annual loves habitats challenging to other plants—thin, rocky soil in fields, vacant lots, gravelly roadsides, sidewalks, gardens, driveways, and other disturbed sites.

Pineapple weed has shallow roots and branched, leafy stems. The leaves are very finely dissected and strongly scented, reminding people of pineapple or chamomile. The whole plant feels somewhat sticky to the touch.

The dull yellow, button-like flowers are borne in open, terminal clusters. The seeds are gelatinous when wet, which aids their dispersal; they stick to animals, people, and machines, as well as being carried along by water.

The plant looks so dinky (weak, slender stems and leaves) that one might be inclined to ignore it at first, but it can quickly become an aesthetic nuisance, at least. Mowing is ineffective, but the roots of this plant are shallow and easy to pull or hoe out when the soil is moist. Follow with mulching, to prevent sprouting of any seeds that have been shed.

# *Mycelis muralis*

## WALL LETTUCE

Non-native annual or biennial, to 3 ft. Flowers yellow, daisy-like, 5-petaled, to 0.5 in.; midsummer–autumn. Leaves to 7 in. Parts edible.

*Mycelis muralis* (syn. *Lactuca muralis*) is a nondescript weed with weak stems and small flowers. One early summer morning, seemingly overnight, it arrives: wall lettuce, in its legions. Basal leaves are soon followed by flowering stems, springing up on roadsides and woodland edges, yards and gardens, and wetlands. Wall lettuce is widely introduced from Oregon to Alaska and from northeastern US to eastern Canada. In the PNW and Alaska, it's considered invasive. It tolerates wet or dry conditions, full sun to full shade.

The basal and lower stem leaves are pinnately lobed with a jagged outline, with a larger triangular terminal segment. Leaves higher on the stem are reduced in size and simpler in outline. The multiple small flowers appear in open clusters at angles to the main stem. Each flower-head has 5 small petals, and each petal has 5 teeth.

The flowers give way to as many as 10,000 seeds per plant, each seed aided in dispersal by a feathery pappus. Owing to this copious seed production, a site with favorable conditions can be overrun quickly, crowding out small native plants.

The leaves of wall lettuce, fairly unique in outline, are easy to recognize once you've met them. The plants are very easy to uproot by hand or with any scraping tool. A layer of mulch or competitive groundcover will prevent their return.

# *Onopordum acanthium*

## SCOTCH THISTLE, SCOT'S THISTLE, COTTON THISTLE

Non-native annual or biennial, to 8 ft. Flowers purple, pink, red, heads to 2.5 in.; midsummer. Leaves spiny, to 2 ft. Parts edible/medicinal with caution. Noxious in BC, WA, OR, CA.

Scotch thistle is introduced over most of North America and is listed as a noxious weed in several states. It's an aggressive weed of dry and moist habitats, including riparian zones, rangeland, roadsides, fields, gardens, and agricultural land. It forms stands of large, unpleasantly spiny vegetation that effectively block access and use of land and bodies of water by people and livestock.

The gray-green, woolly leaves of *Onopordum acanthium* are toothed to lobed and very spiny; the stems are also hairy and spiny. The flowerheads are borne singly or in small clusters at the ends of branches. The plants can be large and branchy, thus bearing many flowers and producing as many as 40,000 seeds in a season. The seeds are aided in wind dispersal by pappuses and can remain viable in the soil for years, germinating when water becomes available.

The good news about this ubiquitous and prickly invader is that, as a biennial or annual, it dies. Its seeds are the key to its success and to any control strategy. Young plants are easy to pull, but wear gloves because they are painful to handle. More mature plants can be eradicated by digging; take care to remove the taproots. Also be sure to remove any flowerheads on dislodged plants from the site, as they can continue to ripen seeds after being uprooted. A larger infestation can be eliminated by repeated mowing, a few times yearly, sometimes for a few years as more seedlings come up. Sheep and goats will graze the plants without harm. Once a patch is cleared, mulch deeply.

# Rhaponticum repens

## RUSSIAN KNAPWEED, HARDHEADS

**Non-native perennial, to 3 ft. Flowers purple, pink, red, heads to 0.5 in.; summer. Leaves alternate, to 4 in. Toxic to horses. Noxious in BC, WA, OR, CA.**

*Rhaponticum repens* (syn. *Centaurea repens, Acroptilon repens*) hails from central Asia and Russia and has spread all over the world, probably introduced accidentally as a contaminant in agricultural seed. It has invaded most of North America, excluding the east and southeast coasts. It is listed as noxious or invasive in a few Canadian provinces and in several US states. Found on dry slopes, meadows, woodland edges, fields, roadsides, and clearcuts, this weed is large, robust, fast-spreading, long-lived, and difficult to eradicate. It forms large colonies that displace agricultural and native plants and is profoundly toxic to horses.

The stems are branched, the stems and leaves hairy. The basal leaves are lobed; the stem leaves are progressively simpler in shape and reduced in size. The numerous flower-heads are borne in open terminal clusters, one plant bearing up to 1,000 seeds in a year. The seeds are attached to pappuses that aid in wind dispersal. Seeds are also dispersed when eaten and then deposited by birds or mammals.

The predominant means of dispersal is vegetative; Russian knapweed forms a very deep taproot that can reach 15 ft. down in its second year, and long rhizomes spread out many feet and produce buds from which new plants arise.

Due to its deep rhizomes and roots, Russian knapweed is extremely difficult to eradicate once established. Early on, young plants can be pulled or dug out, before the taproots and rhizomes are too long. Any piece of rhizome left behind can resprout. Even a small patch that has had time to mature may require an integrated approach (e.g., digging plus herbicide) and repeated efforts multiple times yearly over a period of a few years.

# Senecio sylvaticus

## WOOD GROUNDSEL

**Non-native annual or biennial, to 3 ft. Flowers yellow, heads to 0.2 in.; early spring–autumn. Leaves alternate, to 4.75 in. Poisonous. Toxic to horses, cattle, sheep, goats.**

Wood groundsel, one of several similar-looking, weedy *Senecio* species in our region, has a limited distribution, mostly on the west side in the PNW from BC to California, plus a few states in the northern Midwest and northeastern US. It can be seen on roadsides, woodland edges, fields, logged or burned coniferous woodland, vacant lots, and yards. The plant is toxic when grazed and competes with native vegetation, particularly in early succession, when it's at an advantage in populating disturbed or bare soil.

Growing from a taproot and scant fibrous roots, the plant sends up a single, often unbranched stem. The greenish-gray leaves are narrow and pinnately lobed, the largest to about 1.5 in. wide, becoming reduced in size upward. Stems and leaves are all finely pubescent and foul-smelling. The branched inflorescence consists of many small heads; these appear as button-like centers atop long involucres, sometimes with a few small ray flowers poking out around the central disk. Wind dispersal is aided by a fluffy pappus on each seed. When moist, the seeds become sticky and adhere to passing animals and humans.

Wood groundsel is easily controlled by pulling and hoeing, ideally before seed production. Mulch and replant.

# Senecio vulgaris

## COMMON GROUNDSEL, OLD MAN IN THE SPRING

**Non-native annual or biennial, to 16 in. Flowers yellow, heads to 0.4 in.; year-round. Leaves alternate, to 4 in. Poisonous. Toxic to horses, cattle, sheep, goats. Noxious in WA.**

Common groundsel is a Eurasian weed found throughout North America on roadsides, lawns, vacant lots, and agricultural land, as well as in gardens and nurseries. In addition to competing with desired plants in these settings, it is toxic to livestock and if consumed can cause potentially fatal liver damage.

The plant can have a single unbranched, leafy stem, or it may be multi-branched, growing from a taproot. The leaves are toothed or lobed. The flowerheads are yellow and button-like, enclosed by a cylindrical involucre about 0.5 in. high, composed of about 21 black-tipped bracts. Flowers are followed by many thousands of small seeds per plant, each lofted by a pappus aiding in dispersal over a large area.

*Senecio vulgaris* can be hard to distinguish from several other *Senecio* species and related plants, particularly the weedy *S. sylvaticus*, which has a distinctive foul smell and fewer involucral bracts. The young leaves of *Jacobaea vulgaris* look similar to those of common groundsel, but the flowers are different.

While the sheer number of plants in a common groundsel invasion can be formidable, they are easy to dispatch by pulling or hoeing. If the plants have bloomed, bag and remove them from the site to prevent new seedlings. A heavy mulch should prevent subsequent generations from sprouting.

# Silybum marianum

## MILK THISTLE, VARIEGATED THISTLE

Non-native annual or biennial, to 6 ft. Flowers red-purple, heads to 2 in.; late spring. Leaves basal to 20 in., cauline alternate. Parts edible/medicinal with caution. Toxic to livestock. Noxious in BC, WA, OR.

Milk thistle is a short-lived but very aggressive weed that has been introduced to (and proved problematic in) many countries. In North America, it's present from BC to California and across the southern and northeastern US and much of southern Canada. The species invades roadsides, fields, and overgrazed pastures, forming dense populations that compete with natives and crowd out desirable forage plants. It is generally unpalatable to livestock, but if they do eat it, can accumulate concentrations of nitrates that are lethal to the animals.

Growing from fibrous roots, the stem of milk thistle is thick, rigid, grooved, and branched. The glossy green leaves, attractively variegated with white mottling, are deeply incised into pointed, irregular lobes, and the margins are irregularly lined with spine-tipped teeth. The basal leaves can be as long as 10 inches and about half as wide. The plant bears large, rounded flowerheads singly at the ends of branches. The involucres are composed of spine-tipped bracts. Milk thistle can produce several thousand seeds per plant and seeds live several years, so any mature plant may be accompanied by a persistent seed bank.

Those contending with larger invasions of milk thistle have used tillage or herbicide. Early mowing prior to bloom may also be an option. These distinctive plants can be recognized early, and early is the best time to intercept them. Wearing thick gloves, pull, hoe, or dig. Clip any mature heads and bag or burn them, to avoid dispersing seed. Mulch well and replant.

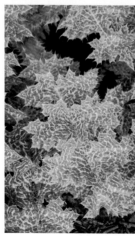

# Soliva sessilis

## LAWN BURRWEED, COMMON SOLIVA, PRICKLY SOLIVA

**Non-native annual, to 2 in. Flowers yellow-green, heads to 0.25 in.; early spring–midsummer. Leaves basal to 0.8 in., cauline alternate. Noxious in BC, WA.**

This South American species is found as a weed along the west coast from BC to California and in the south-central to southeastern US. In the PNW it lives mostly on west-side lowlands, invading roadsides, lawns, golf courses, parks, and other disturbed sites.

This diminutive ground-hugging annual stays very low but spreads sideways to 6 in. The small leaves are feathery-looking, pinnately divided into thin segments, resembling some other familiar plants like parsley. A single plant will send out as many as 10 flowering stems, creeping out in a circle. The leaves and stems are variably hairy, and the stems may be purple-spotted. The small button-like, petal-less flowerheads are borne in the leaf axils. The seeds are tiny, spiny, and bur-like, which aids in their dispersal.

This is particularly a weed of lawns and therefore a concern for managers of commercial or public recreational turf, where mulching and various mechanical means of extraction may be impracticable. In those situations, pre-emergent herbicides are often used, and people are advised that thicker, healthier lawns will outcompete the weed. When lawn burrweed shows up in a garden, pull or hoe when the soil is moist, mulch, and monitor. Most garden plants will outcompete it.

# Sonchus arvensis

PERENNIAL SOW-THISTLE, CORN SOW-THISTLE, FIELD SOW-THISTLE

Non-native perennial, to 6 ft. Flowers yellow, dandelion-like, to 2 in.; midsummer–autumn. Leaves to 16 in. Parts edible/medicinal. Noxious in BC, WA, CA.

Perennial sow-thistle, native to Eurasia and Africa, is now found throughout most of North America, most often on moist soil in prairies, woodland edges, roadsides, yards, beaches, lakeshores, and agricultural fields. It's another dandelion lookalike but much taller and with a branched multi-flower inflorescence, as opposed to the single flowerhead of *Taraxacum officinale*. *Sonchus arvensis* is listed as noxious or invasive in a few Canadian provinces and in several US states. It's an invasive plant that displaces agricultural crops and causes economic losses.

The leaves of perennial sow-thistle are prickly, the lower ones large with pointed lobes. Higher on the stem, they are smaller and simpler in shape. The hollow stem is unbranched, except in the terminal inflorescence, which may bear as many as 150 flowerheads. The flowers open in the morning and close by about noon. *Sonchus arvensis* multiplies by profligate seed production; as many as 10,000 or more seeds per plant are bird-planted or dispersed on the wind with feathery pappuses. It also spreads vegetatively from horizontal, rhizome-like roots.

In addition to the creeping horizontal roots, this perennial has very deep vertical roots, making it a challenge to remove. Pulling and digging must be done with care to get the roots. Root fragments left behind can resprout. For large stands, deep tillage can be effective.

Ruminants will eat it (and it's nontoxic), so sheep, cattle, or goats may be helpful. Herbicides may not help and should probably be avoided: *Sonchus arvensis* is one of several species in the genus which have become genetically resistant to some common herbicides.

# Sonchus asper

## PRICKLY SOW-THISTLE

Non-native annual or biennial, to 40 in. Flowers yellow, dandelion-like, to 1 in.; summer–autumn. Leaves alternate, to 12 in. Parts edible.

*Sonchus asper* is a Eurasian weed that has spread worldwide. It is known to have been in the US by the early 1800s and now occurs throughout North America. Prickly sow-thistle is found on woodland edges, rocky montane slopes, riparian areas, roadsides, agricultural fields, prairies, clearcuts, and other disturbed sites.

*Sonchus asper* is a host to pests and diseases of economically important food crops. The tiny seeds are a common contaminant in seed crops. The plant can compete with crops and reduce yields. In natural landscapes it may form dense patches that crowd out and displace native plants.

The leaves of prickly sow-thistle are usually pinnately lobed but may be oval and without lobes. The auricles are rounded, different from the pointy auricles of its cousin, *Sonchus oleraceus*. Its leaves are more conspicuously prickly all along the margins and are thicker than the leaves of *S. oleraceus*.

Like common sow-thistle, prickly sow-thistle bears open clusters of dandelion-like flowers. A single plant may produce over 20,000 seeds. These are dispersed by wind and water, by sticking to animals, people, or equipment, and by being consumed and then deposited by birds, small mammals, or livestock.

Control strategies are the same as for other *Sonchus* species. Pulling and digging can be effective for small infestations, though gloves are a good idea because the plant can be unpleasantly prickly. Larger patches can be suppressed by grazing animals. Thick mulch will prevent new germinations.

# *Sonchus oleraceus*

## COMMON SOW-THISTLE

Non-native annual or biennial, to 3 ft. Flowers yellow, dandelion-like, to 1 in.; midsummer–autumn. Leaves alternate, to 12 in. Parts edible/medicinal. Noxious in BC.

Like its cousin *Sonchus asper*, *S. oleraceus* is a globetrotting Eurasian weed. It is often a contaminant in seed crops, which may be how it has conquered nearly every continent worldwide, including Antarctica and many islands. It is present throughout North America, usually on disturbed sites, inhabiting roadsides, prairies, dunes, clearcuts, rocky slopes, riparian zones, woodland edges, yards, gardens, and agricultural fields.

In addition to directly competing with and contaminating agricultural crops, common sow-thistle is host to several insect pests of common food crops.

Common sow-thistle looks similar to a few other weeds of our region. It differs from perennial sow-thistle in having smaller flowers and being a smaller plant overall; it is not as prickly as *Sonchus asper* and also differs in having softer, thinner leaves. The flowers of all sow-thistles resemble common dandelion, but low-growing *Taraxacum officinale* has an unbranched stem bearing a single flowerhead, whereas *Sonchus* species all bear multiple flowers in branched inflorescences at the tops of tall stems.

Common sow-thistle grows from a long, branched taproot. Lower leaves have deeply incised, triangular lobes that point backward toward the petiole; upper leaves are simpler and reduced in size. All leaves have soft prickles along the margins, and leaf bases have prominent, pointed auricles. The flowers of a single plant can produce as many as 6,000 tiny seeds, which are dispersed by birds and by the wind.

*Sonchus oleraceus* can be controlled by digging and pulling, ideally before seed set. Take care to remove the taproot. Prevent its return by mulching heavily and monitoring for seedlings.

# Tanacetum vulgare

## COMMON TANSY, GARDEN TANSY

Non-native perennial, to 5 ft. Flowers yellow, heads to 0.5 in.; midsummer–autumn. Leaves alternate, to 8 in. Parts medicinal with caution. Toxic to livestock. Noxious in BC, WA.

*Tanacetum vulgare* (syn. *Chrysanthemum vulgare*) is an old-fashioned garden plant, long grown as an ornamental. It was first brought from Europe to North America in the 1600s and has since invaded most of the continent as a garden escape. Tansy occurs on roadsides, streambanks, and coastal dunes as well as in fields, pastures, and yards. Unfortunately, seeds of this species are still offered for sale by several US companies.

Tansy is toxic to humans and livestock. Although its foul odor often protects the plant from heavy grazing, the toxicity can be cumulative as well as acute and sometimes fatal.

*Tanacetum vulgare* is not to be confused with another notorious noxious weed, tansy ragwort (*Jacobaea vulgaris*), which is often inaccurately called simply "tansy." A native beach plant, *T. bipinnatum*, differs from common tansy in being more sprawling in habit and much shorter.

Common tansy grows from a thick, branched rhizome, from which several shoots arise. The leaves are fern-like, bipinnately divided, and have a strong, unpleasant odor. A plant may bear as many as 200 button-like flowerheads in clusters atop the stems. A single plant may produce 2,000 seeds. New plants are produced from seeds and rhizomatous spread.

Small patches are easily removed by pulling and digging. Wear gloves to avoid dermatologic reactions, and take care to remove all rhizomes and root fragments; monitor the site for recurrence of seedlings or sprouting from root fragments left behind. Mowing and burning are both ineffective controls, as they can leave behind root fragments. Herbicide may be an option for large infestations.

# Taraxacum officinale

COMMON DANDELION

Non-native perennial, to 20 in. Flowers yellow, heads to 1.4 in.; year-round. Leaves basal, to 15 in. Parts edible/medicinal.

Common dandelion is probably the most broadly familiar garden weed. It inspires wrathful invectives from those who value a pristine lawn and romantic encomiums on its virtues (real, exaggerated, or invented) from online influencers. Everyone knows it, sort of, though it's often confused with many of its weedy fellow DYCs ("damned yellow composites," the old botany joke about this difficult-to-ID family), particularly the "false dandelions" of *Hieracium* and *Hypochaeris*.

*Taraxacum officinale* is a European invader over most of North America. There are as many as eight native alpine *Taraxacum* species in the PNW, at least one of which is in California, but they're not likely to show up in your lawn.

*Taraxacum officinale* has been used medicinally and for food and beverages since antiquity; it first came to this continent, cultivated for these purposes, in the 1600s. Dandelions are common on moist, disturbed ground in sun—fields, lawns—from low to high elevations. They are a pest of commercial turf, orchards, and gardens. Dandelions possess several features ideal for an invasive career: they are long-lived; they are capable of producing seeds without pollination; and each seed is attached to a fluffy pappus that can carry it on the wind for miles.

The dandelion plant grows from a deep taproot, producing a cluster of basal leaves and a leafless, hollow stem bearing a single flower. The leaves have pointed lobes angling backward, their deep serrations inspiring the common name (from the French, *dent de lion*, "lion's tooth").

Very young plants can be pulled, but as they mature, more care is needed: any part of the crown or taproot left behind can resprout. Several long- and short-handled tools are recommended for extracting the taproots. Mowing is ineffective because it leaves crowns and taproots behind. Control of dandelions in lawns or gardens may require regular monitoring and grubbing out of seedlings early in each season.

# *Tragopogon dubius*

## YELLOW SALSIFY, YELLOW GOATSBEARD, WESTERN SALSIFY

Non-native annual or biennial, to 30 in. Flowers yellow, dandelion-like, to 2.5 in.; summer. Leaves basal to 1 ft., cauline alternate. Parts edible. Noxious in BC.

*Tragopogon dubius* (syn. *T. major*) is a Eurasian weed, primarily biennial, with yellow flowers and narrow, grass-like leaves that are long at the bottom and shorter higher on the stem. The very similar-looking *T. pratensis* (meadow salsify) can be distinguished from *T. dubius* by its reflexed leaves (vs. the straighter leaves of *T. dubius*). The flower of *T. dubius* is distinguished by several elegant floral bracts extending beyond the petals, whereas the bracts of *T. pratensis* are only as long as, or shorter than, the petals. Both these yellow-flowered salsifies produce a fluffy, spherical seedhead similar to dandelion but larger and somewhat ornate. Both grow on roadsides, fields, and waste places throughout most of North America but are rarely considered aggressive or problematic. They are listed as invasive in a few counties, particularly where they invade rangeland and agricultural fields.

Both species have numerous similar common names, some of which they also share with unrelated plants ("goatsbeard" is a name applied to the salsifies and to *Aruncus*, an entirely unrelated and dissimilar plant).

Yellow salsify spreads by self-seeding. Digging and pulling (particularly before the plants set seed) should be sufficient to remove unwanted plants from limited areas.

# *Tragopogon porrifolius*

PURPLE SALSIFY, OYSTER PLANT

Non-native biennial, to 4 ft. Flowers purple, blue, violet, dandelion-like, to 2 in.; spring–summer. Leaves alternate, to 15 in. Parts edible.

Purple salsify is an attractive Eurasian weed of fields and roadsides, found throughout much of North America. The plant bears a single composite flower atop a mostly unbranched stem. The leaves are long, narrow, and grass-like, their bases clasping the stem. The seedheads of all *Tragopogon* species resemble large, spherical dandelions. Each seed is attached to a pappus that allows it to sail away some distance from the mother plant.

The roots, shoots, flowers, and seeds of purple salsify are edible raw or cooked. Several companies serving home gardeners offer the seeds of wild purple salsify and some named cultivars, particularly strains boasting a large and palatable root. An old common name for all the salsifies is "oyster plant," as the root is said to taste like oysters.

*Tragopogon mirus* (remarkable goatsbeard) has purple flowers with yellow centers. It has been determined through DNA studies to be a hybrid of *T. porrifolius* and *T. dubius*. Its native range is limited to parts of Washington, Idaho, and Arizona.

All *Tragopogon* species are easily controlled in the home garden by pulling, digging, or scraping before they set seed.

# *Tripleurospermum inodorum*

## SCENTLESS MAYWEED, FALSE CHAMOMILE

Non-native annual, to 3.25 ft. Flowers white, daisy-like, heads to 2 in.; early summer–autumn. Leaves alternate, to 3 in. Noxious in BC, WA.

*Tripleurospermum inodorum* (syn. *Matricaria inodora*), a European species, is seen in scattered locations across most of North America, including the PNW. It invades pastures, lawns, riparian areas, roadsides, and farmland, particularly impacting grain and seed crops. Multiplying by prodigious seed output, it can form dense colonies that suppress native vegetation and more desirable forage or landscape plants.

Growing from fibrous roots, the typical scentless mayweed sends up several smooth, multi-branched stems. The leaves are very finely dissected into thread-like segments. The foliage is unscented (thus the specific epithet and common name); this distinguishes it from several very similar-looking relatives that are pungent to malodorous.

Many daisy-like flowerheads are borne singly at stem ends, with the classic daisy/feverfew scheme of white petals and yellow central disk. Seed production in this species has been estimated at up to 1,000,000 (yep, a million) seeds per plant, though it's often a tad less. Seeds do not have pappuses but are easily dispersed by wind, water, animals, and human activity.

Small invasions can be stymied by pulling or grubbing out with a hoe, with care to remove the root crown. Larger patches can be mowed low to slow seed production, but the plants may regrow and bloom very short, so this may be only a temporary fix. Mulch well, replant with competitive species, and monitor for new seedlings.

# Tussilago farfara

## EUROPEAN COLTSFOOT, BUTTERBUR

Non-native perennial, to 18 in. Flowers yellow, daisy-like, to 1.25 in.; early spring. Leaves alternate, to 8 in. Parts edible/medicinal with caution. Noxious in WA, OR.

European coltsfoot was probably brought to North America by early settlers for medicinal purposes; it was present in the US at least from the early 1800s. It has since invaded the PNW from BC to Oregon and is widely introduced in northeastern North America. It's a listed noxious weed in several states.

*Tussilago farfara* is a low-growing rhizomatous perennial that likes moist or partly shaded sites in lawns, riparian zones, marshes, and moist woodlands. It shares with *Petasites* the peculiar habit of blooming before the large basal leaves appear. Flower buds form on the plant's root crown in fall as the leaves die back. In spring, the flower stems elongate, bloom, and set seed, just as the basal leaves are beginning to emerge.

*Tussilago farfara* has very different leaf forms: the leaves on the flower stems are small and ovate to linear; the much larger basal leaves are broadly heart-shaped or oval with long petioles. They are green and hairless on top, woolly on their undersides. The striking yellow flowers are borne singly on each of several erect, unbranched stems arising from a single plant. A plant can produce as many as 3,500 seeds in a season.

European coltsfoot can form dense stands through rapid rhizomatous spread and copious seed production. The best bet for conquering it is early intervention. Pulling can be effective when done before the seedlings develop taproots. When taproots and rhizomes are present, digging must be done carefully. Be sure to remove all rhizome fragments; the rhizomes are deep and brittle, easily breaking off into pieces that can then resprout. Repeated digging may be necessary in subsequent years to clear the site. Large infestations may call for a combined approach using digging and herbicide.

187

# Xanthium spinosum

## SPINY COCKLEBUR

Non-native annual, to 4 ft. Flowers yellow-green, tiny; midsummer–autumn. Leaves to 3 in. Poisonous. Toxic to cats, dogs, horses, cattle, pigs, sheep. Noxious in WA, OR.

This South American species has gained notoriety as one of the worst weeds worldwide. It is scattered over most of North America in damp disturbed sites, including irrigated farmland, fields, and pastures; in the PNW, it is present primarily on the east side. It is a nuisance for farmworkers, and its spiny seedheads get stuck in animal hides and coats, especially sheep's wool. Seedlings and seedheads are toxic to grazing animals. The plant displaces crops and quality forage.

A multi-branched stem arises, erect and rigid, from a taproot and fibrous roots; it is striated, yellowish- or brownish-gray, pubescent, and leafy, with many conspicuous, sharp, 3-pointed spines to 2 in. long in the leaf axils. The leaves are short-petiolate, dark green to gray-green, lanceolate to linear, with a white midrib; they may be entire, toothed, or 3-lobed, with the central lobe much longer than the other two. The tiny flowerheads are borne singly or in clusters. Male flowerheads are at the tops of stems, female heads below them in the upper leaf axils. The seedheads are ovoid, to 0.5 in. long, and covered with hooked spines.

For large patches, farmers and others have found cultivation to be effective in suppressing spiny cocklebur. Burning is also effective. Plants can be pulled when young (wear thick gloves!) or hoed or mowed, preferably before bloom. If seed production has begun, the plant material should be burned to destroy the seeds and avoid spreading them. Mulch heavily and continue to monitor, as the seeds can be viable for several years.

# Xanthium strumarium

## COMMON COCKLEBUR, ROUGH COCKLEBUR

Native annual, 12–60 in. Flowers green, brown, male to 0.75 in., female to 1 in.; late summer–autumn. Leaves alternate, whorled, to 8 in. Poisonous. Toxic to cats, dogs, horses, cattle, pigs, sheep, chickens.

Common cocklebur is a weedy native throughout much of North America, where it inhabits meadows, streambanks, cropland, and other moist, sunny places, often on disturbed ground. It can invade yards and gardens, where its native status may not compensate for its shortcomings.

*Xanthium* (cocklebur) may be confused with the non-native weed *Arctium minus* (common burdock). They grow in similar habitats and are large plants with large, coarse leaves and prickly inflorescences, but important differences may help to distinguish them. *Arctium* is biennial to perennial; *Xanthium* is annual. Both plants are monoecious, but in *Arctium*, each flower has both male and female parts, whereas in *Xanthium* species, male and female flowers are borne separately. *Arctium* flowerheads are purple; *Xanthium* inflorescences are brownish-white (male) or green (female). *Arctium* leaves have wavy or smooth margins; *Xanthium* leaves have shallowly incised, pointy lobes or coarse teeth.

It's good to get clear on the differences, if you graze or have grazing animals, because of another difference: common burdock is edible; cockleburs are toxic for mammals generally, and consumption has caused fatalities in cattle and in humans.

Common cocklebur grows from a stout, somewhat woody taproot. The thick, round stems are somewhat hairy and usually unbranched, except for short side shoots at the axils. The large leaves are more or less oval to heart-shaped and arranged alternately to somewhat whorled on the stem. Racemes to 4 in. long grow from the upper leaf axils. The tiny flowers are borne in heads, the round male heads in the upper half of each raceme, and oblong female heads in the lower half.

Common cocklebur can be unpleasant to work with, the prickly inflorescences sticking to everything. Gardeners who are not charmed by the plant or who have grazing animals on-site or in the neighborhood may wish to discourage this somewhat aggressive native. Pull or dig (easiest when the soil is moist), ideally before seed has been shed; gloves are recommended. If plants have self-sown, seeds can remain viable in the soil for several years, so watch for seedlings and mulch to discourage new volunteers.

# Impatiens capensis

## CAPE JEWELWEED, SPOTTED TOUCH-ME-NOT

Non-native annual, to 5 ft. Flowers orange, to 1 in.; midsummer–autumn. Leaves mostly alternate, to 5 in. Parts edible. Toxic to cats, dogs. Noxious in WA.

*Impatiens capensis* is native to North America east of the Rockies and introduced here in the PNW. Its seedpods—as well as those of *I. glandulifera* and native *I. noli-tangere* (Latin for "touch me not")—are known for their dramatic explosive dehiscence, as the family's common name suggests.

Cape jewelweed is a plant of wet places: moist woods, pond and stream edges, and other wetlands; it is more plentiful on the wet west side of the Cascades. It can be an aggressive weed, crowding out native species in moist habitats.

This tall, branched annual carries bilaterally symmetric flowers in pairs at nodes and at the ends of stems. Flowers may be yellowish to deep orange, with reddish-orange spots. When the seeds are ripe, it takes only the slightest touch to cause them to shoot out forcefully, sometimes landing several feet away. Even for someone having long familiarity with the phenomenon, the effect can be startling.

It can be tempting to indulge this plant when it shows up in the garden, but it spreads so aggressively that it soon wears out its welcome. Luckily, *Impatiens capensis* is shallow-rooted, so it's easy to pull or grub out—just be careful to remove roots. As a couple of our natives have similar yellow to orange flowers, you might want to wait for a flower for a confident ID before you decide what to do.

# *Impatiens glandulifera*

POLICEMAN'S HELMET

Non-native annual, to 9 ft. Flowers white, pink, purple, to 1.5 in.; midsummer–autumn. Leaves alternate, opposite, whorled, to 6 in. Parts edible. Toxic to cats, dogs. Noxious in BC, WA, OR.

*Impatiens glandulifera* is a showy species from India, present as a garden escape in westside PNW as well as in the northeastern US and eastern Canada. It is listed as noxious or invasive in several jurisdictions. This moisture-loving, shade-tolerant plant is found in low-elevation riparian habitats, including moist woodlands and streams. It can form large stands in these areas, displacing native flora and causing a cascade of damaging ecological effects, including increased erosion and decreased water quality.

The stems are succulent, hollow, and often purple-tinged. The bright to deep green leaves are ovate to elliptic, with small, evenly spaced marginal teeth. The bilaterally symmetric flowers are white to pink or purple. A single plant can produce up to 800 seeds. Like other annual *Impatiens* species, *I. glandulifera* has explosive dehiscence that is nothing short of spectacular. When seeds are ripe, they are ejected from the pods with startling force, propelled as much as 20 ft. from the mother plant. (Check online for several great videos of this phenomenon.) Seeds remain viable in the soil for many months.

These plants are shallow-rooted and very easy to pull. Any uprooted plants with mature flowers or seedpods should be bagged and removed from the site. As with any extravagant self-seeder, mulch is your friend, suppressing future germinations.

# Anchusa officinalis

## COMMON BUGLOSS, COMMON ALKANET

---

**Non-native biennial or perennial, to 2 ft. Flowers blue, violet, 5-lobed, to 0.4 in.; late spring–autumn. Leaves basal to 8 in., cauline alternate. Parts edible/medicinal. Noxious in BC, WA, OR.**

---

*Anchusa officinalis* is a Mediterranean species found from BC to California, eastward to the Great Plains, and in much of northeastern North America. An aggressive self-sower and agricultural pest, common bugloss invades roadsides, fields, vacant lots, cropland, pastures, rangeland, and natural areas. It competes with native plants, crops, and desirable forage. It contaminates alfalfa fields, and when inadvertently baled with hay, its succulent stems can cause molding.

From a taproot that grows stout, woody, and deep, the plant may bloom in its first season or may only produce a basal rosette. The next year, it produces several fleshy and hairy flowering stems, clothed in coarse leaves. The plant can spread to 3 ft. or more at maturity. The lower leaves are stalked and lanceolate; the upper ones are more reduced, sessile, and narrower, with margins entire or toothed.

The typical flowers are a striking blue or violet with white throats, though white or pink flowers sometimes occur. They are borne in terminal spiraling or helix-shaped clusters that elongate and straighten with maturity. Each flower produces 4 seeds; a single plant may produce as many as 900 seeds in a season. The seeds remain viable for several years and can be dispersed by wind or by sticking to people, animals, machinery, etc. Most reproduction is by seed, but root fragments can also sprout and produce new plants.

For small invasions, digging can be effective. Be careful to remove the entire taproot, and if seeds have begun to develop, bag and remove from the site. Wear gloves and protective clothing (long sleeves) when working with the plant, because the bristly hairs covering vegetative parts can cause dermatitis. For larger patches, continual mowing can forestall seed set but will not kill the plants. Even when using herbicides, repeated monitoring and additional treatments will likely be necessary. Mulch to prevent subsequent germinations.

# *Asperugo procumbens*

CATCHWEED, MADWORT, GERMAN MADWORT

Non-native annual, to 4 ft. Flowers blue, violet, 5-lobed, to 0.1 in.; late spring–midsummer. Leaves alternate, to 3.5 in.

*Asperugo procumbens* is found in much of North America, excluding the southern states, in open sites on disturbed, moist ground, including roadsides, agricultural land, fields, and ditches. Rapidly producing a mass of reclining vegetation, it competes with desired plants for light, space, water, and soil nutrients. It can become an agricultural pest, its long stems wrapping around wheels and gears of harvesting machinery.

The weak, scrambling/climbing stems bear tiny backward-pointing prickles, enabling them to stick to things they clamber up on. The spoon-shaped leaves are thin, somewhat hairy on their surfaces, and fine-bristled on the margins; the lower leaves are petiolate, leaves higher on the stem reduced in size and sessile. Both flowers and seeds are very small; the latter are barbed nutlets that stick to animals, people, machinery, etc., and thus are dispersed.

Pull catchweed, the sooner the better. As the whole plant and its seeds are "catchy," dress accordingly. Mulch or replant with competitive groundcovers.

# Cynoglossum officinale

## BURGUNDY HOUNDSTONGUE, COMMON HOUNDSTONGUE, GYPSYFLOWER

Non-native biennial or perennial, to 4 ft. Flowers purple, 5-lobed, to 0.5 in.; midspring–midsummer. Leaves basal to 12 in., cauline alternate. Parts edible/medicinal with caution. Toxic to sheep, horses, cattle, deer, chickens. Noxious in BC, WA, OR.

*Cynoglossum officinale* is a Eurasian species that has become a problematic noxious weed in much of North America, invading roadsides, fields, moist grasslands, and woodland edges. This species competes with desirable native or agricultural plants, reduces biodiversity, and degrades forage for livestock and wild grazers. It is seriously toxic to grazing animals and chickens. In addition, the plant and its seeds—small, stickery nutlets—can irritate the skin of people and animals.

Burgundy houndstongue grows from a thick, branched taproot, from which rises a single, erect stem. The basal leaves are large, gray-green, and rough-textured, with petioles. Higher on the flowering stem, the leaves are progressively smaller and more sessile. The stems and leaves are hairy. The plant bears axillary and terminal clusters of dark reddish-purple (rarely white) funnel-shaped flowers. A plant can produce up to 3,000 seeds, which can remain viable in the soil for a few years.

Small infestations can be pulled and dug; take care to remove the taproots. First-year basal leaf rosettes can be cut below the root crown. The key to successful control is monitoring for seedlings and preventing blooming/self-sowing cycles. Uprooted plants that have begun to make seeds should be bagged and burned or removed from the site. Wear gloves when handling this plant.

# *Echium vulgare*

## VIPER'S BUGLOSS, BLUEWEED

Non-native biennial or perennial, to 3 ft. Flowers blue, violet, to 0.8 in.; summer. Leaves basal to 10 in., cauline alternate. Poisonous. Toxic to horses, cattle. Noxious in BC, WA.

*Echium vulgare* is a Mediterranean species that has spread through most of North America, including the PNW. It is found in open woodland and disturbed sites, like roadsides, fields, pastures, and cropland. In pastures, it is toxic and outcompetes quality forage for livestock and wildlife. It is also host to several fungal pathogens affecting economically important crops.

The plant grows from a taproot that can reach as far down as 32 in.; it has a large fibrous root system as well. The basal leaves are simple, large, and stalked. In the second year, one to many flowering stems arise. Stem leaves are alternate, progressively smaller, and more sessile. The showy inflorescence consists of a series of short branches, each bearing a spiraling or helix-shaped cluster of bright blue or violet (sometimes pink or white) flowers. A single plant may produce 2,000 seeds. These are small nutlets that can be dispersed via water, catch a ride on the coats of animals (or people), or be consumed by animals and then "planted" after passing through the GI tract.

Pull or dig viper's bugloss when the soil is moist, being careful to remove all the roots. If the plants have begun to bloom, uprooted plants should be bagged and removed or burned, to avoid shedding seeds. Wear gloves and protective clothing (long sleeves and pants) when handling this plant, as it can cause significant dermatitis.

# *Lycopsis arvensis*
## ANNUAL BUGLOSS

**Non-native annual, to 2.5 ft. Flowers blue, 5-petaled, to 0.25 in.; summer. Leaves basal to 6 in., cauline alternate. Noxious in WA.**

*Lycopsis arvensis* (syn. *Anchusa arvensis*) is found along the west coast from BC to California and across the northern US and southern Canada, plus much of the US east coast. This annual forget-me-not relative invades pastures, farm fields, and roadsides; it can be an agricultural pest, reducing yields.

Annual bugloss grows from a short taproot, with a basal rosette of many hairy, petiolate, lanceolate leaves. The plant is typically under 1.5 ft. but can be twice as tall. Leaves on the flowering stem are reduced in size and more sessile upward. The small, sky-blue, funnel-shaped flowers, subtended by leafy bracts, are borne in terminal spiraling clusters. A single plant may produce 250 seeds in a season.

This plant is easy to overlook or underestimate. The best intervention is prior to the arrival of a multitude of seedlings. A small invasion of annual bugloss is easily eradicated by pulling, hoeing, and digging when the soil is moist; take care to extract the taproots. Mulch and replant.

# Myosotis discolor

YELLOW AND BLUE FORGET-ME-NOT, CHANGING FORGET-ME-NOT,
YELLOW AND BLUE SCORPIONGRASS

**Non-native annual or biennial, to 20 in. Flowers blue, 5-petaled, to 0.10 in.; early spring. Leaves alternate, to 1.5 in.**

This tiny European plant is one of several weedy *Myosotis* species common in our region. It occurs over much of western and eastern North America, skipping a north-south corridor through the middle. In the PNW, it's more common on the west side of the Cascades, particularly around the Puget Sound. It's a common weed of roadsides, yards, and gardens—relatively bare places where this diminutive plant will not easily be outcompeted.

Yellow and blue forget-me-not is fuzzy all over, with sparsely leafy, very slender, lax and floppy stems. The tiny flowers begin yellow but age to blue. They are striking at close range in that one often sees both yellow and blue flowers in a single cluster, due to differences in age.

This mildly entertaining, nondescript weed can nevertheless get a little annoying in numbers. The fibrous roots are weak, and the plant is easily scraped away with the side of a foot or hand or hoe. Mulch or competitive plantings will stop it.

# *Myosotis micrantha*

## SMALL-FLOWER FORGET-ME-NOT, MOUSE EAR, BLUE SCORPIONGRASS

**Non-native annual, to 8 in. Flowers blue, violet, 5-petaled, to 0.1 in.; late spring. Leaves alternate, to 0.8 in.**

*Myosotis micrantha* (syn. *M. stricta*) is introduced over much of North America, with the exception of the southern US and central Canada. In the PNW, this tiniest of the forget-me-nots is found mostly east of the Cascades, on roadsides, streamsides, grasslands, and other open sites.

A single plant may produce several erect stems, mostly unbranched, thin, and fuzzy. The tiny flowers, a pretty sky-blue, are borne in small, downward-curving clusters at the tops of the delicate stems.

*Myosotis micrantha* is unlikely to cause much trouble for any but the most fastidious of gardeners. Plants are easy to remove by scraping with anything handy. Mulch to defeat future seedlings.

# Myosotis scorpioides

COMMON FORGET-ME-NOT, TRUE FORGET-ME-NOT, MARSH FORGET-ME-NOT

**Non-native perennial, to 20 in. Flowers blue, 5-petaled, to 0.3 in.; midsummer. Leaves alternate, to 3 in. Unpalatable.**

Garden escape *Myosotis scorpioides* has invaded most of North America, with the exception of a north-south slice through the middle of the US and Canada. The plant is a listed invasive and is banned in Connecticut and Massachusetts. In the PNW, it is abundant on the west side, up through BC and Alaska.

Common forget-me-not differs from several of its very similar-looking relatives in being water-loving, less hairy, more perennial, and stoloniferous. It is found in or near water, in wet to moist soil or standing water, on the edges of springs, ponds, slow streams, and freshwater marshes.

Plants have shallow, fibrous roots like most other *Myosotis* species, as well as creeping stolons that can produce offsets, potentially forming colonies. The stems are long, delicate, and leafy, branched or unbranched. The flowers are light blue with yellow centers and borne in terminal racemes that curve downward, thus *scorpioides*, suggesting a resemblance to scorpions.

To combat common forget-me-not, pull or hoe and watch for stolons and seedlings. If the invaders are not in a pond but in well-watered garden soil, withholding water will slow them down. Mulch and competitive plantings will help to discourage further incursions.

FORBS/HERBS AND VINES

# Myosotis sylvatica

### WOODLAND FORGET-ME-NOT, WOODS FORGET-ME-NOT

**Non-native perennial, to 12 in. Flowers blue, 5-petaled, to 0.4 in.; late spring–midsummer. Leaves basal to 3 in., cauline alternate.**

Woodland forget-me-not is an old-fashioned garden plant that has escaped cultivation widely in northeastern North America, the midwestern US, and California, Washington, and BC. In Washington, it is found mostly west of the Cascades, often on moist woodland edges and roadsides.

A single plant will send up several branched stems from fibrous roots. Basal leaves are stalked, stem leaves alternate, smaller, and sessile. Stems and leaves are very fuzzy. The flowers are usually blue (with yellow centers) but sometimes white.

Though widely considered weedy, *Myosotis sylvatica* nevertheless captures the affection of many gardeners, and the seeds are still sold by many companies in the US. The plants self-seed and will persist in the garden for years, sometimes to the ultimate regret of the gardener. For those who like the plants but not in the millions, deadheading is key. When unwanted, invading plants are easily pulled or scraped away, most effectively before self-sowing has occurred. Thick mulch and competitive plantings will discourage new seedlings.

# *Pentaglottis sempervirens*

## GREEN ALKANET, EVERGREEN BUGLOSS

Non-native perennial, to 40 in. Flowers blue, 5-petaled, to 0.4 in.; midspring–midsummer. Leaves basal to 16 in., cauline alternate. Parts edible.

*Pentaglottis sempervirens*, the only species in its genus, is a European borage relative that has invaded wild lands in scattered locations along the west coast from BC to California. It grows in light shade in gardens, woodlands, riparian margins, and roadsides. Because it has demonstrated a propensity to spread rapidly by seed, it is on the monitor list for Washington.

Green alkanet grows from a thick taproot that can extend 20 in. down into the soil. Erect and coarsely hairy stems rise above ovate, long-stalked, basal leaves. Cauline leaves are progressively reduced and more sessile upward on the stem. Clusters of sky-blue flowers with white centers are borne on long, slender stalks in leaf axils and on the ends of stems. Plants reproduce primarily from seed, though severed root fragments can also resprout.

Gardeners may be charmed by this admittedly attractive plant and be tempted to let it go. But keep in mind: many related species and cultivars with the same blue flowers are often rambunctious but less prone to outright invasion. Control is best accomplished before the plant sets seed. Dig it up, removing as much as possible of the taproot, then mulch and monitor. The plants are covered with small, prickly hairs, so gloves are advised for pulling. They are deep-rooted, and herbicide may be the better option for some.

# Symphytum officinale

## COMMON COMFREY

**Non-native perennial, to 5 ft. Flowers blue, pink, 5-lobed, to 0.6 in.; late spring–midsummer. Leaves basal to 12 in., cauline alternate. Parts edible/medicinal with caution. Toxic to horses, chickens.**

This common herb from Europe has escaped cultivation and become a sometimes invasive weed over much of North America, often in damp or partly shady, disturbed sites, such as woodland edges or roadside ditches. It is widely planted in gardens and spreads by self-seeding and by robust, long rhizomes. In recent decades this "medicinal" species has become controversial, as it contains alkaloids that can cause liver damage and cancer in humans or livestock. It is toxic not only by ingestion but by contact.

*Symphytum officinale* grows from a deep taproot, from which arise several thick stems. The basal leaves are broad and stalked; cauline leaves are gradually reduced and more sessile. All stems and leaves are coarse and hairy. The bell-shaped flowers, typically blue or pink (sometimes yellowish-white or purple), are borne in pendent clusters.

As a garden plant, *Symphytum officinale* is ornamental but very aggressive, rapidly claiming large areas of real estate. Gardeners who like the look might do well to grow it in a container or with barriers, or seek out its slightly less aggressive cousin, *S. ×uplandicum* (Russian comfrey), and some cultivars.

Once established, common comfrey is difficult to combat, due to the long, deep rhizomes. When digging, wear gloves because of the potential for skin absorption of its toxic properties. Take care to remove as much of the rhizomes as possible, plus any seeds or flowers. Monitor for new sproutings and be prepared for repeated efforts.

# *Alliaria petiolata*

GARLIC MUSTARD

---

Non-native biennial, to 4 ft. Flowers white, 4-petaled, to 0.4 in.; early–midspring. Leaves basal to 5.5 in., cauline alternate. Parts edible/medicinal. Noxious in BC, WA, OR.

---

*Alliaria petiolata* (syn. *A. officinalis*) is a widespread weed over much of North America, with the exception of the Southwest. It is a listed noxious weed in several jurisdictions, gaining its place near the top of the list of herbaceous invasives due to its profligate self-seeding. A single plant can produce hundreds of small seeds, which can be scattered widely and remain viable in the soil for several years. Garlic mustard invades wooded understory tracts, including parks, and may be found on roadsides, in fields, and in riparian zones.

The species can come to dominate woodland understories, thus competing with native flora and reducing biodiversity. It has no known benefit to wildlife and is toxic to the larvae of some native butterflies, while displacing the particular native plant species they require. In addition to formidable reproduction, *Alliaria petiolata* has been studied for possible allelopathic properties, suppressing germination of other species.

As is typical for biennials, garlic mustard begins its two-year life as a taprooted basal rosette of kidney-shaped leaves with scalloped margins, then blooms in its second year, bearing dense clusters of small white flowers. All parts of the plant smell strongly of garlic, and it is edible. Its use as a flavoring in food dates back to antiquity in Europe, and early settlers in North America brought it here for that purpose.

Small infestations of garlic mustard can be removed by pulling and digging, though care must be taken to remove the taproot, which can resprout. Thick mulching should help prevent germination from the seed bank. Burning has been a successful strategy for larger areas, where appropriate, but must be hot enough to kill taproots.

# *Alyssum alyssoides*

## YELLOW ALYSSUM, PALE MADWORT

---

Non-native annual or biennial, to 12 in. Flowers yellow, white, 4-petaled, to 0.1 in. wide; late spring–midsummer. Leaves alternate, to 1 in. Parts edible.

---

Yellow alyssum is a European species present in the US and Canada since the 1800s and now introduced over much of North America. In the PNW, this drought-tolerant plant is found mostly east of the Cascades. It's an inconspicuous weed of roadsides, woodland edges, rangeland, and cropland. In dry habitats, it competes for available soil moisture with natives or desirable forage plants. It is shallow-rooted and can contribute to soil erosion.

Yellow alyssum often grows as a winter annual, germinating in fall and overwintering as a leaf rosette, then resuming growth in spring. A single plant typically produces multiple erect stems, unbranched or branched. Leaves are small, simple, and more or less spatulate or lanceolate, and woolly, as are the stems. Each stem bears 30–40 pale flowers in a dense, erect spike.

Pull or scrape with a hoe or similar tool. Mulch and/or replant with competitive groundcovers.

# *Arabidopsis thaliana*

## THALE CRESS, MOUSE-EAR CRESS

Non-native annual, to 16 in. Flowers white, 4-petaled, to 0.1 in.; spring. Leaves basal to 1.5 in., cauline alternate. Parts edible.

*Arabidopsis thaliana* is a cosmopolitan weed distributed worldwide, throughout most of North America, and in most of the PNW. It is found on disturbed sites, including roadsides, agricultural land, yards, and gardens. It's important in botany for reasons that are only tangentially related to its weed status: it was the first plant to have its genome sequenced and has been much used as a model for studying the genetics and biology of plants.

This small weed produces a basal rosette of many narrow, somewhat hairy, stalked leaves; these may die back as the plant develops. Leaves on the flowering stem are sparse, smaller, mostly not hairy, and sessile. The stem is erect and often branched, bearing open clusters of many small flowers at the upper ends of branches. These are followed by narrow siliques to about 0.7 in. long, each containing as many as 25 seeds. Mature plants may bristle with many of these skinny appendages, which are green before they ripen. A single plant may produce tens of thousands of seeds.

As with shotweed, this is a small plant that can soon give rise to an army of offspring. It takes only 6 weeks for a generation to pass from germination to blooming and setting seed. Pull or scrape away plants before they bloom, or take care to remove uprooted flowers and siliques from the garden. Mulch and watch for new seedlings.

# Barbarea verna

## EARLY YELLOWROCKET, EARLY WINTER CRESS, AMERICAN CRESS

**Non-native biennial, to 1 ft. Flowers yellow, 4-petaled, to 0.4 in.; early spring. Leaves basal to 7 in., cauline alternate. Parts edible.**

Early yellowrocket is a weedy mustard found in scattered locations from BC to Oregon and a limited area of California, as well as in much of the eastern US. While it has not yet become commonplace in the west, its wide distribution in the east suggests we may see more of it in coming years.

*Barbarea verna* has numerous common names, all of them shared in part or in full with other mustard species, and it can be challenging to distinguish it from many other yellow-flowered mustards. Leaf shape may be helpful: in this species all leaves are pinnately lobed, with the upper cauline leaves reduced in size and having narrower lobes. The flowers are borne in tight terminal clusters. Leaves and seeds or seedpods are edible, and the species has been cultivated as a food crop in western Europe since the 1600s.

*Barbarea verna* is a small plant growing from a taproot. It's easy to pull or grub out with a hoe; take care to remove the roots and any seedpods that have formed.

# Barbarea vulgaris

## YELLOW ROCKET, BITTER WINTER CRESS

Non-native biennial, to 2 ft. Flowers yellow, 4-petaled, to 0.4 in.; early spring–midsummer. Leaves basal to 5 in., cauline alternate. Parts edible/medicinal with caution.

*Barbarea vulgaris* is a European species introduced over most of North America. A plant of moist places, in the PNW it is found mainly west of the Cascades. It's a garden escape that has found its way to roadsides, cropland, and vacant lots. It displaces native plants and agricultural crops, contaminates hayfields, and causes problems in gardens, commercial turf, and nurseries. This species has several common names, most of which are similar or identical to other species in the mustard family. In the PNW, watch out particularly for the similar-looking western native, *B. orthoceras* (American yellow rocket). It's hard to distinguish from *B. vulgaris*, except that the native has a fringe of hairs around the basal auricles of the stem leaves.

The weedy, non-native yellow rocket is taprooted, with multiple erect, branched stems. Basal leaves are long-stalked and lyre-shaped to pinnately lobed, with a large, rounded terminal lobe. Cauline leaves are alternate, the lower ones lobed then simpler and smaller higher up on the stem. They are more sessile, with auricles clasping the stem. Leaf shapes overall are variable. Leaves and stems are glossy and hairless. The bright yellow flowers are borne in dense, rounded clusters at the tops of stems and as smaller clusters in leaf axils. Seeds develop, single file, in long, very slender siliques.

For small invasions, pull or dig, taking care to remove taproots, and bag any seedpods. Larger patches can be prevented from setting seed by mowing. Mulch and monitor for seedlings.

# Berteroa incana

## HOARY ALYSSUM

Non-native annual, biennial, or perennial, to 3 ft. Flowers white, 4-petaled, to 0.2 in.; midspring–autumn. Leaves basal to 3 in., cauline alternate. Toxic to horses, cattle. Noxious in BC, WA, OR, CA.

*Berteroa incana* is a European weed widely distributed over much of North America. It's a listed noxious weed in BC and in several western states. In the PNW, it is found primarily in northeast and central Washington and in Wallowa and Deschutes counties, Oregon. The common name can be confusing: *B. incana* is not in the same genus as the familiar garden-plant alyssum, though they are in the same family.

Hoary alyssum invades waste places, pastures, agricultural land, and roadsides. It is particularly competitive in very hot, dry areas and thrives in sandy, gravelly, poor, often alkaline soils. It may invade grasslands and woodlands, displacing native flora, but much of the concern about this species is due to its severe toxicity and potential lethality to horses and cattle.

*Berteroa incana* is a slender, taprooted plant 1–3 ft. tall, usually branched, with grayish, hairy, simple leaves. Its small terminal clusters of tiny white flowers with deeply notched petals are followed by flat, oval seedpods.

Homeowners are encouraged to eradicate any hoary alyssum plants to prevent spread to agricultural lands. Pulling or scraping and mulching should suffice for small areas. On larger properties, including farmland or pastures, the weed can be difficult to detect and control before a persistent seed bank accumulates. Eradication may require regular monitoring, tilling, and repeated herbicide applications.

# *Brassica nigra*

## BLACK MUSTARD

Non-native annual, to 7 ft. Flowers yellow, 4-petaled, to 0.3 in.; midspring–midsummer. Leaves basal to 10 in., cauline alternate. Parts edible/medicinal with caution. Toxic to cattle, sheep, goats.

Black mustard is a Eurasian plant that has spread throughout much of the world, including most of North America. It has long been cultivated for its black seeds (hence *nigra*, "black"), which are used as a spice.

It is present in scattered areas in the PNW and is particularly problematic in California. It can be found, often in large populations, on roadsides, grasslands, shrublands, riparian zones, and other open, disturbed areas. It competes for space with more desirable plants, particularly natives, and may have allelopathic effects that suppress germination of other species. It often fills in quickly on recently burned sites and, in turn, increases fire risk. Livestock grazing heavily on *Brassica nigra* and other mustards are at risk for poisoning.

Black mustard grows from a taproot, from which arises an erect, often branched flowering stem. The lower leaves of black mustard are pinnately lobed; upper stem leaves are reduced in size and simpler in shape. The bright yellow flowers bloom in terminal racemes up to 2 ft. long, followed by narrow siliques up to 1 in. long, each containing 2–10 seeds. The seeds can last for decades in the soil.

*Brassica nigra* has little capacity for distance dispersal, so most seedlings occur near the parent plant. For effective control, pull or grub out young plants before they bloom, then mulch. Once a seed bank has formed, annual monitoring and pulling may be required for several years.

# Brassica rapa

## WILD MUSTARD, WILD TURNIP, WILD RUTABAGA

**Non-native annual or biennial, to 3.5 ft. Flowers yellow, 4-petaled, to 0.4 in.; spring. Leaves basal to 12 in., cauline alternate. Parts edible/medicinal. Toxic to horses, cattle, sheep, goats.**

*Brassica rapa* (syn. *B. campestris* var. *rapa*) is a cosmopolitan weed and agricultural product, cultivated for food, seeds, oil, and forage since antiquity. The species and its cultivars possess a multitude of common names, most of which refer to food plant variations: broccoli raab, Italian kale, bok choi, etc. *Brassica rapa* is introduced in the PNW from Alaska to California and throughout North America. It is listed as invasive in several regions of Canada and the US.

*Brassica rapa* inhabits roadsides, cropland, woodland edges, yards, gardens, orchards, fields, and waste places. It can displace desirable crop and forage plants, or natives. Dry end-season plants can also become fire hazards. The species can form dense stands that compete with natives, but most of its growth is in winter, so competitive harm is limited. Though widely used for livestock and human food, the species contains potentially toxic compounds. When consumed in excess, the seeds in particular can cause GI and thyroid problems in cattle and especially in horses.

Wild mustard usually grows as a biennial, beginning as a rosette of basal leaves with a substantial taproot, and not blooming until its second year. The basal leaves are pinnately lobed and stalked. Stem leaves are alternate, smaller, simple, and sessile. The terminal flower clusters are followed by slender siliques to 4 in. long. Seeds can remain viable in the soil for decades.

Unwanted wild mustard can be pulled, preferably when young and before forming seed. Repeated mowing can avert seed set and exhaust the plant. Herbicides should not be required for a short-lived plant in the home garden, but note: some cultivars of this plant have developed glyphosate resistance.

# Cakile maritima

## EUROPEAN SEAROCKET

Non-native annual or perennial, to 20 in. Flowers lavender, pink, white, 4-petaled, to 0.6 in.; midspring–autumn. Leaves alternate, to 3 in. Parts edible.

*Cakile maritima*, a European species, is introduced on dunes of marine waters on the east, west, and southern coasts of North America, as well as on the beaches of Puget Sound in the PNW. It's very similar to another introduced *Cakile*, *C. edentula*, which occupies the same range along the west coast. These weedy plants have traveled worldwide thanks to tides and rides hitched in ship ballast.

Given its strong preference for sand dunes, European searocket is unlikely to show up unless you have a sandy waterfront yard or garden. It's a very common sight on sandy beaches of the west coast, usually as isolated, transient clumps. The plant is well suited to the beach environment, with a taproot to 16 in. to anchor it and derive any available moisture, succulent foliage to conserve water, high salt tolerance, and corky seeds that float.

The branched stems are succulent to corky, and may sprawl horizontally or be semi-erect, often creating a mound up to 3 ft. across. The fleshy, hairless, light green leaves are variable in shape, both within individual plants and among or within populations. Leaves can be spoon-shaped and entire, or dissected almost to the midvein, with very narrow lobes. Some have slight, wavy to rounded marginal dentition; others have rounded pinnate lobes. Lower leaves are more likely to be stalked; higher on the stem, they are more sessile and simpler.

The flowers eventually form distinctive cylindrical 2-seeded capsules, the outer half of which breaks away when the seeds are ripe, carrying one seed with it, while the other seed remains attached to the plant.

Unwanted volunteers are easy to pull from the sand, perhaps with some help from a trowel to dislodge the taproots. Bag any seed capsules to avoid spreading them about.

# Capsella bursa-pastoris

## SHEPHERD'S PURSE

**Non-native annual, to 20 in. Flowers white, 4-petaled, to 0.1 in.; spring–summer. Leaves basal to 4 in., cauline alternate. Parts edible/medicinal with caution.**

Shepherd's purse is a Eurasian weed that has naturalized in many areas of the world, including throughout North America and the PNW. It is very common, especially on dry and disturbed ground—roadsides, yards, gardens, pastures, and waste places. This species has long been used in European and Asian cuisines, for animal fodder, and in herbal medicine, but in excess can have toxic effects.

Growing as either a summer or winter annual, *Capsella bursa-pastoris* has a taproot from which sprout basal leaves in a tidy circular rosette. These are stalked and may be shallowly or deeply lobed or dentate. One to a few flowering stems, simple or branched, bear much smaller leaves that are alternate, sessile, and entire to slightly dentate. Terminal elongated racemes of tiny white flowers are followed by the most recognizable feature of this plant, giving it its common and species names (from the Latin *bursa* "purse," *pastoris* "shepherd").

The silicles are triangular to heart-shaped, flat, about 0.1 in. across, resembling tiny purses. Each "purse" carries about 20 seeds, and a single plant can produce tens of thousands of seeds, making shepherd's purse a formidable self-seeder. Seeds are dispersed by being eaten and then excreted by deer or birds. They also remain viable in the soil for a long time.

Despite its undeniable charm, this little weed can quickly wear out its welcome by dint of numbers. Pull or grub out when the soil is moist, and follow with mulch or ground-covering competitive plantings.

# *Cardamine hirsuta*

## SHOTWEED, HAIRY BITTERCRESS

Non-native annual or biennial, to 10 in. Flowers white, 4-petaled, to 0.2 in.; early spring–midsummer. Leaves basal to 4 in., cauline alternate. Parts edible.

Shotweed is a ubiquitous small weed familiar to most gardeners in the PNW west of the Cascades. It seems to show up the minute a cultivated plot or container is initiated. While not a threat to most garden plants and easy to dislodge, it can be an aesthetic issue. The common name "shotweed" refers to its extravagantly explosive dehiscence: barely brush against a mature plant, and tiny seeds shoot out in all directions. "Cress" is a name applied to many edible plants in the mustard family with leaves used as potherbs and salad vegetables. This species is one of these: to many palates, it is not bitter, just pleasantly peppery or radishy-tasting.

This fairly delicate, lightly rooted plant makes up in reproductive capacity what it lacks in size or robustness. The sheer number of plants, rapidity of population growth, and nearly year-round presence can be vexing. Leaves are pinnately compound, with numerous rounded leaflets. Flowers are minute and white, in small terminal racemes.

*Cardamine oligosperma* (little western bittercress), a native species, is extremely similar to shotweed, with a few differences that may be difficult to discern. It is more likely to be biennial (or sometimes perennial) and is taprooted. It may have several stems arising from the base. Seeds are slightly larger. It is more likely to be found in moist montane environments, whereas *C. hirsuta* is largely confined to lower elevations on disturbed ground.

Shotweed is a persistent weed in gardens; it can multiply exponentially, seemingly overnight, but is easy to remove with light pulling or scraping.

BRASSICACEAE (mustard family)

# *Chorispora tenella*

## BLUE MUSTARD, CROSSFLOWER

Non-native annual, to 12 in. Flowers pink, purple, violet, 4-petaled, to 0.4 in.; late spring–early summer. Leaves basal to 3 in., cauline alternate. Parts edible. Noxious in CA.

*Chorispora tenella* (syn. *Raphanus tenellus*), an Asian radish relative, has moved into dry habitats in many parts of the world, including most of North America, especially the western and central regions. In the PNW, it is found mostly on the dry east side. It invades both native and disturbed landscapes, including shrub steppe, pastures, cropland, yards, and roadsides. It affects milk quality when cattle graze it.

Blue mustard often grows as a winter annual, with seeds germinating in winter and then growth resuming in early spring. From a thick taproot arise a few basal leaves and the leafy, branched flowering stem, which may be more or less erect to prostrate. The leaf margins are typically wavy and irregularly toothed, and most are stalked. Stems and leaves are somewhat hairy and sticky/glandular to the touch. The foliage has a musky odor. The small flowers are borne in terminal clusters; they look very much like those of *Raphanus raphanistrum* (wild radish), which is no accident: this species was originally placed in that genus. Seeds are borne in silicles.

*Chorispora tenella* is a vigorous self-sower, so the best time to control it is before it makes seed. Small infestations can be controlled by digging, grubbing with a hoe, or pulling when the soil is moist. Remove any plants that have bloomed, to reduce seeding. Mulch and/or plant with competitive ground-hugging plants.

# *Descurainia sophia*

FLIXWEED, HERB SOPHIA

Non-native annual or biennial, to 40 in. Flowers yellow, 4-petaled, to 0.15 in.; early spring. Leaves alternate, to 4 in. Parts edible/medicinal. Toxic to horses, cattle, goats.

*Descurainia sophia* (syn. *Sisymbrium sophia*, *Arabis sophia*) is a Eurasian weed present in North America since the 1800s and now found in drier regions throughout most of the US and Canada, including east of the Cascades in the PNW. It invades roadsides, deserts, grasslands, woodland edges, overgrazed rangeland, and cropland and shows up as an early volunteer on soil cleared for ecorestoration. The plant is particularly troublesome as it can cause serious poisoning if grazed in quantity by livestock. However, the seeds are edible, used similarly to black mustard seed, as a spice.

Growing from a short taproot, *Descurainia sophia* begins as a rosette of leaves, sending up leafy stems in early spring. The stems are branched, and the herbage is grayish and hairy. The leaves are pinnately compound, divided twice to three times into short linear segments that can resemble fern or conifer foliage from a distance. The flowers are borne in long, slender terminal racemes. Flowers are followed by siliques to 1 in. long and 0.5 in. wide, each containing up to 20 seeds. A single plant can produce as few as 75 or as many as several hundred thousand seeds. Seeds are dispersed by wind and water and by sticking to animals or machinery.

Prescribed burning, mowing, or cutting can all result in stimulating regrowth of taproots. Small invasions can be removed by pulling, hoeing, and digging. Though less than ideal for soil structure, large patches can be effectively removed by tillage.

# Diplotaxis tenuifolia

## SLIMLEAF WALL ROCKET, SAND ROCKET, PERENNIAL WALL ROCKET

**Non-native perennial, to 30 in. Flowers yellow, 4-petaled, to 1 in.; midspring–autumn. Leaves alternate, to 7 in. Parts edible with caution. Toxic to cattle.**

*Diplotaxis tenuifolia* (syn. *Sisymbrium tenuifolium*), a Eurasian mustard, is found as a weed along the west coast from BC to California, as well as being widely distributed in the northeastern US and Canada. It's a problematic invasive on the southern California coast. The species is found primarily in open, disturbed habitats,

including grasslands and roadsides; it is an agricultural pest, invading pastures and competing with crops. The seeds can contaminate grain crops and hay. When grazed by cattle, it causes meat and dairy products to be tainted. Although cultivated, particularly in Europe, as a food crop for human consumption, it can accumulate nitrates and has been suspected of poisonings in cattle.

The seeds of slimleaf wall rocket often germinate in fall, forming rosettes over the winter. A deep taproot is then formed, and the plant dies back aboveground in the fall, returning again the next spring. The basal leaves exist only in seedlings; after that, all leaves are cauline. The stem and leaves are hairless and glaucous. Lower leaves are long and stalked; higher on the stem, the leaves are reduced in size and more sessile. Leaves are variable in shape, from pinnately divided to somewhat lobed to coarsely toothed or entire. They have a strong mustard scent. Flowers are borne in loose terminal racemes that elongate as the seedpods form. The siliques are narrow, up to 2.5 in. long, and beaked at the end.

The weed reproduces by seed and by root fragments, and these may both be dispersed by agricultural activities. Repeated tillage has been used successfully to combat *Diplotaxis tenuifolia* invasions in agriculture. Herbicides are used, but the species has developed resistance to some herbicides.

For small invasions in the home garden, pulling and hoeing can be effective; take care to remove all taproots and any seedpods that have formed. Mulch to prevent future seedlings.

# *Draba verna*

SPRING DRABA, COMMON DRABA, SPRING WHITLOW-GRASS

Non-native annual, to 6 in. Flowers white, 4-petaled, to 0.12 in.; early spring. Leaves basal, to 0.75 in. Parts edible.

This tiny European weed is widely introduced throughout most of North America and much of the world. A plant of dry places, it can be found throughout the PNW, most abundantly on the east side. It lives in shrub steppe, grasslands, and other dry, sunny places. Even on the west side, it's a common weed of gravel driveways. The "whitlow" portion of one of its common names comes from an early medicinal use in treating a finger or toenail inflammation.

The leaves are all basal; they are variably hairy, usually with smooth margins but sometimes with 1–2 coarse teeth along the sides. From the small, circular basal rosette rise one to a few wiry, leafless, unbranched stems. The tiny white flowers are borne in terminal racemes; each flower has the 4 petals characteristic of this family, but they are so deeply notched that they may appear to be 8 in number. The siliques are oval and flattened, about 0.3 in. long, each containing as many as 40 small seeds.

Being tiny and annual, spring draba is unlikely to be a significant problem. It can easily be removed with hoeing or pulling; take care to remove any plants on which seed capsules have formed.

# Hesperis matronalis
## DAME'S ROCKET, SWEET ROCKET, MOTHER-OF-THE-EVENING

**Non-native biennial or perennial, to 4 ft. Flowers purple, 4-petaled, to 1 in.; early summer. Leaves alternate, to 6 in. Parts edible with caution.**

*Hesperis matronalis* is a garden escape that has naturalized widely in the northeastern US and the northern Midwest, as well as the near-coastal west from BC to California. It is common in scattered populations on the PNW westside, on roadsides, forest edges, and vacant lots. Many wildflower seed mixes include this old-fashioned garden plant, leading people to believe it's native. It is not, and as a prolific self-sower, it can be invasive.

Plants grow from a taproot with substantial fibrous roots, from which arise one or several tall, erect stems, which may be unbranched or somewhat branched. The hairy leaves are lanceolate to oval, with toothed margins, the lower leaves long-stalked and the upper ones sessile. The flowers are typically purple but may be pink or white; they are followed by slender siliques to 4 in. long.

Dame's rocket is easy to confuse with *Lunaria annua*, a mustard family relative with similarly colored flowers, of similar height, and growing in similar habitats, but *Hesperis matronalis* is a perennial with slender siliques; *L. annua* is an annual with coin-shaped pods.

Its attractive and fragrant flowers may beguile gardeners, but dame's rocket will displace natives in wild landscapes. If grown in a garden, plants should at least be thoroughly deadheaded. If you are not so beguiled, pull or dig them out, taking care to get all the roots, and remove seedpods from the site.

# Isatis tinctoria

## DYER'S WOAD

Non-native biennial or perennial, to 4 ft. Flowers yellow, 4-petaled, to 0.25 in.; mid–late spring. Leaves basal to 7 in., cauline alternate. Parts medicinal. Noxious in BC, WA, OR, CA.

*Isatis tinctoria*, a European weed, is widely introduced in the western US and Canada, along with northeastern US and northeastern Canada. It is a listed noxious weed in several jurisdictions. Dyer's woad, used for blue dye and medicinals in Europe since the 1200s, was brought to North America in the 1600s by early settlers; by the 1800s, it was being offered in New England seed catalogs. This drought-loving plant makes itself at home in dry habitats, including rangeland, woodland, roadsides, and sagebrush communities. It has invaded thousands of acres in the west.

Plants spread entirely by seed, and the heavy seeds have little means of dispersal except by hitching rides—on animal coats, vehicle tires, etc. A major vector of dispersal happens when the seeds end up contaminating hay bales or various seed crops.

*Isatis tinctoria* starts out as a basal rosette in its first year, developing a taproot that can be as long as 5 ft., plus a system of smaller lateral roots. The basal leaves are long-stalked; the stem leaves are alternate and sessile. All leaves are blue-green with a pale midvein. One to several flowering stems are branched near the top. The terminal flower clusters are followed by plump seedpods, bearing from several hundred to several thousand seeds per plant.

The best option for eradication of dyer's woad may be pulling, after the plant has bloomed but before seed production. Larger patches can be prevented from blooming and exhausted by regular mowing. These strategies take advantage of a biennial's limited time frame for viability and reproduction.

# Lepidium appelianum
## GLOBE-PODDED HOARYCRESS

**Non-native perennial, to 4 ft. Flowers white, 4-petaled, to 0.16 in.; mid–late spring. Leaves basal to 4 in., cauline alternate. Parts edible. Noxious in BC, WA, CA.**

*Lepidium appelianum* (syn. *Cardaria pubescens*) is one of approximately 17 *Lepidium* species that occur in the PNW. About 6 are native; the rest are introduced. This Asian weed is widely distributed over much of North America in disturbed soils moist or dry; in the PNW, it is found more often east of the Cascades. It invades pastures, rangeland, farmland, and riparian zones. Aggressively spreading through seed and rhizomatous proliferation, it can form dense colonies that degrade wildlife habitat, compete with more desirable forage plants, and impact important food crops.

Multiple erect to nearly prostrate stems rise from a woody crown with a spreading root system and many creeping rhizomes. The leaves are oval to broadly lanceolate, with smooth or irregularly toothed margins. Lower leaves are stalked; leaves higher on the stem are reduced in size, sessile, and clasping. The plant bears terminal racemes of up to 30 flowers each. These are followed by small (to 0.25 in. wide), finely hairy, oval to round, pillow-like seedpods. A single plant may produce as many as 2,000 seeds in a season.

The best management strategy is early intervention. Hoe, pull, and dig, preferably when the soil is moist, to facilitate extraction of roots and rhizomes. Mulch, replant with desired competitive plants, and monitor.

# *Lepidium campestre*

## FIELD CRESS, FIELD PEPPERGRASS, POOR MAN'S PEPPERGRASS

**Non-native annual, 8–16 in. Flowers white, 4-petaled, to 0.12 in.; late spring–early summer. Leaves basal to 4.5 in.; cauline alternate to 3 in. Parts edible.**

Field cress is introduced throughout most of North America, including the PNW. It's found on open, often dry sites, including roadsides, meadows, and fields, as well as in riparian zones.

This plant closely resembles other *Lepidium* species; its most distinguishing feature is the gray fuzziness of stems and leaves. The basal leaves are oblong and may have lyrate outlines; they may wither away as the flowering stems rise. The cauline leaves are sessile, clasping, narrow, and arrowhead-shaped, with small marginal teeth.

The tiny white flowers are borne in terminal, often compound racemes (several small flowering spikes emerging from the top of the main stem). The oval, somewhat flattened seedpods are about 0.25 in. long. The seeds are pungent and edible.

Field cress is a generous self-sower and can form colonies. Eradicate plants by pulling and grubbing them out with a hoe, then mulching.

# Lepidium chalepense

## LENS-PODDED HOARYCRESS, CHALAPA HOARYCRESS, ASIAN WHITETOP

**Non-native perennial, to 2 ft. Flowers white, 4-petaled, to 0.08 in.; early summer. Leaves basal to 4 in., cauline alternate. Parts edible. Noxious in BC, OR, CA.**

*Lepidium chalepense* (syn. *Cardaria chalepensis*), one of our several introduced *Lepidium* species, is found over much of North America and in the PNW is primarily on the east side. It is principally an agricultural weed but is found in various disturbed, often dry, habitats—farmland, rangeland, yards, gardens, and roadsides.

With long, robust rhizomes, this plant can spread vegetatively as much as 6 ft. a year. The stems are somewhat pubescent, erect, and branched mostly at the top, in the inflorescences. The basal leaves are oblong, to 1.5 in. wide, and stalked, with dentate margins. Stem leaves are shorter and wider, and higher on the stem become stalkless and clasping, with auriculate bases. The tiny white flowers are borne in terminal racemes. The silicles are round and pillow-like, and lack the hairiness found in some of our other *Lepidium* pods.

Small invasions, if intercepted early, can be pulled or dug out. As the plant matures, its rhizomes make this a formidable task. Repeated mowing can at least forestall seed set. Land managers coping with large populations use herbicides, but these can require repeated application. After clearing the area, mulch well and monitor for recurrences.

# Lepidium draba

## WHITETOP, HEART-PODDED HOARYCRESS, HOARY PEPPERWORT

**Non-native perennial, to 2 ft. Flowers white, 4-petaled, to 0.25 in.; spring–summer. Leaves basal to 4 in., cauline alternate. Parts edible. Toxic to livestock. Noxious in BC, WA, OR, CA.**

*Lepidium draba* (syn. *Cardaria draba*) is a Eurasian weed that has spread to all continents and is widely introduced throughout most of North America. It is a listed noxious weed in several jurisdictions. Whitetop can form dense monocultural mats, displacing native vegetation and crops or pasture plants. It contaminates wheat crops and causes GI irritation when grazed by livestock. It invades roadsides, pastures, agricultural land, riparian areas, grasslands, and other habitats, often on saline soils.

Whitetop grows from a thick rhizome and has an aggressive root system that spreads several feet vertically and horizontally. It typically forms a leaf rosette and does not bloom in its first year. Flowering stems, which rise from buds on the rhizomes, may be erect or trailing, often branched. The lower leaves are stalked; the upper are more sessile and clasping.

The small white flowers bloom in flat-topped clusters. They are followed by plump, heart-shaped silicles about 0.2 in. across. One plant can produce several thousand seeds in a season. The species self-sows freely but may spread more aggressively via rhizomes.

Very small infestations can be dug up. Be sure to cut mature plants as far as 20 in. below the soil surface, to reduce resprouting of rhizomes. Any broken pieces of roots and rhizomes must be removed. Monitor the site for seedlings and be prepared to continue the process for a few years if a seed bank has accumulated. Larger infestations may be both very difficult to remove and the removal very disruptive to the soil and other vegetation, so herbicide may be something to consider. Another option is to mow frequently to prevent seeding and remove all green repeatedly, thus eventually starving the root system.

# Lepidium latifolium

## BROAD-LEAVED PEPPERGRASS

Non-native perennial, to 5 ft. Flowers white, tiny; summer–autumn. Leaves basal to 12 in., cauline alternate. Parts edible. Noxious in BC, WA, OR, CA.

Broad-leaved peppergrass is a Eurasian species found widely distributed along the west coast from BC to California, and over much of North America. It invades a variety of disturbed habitats, from beaches and coastal and inland wetlands to riparian zones and irrigated farmland to roadsides and dry upland areas, montane meadows, and high desert. It can form dense monocultural colonies that displace desirable forage in pastures, crowd out native vegetation, and degrade wildlife habitat in natural areas.

Growing from a large root mass and rhizomes that can extend to 6 ft. horizontally, the woody crown can send up multiple tall stems. The leaves are waxy, with prominent pale midveins. Basal and lower stem leaves may be 3 in. wide with dentate margins and long petioles. Higher along the stem, they are reduced in size and nearly sessile, with smooth margins. The many tiny white flowers bloom in terminal arrays of multiple compound racemes, which are dense and rounded. These are followed by clusters of small oval silicles (to 0.08 in.), somewhat compressed and slightly hairy, each containing 2 seeds. A single plant can produce thousands of seeds in a season. Despite abundant seed reproduction, the majority of population expansion is often by creeping rhizomes and sprouting of buds on roots and root crowns.

Small invasions of broad-leaved peppergrass can be pulled, grubbed out with a hoe, or dug, with care taken to remove all roots. Replant with more desirable and competitive plants, and mulch well, monitoring for resproutings. Land managers report less than satisfactory results in combatting large infestations of this weed with herbicide; too often, underground fragments survive and resprout.

# Lepidium perfoliatum

CLASPING PEPPERGRASS, PEPPERWORT

Non-native annual, to 24 in. Flowers yellow, 4-petaled, to 0.12 in.; midspring–midsummer. Leaves basal to 5 in., cauline alternate. Parts edible.

This annual weed is distributed throughout North America and in the PNW occurs mostly east of the Cascades, on dry soils and degraded habitats.

The stems may be branched or not, with pinnately dissected basal and lower stem leaves. Higher on the stem, leaves are smaller, simpler, round in shape and tightly clasp the stem, appearing perfoliate. The many tiny yellow flowers are borne in dense terminal racemes. They are followed by oval silicles to 0.15 in. long. This is a fast-growing, short-lived plant producing many seeds, so removing before seed set is key to control.

This weed is easy to control by hoeing or pulling; take care to remove any seedpods from the site. Large infestations may be combatted by mowing just before plants bloom.

# Lepidium virginicum

## TALL PEPPERWEED, COMMON PEPPERGRASS

Native annual or biennial, to 1.5 ft. Flowers white, 4-petaled, to 0.1 in.; midspring–midsummer. Leaves basal to 3 in., cauline alternate. Parts edible/medicinal.

*Lepidium virginicum* is a widely distributed, weedy native in much of North America; it is considered a problematic invasive in parts of the US as well as in Europe. In the PNW, it is most common in westside lowlands. It invades native prairies and other wild-lands but most often is found in more developed or disturbed habitat, including lawns, roadsides, vacant lots, and pastures.

From a slender, branched taproot the plant begins as a basal rosette of narrow, toothed or shallowly pinnately lobed leaves. Cauline leaves are reduced in size, more sessile, and more often simpler in outline. Stem leaves are slightly hairy; as in many related plants, they are peppery-tasting and palatable as salad greens. The stems are usually branched, giving the plant a bushy appearance. Upper stems bear terminal racemes of many tiny flowers, which are followed by distinctive seedpods, oval and somewhat flattened, notched silicles. The seeds, as with several *Lepidium* species, are used as a source of peppery seasoning in food.

This weed has developed herbicide resistance in agricultural settings where growers are embattled by large *Lepidium* populations. The key to control of this annual is to get it before seed set. For home gardens, it should be sufficient to pull, hoe, or mow, followed by mulch.

# Lunaria annua

MONEY PLANT, HONESTY, SILVER DOLLAR PLANT

Non-native annual or biennial, to 3 ft. Flowers purple, 4-petaled, to 0.75 in.; spring. Leaves mostly alternate, to 4 in. Parts edible.

Money plant is a non-native garden plant that has escaped widely in the Midwest and northeastern US and particularly in the west, from BC through west-side Washington and Oregon to coastal California. It invariably finds its way to forest edges, roadsides, and other moist, disturbed areas. It rarely forms dense patches and often seems so at home in the dappled shade of woodlands that many people believe it's native. The seeds are widely sold to gardeners.

*Lunaria annua* grows rapidly with semi-erect, branched stems bearing oval leaves with toothed margins. The bluish-purple to deep reddish-purple (occasionally white) flowers are followed by the seedpods, whose unique appearance inspired the genus name (*Lunaria*, "moon") and common names referring to coins. The pods are oval to perfectly round, very flat, and, as they mature, papery and translucent. Late in the season, they make pleasant light rattling sounds in a breeze, and they are valued for dried flower arrangements.

Some plant ecologists in Oregon and Washington are concerned about the expanding populations of this species. It has not yet made the noxious weed lists and may never do so; its real impact on native flora is not clear. However, it is inevitably true that for every patch of *Lunaria annua*, we potentially lose many small woodland or meadow natives. If your garden is not devoted to natives, you may view any money plant that shows up as a welcome volunteer. If you want only natives, or you're growing small things that will be bullied by the larger plant, or you're adjacent to wild land and want to maintain the integrity of the native ecosystem—then, it's a weed. Either way, please don't let the seeds disperse.

Pull or hoe out unwanted volunteers, being sure to collect any seedpods. (You might want to harvest them for your own or your friends' arrangements.) Mulch and competitive plantings appropriate to the site should discourage subsequent intrusions.

# Raphanus raphanistrum

## WILD RADISH

**Non-native annual or biennial, to 30 in. Flowers yellow, white, violet, 4-petaled, to 0.75 in.; midspring–autumn. Leaves basal to 8 in., cauline alternate. Parts edible with caution. Toxic to horses, cattle, chickens.**

This wild cousin of the familiar garden radish is a common weed, seen in scattered sites across most of North America. It can be found in yards, vacant lots, orchards, farmland, fields, parks, roadsides, and other open, disturbed ground. It's a problem weed in agriculture, showing up among many grain and vegetable crops.

Growing from a small taproot, the stems are sparsely pubescent and well branched toward the top. The basal leaves are stalked and pinnately divided, with a large, rounded terminal lobe, the other lobes smaller and deeply incised. The cauline leaves are reduced in size, simpler in outline, and shorter-stalked. The flowers are stalked and borne in loose terminal racemes. They have clawed petals and are variable in color, often pale yellow but also white, pink, or lilac, with purple veining. The seedpods are narrow siliques to 2 in. long, with tapered beaks, and each contains up to 10 seeds.

In the home garden, wild radish is easy to pull or grub out with a hoe. Mulch and replant.

# *Raphanus sativus*

## GARDEN RADISH, WILD RADISH, JOINTED CHARLOCK

Non-native annual, to 2.5 ft. Flowers pink, purple, yellow, white, 4-petaled, to 0.5 in.; spring–summer. Leaves basal to 7 in., cauline alternate. Parts edible/medicinal with caution.

This Eurasian plant has been widely grown for food since antiquity. It occasionally escapes cultivation and is found as a weed across North America in scattered locations on roadsides, vacant lots, and garden edges; it also hybridizes with its wild cousin, *Raphanus raphanistrum*.

Growing from a stout taproot, garden radish begins as a rosette of basal leaves, oblanceolate and pinnately lobed, with coarsely scalloped margins. Stem leaves are similar but reduced in size and less deeply incised.

The plant's flowers are borne in terminal racemes on central and upper stems. They are followed by short siliques, each containing 2–3 seeds. Garden radish can be distinguished from wild radish by the size of its root and the silique, which has fewer seeds and is not as long and slender as that of wild radish.

Garden radish is obviously edible, though the root becomes less palatable when the plant blooms. If it's too late to harvest or you're not a fan of this pungent root vegetable, it's easy enough to pull, hoe, or dig it out.

# Rorippa curvisiliqua

## CURVEPOD YELLOWCRESS, WESTERN YELLOWCRESS

**Native annual or biennial, to 18 in. Flowers yellow, 4-petaled, to 0.08 in.; spring–summer. Leaves basal to 2.75 in., cauline alternate. Parts edible.**

This native plant has a limited range in western North America, from Arizona to Alaska; it is widely distributed in the PNW. It is found on wet soil in moist meadows and on lakeshores and streambanks.

Growing from a taproot, the prostrate to erect stems can extend to at least 2 ft. long. They are sparingly branched, or may be branched only at the top of the plant. Leaves both basal and cauline are variable and may be pinnately lobed, dentate, or entire. The leaves of the basal rosette wither away by the time the plant reaches maturity.

Flowers are borne in long racemes at the ends of stems and in the upper leaf axils. The flowers are followed by narrow seedpods that are usually curved (hence *curvisiliqua*). These small plants are easily removed by pulling or grubbing out with tools, preferably before seed set. Be sure to remove any pods that have formed.

# Sinapis arvensis

WILD MUSTARD, CHARLOCK MUSTARD, CORN MUSTARD

Non-native annual, to 3 ft. Flowers yellow, 4-petaled, to 0.5 in.; midspring–autumn. Leaves basal to 7 in., cauline alternate. Parts edible with caution. Toxic to horses, cattle. Noxious in BC.

*Sinapis arvensis* (syn. *Brassica kaber, Rhamphospermum arvense*), a Mediterranean weed, has been present in North America for at least 400 years. It is found throughout much of the continent, often on disturbed ground in waste places, yards, gardens, and farm fields, where it can be an agricultural nuisance. Note: the common names "charlock" and "wild mustard" are given to several related plants as well.

Growing from a short taproot, this wild mustard produces a rosette of stalked basal leaves that vary greatly in shape, from broadly oval with coarsely toothed and wavy margins to more lanceolate and pinnately lobed with a larger terminal lobe. Stems and leaves are variably hairy. Cauline leaves become reduced in size upward on the stem, simpler, and shorter-stalked, sometimes sessile or clasping. The terminal racemes of bright yellow, somewhat showy flowers on the upper stems are followed by siliques to 1.5 in. long, tapering to short beaks. A single plant may produce as many as 3,500 seeds, which can remain viable for decades.

Pull, hoe, or dig out plants when the soil is moist and before seed set, taking care to extract the taproot and to remove any seedpods from the site. Mulch, and monitor for subsequent seedlings.

# Sisymbrium altissimum

## TUMBLE MUSTARD, JIM HILL MUSTARD, TALL TUMBLE MUSTARD

Non-native annual or biennial, to 5 ft. Flowers yellow, 4-petaled, to 0.33 in.; midspring–autumn. Leaves alternate, to 8 in. Parts edible.

This very aggressive weed has worldwide distribution and is found all over North America. In the PNW, it's most common on the east side of the Cascade crest. Well adapted to dry and disturbed habitats, it invades shrub steppe, grasslands, pastures, cropland, nurseries, and waste places. It displaces native plants and desirable agricultural or forage plants and serves as an alternate host to diseases affecting important crops.

*Sisymbrium altissimum* has multiple traits ideal for an invasive career, including early germination, rapid growth, and a long period of seed dispersal. Its populations explode following rangeland fires, and it benefits from overgrazed habitats. When a plant has bloomed and is drying at the end of its life cycle, it can break off and tumble over the landscape, thus dispersing seeds. Seeds are also dispersed when they stick to animals, people, vehicles, or machines. A major historic vector of dispersal was along railroads (hence Jim Hill mustard, after railroad magnate James J. Hill).

Tumble mustard produces a rosette of leaves, followed by a single, multi-branched stem. Its taproot can reach 20 in. at maturity. Lower leaves are stalked and deeply divided into pinnate, roughly triangular lobes. Higher on the stem, the leaves are more finely divided, the segments more linear. Lower stems and leaves are hairy, the upper ones hairless.

Flowers are borne in small terminal clusters, followed by narrow siliques that can hold 120 or more seeds each. A single plant can produce thousands of siliques and over a million seeds, which may last in the soil for decades.

The good news for the dryland home gardener is that these plants have only their self-sowing to rely on for grabbing real estate. Pull new rosettes when they appear in fall or early spring. Be vigilant in collecting any siliques that have formed. If this is not the first appearance of *Sisymbrium altissimum* on the site, continue to monitor for seedlings and be prepared to keep pulling.

# Sisymbrium loeselii

TALL HEDGE MUSTARD, FALSE LONDON ROCKET, LOESEL'S TUMBLE MUSTARD

Non-native annual, to 4 ft. Flowers yellow, 4-petaled, to 0.3 in.; late spring–early summer. Leaves basal to 6 in., cauline alternate. Unpalatable.

Tall hedge mustard is found across North America, with the exception of the southernmost US and northernmost Canada. It is most competitive in dry areas, and in the PNW is found mostly on the east side, invading fields, woodland edges, pastures, gardens, commercial landscapes, roadsides, and other disturbed sites.

Growing from a taproot, tall hedge mustard begins life as a basal rosette of pinnately notched leaves, sending up flowering stems in summer. The stems are upright, often branched toward the top, mostly hairless higher on the plant and hairy toward the base. The lower leaves are triangular to lanceolate, short-stalked, and pinnately divided into wedge-shaped lobes, often pointed backward toward the petiole, with margins coarsely dentate. Leaves higher on the stem are reduced in size and short-stalked to sessile, with fewer lobes.

The terminal inflorescences begin as congested, rounded clusters, elongating with maturity to 16 in. Individual flowers are borne on slender stalks and have spatulate petals. The flowers are followed by linear siliques to 1.5 in. long. The small seeds are dispersed by wind, water, animals, vehicles, and farm machinery.

This weed reproduces only through seed dispersal and is easy to dislodge by pulling or hoeing, going below the crown to sever the taproot, ideally prior to seed set. Larger patches can be eradicated by repeated mowing to prevent blooming and self-sowing.

# Sisymbrium officinale

## HEDGE MUSTARD, HEDGEWEED

Non-native annual, to 2.5 ft. Flowers yellow, 4-petaled, to 0.16 in.; spring–summer. Leaves basal to 8 in., cauline alternate. Parts edible/medicinal.

Hedge mustard is a very widespread annual weed of roadsides, fields, and cropland throughout most of North America. In the PNW, it occurs mostly west of the Cascades. It can be a troublesome weed of agricultural crops.

The strong, wiry stems of this species are very hairy and may be unbranched to multi-branched. The stems spread out and curve upward, producing a sometimes bushy candelabra shape. The basal leaves are somewhat variable in shape and marginal dentition. They are typically pinnately cut almost to the midvein, forming a series of jagged lobes. Stem leaves are sessile and much reduced in size, with much narrower, sometimes linear lobes.

The flowers have pale to bright yellow, well-separated petals and are borne in small, initially rounded terminal clusters that elongate as they mature. They are followed by narrow siliques to 0.6 in. long, tapered at the ends.

In the home garden, hedge mustard can be controlled by pulling or hoeing; take care to remove any siliques that have formed. Mulch to discourage future seedlings.

# *Teesdalia nudicaulis*

## SHEPHERD'S CRESS, BARESTEM TEESDALIA

Non-native annual, to 8 in. Flowers white, 4-petaled, to 0.08 in.; early spring. Leaves basal, to 2 in.

*Teesdalia nudicaulis* is a Eurasian weed with a limited North American distribution. It is found from BC to Washington, Oregon, and Idaho in the PNW, as well as in a few midwestern states and along the east coast.

Shepherd's cress has a rosette of pinnately lobed or dissected leaves with rounded segments. Stems may be branched or not and may be leafless (hence *nudicaulis*) or bear scant, bract-like leaves on the upper portions.

The flowers are borne in terminal racemes, rounded at the top. Individual flowers are asymmetric, with 2 petals on the outer half being nearly twice as long as the 2 inner petals. The silicles are very small and oval, containing up to 4 seeds each—not a heavy self-sower.

With limited seed output and a short season, this weed is easily controlled by hoeing, pulling, and mulching.

# *Thlaspi arvense*

## FIELD PENNYCRESS, FANWEED

Non-native annual, to 20 in. Flowers white, 4-petaled, to 0.12 in.; midspring–midsummer. Leaves basal to 2.5 in., cauline alternate. Parts edible/medicinal with caution. Toxic to horses, cattle, pigs.

*Thlaspi arvense* is found nearly everywhere in North America, including the PNW. It goes by a host of different common names, most shared in full or in part with other plants, so confusion is possible.

Field pennycress grows from a taproot, with a few basal leaves that can wither away early. The stem may be branched or unbranched, with lower leaves stalked and with scalloped outlines similar to the basal leaves. Higher leaves are reduced in size, sessile, and more lanceolate.

The small flowers, borne in elongating terminal racemes, are followed by oval to heart-shaped silicles, compressed and with a thinner, winged margin. A single plant may produce as many as 20,000 seeds, and those seeds can remain viable for 20–30 years.

Owing to its exceptional reproductive capacity, *Thlaspi arvense* can be a significant pest of many commercially important crops. When it contaminates animal feed, it can cause serious, potentially fatal poisoning in cattle, though the leaves and seeds have been used in cooking in some European and Asian traditions.

In larger infestations, tillage is sometimes recommended for control but should be avoided where possible. In most home gardens, pulling and hoeing should suffice, with care taken to remove from the site any plants that have grown seedpods.

# *Arenaria serpyllifolia*

## THYME-LEAF SANDWORT

Non-native annual, to 10 in. Flowers white, 5-petaled, to 0.2 in. wide; midspring–midsummer. Leaves opposite, to 0.3 in. Parts edible/medicinal.

Thyme-leaf sandwort is a small weed introduced through most of North America and across the PNW. It inhabits a variety of disturbed sites, including fields, cliffs, roadsides, and sidewalk cracks. It is most successful on sites where competition from other plants is minimal.

Multiple erect to sprawling slender stems rise from a taproot. The stems are deep purple and slightly fuzzy, often branched at the base, producing a tangled mat. The leaves are small and oval in opposite pairs, well separated along the stems.

The flowers are stalked and borne in terminal clusters and singly in the leaf axils. Unlike some similar-looking plants, the flowers of thyme-leaf sandwort have unnotched petals.

*Arenaria serpyllifolia* is easy to overlook and is unlikely to be much of a problem once the gardener decides it is unwelcome. Pull or hoe when the soil is moist, then mulch or fill in with perennial groundcover or other larger plants.

# Cerastium fontanum subsp. vulgare

## MOUSE-EAR CHICKWEED, COMMON CHICKWEED, BIG CHICKWEED

**Non-native annual, biennial, or perennial, to 20 in. Flowers white, 5-petaled, to 0.25 in.; spring–autumn. Leaves opposite, to 1.5 in. Parts edible.**

A well-known Eurasian weed, *Cerastium fontanum* subsp. *vulgare* (syn. *C. vulgatum*) is widely distributed throughout North America. It is found on moist, disturbed ground everywhere: agricultural land, residential and commercial turf, orchards, woodland edges, wetland margins, fields, yards, and gardens. The genus includes several other weedy species and some North American natives, as well as popular garden plants.

Mouse-ear chickweed is sometimes grown for its edible leaves. Though its ubiquity and near-universal presence in well-watered gardens makes one laugh at this: yes, you can buy seeds. Another well-known edible weed is *Stellaria media*. Both species are sometimes called "common chickweed," and both are very common garden weeds. They are closely related but distinct in appearance, with mouse-ear chickweed being much fuzzier.

Mouse-ear chickweed is primarily a short-lived perennial, possibly a biennial, and may sometimes be an annual or look like one, with its dinky stature, weak stems, and sometimes first-year bloom. The stems are noticeably fuzzy, recumbent, and mat-forming. The small, sessile leaves are variable in shape, oval to spatulate. Flowers are borne in open, terminal clusters. As with many species in this family, the 5 petals are so deeply notched, they may look as if they are 10 in number.

This little weed reproduces mostly by self-sowing but can also sometimes form new plants when the trailing stems root at the nodes. While a happy population that has had time to be fruitful and multiply can

be momentarily annoying, control is easy. Moisten the soil, pull or scrape the plants away with a hoe, mulch to prevent new seedlings.

# *Cerastium glomeratum*

## STICKY MOUSE-EAR CHICKWEED

Non-native annual, to 15 in. Flowers white, 5-petaled, to 0.3 in.; spring–midsummer. Leaves opposite, to 0.6 in. Parts edible/medicinal.

*Cerastium glomeratum* (syn. *C. viscosum*) is a very common weed along the west coast from Alaska to California and through much of the US as well as eastern Canada. This small plant can be seen on roadsides and in fields, yards, gardens, vacant lots, and agricultural land.

From a slender taproot arise one to several branched stems, erect or sprawling, which may root at the nodes. Stems, leaves, and calyces are noticeably fuzzy and glandular, making them a little sticky to the touch. Basal and lower cauline leaves are small and tapered to short stalks. Leaves higher on the stem are sessile but a little larger. The numerous white flowers are borne in tight terminal clusters. The petals are nearly equal to the green sepals and usually notched deeply, sometimes cleft so far that they appear to be doubled in number.

Sticky mouse-ear chickweed is easy to remove by pulling or scraping with a hoe or trowel. Follow with competitive plantings and mulch.

# Dianthus armeria

## DEPTFORD PINK, GRASS PINK

**Non-native annual or biennial, to 2.5 ft. Flowers pink, red, 5-petaled, to 0.5 in.; mid–late summer. Leaves basal to 4 in., cauline opposite. Poisonous.**

This charming, delicate weed, found in most of North America, is scattered across the PNW, invading fields, woodland edges, and roadsides.

A slender taproot gives rise to a basal rosette of grass-like leaves and stiff, slender stems, often sparingly branched. Leaves and stems are hairy. The bases of each pair of cauline leaves form a sheath around the stem. The flowers are borne in tight, mostly terminal clusters of 3–5. They are bright pink to red with toothed margins and tiny white spots.

This attractive plant might begin as a welcome guest and then wear out its welcome with overgenerous self-sowing. Gardeners living near wild lands might particularly want to suppress this potential competitor with native flora. Pulling or hoeing followed by mulch should do the trick.

# *Gypsophila paniculata*
## BABY'S BREATH

Non-native perennial, to 2.5 ft. Flowers white, 5-petaled, to 0.25 in.; midsummer–autumn. Leaves opposite, whorled, to 4 in. Unpalatable. Noxious in BC, WA, CA.

Baby's breath is a popular plant of gardens and florist arrangements that has escaped into wild places over much of North America, with the exception of several far-southern states. It prefers sunny sites in dry regions, invading roadsides, meadows, and agricultural land. In the PNW, it occurs most commonly on the east side.

Plants grow from a thick crown and rhizome, with roots extending downward as far as 13 ft. The leaves are simple, linear, and opposite to nearly whorled on one to many multi-branched stems. Many small flowers are borne in open panicles, giving a frothy appearance. A single plant may produce 14,000 seeds in a year; the seeds are tiny and easily wind-borne for great distances. As a plant matures, stem numbers and thus flowers and seeds produced only increase.

Its deep root system gives baby's breath drought tolerance—a competitive advantage in arid regions, where it crowds out other plants. Given a chance to spread, plants can form dense stands that are resistant to most methods of control. As seedlings mature, their deep roots make pulling impossible and digging labor-intensive. To prevent regrowth, the rhizome and crown must be removed, which may require digging down 6–12 in. Mowing has proven ineffective in efforts to remove stands from public lands. For large stands, repeated disking can prevent regrowth of old plants and germination of new ones; heavy, repeated grazing has been effective in preventing seed set and reducing plant vigor.

# Holosteum umbellatum

## JAGGED CHICKWEED, UMBRELLA SPURRY

Non-native annual, to 8 in. Flowers white, 5-petaled, 0.25 in.; late spring–early summer. Leaves basal to 0.8 in., cauline opposite.

Jagged chickweed has been present in the US at least since the mid-1800s, probably introduced accidentally, perhaps as a plant-seed contaminant. It's now found throughout much of North America, including the west coast. In the PNW, it's found mostly on the east side of the Cascades, invading dry, open areas, including high deserts, roadsides, fields, and vacant lots.

From a taproot, the plant produces one to several erect stems, typically unbranched or branched only at the base. The leaves are oval to lanceolate with a prominent central vein, stalked in the basal rosette and more sessile and scant above. The specific epithet and the common name "umbrella spurry" refer to the arrangement of the inflorescence: a terminal umbel of a few flowers on slender pedicels. The petals have toothed margins on their tips (thus "jagged" chickweed).

Jagged chickweed gets around by seed dispersal. Pull or hoe when the soil is moist, dislodging the taproots, then follow with mulch or competitive planting of larger plants or groundcover.

# *Lychnis coronaria*

## ROSE CAMPION, MULLEIN PINK

Non-native biennial or perennial, to 3.5 ft. Flowers pink, red, 5-petaled, to 1.25 in.; summer. Leaves basal to 4 in., cauline opposite. Unpalatable.

*Lychnis coronaria* (syn. *Silene coronaria*) is present as a garden escape along the west coast from BC to California and in much of eastern North America. It remains a popular garden plant, but rose campion can be invasive both in and out of gardens. Being moderately tolerant of drought and a prolific self-seeder, it is particularly problematic on dry sites west of the Cascades.

The common name "mullein pink" has potential to confuse; this plant is not related to mullein (*Verbascum*), but small seedlings are often mistaken for other fuzzy, simple-leaved plants, like *Stachys byzantina*.

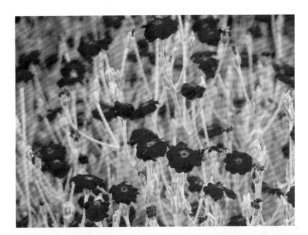

The most noticeable features of the plant are its gray, short-woolly leaves and stems. All leaves are simple and more or less lanceolate, the upper ones reduced and clasping the stem. Multiple stems rise from the branched crown, bearing many showy and sweet-smelling flowers.

This rambunctious garden plant is loved by many and feared by some for its persistent fecundity. Even the initially charmed gardener may tire of it, and many gardens come with an old population already present in the seed bank. It also may jump the fence into wild lands, displacing native flora.

If you wish to keep the plant but prevent it from taking over, arduous deadheading of the many flowers or cutting to the ground after bloom are both options. For more thorough removal, pulling or grubbing out with a hoe should work, facilitated by first moistening the soil. Apply some heavy wood mulch and monitor for seedlings.

# Sagina apetala

## ANNUAL PEARLWORT

**Non-native annual, to 5 in. Flowers green, white, 4-lobed, to 0.1 in.; early summer. Leaves opposite, to 0.5 in.**

This delicate European weed has a very limited North American distribution, from BC (where it is listed as native) through Washington and Oregon on the west side, to California and a handful of other states. It takes advantage of low competition on moist, disturbed, bare soil in gardens, lawns, streambanks, sidewalk cracks, roadsides, and paths.

Annual pearlwort grows from a small taproot with numerous thread-like, branched, procumbent stems that root at the nodes. The leaves are tiny and linear, to 0.5 in. long. In early summer, minute, terminal or axillary apetalous flowers (no petals, only sepals) bloom on slender stalks to 0.2 in. long.

This plant has minor entertainment value for its sheer teensiness. When that ceases to amuse, it's easily ripped out by hand or hoe, or you can smother it with thick mulch.

# Sagina procumbens

## BIRD-EYE PEARLWORT, PROCUMBENT PEARLWORT

Non-native biennial or perennial, prostrate to 6 in. Flowers white, 4-petaled, to 0.2 in.; midspring–autumn. Leaves basal to 0.7 in., cauline opposite.

*Sagina procumbens* is a tiny but surprisingly aggressive weed distributed over much of North America. It's found across the PNW but is more common on the west side. Bird-eye pearlwort invades both natural and disturbed sites—gardens, lawns, woodlands, streamsides, ditches, nursery containers, and plantings. Owing to its delicate appearance and its preference for moist places, it is often mistaken for moss, and indeed one of its close relatives, *S. subulata* (Irish moss) is a horticultural plant.

Growing from a slender, shallow taproot, a basal rosette of small linear leaves may give rise to multiple branched stems. The very slender, lax stems trail across the ground and root at nodes, quickly forming a mat. The cauline leaves are opposite but may appear whorled; flowers are borne singly or in small clusters at the ends of stems. The tiny white flowers may sometimes lack petals, consisting only of the green sepals.

It's easy to underestimate at first, but this plant produces large numbers of tiny seeds that are easily dispersed by wind, water, and animals. New plants reach reproductive age and start producing seeds and seedlings within a few months. The many seeds are long-lived in the soil and can form a lasting seed bank. In commercial settings, herbicides are often recommended because of the labor-intensiveness of removing large populations by hand. For the home gardener, control will usually be easy enough with pulling, scraping with hoes or trowels, and following up with a preventive layer of mulch. The presence of *Sagina procumbens* is often an indicator of excess moisture, so evaluate your watering regimen.

# *Saponaria officinalis*

## SOAPWORT, BOUNCING-BET

Non-native perennial, to 3 ft. Flowers white, pink, 5-petaled, to 1 in.; summer–autumn. Leaves opposite, to 4 in. Parts medicinal with caution. Toxic to horses, cattle, sheep, chickens.

Soapwort is an old garden favorite, long grown in Europe and the Americas for its fragrant flowers and for use in making soap. ("Bouncing Bet" is an old term for a laundry woman.) It has escaped cultivation and is now naturalized all over North America and throughout the PNW, with a preference for drier areas. It inhabits sandy or gravelly streambanks, woodland edges, and roadsides.

This species produces many orange rhizomes, from which rise one to several very leafy stems. The stems are usually unbranched, or with short branches extending from the upper leaf axils, and are swollen at the leaf nodes. The leaves all have 3 prominent, parallel veins and are simple, oval to lanceolate, and either sessile or with short petioles. The flowers, borne in terminal clusters, may be white to deep pink and have deeply cleft petals and tubular, inch-long calyces.

*Saponaria officinalis* spreads aggressively via seed and rhizomes, forming dense colonies that crowd out other species and are difficult to eradicate. The persistent rhizomes defeat methods like cutting, mowing, or burning. Grazing is not recommended: plants are toxic to grazing animals. Herbicides have been preferred where large infestations cause problems for agriculture. The rhizomes resprout, so care must be taken to remove them when pulling or digging, and repeated diggings may be required.

# Silene latifolia

### WHITE CAMPION, EVENING CATCHFLY, WHITE COCKLE

Non-native biennial or perennial, to 3.5 ft. Flowers white, 5-petaled, to 1.2 in.; summer. Leaves basal to 4 in., cauline opposite. Parts edible with caution. Noxious in BC, WA.

*Silene latifolia* (syn. *S. latifolia* subsp. *alba*, *Lychnis alba*) is a widespread weed over most of North America, with the exception of some far-south states. It invades roadsides, meadows, pastures, woodland edges, waste places, grasslands, and agricultural land, preferring somewhat moist, cooler regions. About 20 *Silene* species are found in the PNW, about half introduced and half native. This species is a significant pest of numerous economically important grain and seed crops and is also a threat to native vegetation, particularly the rare PNW native, *S. spaldingii*.

From a branched crown, several unbranched stems arise. The stems are hairy, jointed, and may be spreading (reaching out more horizontally) or semi-erect. Leaves are slightly hairy and simple, oblong to lanceolate; stem leaves are smaller and more sessile than the basal leaves.

White campion is dioecious. The flowers are white to light pink, with the petals deeply notched; they are borne in small, open terminal clusters, or singly in the upper leaf axils. Female flowers, if pollinated, will produce as many as 24,000 seeds for a single female plant in a season. Most reproduction is through seed dispersal, but there is also vegetative sprouting from the short rootstocks.

Deep tillage has been used to combat invasions of *Silene latifolia* in agriculture and environmental restoration, but this may not be desirable or possible in home gardens. Mowing delays seed set but has not been successful in discouraging the persistence of roots. For small invasions, pulling or grubbing out with tools is effective; take care to remove all the roots.

# Silene noctiflora

## NIGHT-FLOWERING CATCHFLY

**Non-native annual, to 30 in. Flowers white, 5-petaled, to 1 in.; mid–late summer. Leaves basal to 5 in., cauline opposite. Noxious in BC.**

*Silene noctiflora* is a European species found in scattered sites across North America, invading disturbed ground in farm fields, meadows, gardens, and plant nurseries.

From a slender taproot it produces a few basal leaves and up to 3 stems, hairy and branched or unbranched, and swollen at the nodes. The basal and lower cauline leaves are long-stalked, oval to lanceolate, to 1.5 in. wide. Upper cauline leaves are reduced in size and nearly sessile. Open clusters of up to 15 flowers bloom at branch ends and in upper leaf axils. The flowers are white to pinkish and fragrant, with deeply notched petals. Flowers are followed by erect, ovoid seed capsules to 0.75 in. long, ripening to light brown and splitting at the tops.

*Silene noctiflora* can be confused with *S. latifolia*, another white-flowered species. But *S. noctiflora* has seed capsules with 6 triangular, reflexed teeth at the top; in *S. latifolia*, there are 10 teeth. *Silene noctiflora* (as the epithet suggests) is also a night-bloomer that closes in the morning.

Pull, hoe, or dig *Silene noctiflora* when the soil is moist. Mulch and replant.

# Silene vulgaris

## BLADDER CAMPION

Non-native perennial, to 3 ft. Flowers white, 5-petaled, to 0.75 in.; early–midsummer. Leaves opposite, to 2.5 in. Parts edible with caution. Noxious in BC.

This European species was probably introduced to North America as a garden plant. It has escaped cultivation, naturalizing across most of the continent in fields, roadsides, vacant lots, and sandy beaches.

From a deep, stout taproot and short rhizomes rise several upright, branched stems. The leaves are pale green to gray-green, hairless to slightly pubescent, with smooth ciliate margins. They are pointed at the tips, rounded at their bases, oblanceolate to narrowly lanceolate or elliptic, and mostly sessile.

Bladder campion is gynodioecious. The axial and terminal panicles of flowers are so numerous that plants often lean over from their weight. The flowers are white with 5 deeply cleft petals, rounded at the tips, forming a bell-shaped corolla about an inch long, atop a long involucre. Ten white stamens with dark tips extend outward from the corollas of bisexual flowers. The calyx is inflated, pale green to dull pink, with 5 triangular lobes. Flowers are followed by smooth, rounded seedpods, held erect and maturing to tan, with a 6-pointed opening at the top.

These can be charming but are weedy, being prolific self-sowers. Deadheading can prevent the production of baby bladder campions. Unwanted plants can be removed entirely by pulling, hoeing, and digging; be certain to extract the taproot, and remove all seedpods from the site.

# Spergula arvensis

## CORN SPURRY

**Non-native annual, to 20 in. Flowers white, 5-petaled, to 2.5 in.; early spring–autumn. Leaves whorled, to 1.5 in. Parts edible with caution. Toxic to cattle.**

This small but troublesome European weed is found primarily in northeastern North America, along the west coast, and in the upper Midwest. It inhabits vacant lots, roadsides, cropland, orchards, gardens, sand dunes, and woodlands. The species is a troublesome agricultural weed in several countries, competing with many crops. It is a host of several crop pathogens, and it is toxic to cattle if consumed in quantity.

Corn spurry grows from a branched taproot with freely branched lateral roots. The stems are spreading to semi-erect, branching at the base of the plant. The leaves are bright green, somewhat fleshy and sticky to the touch, arranged in whorls. A plant matures from seed to bloom in 8 weeks, with mature seeds soon after. A multi-branched plant can produce 7,500 seeds, which can persist in the soil for years.

Integrated pest management strategies in agriculture have combined pre-emergent herbicides with cultural practices like increased nitrogen fertilization. The home gardener can take a tip from these strategies; in most cases, small invasions can be eradicated through pulling and hoeing, followed by mulch to prevent new germinations.

# *Spergularia rubra*

RED SANDSPURRY, RUBY SANDSPURRY

Non-native annual or biennial, to 12 in. Flowers lavender, pink, 5-petaled, to 0.25 in.; year-round. Leaves opposite, whorled, to 0.6 in. Parts medicinal.

*Spergularia rubra* is a small, delicate weed found in northeastern North America and much of the continent's western half. It likes well-drained, often sandy soil in sun and tolerates poor soil well, so it inhabits roadsides, parking lots, fields, and other disturbed sites, particularly those with sparse vegetation. This plant resembles several close relatives that are similarly diminutive and weedy.

Red sandspurry's taproot may be slender or thick and semi-woody, extending several inches into the soil. The plant sends up many slender, pubescent stems. They are typically branched at the base and more or less erect to sprawling or prostrate, creating mats. The leaves are linear and sharp-tipped, opposite or whorled, sometimes irregularly clustered in groups of 3–5, and subtended by prominent, pointed, whitish stipules.

The flowers are tiny but showy up close, with 5 long, pointed green sepals visible and alternating with the bright pink (not really red) petals. They are borne on slender pedicels in terminal clusters and singly in the leaf axils.

Pull or hoe this weed when the soil is moist, giving the taproots an extra tug, then apply a thick mulch or competitive planting.

# Stellaria graminea

## LESSER STITCHWORT, GRASS-LEAF STARWORT

Non-native perennial, to 40 in. Flowers white, 5-petaled, to 0.5 in.; midspring–midsummer. Leaves opposite, to 1.5 in. Parts edible with caution. Toxic to livestock.

This Eurasian weed has a limited distribution on this continent, occurring mostly in northeastern North America. In the PNW, it is found scattered from BC to California, in somewhat moist, disturbed habitat, including fields, pastures, roadsides, cropland, lawns, and gardens. *Stellaria graminea* can contaminate grain crops and plants grown for fodder. It is toxic if consumed in quantity, due to the presence of saponins, common to many pink family members.

Lesser stitchwort grows from a branched rhizome, with a long, branched stem that is 4-angled, weak, and slender. It is prostrate or trailing, sometimes sprawling over larger plants. The leaves are opposite and narrow, with prominent central veins. The flowers, borne in terminal, branched clusters, have petals so deeply notched that 5 petals look like 10.

*Stellaria graminea* spreads by seeds and also reproduces vegetatively when the rhizomes give rise to new plants. It is usually found in small patches. Control efforts in agriculture have employed deep cultivation and herbicides. For small invasions in home gardens, pull, hoe, or dig young plants when the soil is moist, taking care to remove the rhizomes. For more mature plants or larger stands, frequent cutting close to the ground will prevent seed production and eventually starve the rootstocks.

# *Stellaria media*

## COMMON CHICKWEED

Non-native annual, to 20 in. Flowers white, 5-petaled, to 0.3 in.; early spring–autumn. Leaves opposite, to 0.8 in. Parts edible/medicinal with caution.

Common chickweed is one of the most well-known garden weeds, common across North America and in the PNW. It could have been introduced accidentally, or may have been planted in gardens by early European settlers, as it has long been used medicinally and for food. Though the leaves are edible, the plant should be used conservatively, as it contains saponins, which are toxic. *Stellaria media* is found in semi-shady, moist locations (sometimes simply the shade of a slightly larger plant will do), in fields, vacant lots, yards, gardens, and cropland. Note: *Cerastium fontanum* subsp. *vulgare* (mouse-ear chickweed), another very common weed, is found in similar places.

Common chickweed has shallow, fibrous roots and weak, slender, trailing stems. The stems may root at the nodes, thus producing new plants vegetatively. Stems are slightly fuzzy; buds and calyces are hairy. The leaves are oval and pointed at the tips. The flowers are borne in the leaf axils and at the ends of stems. Their 5 petals are so deeply cleft that they appear doubled in number. The flowers open only on clear mornings and close after about 12 hours. The leaves also fold up at night, protecting new buds.

*Stellaria media* is an awesome reproducer; first flowers may appear within weeks of germination and produce mature seeds shortly after. Seed production is prodigious, and seeds may persist in the soil for decades. Seeds are dispersed by animals, wind, water, and agricultural activities. In addition to competing with crop plants, this weed is a problem for agriculture because it is a host to several pathogens affecting crop plants.

Farmers have used several control methods successfully, particularly cultural practices like increased nitrogen fertilization and increased crop density to outcompete this weak and dinky weed. Flame weeding has been used successfully and may be a practice workable for home gardeners when the plant invades spaces where it's safe and practical. Otherwise, pulling and hoeing are effective for most garden settings and can be followed by thick mulch to prevent new seedlings.

# Calystegia sepium

## HEDGE BINDWEED, HEDGE MORNING GLORY, DEVIL'S VINE

Native perennial vine, to 10 ft. Flowers white, 5-petaled, to 3 in.; late spring–autumn. Leaves alternate, to 4 in. Parts edible/medicinal with caution.

*Calystegia sepium* (syn. *Convolvulus sepium*) is one of several species within two or three genera that people may call "morning glory." This one is large and showy, and different authorities call it native, non-native, or both. Hedge bindweed is found across the PNW, from BC to Oregon, and in scattered areas across the continent, particularly in northeastern North America. It's also native to Europe, so there may be a mix of native and non-native populations.

The plant prefers moist to mesic conditions and often climbs trees, shrubs, fences, and other vertical objects. It is found in prairies, woodland edges, parks, riparian areas, floodplains of rivers and lakes, wetlands, cropland, fields, roadsides, vacant lots, vineyards, and orchards.

Underground, this plant has shallow, fibrous roots and fleshy white rhizomes that can be 10 ft. long. The twining, herbaceous aboveground stems are green to red and multi-branched. The leaves may be sagittate or hastate and are borne on slender petioles to 3 in. long.

The flowers are large and numerous, but each individual flower opens in the morning and lasts only one day. Flowers are mostly single in the leaf axils, borne on short, slender stalks. The corollas are trumpet-shaped with 5 fused petals, bright white or pale pink with white stripes following the divisions between the lobes. An average plant may produce 550 seeds in a season; these can remain viable in the soil for decades.

Hedge bindweed reproduces vegetatively, with frequent budding on the rhizomes, and spreads via self-seeding. Multiple strategies—withholding water, introducing fungal pathogens, solarization to kill the roots and rhizomes, applying herbicides—have been used to fight it, often with only partial success. Repeated tillage during the early weeks after germination has been effective. Authorities on weed control warn that the species may be virtually impossible to eradicate from any site where it is established; suppression is the most realistic goal in such cases and may require ongoing efforts. Gardeners facing small invasions may have some hope of winning by employing any of the aforementioned techniques, or simply pulling and digging . . . a lot. (Or moving!)

# *Convolvulus arvensis*

FIELD BINDWEED, FIELD MORNING GLORY, LESSER BINDWEED

Non-native perennial, to 7 ft. Flowers white, pink, 5-lobed, to 1 in.; spring–summer. Leaves alternate, to 2.5 in. Parts medicinal. Toxic to horses. Noxious in BC, WA, OR, CA.

Field bindweed, widespread across the PNW and all North America, is one of the most common and loathed garden weeds. It invades agricultural fields, roadsides, nurseries, gardens, yards, and other open, disturbed sites. In addition to causing grief among gardeners, it impacts crop yields, contaminates seed crops, and displaces native vegetation.

*Convolvulus arvensis* is one of several native and non-native "morning glories," the other most common one in our region being *Calystegia sepium* (hedge bindweed), which has much larger leaves and flowers than field bindweed.

What field bindweed lacks in size of aboveground parts (vs. hedge bindweed), it compensates for by the sheer immensity of its root and rhizome systems. Its vertical roots extend downward as far as 25 ft. The lateral root system may occupy the upper 2 ft. of soil, with rhizomes extending 30 in. or more from the mother plant and often rooting and sending up additional shoots, so that a single plant may spread to 10 ft. in diameter in a season. The main stem is slender, deciduous, sometimes twining, and may trail across the ground for as much as 7 ft. The leaves are petiolate and narrowly arrowhead-shaped.

The funnel-shaped flowers are white to pale pink, stalked, and borne singly in the leaf axils. A single plant may produce as many as 550 seeds, which can persist in the soil and remain viable for decades.

An established population of field bindweed can develop with startling speed and will soon be resistant to most eradication strategies, so the best strategy is vigilance and swift response. Know what the seedlings look like, and remove any you see immediately. Pull when the soil is moist, removing all roots and rhizomes, and do not compost: send to the landfill. Because of the deep and vigorous underground parts that can resprout, almost any organic method of removing an established patch has potential to stimulate new growth and may be a never-won battle. One method that is not entirely futile is "cooking" the weeds with black plastic, but this is less than ideal for the soil and may need to be done for several years. For organic gardens, be prepared for an ongoing campaign. Mulch heavily, monitor regularly.

# *Bryonia alba*

## WHITE BRYONY, NORTHWEST KUDZU

**Non-native perennial vine, to 60+ ft. Flowers greenish, white, 5- or 6-petaled, to 0.5 in.; late spring–autumn. Leaves alternate, to 6 in. Poisonous. Toxic to horses, livestock. Noxious in WA, OR.**

White bryony is an aggressive European vine limited to scattered locations in eastern Washington, Oregon, Idaho, Utah, and Montana. Grown in the past as an ornamental, it has escaped cultivation and invaded riparian zones, roadsides, and other disturbed areas. This rapidly growing vine can form dense mats, smothering and shading out other plants. It climbs shrubs, trees, buildings, and fences. It can damage trees, especially when weighed down with snow. All parts of the plant are highly toxic to humans and to animals, including livestock that may graze it. It is dispersed by songbirds, which are immune to the toxicity.

White bryony grows from a yellowish, turnip-like tuberous root that can reach 18 in. long. A plant may have one to several thick, non-woody stems that can grow as much as 6 in. in a day. The leaves are about half as wide as long, palmate or hastate and 3- to 5-lobed; they are stalked, dotted with white glands, and coarsely toothed along the margins. Long, curling tendrils aid the vine in climbing. The flowers are borne in axillary clusters. Male and female flowers are separate but on the same plant, the male flowers larger. Flowers are followed by blue-black berries to 0.3 in. in diameter, containing up to 6 seeds each. When crushed, they emit a foul odor. They are particularly toxic, and ingestion of less than 40 berries is sufficient to kill an adult human.

The best option for control is to pull or dig it up when possible, or to cut the roots several inches below the soil surface, removing the crown. Wear protective clothing, as the plant can cause skin irritation. Eradication may require frequent and repeated efforts to intercept resprouting and new seedlings. Even with herbicide, repeated applications will be required. Take care to remove from the site any berries that have formed, monitor the area for new seedlings, and mulch.

# Pteridium aquilinum

## BRACKEN FERN

Native perennial, to 6 ft. No flowers. Leaves opposite. Parts edible/medicinal with caution. Toxic to horses, cattle, pigs, sheep, chickens.

This large deciduous fern is native to most of North America and common across the PNW, where it is seen in woodlands and in open sites on moist to somewhat dry ground. Though native, it is widely considered weedy and often aggressive in its conquest of territory. Bracken fern is a very common volunteer in PNW gardens and a problematic weed for agriculture, particularly for those who keep livestock, because the plants are toxic and carcinogenic. Although some people eat the young fiddleheads, the fern is also carcinogenic for humans; even its spores have been found to be carcinogenic.

The sometimes very tall, branched fronds of bracken fern arise singly from deep underground rhizomes. The blades are triangular, often held horizontally, and borne opposite each other along a central stalk (stipe). Spores are shed summer to fall by the sori, which appear as narrow bands on the margins of the undersides of the leaf segments.

Efforts to control invasions of bracken in agriculture have employed a number of strategies. Burning was ineffective because of the persistence of the roots and rhizomes. Digging of mature plants is labor-intensive because of the deep roots. Herbicides have not been entirely successful and cannot always be used. Crushing and trampling under the hooves of animals has been successful but is not always practicable. The most useful method has been cutting, which, if done repeatedly for several years, eventually exhausts the plant.

# Dipsacus fullonum

## FULLER'S TEASEL, COMMON TEASEL

Non-native biennial or perennial, to 7 ft. Flowers blue, violet, heads to 4 in.; summer. Leaves basal to 12 in., cauline opposite. Parts medicinal. Noxious in BC, WA.

*Dipsacus fullonum* (syn. *D. sylvestris*) was introduced as an agricultural product in the 1700s, when the dried flowerheads were used for carding in the wool textile industry. The seeds are much liked by birds, which has probably contributed to the plant's invasive habits: fuller's teasel forms large stands where conditions are favorable. The plant is grown in gardens as an ornamental or to attract birds, and it adds drama to dried flower arrangements. This widespread weed is problematic due to its invasion of wild areas and agricultural fields. The white-flowered *D. laciniatus* is also invasive.

With its prickly leaves, stems, and bracts and its spiny inflorescence, Fuller's teasel is often mistaken for a thistle but is not related to the true thistles. The plant starts life with a basal rosette of leaves in its first year, then a flowering stem with shorter, sessile leaves in the second year. The simple leaves bear a distinctive line of prickles along the underside midvein. Atop the tall plant, an egg-shaped inflorescence bears up to 1,500 tiny florets. They open in spiraling lines up and down the inflorescence, beginning at the middle, each floret lasting only a day and producing a single seed after pollination.

Small populations can be eradicated easily by digging and pulling, preferably before seed set. Larger problem areas are sometimes treated with herbicides. When a seed bank has been produced, several years may be required to eliminate the plants.

# Equisetum arvense
## FIELD HORSETAIL, COMMON HORSETAIL

Native perennial, to 20 in. No flowers. Fertile stems white, pink, tan, to 12 in.; sterile stems green, to 20 in. Parts edible/medicinal with caution. Toxic to horses, cattle, sheep, chickens.

*Equisetum* species are found throughout most of North America, as well as on most other northern hemisphere continents. Though native everywhere, the horsetails are so ubiquitous and so aggressive that they are widely treated as weeds. They are nearly impossible to eliminate from a site once established and are toxic to livestock, which may consume them when the plants are inadvertently baled with hay. They are also a troublesome weed of many economically important crops. Field horsetail is one of at least a dozen *Equisetum* species found in the PNW. It is widely distributed on both sides of the Cascades, favoring moist, sandy places, though it can also tolerate moderate dryness. It's a common sight on riverbanks, moist woodland edges, wetlands, and roadsides, as well as in drainage ditches, fields, gardens, and yards.

*Equisetum arvense* grows from a network of rhizomes, spreading laterally and vertically. These can go as deep as 20 ft. into the soil, contributing to the plant's tolerance of drought and its great resistance to eradication attempts, including tillage and herbicides. New plants can develop from buds on the rhizomes. Underground tubers also develop, serving both as storage organs and potential propagules for new plants.

In spring, the cylindrical stems arise, ridged and rough to the touch thanks to their high silicate content. The fertile, spore-bearing stems appear first; these are non-photosynthetic and unbranched. They may be off-white to pink or tan and are topped by brown cone-shaped structures that produce the spores that, for ferns, are analogous to seeds in the flowering plants.

After shedding spores, the fertile stems will wither and are replaced by the sterile, photosynthetic ones. These are green, hollow, and divided into as many as 20 segments, with short, slender, green branches in whorls at segment joints. The sterile stems persist until frost.

Once field horsetail is established on a site, eradication is widely considered to be impossible; the best that can be hoped is to keep it at bay and prevent it from crowding out other plants. The rhizomes are too deep to dig out; tillage has little effect and may actually increase populations. *Equisetum arvense* is resistant to many herbicides, and even the more effective herbicides may only slow it down, with repeat applications. Small patches may be discouraged, though probably not vanquished, by persistent pulling. Or you could move.

# Equisetum telmateia

## GIANT HORSETAIL

Native perennial, to 9 ft. No flowers. Fertile stems yellow, tan, to 2 ft.; sterile stems green, to 9 ft. Parts edible with caution. Toxic to horses, cattle, chickens.

Giant horsetail is the largest of the *Equisetum* species occurring in the PNW. This one has a limited distribution, found coastally from BC to California, in Idaho, and in a disjunct region in Michigan. It is also native to parts of Europe, Asia, and Africa. The plant lends an almost prehistoric look to the shady, moist, open woods where it grows, often in large colonies formed by rhizomatous spread.

The fertile stems appear in early spring, cylindrical and pale yellow, with several brown bands of scale-like leaves and a terminal brown cone-shaped structure to 3 in. long, which produces the spores. The fertile stems wither after shedding their spores, and the sterile stems rise up. These are photosynthetic, green, and much taller than the fertile stems, ringed with whorls of thin green branches. In addition to releasing spores that can start new plants, giant horsetail spreads laterally through the soil via rhizomes, generating more plants.

As with *Equisetum arvense* and other species in the genus, *E. telmateia* is very difficult to control and may be impossible to eradicate. Pulling or digging plants as soon as they poke up through the soil in early spring will give the best hope of at least slowing them down. Herbicides may help at the earliest stages. Removing fertile stems before they can produce spores is ideal, though vegetative spread will continue.

# Euphorbia cyparissias

## CYPRESS SPURGE

Non-native perennial, to 12 in. Flowers yellow-green, to 0.13 in.; late spring–midsummer. Leaves alternate, opposite, whorled, to 1 in. Poisonous. Toxic to cats, dogs, horses, cattle, sheep, chickens. Noxious in BC.

Cypress surge has been a garden plant in North America since the late 1800s and is widely naturalized over much of the continent. It's listed as a noxious weed in several states, but it is still available in many nurseries. As a garden escape, it competes with native flora. Like other *Euphorbia* species, the plant is toxic to grazers and can cause dermatological reactions for gardeners.

*Euphorbia cyparissias* spreads via rhizomes and self-seeding. Fans of the species praise its speed in forming a tidy, thick, low groundcover over large areas, particularly in full sun and regardless of poor soil. Ex-fans speak of thousands of seedlings pulled out over decades.

The common and species names refer to the cypress-needle-like leaves, fleshy, linear, and often blue-green. Lower leaves are alternate; those higher on the stem are whorled to opposite. Many gardeners encounter cypress spurge as 'Fens Ruby', a cultivar with a reddish tinge as new leaves emerge in spring and again at the end of the growing season. Flowers are bright yellow; foliage is bluish. Some say 'Fens Ruby' is less aggressive than the species; others say it's aggressive enough.

Cypress spurge control, best begun before a large area has been invaded, may require persistent digging, pulling (wear gloves!), and heavy mulching. Larger infestations can be daunting and may call for herbicide.

# Euphorbia maculata

## SPOTTED SPURGE, SANDMAT, MILK SPURGE

Non-native annual, to 16 in. Flowers pink, white, to 0.06 in.; summer–autumn. Leaves opposite, to 0.7 in. Poisonous. Toxic to horses, cattle, sheep, chickens.

*Euphorbia maculata* (syn. *Chamaesyce maculata*, *E. supina*) is found throughout North America and considered native to the eastern US. It is a widespread annual weed of sunny ground, on varied but often sandy or dry soils, invading roadsides, waste places, and driveways.

The tiny leaves and long, trailing, frequently branching, prostrate stems can be mistaken for a few other *Euphorbia* species, including *E. glyptosperma*, which is native to much of North America, including the PNW, and California natives *E. prostrata* and *E. serpens*. Spotted spurge is distinctive compared to these and other *Euphorbia* species for the dark leaf blotches that inspired its common and species names (*maculata* means "spotted"). The tiny flowers are pink or white, in small clusters. Like others in the genus, this plant exudes a toxic milky sap that can cause dermatological reactions in sensitive individuals.

Control spotted spurge by pulling (wear gloves!) or scraping, and mulching. It's easy enough to remove but if given a head start, it can cover a lot of ground quickly.

# *Euphorbia myrsinites*

MYRTLE SPURGE, BLUE SPURGE, DONKEYTAIL SPURGE

Non-native biennial or perennial, to 12 in. Flowers yellow-green, to 0.04 in.; late spring–early summer. Leaves whorled, to 0.75 in. Poisonous. Toxic to horses, cattle, sheep, chickens. Noxious in WA, OR, CA.

Myrtle spurge is an attractive ornamental that has become an invasive pest in the PNW. An aggressive groundcover in gardens, it has escaped in many western states and become a weed of fields, farmlands, roadsides, and waste places. In the PNW, it is invasive as a garden escape mostly east of the Cascades; gardeners with wetter gardens have little trouble with it.

*Euphorbia myrsinites* is a mostly herbaceous plant growing from a somewhat woody base, remaining low but spreading 18 in. horizontally with trailing stems. The succulent gray-blue leaves are arranged in tightly spiraling whorls (thus "donkeytail"). The plant produces clusters of yellow-green flowers inside bright yellow bracts. Myrtle spurge owes its awesome reproductive prowess to its explosive seed dehiscence, a talent it shares with other plants in the genus: as seed capsules ripen and split, the small seeds can shoot as far as 15 ft. from the mother plant—and remain viable in the soil for several years. Broken-off bits of stem can also root and make new plants.

Many gardeners who at first appreciated the aesthetic, uniqueness, and drought tolerance of this plant were ultimately disenchanted by its rapid conquest of ground. Eradication is only a matter of pulling (wear gloves!) or digging, but persistence is required, and some embittered gardeners report battling it for years. Once it's cleared from an area, monitor for new seedlings and mulch to prevent germination of the many seeds left behind.

# *Euphorbia oblongata*

## BALKAN SPURGE, EGG-LEAF SPURGE

---

**Non-native annual, to 3 ft. Flowers yellow, tiny; late spring–midsummer. Leaves alternate, to 2.6 in. Poisonous. Toxic to horses, cattle, sheep, chickens. Noxious in BC, WA, OR, CA.**

---

*Euphorbia oblongata* is a European species that has escaped cultivation and become an increasingly troublesome weed in the PNW, where it appears in scattered sites from southwestern BC to California. It can be found in a wide range of habitats both moist and dry, invading meadows, riparian areas, woodlands, roadsides, and other disturbed ground. The species is toxic and displaces native vegetation and other desirable plants.

Growing from a large, woody, branched taproot, as many as 20 upright stems may be produced from a single crown. These are covered in fine white hairs, branched at the tips. The oval leaves are smooth and hairless, with distinct midveins and finely dentate margins. The tiny flowers are borne in terminal clusters surrounded by brilliant yellow to yellow-green bracts. These are followed by waxy, 3-lobed seedpods that expel their seeds explosively when ripe. In addition to this energetic self-seeding, the plant reproduces vegetatively by budding from the root crown.

The best defense against Balkan spurge is very early detection. Mowing will not work, as plants will resprout from crowns and taproots. Pull young seedlings, wearing gloves to protect against the toxic sap; dig up rooted plants, taking care to remove all taproots. Mulch the area well, and monitor.

# *Euphorbia peplus*
## PETTY SPURGE, CANCER WEED

Non-native annual, to 8 in. Flowers green, to 0.03 in.; spring–summer. Lower leaves alternate, upper opposite, to 1 in. Poisonous. Toxic to horses, cattle, sheep, chickens.

This small species, native to Africa and Eurasia, is naturalized over much of the world, including North America. It is very common to gardens in the PNW, particularly on the cool, rainy west side. Plant a garden and this delicate, light-rooted weed will appear, seemingly out of the ether, filling in any shady, moist niches. The common name "cancer weed" refers to its use in treating skin disorders and potentially some forms of skin cancer.

*Euphorbia peplus* is soft-textured and light green, the flowers tiny and light green, in 3-pointed umbels.

It's not unattractive and is unlikely to overwhelm or compete much with other plants. But it is toxic to any grazing animals, and it blooms and sets seed prolifically throughout the growing season. Like any weed, if given an inch, it could quickly become an annoyance.

Fortunately, petty spurge is easy to pull or scrape away. Pulling should be approached with caution, however, as its milky sap is toxic and can cause dermatitis.

# *Euphorbia virgata*

## LEAFY SPURGE, WOLF'S MILK

Non-native perennial, to 3 ft. Flowers yellow-green, to 0.15 in.; late spring–midsummer. Leaves alternate, to 3 in. Poisonous. Toxic to horses, cattle. Noxious in BC, WA, CA.

*Euphorbia virgata* is a Eurasian weed that is listed as noxious in several North American jurisdictions, due to its high invasiveness and toxicity to cattle, horses, and humans. It's found primarily on dry sites, and in the PNW it prefers the east side, where it invades roadsides, prairies, cropland, pastures, and rangeland. It displaces better forage and causes economic losses due to impacts on cattle, including fatalities. In older references, this species may be misidentified as the similar-looking *E. esula*.

Leafy spurge grows from a taproot that can reach a formidable depth of 15 ft. into the soil, and its woody, rhizomatous root system can extend to a diameter of 20 ft. The plant can form dense colonies by vegetative spread. Multiple erect stems rise from a tough root crown. The smooth, blue-green leaves are sessile and oblong to linear. Those lower on the stem are greatly reduced; those at the top are broader and more ovate. All stems and leaves exude a toxic milky latex sap when crushed or broken.

The stems are branched only toward the top, where they bear umbellate clusters of tiny cup-like flowers, each cluster subtended by showy yellow bracts. The flowers are followed by seed capsules that expel seeds explosively when ripe. A single plant may produce 200 seeds.

Wear gloves and protective clothing for coping with this species, as its sap can cause significant dermatologic reactions. For limited invasions, pull or dig seedlings before they go deep, and mulch heavily.

Unfortunately, most mechanical means (burning, tillage, etc.) for controlling larger patches can stimulate vegetative growth. Herbicide is often used. Competitive planting and several biocontrols—insects attacking different parts of this plant—have proven successful. Goats and sheep are not harmed by grazing leafy spurge, and grazing can be helpful in suppressing it.

# Galega officinalis
## GOATSRUE, PROFESSOR-WEED

Non-native perennial, to 6 ft. Flowers purple, pink, white, 5-lobed, to 0.5 in.; midsummer. Leaves alternate, to 8.5 in., leaflets to 2 in. Parts edible/medicinal. Toxic to horses, sheep. Noxious in BC, WA, OR, CA.

*Galega officinalis* hails from Eurasia and is recently introduced in North America. In addition to the PNW, it is present in a handful of northeastern states and in Utah, Colorado, and Nebraska. It is already a listed noxious weed in several jurisdictions because of concerns over its rapid and aggressive takeover in landscapes. The species invades roadsides, irrigated farmland, pastures, and wetlands. It can form extensive stands that displace native flora and impact wildlife habitat. It is also very toxic to grazers.

Goatsrue looks very similar to vetches, which clamber by means of tendrils, but goatsrue stands erect, without tendrils. With a deep taproot and thick root crown, a single plant can send up as many as 20 hollow, branched stems. The leaves are alternate and odd-pinnately compound, having a terminal leaflet and 6–10 pairs of opposite leaflets. The tip of each leaflet narrows to a fine hair-like point.

The narrowly bell-shaped flowers are borne in erect, terminal and axillary racemes to 4 in. long, with up to 50 flowers each. They are followed by inch-long pods carrying about 8 seeds each; a single plant may produce as many as 15,000 seeds in a year. Goatsrue spreads only by seed, but with such copious seed output and seeds that persist in the soil for several years, it can establish a persistent seed bank.

Control of large established populations is challenging, requiring multiple strategies over a few years, including cultivation and herbicides. Cutting and mowing have proven ineffective, as the plant can

bloom and set seed even when cut very low. For small invasions, clipping off and disposing of seedpods can be a temporary fix to prevent seed production. Young plants can be pulled or hoed and dug out; take care to remove the taproots. As with any plant whose reproduction depends upon copious self-seeding, follow with mulch and monitoring.

# *Lathyrus latifolius*

## PERENNIAL SWEET-PEA, EVERLASTING PEA

**Non-native perennial, to 6 ft. Flowers pink, red, white, 5-lobed, to 1 in.; spring–summer. Leaves alternate, to 6 in., leaflets to 3 in. Poisonous. Toxic to cats, dogs, horses, cattle, pigs, sheep. Noxious in OR.**

This very widespread weed can be seen on roadsides, fields, and woodland edges throughout North America. It is on the monitor list in Washington, where it has been found invading natural areas. It can form broad thickets, competing with native vegetation. It is toxic to cattle and particularly to horses, and the seeds can be toxic to humans if consumed in large amounts. The plant is still used as an ornamental and is widely available in seed packets. The flowers are pretty but are not "sweet" (like those of *Lathyrus odoratus*, a favorite, fragrant garden annual).

The stems of perennial sweet-pea are long, with broad wings, like longitudinal flaps. They scramble over the ground and other vegetation, or climb with the help of strong tendrils. The leaves are pinnately compound, each with 2 lanceolate to elliptic leaflets and a 3-parted tendril between them. The plants bear long-stalked axillary racemes of up to 15 flowers each. The flowers are typically pea-like, with bilateral symmetry. They are followed by narrow pods to 4 in. long, holding up to 15 seeds each. The plant self-seeds, but its primary means of expanding its territory is rhizomatous spread.

Pull or grub out small seedlings with a hoe. More mature plants can be deep-rooted and may require some arduous and repeated digging to remove the roots and rhizomes.

# *Lotus corniculatus*
## BIRD'S-FOOT TREFOIL, BIRDFOOT DEERVETCH

Non-native perennial, to 2 ft. Flowers yellow, 5-petaled, to 0.6 in.; summer. Leaves alternate, leaflets to 0.75 in. Poisonous. Toxic to cattle, sheep.

Bird's-foot trefoil was introduced to North America for cattle forage and erosion control. It has become very widespread throughout most of the US and Canada, a common weed in pastures, prairies, lawns, and roadsides.

Growing from a taproot, the plant stays low, with sprawling, trailing, multi-branched stems that can root at the nodes. The leaves are compound, composed of 3 upper leaflets that resemble clover, with 2 additional lower leaflets. The bright yellow flowers, often with touches of red, are borne in small, round, umbel-like clusters of 3–12. These are followed by dark-colored, flat and narrow pods to 1.5 in. long, each bearing about 20–25 seeds. The plant spreads aggressively by seeds, rhizomes, and stolons, forming dense mats that compete with native or intentionally planted vegetation.

For an established patch of *Lotus corniculatus*, be prepared to repeat control measures annually for some time. Dig up plants with a digging fork, removing all roots. Plants may be cut at the root collar repeatedly, followed by heavy mulching. Bag all plant parts and remove from the site. Keep larger patches very closely mowed for several years. Burning is counter-productive, as it facilitates seed germination.

# *Medicago lupulina*

## BLACK MEDIC, HOP CLOVER

Non-native annual or perennial, to 30 in. Flowers yellow, to 0.1 in.; midspring–autumn. Leaves trifoliate, to 0.75 in. Parts edible/medicinal.

*Medicago lupulina* is found throughout North America, including the PNW, in a variety of sometimes moist but often dry habitats, including roadsides, vacant lots, fields, and lawns. It can be hard to distinguish from *Trifolium dubium*, another small weed. Both plants start out small and largely prostrate, but *M. lupulina* grows to three times the height of the *Trifolium* and is multi-branched, remaining somewhat sprawling, or becoming semi-erect. Its leaves and stems are downy, and the leaflets have tiny points at the tips (*T. dubium* leaflets do not have points).

Black medic bears spherical, tight clusters of small bright yellow flowers. These are followed by the distinctive twisted, black pods that give the species its most-used common name. Each contains a single seed.

Though lightly taprooted, *Medicago lupulina* is easy to pull or scrape away. It spreads via prolific self-seeding, and seeds remain viable for years, so control is best applied before the plants bloom. After an area has been cleared, a heavy mulch may help to suppress germination of remaining seeds.

# Medicago sativa

## ALFALFA

Non-native perennial, to 3 ft. Flowers blue, violet, pea-like, to 0.4 in.; spring–summer. Leaves trifoliate, leaflets to 0.5 in. Some portions edible or medicinal with caution. Toxic to horses, cattle, sheep, chickens.

Alfalfa has been used as forage worldwide since antiquity. It was introduced to eastern North America in the 1700s and has been important to agriculture here ever since. In the US, alfalfa has been grown predominantly in northern and western regions, and the leading producers are California, Idaho, and Montana. The species is very deep-rooted and drought tolerant and has been useful in soil stabilization and nitrogen fixation. In addition to livestock feed, sprouted raw alfalfa seeds are eaten by humans, but unsprouted raw seeds are toxic to primates, including humans.

Alfalfa is a fine animal feed when harvested, preserved, and fed in appropriate amounts. Fresh legume forage (alfalfa, red and white clovers mostly) is notorious for causing bloat in ruminants, even to the point of threatening life in some cases.

*Medicago sativa* can escape from cultivation and be invasive in moist meadows and disturbed sites at mid-elevations. It is a fairly long-lived perennial, herbaceous except for a woody crown, with a stout taproot that can extend several yards into the soil. The inflorescence is a cluster of 5–50 small flowers, usually purple (sometimes violet, green, or yellowish). The leathery pods are crescent-shaped to spiraling and contain 6–8 seeds each.

Eradication of small invasions is relatively easy by pulling and digging when the soil is moist. Care must be taken to destroy the crown, which can resprout. Larger infestations may require tilling to break up crowns and bring roots to the surface, combined with herbicide application.

271

# Melilotus albus

## WHITE SWEET-CLOVER

Non-native annual, biennial, or perennial, to 9 ft. Flowers white, to 0.33 in.; early summer–autumn. Leaves alternate, trifoliate, to 1 in. Parts edible/medicinal with caution. Toxic to horses, cattle, sheep.

Both *Melilotus albus* (syn. *Melilotus alba*) and *M. officinalis* are tall, erect, freely branched, taprooted plants with attractive and very sweet-smelling flowers and foliage. Each plant bears multiple racemes, each with as many as 30–70 flowers. Some botanists have classified them as two forms of the same species.

Apart from flower color, white and yellow sweet-clovers differ in a few ways. White sweet-clover is generally taller than its yellow cousin and blooms a few weeks later. Its flower racemes are longer (8–10 in.) than those of *Melilotus officinalis* (6 in. long). The leaflets of white sweet-clover are narrower, often half as wide as those of yellow sweet-clover.

In *Melilotus*, flowers are followed by oblong "pea-pods," each about 0.13 in. long and typically containing a single seed. Seed production is large, with an average of about 5,000 seeds per plant. The result with an established population is a large seed bank in which thousands of seeds can remain viable for decades.

Plants are easily uprooted by pulling or digging, but with such prolific seed production, success will be better if they are removed before seed set.

# Melilotus officinalis

## YELLOW SWEET-CLOVER

Non-native annual, biennial, or perennial, to 6 ft. Flowers yellow, to 0.2 in.; summer. Leaves alternate, trifoliate, to 0.75 in. Parts edible/medicinal with caution. Toxic to horses, cattle, sheep.

*Melilotus officinalis* and *M. albus* are both tall, slender plants with long spikes of very fragrant flowers. They are both Eurasian weeds present in North America since the 1600s and now widespread throughout the continent. Both species can be found on disturbed sites, in riparian zones, near water in arid regions, on coastal dunes, and in grasslands, particularly at more northern latitudes in North America.

By the early 1900s, *Melilotus* was planted for honey production and for reclamation of agriculturally depleted soils. In the mid to late 1900s, even as concerns about invasiveness and other problems grew, *Melilotus* was planted as forage for livestock and intermittently for roadside bank stabilization and revegetation. Both white and yellow sweet-clover can be invasive and potentially competitive with native flora, as well as being an agricultural pest and potential threat to livestock. *Melilotus* is grazed by livestock and wildlife, but when damaged or moldy, the coumarin content in the plant is broken down into a toxic compound similar to rodenticide, potentially causing serious damage if grazed in quantity.

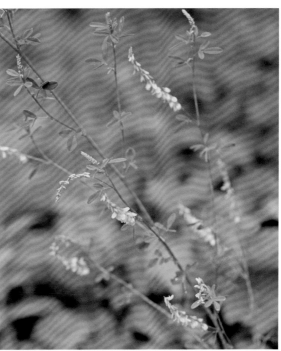

# *Onobrychis viciifolia*

## SAINFOIN, HOLY-CLOVER

Non-native perennial, to 30 in. Flowers pink, red, to 0.5 in.; early–midsummer. Leaves alternate, pinnate, leaflets to 0.8 in. Unpalatable.

Sainfoin, a European plant sometimes grown for livestock feed, has escaped cultivation and is found on roadsides, fields, and other disturbed sites across much of the western and midwestern US and southern Canada, as well as in Alaska.

Sainfoin grows from a branched taproot that can be as deep as 6 ft. at maturity and sends up stout, erect, hollow stems from a branched root crown. The leaves are odd-pinnate, with typically up to 17 but sometimes as many as 27 leaflets; these are elliptic to oblanceolate and apiculate. The axillary and terminal spike-like racemes on long peduncles bloom with up to 50 flowers each. The showy flowers are pea-like, with prominent deep reddish-magenta lines running vertically up the reflexed banners (upper petals). Flowers are followed by fuzzy oval pods to 0.3 in. long, each holding a single seed.

For small invasions of sainfoin, pull, hoe, or dig when the soil is moist. Taproots on mature plants may not be possible to fully extract mechanically or manually without considerable labor and disturbance to the soil. Follow with mulch and monitor.

# *Securigera varia*

## PURPLE CROWN VETCH

Non-native perennial vine, to 6 ft. Flowers purple, violet, pink, to 0.5 in.; summer. Leaves alternate, to 5 in., leaflets to 0.75 in. Poisonous. Toxic to horses, pigs, chickens.

*Securigera varia* (syn. *Coronilla varia*), an aggressive European relative of clovers, is found across North America, invading roadsides, riparian zones, woodland edges, fields, and gardens. Purple crown vetch has only been here since the 1950s but has gained noxious or invasive status in several states. It has been widely planted as a landscape ornamental and for erosion control, soil improvement, fodder, and forage. With aggressive rhizomatous spread, a single plant can cover 300 square ft. in a few years, forming dense thickets that crowd out natives and alter local ecosystems.

Rising from highly branched rhizomes as long as 9 ft., a single plant may have many branched, ascending stems that often sprawl and lean on other plants for support. The pinnately compound leaves are mostly sessile, with up to 25 pairs of leaflets, and a terminal leaflet with no tendril. Showy flower clusters bloom on stalks to 6 in. long, rising from the upper leaf axils. Each cluster is round and umbel-like, to 1 in. across, bearing up to 25 pea-like flowers. The flowers are fragrant and bilaterally symmetric. Flowers are followed by clusters of pods in crown-like or hand-like arrays. Each pod is segmented, pointed, to 2 in. long, and may contain up to 12 seeds.

Large, persistent invasions of purple crown vetch are very difficult to eradicate, and herbicides are often used. Effective manual control requires pulling or digging out the entire plant with as much of the rhizome network as possible. Remove all stems and rhizomes from the site, and monitor, as seeds in the soil may remain viable for several years.

# Sphaerophysa salsula

## ALKALI SWAINSONPEA, RED BLADDER-VETCH

**Non-native perennial, to 3 ft. Flowers red-purple, 5-lobed, to 1 in.; early–midsummer. Leaves alternate, pinnate, to 4 in., leaflets to 0.8 in. Noxious in WA, OR, CA.**

This Asian plant has been present in the PNW at least since the 1930s and is now found in nearly all western US states, plus Saskatchewan. It inhabits roadsides, fence lines, farm fields, and pastures. It is a problem in agriculture because it is a frequent contaminant in clover and alfalfa seed, hard to separate because of similar size and shape.

From deep and vigorous woody rhizomes and taproot, alkali swainsonpea sends up one to several stems, branching from the base and creeping or spreading. The pinnately arranged leaflets are oval or oblong to elliptic and covered with silvery hairs. The plant bears loose axillary racemes of up to 12 flowers each. Flowers are pea-like, with bell-shaped, 5-lobed calyces. They are followed by translucent, inflated, membranous pods to 1 in. long and 0.4 in. across, each bearing many seeds.

Due to its long creeping rhizomes, alkali swainsonpea is hard to eradicate. Mowing and burning may delay seed production but will not kill the plant, and mowing can disperse rhizome fragments that may resprout. Large invasions are typically handled with herbicides. Small invasions in home gardens can be combatted with pulling and digging. Remove as much of the roots and rhizomes as possible, and then monitor for seedlings and resprouting of rhizome fragments.

# Trifolium arvense

## RABBITFOOT CLOVER

**Non-native annual, to 16 in. Flowers pink, white, heads to 1.5 in.; midspring–midsummer. Leaves alternate, trifoliate, leaflets to 0.75 in.**

Rabbitfoot clover is a Eurasian weed that often colonizes disturbed, sandy, or otherwise barren ground. It is found over much of southern Canada and the eastern US and along the west coast from BC to California, eastward through Idaho, Montana, and North Dakota.

The plant sends up one to several, often multi-branched stems, erect to ascending. They are initially densely pubescent but may become hairless with age. The leaves are trifoliate, sparsely hairy on top and densely hairy below, with fine ciliate hairs along the margins and short, fuzzy stalks. The leaflets are linear to lanceolate, tapered at the base and blunt or rounded at the apex. The flowers are borne in round to cylindrical, axillary and terminal heads to 1.5 in. long and 0.5 in. across, on short stalks. The minute florets are white to pale pink and partially hidden by the feathery pink/gray calyces. The fuzzy calyces are persistent, remaining on the plant and enclosing the tiny developing seedpods.

These plants are likely what you're seeing on the sides of highways, in swaths of delicate gray and pink fuzz. We find them more attractive than bare grit and dead grass on roadsides, but they could become a nuisance if they decided to take over a rock garden. Pull and hoe, mulch and replant.

FORBS/HERBS AND VINES

# Trifolium campestre

## HOP CLOVER, FIELD CLOVER

**Non-native annual, to 12 in. Flowers yellow, heads to 0.5 in.; midspring–summer. Leaves alternate, trifoliate, leaflets to 0.75 in. Parts edible.**

Hop clover is a small European annual found over much of North America. It is sometimes grown for forage and elsewhere inhabits fields, pastures, trail edges, and other disturbed sites.

Growing from a taproot, the plant typically produces several pubescent or hairless, procumbent to ascending, often sprawling, multi-branched stems. The leaves are trifoliate with long petioles, their leaflets oblong to oval or oblanceolate and finely serrated along the upper two-thirds of their length. The petiole of the terminal leaflet is at least twice as long as those of the lateral leaflets. Spherical flowerheads are borne singly on long axillary peduncles. The petals are persistent after bloom, turning from their bright lemon-yellow to a faded whitish or light brown. Hop clover spreads by seed, often forming colonies.

This species can be confused with a few yellow-flowered relatives. *Trifolium dubium* looks similar, but its middle leaflet petiole is no longer than the lateral petioles. *Medicago lupulina* is very similar-looking, but it has distinctive coiled, black seedheads, and the tips of its leaflets end in a pin-like point.

Pull and hoe hop clover before it gets away from you. It's easy to remove before there are hundreds. Mulch and replant.

# *Trifolium dubium*

## LESSER TREFOIL, SMALL HOP CLOVER

Non-native annual or perennial, to 10 in. Flowers yellow, to 0.1 in.; summer. Leaves trifoliate, to 0.75 in. Parts edible with caution.

*Trifolium dubium* is introduced widely in much of North America, with the exception of central Canada. In the PNW, it's less widespread than its lookalike *Medicago lupulina* and is found mostly west of the Cascades.

Shorter than the *Medicago*, this little weed also differs in being nearly hairless, the stems often reddish. Its flowers are very similar, but they are somewhat paler yellow, with fewer flowers per cluster. The flowers are followed by a straight pale pod (vs. the curved black pod of *Medicago lupulina*).

Lesser trefoil is a minor nuisance that is easy to remove by scraping or hoeing, but prolific self-sowing can make for repeated emergence. Heavy mulch should suppress future outbreaks.

# Trifolium pratense

## RED CLOVER

---

Non-native perennial, to 3 ft. Flowers red, pink, heads to 1.5 in.; midspring–midsummer. Leaves alternate, trifoliate, leaflets to 2.5 in. Parts edible/medicinal with caution. Toxic to horses, cattle, sheep.

---

This European species is often planted as a forage crop. It has escaped cultivation and is common across most of North America, invading roadsides, lawns, gardens, meadows, and clearcuts. It can form dense stands, altering soil chemistry due to nitrogen fixation and competing with native seedlings. In hot humid weather, it can become infested with a fungus that is toxic to horses grazing the plants.

Red clover is a short-lived perennial that grows from a short taproot and shallow fibrous roots. The plant typically sends up several stems, with alternate, palmately trifoliate leaves, the lower ones stalked. Leaves and stems are covered with soft hairs. The leaflets are elliptic to oval, with minutely serrated margins. Every leaflet bears a light-colored, V-shaped pattern. The terminal, short-stalked to sessile flowerheads are spherical to conical in shape, red or pink to purple, each subtended by a pair of leaves. The flowers are followed by oval pods, each containing 2 seeds. A plant may produce as many as 1,000 seeds in a season.

When *Trifolium pratense* is a pest in lawns, the best recourse is to encourage the grass to grow taller, shading out the clover. Small invasions can be manually extracted by pulling or digging out with a fork; take care to remove the roots. Larger patches can be suppressed by cutting to the ground and burying with a few inches of woody mulch.

# *Trifolium repens*

## WHITE CLOVER, DUTCH CLOVER, WHITE LAWN CLOVER

**Non-native perennial, to 2 ft. Flowers white, heads to 0.5 in.; midspring–autumn. Leaves alternate, trifoliate, leaflets to 0.75 in. Parts edible/medicinal with caution. Toxic to horses, cattle, sheep.**

White clover, a European species grown as a forage crop in North America at least since the 1700s, is now found across most of the continent. With prolific self-seeding as well as vegetative spread, it can form colonies that quickly dominate disturbed sites, impeding establishment of native seedlings. It's a common weed of roadsides, meadows, lawns, vacant lots, woodland trails, and pastures.

White clover grows from a shallow, branching taproot and sends out creeping stolons that root at the nodes. The stems are mostly hairless, sometimes erect but more often decumbent. The alternate, palmately trifoliate leaves are borne on vertical petioles to 8 in. long. Leaflets are oval to obcordate, with minutely serrated margins. As in many clovers, the leaflets often bear whitish chevron markings, but these may be irregular or missing. The spherical flowerheads are held above the foliage on long, vertical stalks. The flowers are white to cream, aging to dingy pale pink.

For small invasions, pull or dig out each plant along with its taproot and stolons. The large numbers of tiny seeds will be your main problem; mulch and competitive plantings will suppress the next white clover generation.

# Trifolium subterraneum

## BURROWING CLOVER, SUBTERRANEAN CLOVER

Non-native annual, to 15 in. Flowers white, in heads; midspring–early summer. Leaves alternate, trifoliate, leaflets to 0.5 in. Parts edible. Toxic to cattle, sheep.

This small European clover is found along the west coast from BC to California, as well as in the Southeast. Grown agriculturally, it escapes cultivation and invades lawns, farm fields, and pastures. It can be a significant pest, competing with native vegetation in some areas.

Growing from a taproot and unusually robust (for a clover) fibrous roots, it sends out non-rooting runners as long as 3 ft. The trifoliate leaves are borne on petioles longer than the blades. Leaflets are obovate to obcordate. The small white flowers, sometimes veined in pink, are borne beneath the foliage, so may be inconspicuous. The inflorescence is a head of 3–4 (sometimes as many as 7) florets. After pollination, the burr-like seedhead is pushed down into the soil by elongation of the peduncle.

Pull, hoe, or dig, taking care to remove roots and seedheads.

# Vicia hirsuta

## HAIRY VETCH

Non-native annual vine, to 28 in. Flowers blue, white, 5-lobed, to 0.15 in.; midspring–early summer. Leaves alternate, pinnate, leaflets to 0.75 in. Parts edible. Toxic to horses, chickens.

*Vicia hirsuta* is a European weed found along North America's east coast, the west coast from BC to California, the southern coast from Texas to Florida, and across eastern Canada and much of the northeastern US. It typically inhabits moist soil on roadsides, meadows, woodland edges, and other disturbed sites.

This small, shallowly taprooted annual has slender, slightly pubescent, branched stems that clamber over other plants. The pinnately compound leaves have up to 18 well-spaced, linear leaflets. The leaflets often have retuse ends with a tiny needle-like tip at the apex and a rounded, tapered base. At the end of every leaf is a forked tendril that aids in climbing. The plants bear axillary racemes of up to 8 tiny, bilaterally symmetric, white to pale blue flowers. These are followed by flat, hairy, 2-seeded pods that age from green to brownish-black.

*Vicia hirsuta* looks similar to *V. villosa* (with which it shares its common name), but the latter has very hairy stems; those of *V. hirsuta* are much less so. Hairy vetch is also easily confused with *V. tetrasperma*, but that tiny vetch has hairless pods containing 3–5 seeds.

Pull and hoe away *Vicia hirsuta*, ideally before it produces seed; mulch and replant.

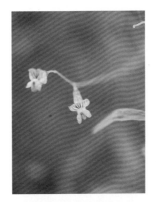

# *Vicia sativa*

## COMMON VETCH

**Non-native annual vine, to 3 ft. Flowers lilac, purple, 5-lobed, to 1 in.; late spring–early summer. Leaves alternate, to 5 in., leaflets to 1.25 in. Parts edible with caution. Toxic to horses, cattle, chickens.**

Introduced from Eurasia, common vetch is present as a weed across most of North America. It's sometimes grown for forage or green manure but has escaped widely into lawns, gardens, farm fields, woodland edges, and roadsides.

This taprooted annual can be hairless or hairy, with thin, weak, slightly branched stems that are semi-erect, often leaning on and clinging to nearby plants via tendrils. The leaves are pinnately compound, with up to 14 leaflets, linear or oval to somewhat lanceolate. Leaflet ends are varied, from rounded to broadly notched or truncated to gradually narrowing to a point, often apiculate. Each leaf ends with a forked tendril.

The axillary flowers, often hidden by the foliage, are borne singly or in clusters of up to 3, on short peduncles. The bilaterally symmetric flower is pale lilac to purple in the erect upper petal, often with the oval lateral lobes reddish. The flowers are followed by flattened seedpods as long as 2.75 in. Seedpods are initially green but fatten and turn tan at maturity; each contains up to 12 round, pea-like seeds.

*Vicia sativa* can be pulled when the soil is moist, or grubbed out with a hoe; take care to remove the taproot. Watch for pods, and dispose of them.

# *Vicia tetrasperma*

## SLENDER VETCH, LENTIL VETCH, SMOOTH VETCH

Non-native annual vine, to 2.5 ft. Flowers lilac, violet, white, 5-lobed, to 0.2 in.; summer. Leaves alternate, leaflets to 1 in. Parts edible. Toxic to horses, chickens.

*Vicia tetrasperma* is a European introduction found along the west coast from BC to California, as well as in Idaho, Montana, and much of eastern North America. It inhabits woodland edges, roadsides, abandoned farm fields, and other disturbed habitats.

On very slender and weak stems, the short leaves each bear 4–10 well-spaced linear leaflets and a terminal tendril. The tiny flowers are borne singly or in clusters of 2–3 on slender axillary stalks. The flowers are bilaterally symmetric and somewhat tubular to bell-shaped, pale lilac or violet to white, with darker purple veining. They are followed by small pods to 0.6 in., each bearing 4(5) spherical seeds (hence *tetrasperma*, "four seeds").

This dinky weed may be untidy but should be easy enough to dispatch. Pull or hoe when the soil is moist. Replace it with preferred plants, or mulch.

# *Vicia villosa*

## HAIRY VETCH, WOOLLY VETCH

Non-native annual or biennial vine, 1–3 ft. Flowers purple, violet, 5-lobed, to 0.75 in.; summer–autumn. Leaves alternate, to 10 in., leaflets to 0.8 in. Parts edible with caution. Toxic to horses, cattle, chickens.

This weed from Eurasia and North Africa is common across most of North America, invading meadows, farmland, and roadsides. The plant is often grown for fodder and as a cover crop and has escaped cultivation widely on all continents. It can crowd out natives and alter soil ecology in natural areas; it's also an agricultural weed, sometimes contaminating seed crops.

*Vicia* is a very large genus of many species that can be challenging to ID, but have no fear: in the PNW we have only perhaps a dozen species, most of them introduced, and only one seems likely to be confused with hairy vetch. Bird vetch (*V. cracca*) has long racemes of similarly colored flowers, but it is much shorter and much less hairy.

Hairy vetch has long, weak, slightly branched stems that sprawl over other plants and climb with the aid of tendrils. It is, as its common and species names suggest, very hairy. The leaves are pinnately compound, each with 10–20 leaflets and a terminal tendril. The flowers are borne in congested one-sided racemes of up to 60 flowers, pendent on ascending axillary peduncles. The flowers are reddish-purple to violet (sometimes pink or white); they have the typical bilabiate pea form, with a reduced upper lip that flares upward and is often more deeply colored than the 2 oval, lateral wing petals that spread outward. The seedpods are typical peapods, about 1 in. long and 0.4 in. wide, containing several round seeds.

Hairy vetch can be removed by hoe when the plants are smaller, or pulled or dug out. Larger patches can be mowed before they go to seed.

# Centaurium erythraea

## COMMON CENTAURY, EUROPEAN CENTAURY

**Non-native annual or biennial, to 20 in. Flowers pink, red, 5-petaled, to 0.5 in.; summer. Leaves basal to 2.5 in., cauline opposite. Parts edible/medicinal with caution.**

*Centaurium erythraea* (syn. *C. umbellatum*), a European species, is found in scattered places near the coast from BC to California, as well as in much of eastern North America. It is also a very widespread weed in Australia. In the PNW, small populations of this delicate weed are found on moist ground in meadows and lawns, mostly on the west side.

Common centaury has fairly short, fibrous roots and sometimes a short taproot. It begins as a basal rosette of oval to oblong, stalkless leaves and then produces one to multiple slender flowering stems, which are often branched. The cauline leaves are opposite, sessile, and similar-looking but narrower and reduced in size upward on the stem. Each leaf has 3–5 somewhat parallel veins. Each plant produces multiple stalkless, pink to light red flowers, in congested clusters at the ends of main stems and side stems.

Common centaury will not crowd out most garden plants but could self-seed where it is not wanted. It's lightly rooted and easy enough to remove by pulling or hoeing. Mulch to prevent future incursions.

# *Erodium cicutarium*

## REDSTEM STORKSBILL, REDSTEM FILAREE

Non-native annual or biennial, to 2 ft. Flowers pink, red, 5-petaled, to 0.6 in.; early spring–midsummer. Leaves basal to 8 in., cauline alternate. Parts edible/medicinal with caution.

*Erodium cicutarium* is a Eurasian weed that was accidentally introduced on the west coast of North America sometime in the early to mid-1700s. It is now present throughout most of the continent, particularly in drier areas, and is listed as invasive or noxious in several states. It's found in the PNW from Alaska to California in fields, meadows, rangeland, cropland, prairies, yards, vacant lots, and roadsides.

Growing from a central taproot with shallow, fibrous lateral roots, the plant first shows up as a basal rosette of varying size, then produces several reddish flowering stems. The leaves are twice pinnately divided, with 9–13 deeply dissected leaflets. The foliage is hairy and pungent, with an ornate, fern-like appearance. The inflorescence is a long-stalked umbel of 5–12 small, pink to purple flowers. These are followed by seeds, as many as 10,000 per plant, which are expelled with a ballistic force that can shoot them as far as 20 in. from the mother plant. Each seed is equipped with a small beak-like projection that aids in dispersal by sticking to things like animals and people; seeds are also easily dispersed by wind and water. With its extravagant seed reproduction, *Erodium cicutarium* can form large, persistent seed banks and dense populations that crowd out agricultural crops or native vegetation.

It would be easy for the uninitiated to overlook a single redstem storksbill, or view it as a "kinda cute" curiosity. Given an inch, it may lose its charm. It's easy to pull, dig, or grub out with a hoe, preferably before seed set. Follow with thick mulch and monitor for new seedlings.

# Geranium dissectum

CUTLEAF GERANIUM, CUTLEAF CRANE'S-BILL

Non-native annual or biennial, to 2 ft. Flowers violet, pink, 5-petaled, to 0.35 in.; midspring–autumn. Leaves alternate, to 2 in. Parts edible/medicinal with caution.

This European species is found in moist places on the west side in the PNW from BC to California, as well as Nevada and much of eastern North America. It's scattered in lawns, fields, roadsides, woodland edges, and agricultural land.

*Geranium dissectum* begins as a rosette of leaves, then sends up delicate stems, branched and typically prostrate to spreading or semi-erect. The stems and foliage are slightly fuzzy. The leaves are long-petiolate, round to heart-shaped in outline, and palmately divided into 5–7 lobes, which are shallowly cut on lower leaves, more deeply cut on leaves higher on the stem. The lobes are further divided into linear segments.

The small flowers are borne singly or in small terminal or axillary clusters, often just 2. The petals are typically notched, with 2 shallow, rounded lobes. Seed number varies with the size of plants, the larger ones producing thousands of seeds per plant. The seeds can last in the soil for years.

The main obstacle in removing cutleaf geranium is that it enjoys the company of other plants, particularly lawn grass, so extricating it can be a bit of a chore. It's otherwise easy to pull, dig, or grub out with a hoe or other tool. Follow with thick mulch where possible, to prevent additional seeds from sprouting.

# *Geranium lucidum*

## SHINING GERANIUM

Non-native annual or biennial, to 20 in. Flowers pink, 5-petaled, to 0.3 in.; midspring. Leaves alternate, to 1.5 in. Unpalatable. Noxious in BC, WA, OR, CA.

Shining geranium is a relatively recent invader on the west coast, from BC to California. In the PNW, it was first seen in 2006 and has since spread so rapidly, particularly west of the Cascades, that it has already hit all our noxious weed lists. The plant invades moist roadsides, yards, fields, open forest, and woodland edges. Covering the ground in early spring, it prevents germination of small natives that depend on spring moisture to get going. It has also invaded some plant nurseries and gotten a boost when gardeners unwittingly take it home along with their purchased plants.

Usually annual, this small plant grows from a shallow taproot and fibrous roots. The stems are slender and brittle, mostly hairless, branching, often reddish, and spreading or semi-erect. The leaves are round to kidney-shaped, with 5–7 lobes dissected more than midway through the leaf, each of these in turn divided into more shallowly cut lobes. The waxy, shiny texture of the leaves inspired the plant's common name. The pink flowers are borne in pairs on peduncles. Shining geranium can be hard to distinguish from dovefoot geranium, another common weed, but that species is fuzzy and has petals that are notched, while *Geranium lucidum* is mostly hairless and its sepals have a visible rib or keel on the back and a bristled tip. Like others of its genus, shining geranium has beaked seedpods that expel their seeds with force when ripe.

Control shining geranium before it sets seed by pulling or digging, taking care to remove the roots; follow with mulch to prevent additional germinations. For larger areas, bury the plants in a deep layer of mulch. A propane burner will also work, where safe and practicable.

# Geranium molle

## DOVEFOOT GERANIUM

Non-native annual, biennial, or perennial, to 16 in. Flowers pink, 5-petaled, to 0.5 in.; spring–summer. Leaves basal to 1.75 in., cauline opposite lower, alternate higher. Unpalatable.

Dovefoot geranium is found all along the west coast, plus Idaho, Montana, and much of northeastern North America. It inhabits moist areas in yards, gardens, roadsides, vacant lots, prairies, and woodland edges.

All vegetative parts of this plant are slightly hairy. The slender stems may be prostrate, sprawling, or semi-erect. The leaves are round or kidney-shaped in outline, palmately divided into 5–7 rounded lobes, each lobe in turn divided into 3–5 narrower segments.

The basal and lower cauline leaves are stalked, the upper leaves sessile. The pink (sometimes white) flowers are borne in terminal and axillary clusters of 2–3. The petals are slightly notched. Flowers are followed by the typical beaked ("crane's bill") seedpods, which open explosively as they dry, releasing as many as 1,500 seeds per plant.

*Geranium molle* is easy to remove when the soil is moist; pull, dig, or grub out with a hoe, and follow with mulch in areas with bare ground.

# *Geranium robertianum*

## HERB ROBERT, STINKY BOB, ROBERT'S GERANIUM

Non-native annual or biennial, to 20 in. Flowers pink, 5-petaled, to 0.5 in.; midspring–autumn. Leaves opposite, to 4 in. Parts edible/medicinal. Noxious in WA, OR.

Herb Robert is common in shady sites on the west side in the PNW and over much of North America. It invades woodland edges and even far into deeply shaded understory, riparian areas, yards, and gardens. The plant, though small and delicate, is a startlingly rapid spreader from seed and is highly competitive with small understory herbs, quickly crowding them out and reducing or wiping out populations.

The plant is low-growing, its thin, hairy, often reddish stems semi-upright or spreading and sprawling. The lacy but foul-smelling foliage is sometimes confused with that of native bleeding hearts. The much-divided leaves begin light green, turning red late in the season or if growing in an overly sunny spot. An individual leaf consists of 3–5 palmately arranged segments, which are in turn pinnately divided, the lobes somewhat rounded at the tips.

The small, bright pink flowers, borne in 2s, are followed by capsules that eject many tiny seeds as they dry. The seeds can land several feet from a mother plant, and last several years in the soil.

Herb Robert is shallow-rooted and very easy to pull or hoe, preferably before the plants go to seed. Mulch well to prevent future germinations.

# Hypericum perforatum

## COMMON ST. JOHN'S WORT, KLAMATHWEED, GOATWEED

Non-native perennial, to 3 ft. Flowers yellow, 5-petaled, to 1 in.; mid–late summer. Leaves opposite, to 1 in. Parts medicinal with caution. Toxic to cats, dogs, horses, cattle, sheep, goats, chickens. Noxious in BC, WA, OR, CA.

Common St. John's wort is a Eurasian weed that has invaded many countries and become a problem, due to its toxicity to livestock and other animals. It is widespread through most of North America and across the PNW. It's a listed noxious weed in several states.

*Hypericum perforatum* may have been introduced in some places as a medicinal plant. It is now found in fields, meadows, roadsides, woodland edges, and rangeland. It competes with native vegetation, desirable forage, and agricultural crops, and is difficult to eradicate once it becomes established. The genus holds several widely used ornamentals and a few western natives; all are easily distinguished from *H. perforatum* by differences in size or habit.

Plants are taprooted and also produce rhizomes and long horizontal roots, from which may sprout additional plants. A single plant may consist of one to several erect, branched stems. The inflorescence consists of multiple terminal clusters of up to 100 flowers each. Both the flower petals and leaves are dotted with glands, visible as small black dots (hence *perforatum*).

In addition to spreading by rhizomes and root fragments, seed output is formidable: a single plant may produce 33,000 or more seeds in a season, and some of these may persist in the environment for decades. In agricultural settings, tillage has proven a successful control, but this is not ideal for care of the soil and often not possible.

For smaller infestations in home gardens, early recognition is key. Pull or hoe when possible, ideally in moist soil, or dig when plants have matured. Take care to extract roots and rhizomes from the soil as much as possible, remove all uprooted plants from the site, and monitor for resproutings. Mulch to discourage new seedlings.

# *Iris pseudacorus*

## YELLOW FLAG IRIS

Non-native perennial, to 3 ft. Flowers yellow, to 4 in.; late spring–early summer. Leaves to 3 ft. Poisonous. Toxic to cats, dogs, horses, cattle, pigs, sheep, goats, chickens. Noxious in BC, WA, OR, CA.

*Iris pseudacorus* is a Eurasian weed introduced to North America as an ornamental over 150 years ago; it is also planted for erosion control and bioremediation. It has escaped cultivation and is a listed noxious weed in several states, invading salt and freshwater marshes, pond and stream margins, irrigation and roadside ditches, and other wet habitats. The plant wreaks environmental havoc, crowding out native flora and changing the ecology of wetlands, even altering the course of streams. It is also toxic to grazing animals and causes skin irritation in humans.

*Iris pseudacorus* grows from short, thick rhizomes; 100 or more individual plants may be connected by the aggressive rhizomatous spread, forming thick, broad mats that alter vegetative structure and water levels. The basal leaves are up to 3 ft. long and 0.6 in. wide, flat and sword-shaped, in a fan-like array. The cauline bracts are much reduced upward on the stems. The stem is erect and once-branched, bearing an inflorescence to 12 in. long. The 6-petaled bilaterally symmetric flowers are yellow with fine brownish markings. The green seed capsules are 3-angled, packed tightly with smooth, brown, disk-like seeds. A single plant may produce hundreds of seeds yearly. Seeds and rhizome fragments are easily transported in moving water, eventually landing in mud and establishing new plants.

Yellow flag iris can be mistaken for a native, but no yellow PNW native irises are this tall or brightly colored. The plant may tempt iris-loving gardeners when it shows up "for free." If you must keep it, remove seed capsules and keep it away from streams.

Young plants are comparatively easy to remove by pulling (wear gloves!) and digging; take care to remove all rhizomes. Large invasions cause significant environmental and property damage and can be nearly impossible to remove manually, so an option is to cut the stem to the base and apply herbicide. Since the plant typically grows in wetlands, herbicide use is subject to regulation; contact your weed local agency for guidance.

# Glechoma hederacea

## GROUND-IVY, GILL-OVER-THE-GROUND, CREEPING CHARLIE

Non-native perennial, 1–6 in. Flowers blue, violet, 5-lobed, to 0.5 in.; spring. Leaves opposite, to 1.5 in. Parts edible/medicinal with caution. Toxic to horses, cattle, goats.

*Glechoma hederacea* was introduced to the US by early settlers, who grew it in gardens as a traditional medicinal herb. It has since spread over most of North America and is listed as an invasive plant in several Canadian provinces and US states. With a preference for moist, shady spots, in the PNW the species is found mostly on the wetter west side, invading woodlands, riparian areas, farmland margins, lawns, gardens, and commercial turf. The plant is still available in the nursery trade, offered as a medicinal and as an attractive groundcover. Note: the common name "creeping Charlie" is shared with at least two other species.

This species grows from shallow fibrous roots. The long-stalked leaves are round to kidney-shaped, with rounded teeth along their margins. The plant bears axillary whorls of 2–6 flowers each. The flowers are bilabiate, with a 2-lobed upper lip and a 3-lobed lower lip. The species produces plentiful seed, but most reproduction is vegetative. It proliferates aggressively by branched stolons up to 7 ft. long, rooting at the nodes. Its lax stems can also root at the nodes when they recline onto soil. Fragmented stolons can take root and become independent plants. By spreading in this way, *Glechoma hederacea* can rapidly form very large mats that crowd out desired plants and are extremely difficult to eradicate.

Mowing, cutting, and burning have all proven ineffective, even in combination, due to the persistence of stolons. Even with herbicides, repeated application and monitoring may be required, due to rapid regeneration of any surviving stolon fragments. Small infestations can be pulled and dug out, but it is imperative you remove every scrap of root and stolon.

# *Lamium amplexicaule*

## GIRAFFE HEAD, COMMON DEAD-NETTLE, HENBIT

Non-native annual or biennial, to 15 in. Flowers pink, red, 5-lobed, to 0.7 in.; spring–summer. Leaves opposite, to 1.2 in. Parts edible.

*Lamium amplexicaule* is a Eurasian weed very similar to *L. purpureum*. It is present over most of North America, though more common in the east and along the west coast. It invades fields, lawns, gardens, and cropland and has been designated as a problematic invasive in several Canadian provinces and US states, due largely to its impacts on agriculture. The plants are strongly competitive with turf grass, ornamental plantings, agricultural crops, and native vegetation.

Giraffe head (the fanciful moniker likely refers to the flower's profile) grows from a taproot and shallow, fibrous root system. Stems and leaves are slightly fuzzy. Lower stems are branching and somewhat prostrate and can root at the nodes; upper stems turn upward. The heart-shaped leaves have rounded teeth along their margins and a crinkly appearance due to indented, reticulate venation. Lower leaves are stalked; upper leaves are lobed, becoming more sessile and very close together toward the stem tips, clasping the stem and appearing whorled. (The specific epithet refers to this quality of leaves enclosing the stem.) The flowers appear in small axillary clusters near the ends of stems. Flowers are tubular and bilabiate. The small seeds are dispersed by wind, animals, human activity, and water.

Small invasions are easily dispatched by pulling, digging, or hoeing. Carefully remove taproots and follow with mulch to suppress seed germination. Larger invasions may be conquered by more of the same, or by smothering with heavy mulch.

# Lamium galeobdolon

## YELLOW ARCHANGEL, YELLOW DEAD-NETTLE

**Native perennial, to 2 ft. Flowers yellow, 4-lobed, to 1 in.; late spring–early summer. Leaves opposite, to 3 in. Parts edible/medicinal. Noxious in BC, WA, OR.**

*Lamium galeobdolon* (syn. *Lamiastrum galeobdolon*) is considered invasive or noxious from BC to California. The form most widely recognized is 'Hermann's Pride', a silver-mottled cultivar. An admittedly beautiful groundcover, yellow archangel spreads with startling speed and aggressiveness, invading woodlands and riparian zones, crowding out native flora.

Plants grow from vigorous but shallow roots and rhizomes, sending out branched, trailing stems that hug the ground or may climb other plants. The semi-evergreen leaves are oval to lanceolate with toothed margins. Stems and leaves are slightly hairy and have a strong, unpleasant odor. The leaves may eventually revert to solid green, the form found growing wild in its Eurasian home range. The bilabiate, somewhat tubular flowers bloom in small whorls at the bases of the upper leaves.

Yellow archangel is extremely difficult to extricate from shrubs and tree roots when it insinuates itself among them, forming dense mats and resprouting from any root or stem fragments left behind, as well as self-sowing. Gardeners who must have it are advised to grow it only with solid containment, watch for wandering stems, and deadhead.

Small invasions can be combatted by pulling; take care to remove all roots and be prepared to repeat this, possibly for years. Bag and remove all plant parts to prevent regeneration. Sheet-mulching, though not generally recommended for overall garden health, may be the best option for large patches. Herbicide may be an option, combined with pulling, digging, and follow-up monitoring.

# *Lamium purpureum*

## PURPLE DEAD-NETTLE, RED HENBIT

Non-native annual, to 12 in. Flowers pink, red, 5-lobed, to 0.5 in.; spring–summer. Leaves opposite, to 2 in. Parts edible.

*Lamium purpureum* is a very widespread Eurasian weed scattered over most of North America and many countries worldwide. In the PNW, it occurs mostly on the west side, invading fields, yards, parks, woodland edges, vacant lots, margins of farmland, gardens, and roadsides. Several *Lamium* species are commonly known as dead-nettles, referring to their supposed resemblance to the unrelated *Urtica dioica* (stinging nettle); but lamiums are "dead" because not stinging.

This very low-growing, quick-spreading plant rises from a taproot and shallow fibrous roots. The stems are square in cross section, creeping out from the crown as far as 2 ft. but staying low and then turning up at their ends. The leaves are heart-shaped, stalked, with blunt or rounded marginal teeth, the upper surfaces looking puckered due to a network of indented veins. Leaves are often lacking on the lower stems; on the upper stems, they are crowded and tinged dull purple. The leaf arrangement is decussate.

The flowers are sessile and borne in small terminal and axillary whorls. They are tubular and bilabiate, with 5 irregular lobes composing a larger upper lip, 2 smaller side lobes, and a 2-lobed lower lip. A single plant may produce over 20,000 tiny seeds in a season, and dense colonies can expand through self-sowing.

*Lamium purpureum* is easily removed by pulling, digging, or hoeing, best done when the soil is moist and before flowering. Larger colonies may be smothered with very thick mulch.

# *Leonurus cardiaca*

## COMMON MOTHERWORT, LION'S TAIL

Non-native perennial, to 5 ft. Flowers pink, violet, to 0.3 in.; summer. Leaves opposite, to 5 in. Parts edible/medicinal.

*Leonurus cardiaca* is an attractive Eurasian plant grown as an ornamental and medicinal and still sold in nurseries for those purposes. It is notoriously aggressive in gardens and potentially invasive in landscapes, occurring as a garden escape in most US states and across southern Canada. It is frequently found near

residential areas and in yards, woodland edges, and degraded wetlands. It is present in scattered locations in the PNW but is more common in the Midwest and northeastern US.

Common motherwort sends up multiple stems from a shallow, fibrous root system and spreading rhizomes. The stems are squarish and hairy, arising from a woody crown, sparingly branched, and initially erect but flopping or sprawling as they mature. The leaves are hairy, palmately veined and cleft, with coarsely toothed margins and wedge-shaped bases. Lower leaves are stalked, 3- to 5-lobed, and nearly as wide as long; higher on the stem, they are smaller, narrower, less petiolate, and simpler in outline.

The tubular flowers are typical of the mint family: 2-lipped and bilaterally symmetric; they are sessile and borne in whorls in the axils of the smaller, upper leaves. The upper lip of the flower is hoodlike, extending beyond the lower portion, with conspicuous fuzzy white hairs covering its outer surface. The lower lip is narrower and deeper in color.

This plant can spread rapidly by seed and can form colonies via rhizomatous spread. If you want it in your garden but also wish to grow other things, consider a container (or other barriers to rhizomatous invasion) and deadheading. Key to stopping uninvited volunteers is early detection and prompt removal. Pull and dig when soil is moist, being careful to remove all roots, rhizomes, and seedheads. Mulch well or use competitive plantings.

# *Marrubium vulgare*

HOREHOUND

Non-native perennial, to 3 ft. Flowers white, to 0.5 in.; summer–autumn. Leaves opposite, to 0.5 in. Parts edible/medicinal with caution.

This Eurasian native has long been used medicinally and has become a widespread weed in many places in the world. It has escaped cultivation and is present as a weed throughout most of North America, excluding northernmost Canada. Horehound tolerates poor soil, often invading bare ground that has been damaged by erosion, overgrazing, or other disturbances. It can form large dense patches, quickly dominating sites, altering floristic structure, and crowding out natives.

With a stout taproot and semi-woody crown, *Marrubium vulgare* sends up several stems, square in cross section and prostrate to semi-erect. The stems and leaves are white-woolly and pungent, with a bitter taste. The odor is intense, variously described as fruity or musky, or resembling cucumber or camphor. The leaves are stalked, oval, nearly as wide as long, the margins with rounded teeth. Upper leaf surfaces are pale green to whitish and corrugated or puckered, the undersides white-woolly.

Flowers are borne in dense axillary whorls, as well as in long terminal clusters. Individual flowers are tubular, with a 2-lobed upper lip and a 3-lobed lower lip, the central lobe broadest and rounded. Each flower is subtended by a calyx of 10 narrow, spiny teeth that hang on after bloom, enclosing the seeds as they develop. A single plant may produce as many as 20,000 seeds per year. The barbed seeds stick to animals, people, and machinery, aiding in their dispersal.

For small patches, pull, hoe, or dig before the plants bloom and set seed. Take care to remove taproots. For larger patches, where practicable, burning has been effective in killing plants and most seeds. Follow with mulch, monitor for new seedlings, and replant with desired species.

# Melissa officinalis

## LEMON BALM

Non-native perennial, to 3 ft. Flowers white, pink, to 0.6 in.; late spring–autumn. Leaves opposite, to 3.5 in. Parts edible/medicinal with caution.

Lemon balm is a European herb that has been grown for medicinal and culinary use for centuries. Long a popular garden plant here, it is a frequent garden escape, found as a weed in scattered locations along the west coast from BC to California, in Idaho and Montana, and over much of eastern North America. An enthusiastic self-seeder, it finds its way to roadsides, vacant lots, yards, gardens, old homesites, driveways, prairies, open woodland, drainage ditches, and pond edges.

*Melissa officinalis* has fibrous roots and woody rhizomes, from which rise erect stems that are square in cross section and usually well branched. They may be smooth or finely fuzzy and are glandular in their upper portions. The leaves, borne on petioles to 1.25 in., are oval to somewhat triangular, a little over half as wide as long. They may be smooth or fuzzy, and their margins are lined with teeth that are blunt or rounded at the tips. They appear somewhat crinkled on the upper surfaces and have a lemony scent. Leaves on the upper stems are reduced in size, with shorter petioles.

The flowers are carried on short stalks in whorls of 4–12 in the axils of upper leaves. The bilabiate corolla is tubular to bell-shaped, with a 2-lobed, flat or hoodlike upper lip and a 3-lobed lower lip, the 2 lateral lobes of which are smaller and spread to either side; the central one is broader. Each flower is subtended by a light green calyx with 3 upper teeth and 2 larger lower teeth.

Gardeners who wish to keep lemon balm for tea and such are advised to keep it contained, in a pot or box to stop rhizomatous spread. Regular deadheading will prevent the self-seeding that can make of your driveway a lemon balm forest. If the plant is in the ground and has already begun to eat your garden, dig and pull, dig and pull. Offer as a U-dig freebie to local herbal tea enthusiasts.

# *Mentha ×piperita*

PEPPERMINT

**Non-native perennial, to 3 ft. Flowers pink, white, blue, to 0.2 in.; midsummer–autumn. Leaves opposite, to 2.5 in. Parts edible/medicinal with caution.**

Peppermint and spearmint are the two mints most familiar as flavoring in teas, candies, and other comestibles. Peppermint is a hybrid of spearmint and is usually sterile, but non-sterile cultivars, which produce seed, are available. It does, however, like its progenitors, spread aggressively by rhizomes. Long grown for culinary and medicinal purposes, it's present as a garden escape throughout North America. Like spearmint, *Mentha ×piperita* likes moist places and can be found in riparian areas, ditches, moist low ground, and old homesites.

The stems are square in cross section, hairless and smooth or glandular. The strongly aromatic leaves are about half as wide as long, oval to lanceolate, with dentate margins. They are stalked (unlike those of spearmint), with petioles to 0.6 in. The flowers are borne in whorls in dense, narrow spikes at the ends of stems, to 2.75 in. long. Individual flowers are 4-lobed and tubular, subtended by 5-lobed calyces.

The best advice for peppermint-loving gardeners is to keep plants contained. If it's too late for warnings and precautions, it may be time to pull and dig it out. Remove the rhizomes as thoroughly as possible, and monitor for recurrence.

# Mentha spicata

## SPEARMINT

Non-native perennial, 1–4 ft. Flowers white, blue, pink, 4-petaled, to 0.12 in.; summer. Leaves opposite, to 3 in. Parts edible/medicinal with caution.

Spearmint is one of the most familiar mints commonly used for culinary and medicinal uses, particularly as a tea. It is often planted in herb gardens and is a common garden escape throughout most of North America. Spreading by seeds and by rhizomes, it invades moist ground in yards, meadows, wetland edges, ditches, and riparian areas. Its dense rhizomatous spread can form nearly impervious mats, crowding out other vegetation.

Growing from vigorous rhizomes and fibrous roots, a single plant produces multiple erect, branched stems, which are square in cross section. The leaves are oval to lanceolate, about 1 in. wide, sessile to short-stalked, and mostly hairless, with toothed margins. They are strongly and pleasantly aromatic. The small flowers are borne in slender, dense spikes to about 5 in. long, rising from the ends of main and lateral branches; smaller spikes may sometimes rise from upper leaf axils. There are often noticeable gaps between whorls along a spike. An individual flower is tubular, nearly symmetrical, and subtended by a 5-lobed calyx. The calyx is persistent, remaining attached to the flowering stem after flowers have withered and seeds have been shed. The small brown seeds can be dispersed by water, animals, and human activity.

This is a delightful herb to grow—in a pot. In the ground, it is a garden-devouring monster. Dig it out, being careful to remove all rhizomes, as any fragments left behind can sprout into new plants. Alternatively, if you have a large patch, offer U-dig plants to local gardeners. After removal, mulch well and monitor for subsequent seedlings or sprouts from the rhizomes.

# *Nepeta cataria*

CATNIP

Non-native perennial, to 4 ft. Flowers white, pink, 5-lobed, to 0.25 in.; summer. Leaves opposite, to 3 in. Parts edible/medicinal with caution.

Catnip has long been grown in gardens for medicinal and culinary purposes, for feline entertainment, and as an ornamental. It has become a widespread weed throughout most of North America and is considered an invasive in several states. It inhabits roadsides, riparian areas, open woodland, fields, old homesteads, and vacant lots. The common names "catnip" and "catmint" (other *Nepeta* species) are often used interchangeably, which can contribute to confusion in identifying these plants.

Growing from a taproot, *Nepeta cataria* sends up several branched, erect stems that are square in cross section. The grayish leaves are stalked, triangular to oval, with rounded marginal teeth. The foliage in particular is aromatic, with a mint-like scent, when bruised. The flowers are borne in spikes to 3 in. long, at the tips of stems and in upper axils; they are bilabiate and tubular, white to pink with purple spotting. The plant spreads via many short rhizomes, sometimes forming broad mats, and produces an abundance of small seeds that are easily dispersed by wind and animals.

Pull, hoe, and dig out catnip, preferably when the soil is moist. Follow with heavy mulch to prevent more seedlings. Large patches may be suppressed by frequent mowing throughout the growing season.

# Origanum vulgare

## OREGANO

Non-native perennial, to 2 ft. Flowers pink, purple, 5-lobed, to 0.2 in.; midsummer–autumn. Leaves opposite, to 1 in. Parts edible/medicinal.

Oregano is a widely used European culinary herb that has escaped cultivation in North America, particularly along the west coast from BC to California, and over much of the northeastern US and eastern Canada. It can be seen on roadsides and old homesites and in fields and woodland edges. The straight species is most often used in cooking, but several more ornamental cultivars are available; all are edible. The common culinary herb sweet marjoram is another species, *O. majorana*.

Spreading by seeds but mostly by creeping rhizomes, the pleasantly aromatic *Origanum vulgare* has the squarish stems typical of its family. The stems are mostly thin and woody twigs, unbranched below the terminal inflorescences; green stems and leaves are slightly fuzzy. There are no basal leaves, but the stems are clothed for most of their length in short-stalked leaves that are oval to somewhat triangular, with smooth margins. They are reduced in size upward on the stem, and clusters of smaller leaves may arise from their axils. The small flowers are borne in dense terminal clusters. The flowers are bilabiate, typical for the mints, with a 2-lobed upper lip; the lower lip has 3 longer, spreading lobes. The flowers are attractive and remain so even after bloom, with persistent, prominent, deeper red to purple calyces with triangular lobes, and below them, leafy bracts in purple to green.

Oregano is still widely used and widely planted, but the problem arises when it has the opportunity to take over patches of wild landscape, or to push aside all other garden plants. Digging up the woody bases, dense fibrous roots, and rhizomes can take a little muscle but is not impossible. Offer the plant as a U-dig to other gardeners and have the work done for you. To retain it but keep it in check, give it a container or separate raised bed. Mulch and monitor for new invasions.

# Prunella vulgaris

SELF-HEAL, HEAL-ALL

Both native and introduced are perennial, to 6 in. Flowers blue, violet, 5-petaled, to 0.5 in.; late spring–autumn. Leaves opposite, to 1.5 in. Parts edible/medicinal.

Self-heal is a European species that has spread worldwide and become a weed of concern in many places. In North America, including the PNW, it is very widespread, but we also have *Prunella vulgaris* var. *lanceolata*, a native variety. The two forms are very similar-looking, with slight but discernible differences. Both are enthusiastic colonizers of lawns, gardens, moist woodlands, meadows, and wetland edges.

*Prunella vulgaris* grows from short rhizomes and fibrous roots, spreading by seed and by stolons. The stems are square in cross section, slightly fuzzy to hairless, short and often prostrate to spreading in the European form, taller (to 20 in.) and more erect in the native form. The leaves are opposite, stalked, and about half as wide as long. In the European variety they are more oval; in the native variety they are more lanceolate (hence *lanceolata*) and slightly longer.

The terminal spikes of whorled flowers are typical for the mint family, being bilabiate and bilaterally symmetric. The upper lip has 2 petals, the lower 3, with the central petal distinctly larger and fringed. The calyces subtending the flowers are bronze-green to reddish-brown and bristly. After bloom, the calyx persists and encloses the seeds as they mature, until they ripen and drop to the ground. A single plant may produce several hundred seeds in a season.

Plants are attractive, particularly in bloom, and can seem like charming visitors at first, but beware: the charm may soon fade. They can spread rapidly, even among nursery pots close enough for seeds to jump around, and their ground-hugging habit and tenacious rhizomes can make them a chore to remove. While they're small enough to not interfere much with larger plants, they cloak the soil so completely that smaller plants and seedlings will be crowded out. Pull, dig, or grub out with a hoe as soon as self-heal appears. Mulch well and plant with things large enough to stand up for themselves.

# Salvia aethiopis

## MEDITERRANEAN SAGE, AFRICAN SAGE

Non-native biennial, to 3 ft. Flowers white, yellow, 5-lobed, to 1 in.; midsummer. Leaves basal to 10 in., cauline opposite. Noxious in BC, WA, OR, CA.

This Mediterranean species was probably introduced to the southwestern US as a contaminant in seed. It now has a limited presence in the PNW, mostly east of the Cascades, inhabiting both dry areas, including roadsides, rangeland, pastures, and riparian zones.

From a stout taproot, Mediterranean sage begins as a basal rosette that can expand to 3 ft. across. Basal and lower stem leaves are stalked, with large oval to oblong blades, having shallow pinnately arranged lobes and finely dentate margins. Cauline leaves are much reduced and give way to sessile bracts. The flowering stem is square in cross section and well branched. The stem and leaves are aromatic and are woolly throughout when young, less so later in the season. The inflorescence is an open panicle with scattered whorls of flowers. Subtended by woolly calyces, the flowers are bilabiate, with an upper lip that is arched and hooded. A single plant can produce as many as 100,000 seeds in a season. Mature plants can break off and tumble across the landscape, scattering their seeds.

Tillage has been effective for larger invasions when practicable, but infestations often occur on rocky ground. For small invasions in the home garden, pull, hoe, or dig out the plants, cutting the roots of the more developed plants below the soil level.

# Salvia sclarea

## CLARY SAGE, CLEAREYE

Non-native biennial or perennial, 4 ft. Flowers purple, white, 5-lobed, to 1 in.; midsummer. Leaves basal to 7.5 in., cauline opposite. Parts edible/medicinal. Noxious in BC, WA.

*Salvia sclarea* has long been grown as an ornamental and medicinal herb and has, in the past, been widely sold in nurseries. It has proved very invasive as a garden escape, particularly in Idaho, and is present in scattered locations in Washington, Oregon, Montana, and a few states across the central US and on the east coast. It is listed as a noxious weed in several jurisdictions due to its displacement of forage plants and competition with native vegetation.

The stems of clary sage are hairy, erect, and well branched. The herbage of the whole plant is hairy and aromatic. The basal and lowest stem leaves are long-stalked, ovate to oblong, and dentate or doubly dentate. Leaves on the flowering stems are reduced upward and shorter-stalked. The small flowers, borne in scattered whorls along the stem, are subtended by large, showy bracts, often papery and purplish. The flowers are bilabiate, purple to white, often with yellow markings. The upper lip is hooded and often purple, the lower white and 3-lobed.

Small invasions of clary sage are easily removed by pulling, hoeing, and digging; this is easiest when the soil is moist and most useful before seed set. Follow with mulch to suppress subsequent seedlings.

# Lythrum hyssopifolia

## HYSSOP LOOSESTRIFE

Non-native annual or biennial, to 16 in. Flowers pink, white, to 0.15 in.; midspring–autumn. Leaves to 16 in. Toxic to sheep, livestock.

Hyssop loosestrife is a diminutive cousin of purple loosestrife, the fearsome noxious weed, with a much more restricted range in North America: it's found in BC, west coast states, and parts of the northeastern US, on moist roadsides, in riparian areas and other wetlands, and in irrigated farm fields. It can be a significant problem due to its toxicity to grazing animals, especially sheep.

This plant has a taproot and fibrous roots. The stems are typically multi-branched and may be erect to sprawling to reclining. The leaves are linear to oblong with smooth margins; they are mostly alternate but may be opposite along the lowest part of the stem. The tiny flowers have 5–7 petals; they are deep pink to white, unstalked, and borne singly in the upper leaf axils. The many very tiny seeds, contained in oval capsules, are dispersed by water, animals, and human activities.

Pull, hoe, or dig when the soil is moist, preferably before seed set. Remove plants with their taproots and any seed capsules from the site. Mulch to prevent subsequent seedlings.

# Lythrum salicaria

## PURPLE LOOSESTRIFE, SPIKED LOOSESTRIFE

Non-native perennial, to 8 ft. Flowers purple, pink, to 0.6 in.; midsummer–autumn. Leaves opposite, whorled, alternate to 4 in. Parts edible/medicinal. Noxious in BC, WA, OR, CA.

Purple loosestrife is a tall, showy, aggressive wetland invader found all across North America. It has been present on the continent at least since the early 1800s and is now listed as a priority noxious weed nearly everywhere it goes. It infests fresh and brackish wetlands, stream edges, marshes, wet meadows, and roadside ditches. It spreads rapidly and dominates wet sites, crowding out native vegetation and changing the structure and hydrology of wetlands in ways harmful to wildlife.

*Lythrum salicaria* grows from a taproot, with a broad root crown, vigorous roots, and rhizomes creating a dense mat around mature plants. A single plant can send up as many as 50 upright stems, which may be branched or not and are 4- to 6-angled in cross section. The leaves are typically opposite and often decussate but may be whorled or alternate. They are stalkless, slightly fuzzy, and lanceolate, with smooth margins. The flowers have 5–7 petals and are borne in terminal spikes to 16 in. long. These are followed by capsules containing many very tiny seeds; a single plant can produce over 2 million seeds in a season.

The species spreads by seed and by vegetative regeneration of root or stem fragments. It is further dispersed by human activity, particularly when seeds and stem fragments get lodged in boats and other equipment used in water. It may also be spread by gardeners disposing of plant material carelessly, or deliberately planting it despite its reputation.

Mowing has proven ineffective in combatting purple loosestrife, due to vegetative regeneration from stem and root fragments. Several biocontrol methods involving insects that attack various plant parts have shown promise. Small invasions can be dug up; take care to remove all roots and dispose of all plant parts. Mulch thickly if possible, and continue to monitor the area for seedlings. Removing larger established patches is very labor-intensive, and herbicides may be the most feasible option, but these are tightly regulated in wetland areas. Contact your noxious weed agency for guidance.

# Abutilon theophrasti

## VELVETLEAF, BUTTERPRINT

Non-native annual, to 6 ft. Flowers yellow, 5-petaled, to 1 in.; mid–late summer. Leaves alternate, to 8 in. Parts edible/medicinal with caution. Toxic to pigs. Noxious in BC, WA, OR.

Velvetleaf was originally brought to North America from Asia in the 1700s in hopes of developing it as an agricultural crop for fiber. That enterprise did not succeed, but the plant escaped cultivation and is now found in southern Canada and all US states, invading farmland, orchards, nurseries, gardens, and roadsides. It's a listed noxious weed in several jurisdictions, though it remains uncommon in the PNW.

*Abutilon theophrasti* grows rapidly from a taproot, sending up a very tall stem that is stout, erect, branched, and softly hairy. The leaves are stalked, velvet, rounded or heart-shaped, and large, to 10 in. wide. All vegetative plant parts have a rank odor when crushed. The flowers are borne on stalks, singly or in small clusters, in the leaf axils. New flowers bloom in rapid sequence.

The flowers are followed by seedpods typical for this family, each forming a ring of segments, with each segment containing several seeds. The pods are distinctive and were in the past used for decorative imprinting of homemade butter or piecrusts. A single plant can produce as many as 17,000 seeds in its short, busy bloom period. The seeds can remain viable in the soil for as long as 60 years.

Small patches of velvetleaf are easily removed by pulling or digging, ideally before seed set. Bag and remove any plant material that might contain seeds, mulch generously, and monitor the site for recurrences. Larger patches can be defeated by close mowing before bloom.

# *Malva moschata*

MUSK MALLOW

Non-native perennial, to 3.5 ft. Flowers white, pink, 5-petaled, to 2.75 in.; late spring–early summer. Leaves basal to 3 in., cauline alternate. Parts edible/medicinal with caution.

Musk mallow is an attractive ornamental introduced by settlers. It has escaped gardens and become invasive in some areas. It's found from BC to California, mostly on the west side in the PNW, as well as in Montana and Wyoming, plus much of eastern North America. The species is short-lived (to 3 years) and spreads only by seeds, with the help of animals and gardeners.

Growing from a deep and stout taproot, the plant sends up one to several erect stems, often branched toward their bases. Stems and leaves are usually some- what hairy. The leaves are roughly round in outline, palmately divided into 5–7 lobes. The basal and lower stem leaves are shallowly divided, with rounded teeth and long petioles. Upper stem leaves are shorter-stalked and deeply divided into narrow segments.

The showy flowers are borne on long stalks, single in the upper leaf axils and often in dense terminal clus- ters. The flowers are white to dark pink, delicate, with petals notched, obcordate or blunted at the apex. After blooming, the calyces go from green to a papery tan, folding over a doughnut-shaped circle of dark brown, kidney-shaped seeds.

Gardeners who deliberately planted musk mallow report that they have come to regret it, as the plant's self-seeding is prolific. Young plants are easily pulled up or scraped away with a hoe when the soil is moist. Take care to dig out the taproots, and follow with thick mulch.

# Malva neglecta

## DWARF MALLOW, CHEESEWEED

**Non-native annual, biennial, or perennial, to 2 ft. Flowers white, 5-petaled, to 0.75 in.; late spring–autumn. Leaves alternate, to 2.5 in. Parts edible/medicinal with caution. Noxious in BC.**

This European species is present and considered invasive over most of North America. It is seen on roadsides, driveways, woodland edges, in fields, vacant lots, cropland, gardens, and lawns—even flourishing in cracks in asphalt parking lots. Though short-lived and non-rhizomatous, *Malva neglecta* is a tough plant that can survive being driven on. With its ground-hugging habit, it suppresses germination or shades out seedlings of native vegetation.

Dwarf mallow grows from a robust, tough, sometimes woody and deep taproot into a spreading, branching vine that can also be bushy, to a height of 2 ft. The leaves, on long petioles, are round to heart-shaped, with 5–7 lobes, wavy margins, and a crinkly look. The 1–3 flowers are borne on inch-long stalks in some of the leaf axils. The flowers vary in color from medium or pale violet to white, with pink or violet stripes running the length of the slightly notched petals. These are followed by round seedpods that resemble cheese wheels (thus "cheeseweed"), with wedge segments containing the seeds.

*Malva neglecta* is best apprehended early, before the taproot can elongate. Pull, dig, or grub out with a hoe, removing the root. For a broader patch, a layer of very thick mulch over months may work to smother the plants.

# *Malva sylvestris*

## COMMON MALLOW, HIGH MALLOW

Non-native annual, biennial, or perennial, to 4 ft. Flowers violet, pink, white, 5-petaled, to 2 in.; midspring–autumn. Leaves basal to 5 in., cauline alternate. Parts edible/medicinal with caution.

This widespread European weed is found scattered over most of North America, with the exception of the northernmost regions, and is considered invasive in many countries. It's an inhabitant of vacant lots, roadsides, woodland edges, and margins of cultivated land. Introduced from the UK as a horticultural plant, it continues to be planted by gardeners and sold in the nursery trade.

Common mallow grows very rapidly from a deep, fleshy, cylindrical taproot. The stems may be unbranched or slightly branched. The coarse leaves are rounded to kidney-shaped, with dentate margins. Basal leaves have 3–7 shallowly to deeply incised, palmately arrayed lobes; cauline leaves are smaller and simpler in outline. The flowers are borne in axillary clusters of 2–4; they are 2–3 in. wide and may be deep violet to pale pink or white, with conspicuous purple longitudinal stripes on the petals; the cultivar 'Zebrina' (a selection of *Malva sylvestris* var. *mauritiana*) has particularly prominent striping. As with dwarf mallow, the seeds of common mallow are found in wedge-shaped segments of a pod resembling a cheese wheel.

This non-rhizomatous plant gets around via seed dispersal and is relatively easy to control. Large patches can be smothered with thick mulch or cut repeatedly to the root crown. Smaller invasions are easily subdued by pulling, digging, or grubbing out with a hoe, preferably when soil is moist and before seed set. Resist the temptation to ignore them; the mallow family is a large one, and there are many less aggressive plants with similar flowers.

# Chamaenerion angustifolium

## FIREWEED

Native perennial, to 8 ft. Flowers pink, red, 4-petaled, to 1 in.; late spring–autumn. Leaves alternate, to 6 in. Parts edible/medicinal.

*Chamaenerion angustifolium* (syn. *Chamerion angustifolium*, *Epilobium angustifolium*) is a circumboreal native, found over most of North America, with the exception of the southeastern US. It is extremely common in the PNW, and its range includes much of the cool temperate northern hemisphere, up to the Arctic. It typically occupies open ground, particularly on burned or logged land, but also woodland edges, gardens, fields, roadsides, meadows, and streambanks.

The roots and rhizomes of fireweed can go down into the soil over 1 ft. deep and creep along under the soil surface to a distance of 20 ft. from the mother plant, budding and sending up additional plants at intervals. The willow-like leaves are narrowly lanceolate, to 0.75 in. wide, with margins smooth or very finely toothed.

The plant bears terminal racemes to 8 in. long, with up to 50 showy flowers blooming sequentially. Opening first at the lower end of the raceme, the flowers may be in yet-unopened buds at the top, while those in the middle are open and those at the bottom have given way to seed capsules. The cylindrical seed capsules are up to 3 in. long, ripening to tan and opening to release as many as 500 seeds each. Each seed is attached to a tuft of silky hairs that aid in wind dispersal. A single plant may produce up to 80,000 seeds in a season. Fireweed reproduces from self-sowing, rhizomatous spread, and the sprouting of rhizome fragments.

This beautiful native is great for the edge of a large yard or semi-wild area but very quickly overwhelms a garden with its rapid conquest of space and sheer biomass. It is so large that it crowds out and smothers many smaller plants. When you've had enough, you can weed it out with a clear conscience. Pull or hoe, dig out, and remove roots and rhizomes. Remove bits of seed-bearing fluff, and mulch well.

# *Epilobium ciliatum* subsp. *watsonii*

## FRINGED WILLOWHERB, WATSON'S WILLOWHERB

Native perennial, to 6 ft. Flowers pink, white, 4-petaled, to 0.3 in.; summer. Leaves basal to 6 in., cauline opposite to alternate.

*Epilobium ciliatum* subsp. *watsonii* is native to much of North America. The plant is so common as a weed that "just shows up" in PNW gardens that many gardeners assume it's non-native. Fringed willowherb has also invaded many other countries and is a problematic weed in parts of Europe. In addition to gardens, in its native range it can be found in moist meadows, wetlands, agricultural land, and riparian areas.

Beginning as a persistent basal rosette of glossy, deeply veined leaves, the plant typically sends up a single stem. Stems are hairless and unbranched below, branched and slightly fuzzy and glandular above. The leaves are oval to lanceolate, sessile to short-stalked, opposite lower on the stem but more often alternate higher up. The small flowers are pinkish (sometimes white) and are borne in terminal racemes. They are followed by linear pods bearing tiny seeds attached to tufts of white hairs. A plant may produce as many as 60,000 seeds in a season.

If you find this plant in your PNW garden (and chances are good that you will), fear not. If it's in the way, you can yank with a clear conscience: though it's native, it is far from rare or threatened. Just be sure to remove the crown, which can resprout. If you like it or want to spare it because of its native status, that's fine, too. It's unlikely to cause much of a problem.

# Epilobium hirsutum

## HAIRY WILLOWHERB, FIDDLEGRASS, CODLINS-AND-CREAM

**Non-native perennial, to 6 ft. Flowers pink, 4-petaled, to 0.75 in.; summer. Leaves opposite, to 4.5 in. Parts edible with caution. Noxious in WA.**

At least 15 *Epilobium* species with small pink flowers occur in the PNW, most of them native. This non-native species is distinguished from most of the others by its hairy ("hirsute") character. It was more widely planted as a garden ornamental in the past and is still sold by some popular overseas sources of garden seed. Occurring from BC to Oregon, the species is still relatively rare in the PNW, more common in the northeastern US. Due to its rapid and aggressive spread in the moist meadows and wetlands where it's happy, *E. hirsutum* is seen as a rising environmental threat. Reproducing by prolific seed output as well as sprouting from rhizomes and stolons, it can form dense colonies, crowding out natives and impeding hydrology.

Growing from shallow but long, fibrous roots and rhizomes, hairy willowherb sends up multiple branching stems that may be erect, or may float or trail in wet environments. Stems and leaves are hairy. The leaves are opposite, sessile, and narrowly lanceolate to elliptic, with minutely serrated margins. The small but showy flowers rising from upper leaf axils have notched petals and white centers. They are followed by long, narrow pods containing many small seeds, each attached to long white hairs that aid in dispersal. A single plant may produce as many as 70,000 seeds.

This weed could easily be underestimated, but don't be fooled into overlooking it on moist ground. Pull or dig, bag and remove, including roots and rhizomes. Composting is not recommended. Mowing does not kill it but can prevent bloom and seed set. Control efforts may need to be repeated over several years. Seeds spread easily on the wind, so if seedpods are present, place a bag over the top of the plant and cut off stems before dealing with the lower portions. Large invasions are often combatted with herbicides, but those must be approved for wetlands, often with required permits.

# *Oenothera biennis*

## COMMON EVENING PRIMROSE

Non-native biennial, to 6 ft. Flowers yellow, 4-petaled, to 1.5 in.; summer. Leaves alternate, to 8 in. Parts edible/medicinal with caution.

*Oenothera biennis* is native to eastern and central North America but has spread throughout the continent and many countries worldwide. It's scattered widely on both sides of the Cascades in the PNW, found in various natural and disturbed or urban habitats, including riparian areas, meadows, woodland edges, vacant lots, roadsides, yards, and farmland. It is still sold in wildflower seed mixes and can easily escape cultivation. Note: common evening primrose looks very similar to the less widespread *O. elata*, but that native plant is a little shorter on average, has somewhat larger flowers, and is more often unbranched.

*Oenothera biennis* is a typical taprooted biennial, appearing as a basal rosette of leaves in its first season, then sending up a single stem (occasionally several) in the second year. The stems are sturdy, hairy, reddish or green, leafy and usually branched. The lanceolate leaves are thin and coarse, with margins smooth or very finely toothed or wavy. They are short-stalked toward the bottom, becoming more sessile higher on the stem. Smaller leaves may appear in the axils of some of the main leaves.

The bright yellow flowers are borne in terminal panicles at the ends of the main stems; they open in the evenings and close in the heat of day (remaining open in cooler or overcast weather). Flowers are followed by tubular, tapered capsules to 1.5 in., turning tan and woody-textured when ripe, opening to spill out many tiny brown seeds, which are easily dispersed by wind and can remain viable in the soil for 70 years.

Common evening primrose is easy to remove by pulling or hoeing, particularly in its first season. In its second year, some digging may be required to remove the taproot. Mulch well to discourage future incursions.

# Oenothera curtiflora

## VELVETWEED, SMALL-FLOWERED GAURA

Non-native annual, to 6 ft. Flowers pink, white, 4-petaled, to 0.25 in.; midsummer–autumn. Leaves basal to 8 in., cauline alternate.

*Oenothera curtiflora* (syn. *Gaura parviflora*) is considered native to the central US but introduced elsewhere in the country. It is present over much of North America; in the PNW, it's found primarily on the east side. An inhabitant of dry, open places, it is often found on roadsides and waste areas.

Velvetweed rises from a stout, branched taproot, with a basal rosette of leaves and a tall stem, unbranched or sparingly so. The basal leaves are spatulate and sessile, glabrous to slightly hairy and velvety, with margins entire or wavy to slightly dentate. Lower stem leaves are oblong; upper stem leaves are reduced and gradually more lanceolate, finally becoming linear bracts subtending the terminal flowers. The inflorescence is a slender, erect raceme as long as 12 in., containing many flowers. Flowers are pink to white, with reflexed sepals. They bloom in sequence beginning at the lower end, each lasting only a day or two. The seedpods are woody and cylindrical, to 0.3 in. long.

With only a few tiny flowers in bloom at any one time, velvetweed is never very showy, so most gardeners will not hesitate to remove it. Pull, hoe, or dig when the soil is moist, taking care to extract the taproot.

# *Epipactis helleborine*

GARDEN HELLEBORINE, BROAD-LEAVED HELLEBORINE

Non-native perennial, to 30 in. Flowers green, pink, brown, to 0.75 in.; summer. Leaves alternate, to 7 in.

Garden helleborine, a Eurasian native, was introduced to North America as an ornamental in the late 1800s. It has since escaped cultivation along the west coast from BC to California and in scattered locations over much of eastern North America. It is on lists in several eastern and midwestern states. In the PNW, it is found mostly on the wetter west side. It invades woodland edges and understories, yards, gardens, wetlands, and roadsides. With aggressive self-seeding and vegetative reproduction, it displaces native species and is very difficult to control.

Several erect stems may arise from the plant's short, fleshy rhizomes. The stems and leaves are slightly hairy. Leaves are rounded to oblong or lanceolate, to 3.5 in. wide, with parallel venation. A stem may bear up to 10 leaves, which are sessile and clasp the stem. The inflorescence is a one-sided raceme of up to 50 flowers. The flowers are bilaterally symmetric, with 2 upper petals that differ in color from the lower one, and an overall color varying from pale green to pinkish to brownish.

Gardeners commonly report that this plant "just showed up," and they are at first pleased—then not so much, as the species spreads. For those who like the look, a similar-looking but larger orchid is the native *Epipactis gigantea*. Eradication of *E. helleborine* can be a challenging, long-term project once plants are established. Dig up each plant, with all its roots and rhizomes. Even with herbicide application, be prepared to monitor and make repeated efforts. Heavy mulch may help to discourage new seedlings.

# *Bellardia viscosa*

## YELLOW GLANDWEED, YELLOW PARENTUCELLIA

**Non-native annual, to 20 in. Flowers yellow, 4-lobed, to 0.6 in.; late spring–midsummer. Lower leaves opposite to 1.5 in., upper alternate.**

*Bellardia viscosa* (syn. *Parentucellia viscosa*) is a Eurasian species found along the west coast from BC to California, as well as in Nova Scotia and several southern states. It invades roadsides, pastures, coastal wetlands, and dunes. With prolific self-seeding (estimated as high as 12,000 seeds per plant), yellow glandweed can form large colonies. It is a hemiparasite, meaning its roots can attach to the roots of other plants, obtaining some nutrients from them and possibly impacting their vigor. Preferred hosts for this species are grasses and legumes.

From fibrous roots, yellow glandweed produces an erect, usually unbranched stem. Stems and leaves are hairy and glandular, feeling slightly rough and sticky to the touch. The leaves are oval to lanceolate, about half as wide as long, with rounded teeth along the margins and prominent venation. Leaves are opposite lower on the stem; they may become alternate higher up. The terminal racemes of many sessile flowers are borne in the axils of leafy bracts. The long tubular portion of the corolla is enclosed by a tubular calyx with 4 V-shaped sepals. The corolla flares at the outer end into a bilabiate structure, with one larger lobe forming a hooded upper lip; the lower lip is formed by the other 3 lobes, smaller and spread apart.

This weed is increasingly on the radar of land managers, who must cope with larger populations and use herbicide. Small invasions can be removed by pulling, hoeing, and digging. Follow with mulch and monitor for new seedlings.

# Euphrasia nemorosa

## COMMON EYEBRIGHT, HAIRY EYEBRIGHT

**Non-native annual, to 14 in. Flowers lavender, white, 5-petaled, to 0.5 in.; midsummer–autumn. Leaves opposite, to 0.75 in.**

This charming plant is found in the PNW and elsewhere in western Canada and Alaska, as well as in parts of the northeastern US and eastern Canada. It's found mostly on our west side, on disturbed sites like fields, roadsides, and sometimes gardens. It is hemiparasitic on the roots of other plants (mostly grasses) for nutrition.

The stems are erect, hairy, brown, and typically branched. The leaves are also hairy and are mostly opposite, with toothed margins; they may be alternate higher on the stems. The flowers, borne in terminal spikes, are bilaterally symmetric, with a 2-lobed upper lip and a larger, 3-lobed lower lip. Each lobe has 3 purple veins, and the central lobe of the lower lip has a yellow splotch.

Common eyebright spreads rapidly from seed on sites with little competing vegetation and so has invasive potential. It has been the focus of some control efforts in Alaska. Due to the abundance of seedlings produced, hoeing may be more effective than pulling, and repeated efforts may be required as more seeds germinate. Mulch heavily and monitor for new sprouts.

# Orobanche minor

## SMALL BROOMRAPE, HELLROOT, CLOVER BROOMRAPE

Non-native annual, to 2 ft. Flowers brown, purple, yellow, white, 5-lobed, to 0.6 in.; late spring–midsummer. Leaves alternate, to 0.75 in. Unpalatable. Noxious in OR.

Small broomrape is a species from the Middle East that was probably introduced here with contaminated seed. Its PNW range is thus far limited to Washington, Oregon, and Idaho; it is also present in Texas and on the east coast. This prolific herbaceous weed can be seen in pastures, cropland, orchards, lawns, gardens, greenhouses, and woodland edges. It's an obligate parasite, particularly infesting legumes and green vegetables, and in large numbers it can cause significant crop losses. In Oregon, it has been found in commercially grown clover crops.

The plant is glandular and fuzzy throughout. By the time it emerges from the soil and blooms, much of its damage to host plants has been done. From short, unbranched roots and a base that may appear bulbous, a slender, unbranched, yellowish to straw-colored or reddish stem arises. The leaves are reduced to small, triangular bracts, crowded and imbricate close to the base, sparser and obviously alternate up the stem. Bloom season is as stated, but any one plant has a very brief bloom, for about a week. The inflorescence is a terminal spike of many small flowers with violet markings. The snapdragon-like flowers are tubular and bilaterally symmetric. A single plant can produce as many as a million dust-like seeds that easily disperse on wind and water, or by sticking to animals, machinery, etc. They may remain viable in the environment for a decade.

The key to preventing a large infestation of small broomrape is vigilance. Seedlings must be pulled or dug up immediately. Mowing larger patches as soon as they emerge can prevent seed production. Any uprooted flowering stalks must be removed from the site, as they can still produce seed.

# Oxalis corniculata

CREEPING YELLOW WOOD SORREL, CREEPING YELLOW OXALIS

Non-native annual or perennial, to 8 in. Flowers yellow, 5-petaled, to 0.25 in.; late spring–autumn. Leaves alternate, trifoliate, leaflets to 0.4 in. Parts edible/medicinal with caution.

*Oxalis corniculata* is widespread in the PNW, throughout North America, and in most countries worldwide. It is often seen in gardens, lawns, greenhouses, pastures, and farmland. Any gardener who purchases nursery plants will eventually bring it home as a stowaway in a plant container. The very dark-leaved form often seen in nursery pots is *O. corniculata* var. *atropurpurea*. The very similar-looking *O. stricta*, also yellow-flowered, is widespread through much of North America. However, *O. stricta* has fleshy rhizomes (which *O. corniculata* lacks) and somewhat reddish leaves; *O. corniculata* often has more purplish foliage and is more prostrate.

This invader has a deep, fleshy taproot, fibrous roots, and aggressive stolons. These trailing stems, above or below the soil surface, root freely and send up shoots wherever they go. The aboveground stems, erect or sprawling, are hairless or slightly fuzzy. Stems and leaves are green or brownish-red to dark purple. The leaves are long-stalked, each composed of 3 heart-shaped leaflets to 1 in. wide; they curl up at night and open again in daylight.

The bright yellow flowers occur in umbel-like axillary clusters of 2–10. The sepals are persistent: after the flowers drop, the calyx subtending them remains. Seeds are carried in cylindrical capsules to 1 in. As the seeds ripen, capsules split open forcefully, expelling seeds to as far away as 16 ft., an adaptation very effective for a plant with a talent for colonizing nursery pots. This species can germinate and mature from seed to flower to

next-generation seed in a few weeks, and seed output is prodigious. In addition to seed reproduction, pieces of taproots or stolons can break off and form new plants.

It's easy to overlook and underestimate this weed, but once established, it is extremely difficult (some land managers say impossible) to eradicate. For small invasions, the key is early intervention. Pulling can be surprisingly tough due to the very tenacious roots and stolons. Dig deep to get as much of the taproot as possible. Continued monitoring and repeated efforts may be required. Pre- and post-emergent herbicides are often used. Mulch well to discourage new germinations.

# Phytolacca americana

## AMERICAN POKEWEED, POKEBERRY

**Non-native perennial, to 9 ft. Flowers pink or white, to 0.25 in.; midsummer. Leaves alternate, to 14 in. Poisonous. Toxic to cats, dogs, horses, cattle, pigs, sheep, poultry.**

This native of the southeastern US is now found in all southern and eastern states, in eastern Canada, and along the west coast from Washington to California. In the PNW, it occurs in scattered sites, mostly on the west side, including roadsides, pastures, waste places, yards, and gardens. American pokeweed is toxic to many animals; yet songbirds are immune to the toxic factor and are the major vector for dispersal of the berries. This pretty and unusual-looking plant is also passed around by unwitting gardeners. But it's invasive and a hazard to pets and other domestic animals and particularly to small children, who may be tempted by the very toxic berries. Some foragers like to extol its edibility, but only young shoots are edible, and preparation requires lengthy boiling, without which it is very toxic.

This robust, shrubby herbaceous perennial grows from a fleshy white taproot, which can reach downward a couple of feet and be 4 in. thick at maturity. The stems are reddish to purple, up to 2 in. in diameter, and partially hollow. The leaves are bright green, lighter on the undersides, with smooth margins; they have an unpleasant odor when crushed. The small, greenish-white flowers have no true petals but 5 petal-like sepals. They are borne in pendent racemes and are followed by purplish-black berries, each about 0.4 in. in diameter and containing 6–10 seeds. Aboveground plant parts die back in winter, but the taproot persists through winter and sprouts another plant in spring.

Small plants can be pulled or dug out, but as they become established, root systems become large and may be difficult to extract. Cutting well below the root crown should kill them. Bag and remove any berries. Mulch the area well, and monitor for regrowth and seedlings, particularly in spots where birds hang out: under trees, along fence lines, and other perches.

# Digitalis purpurea

## PURPLE FOXGLOVE

**Non-native biennial, to 5 ft. Flowers purple, pink, white, to 2.5 in.; late spring–summer. Leaves alternate, whorled, to 14 in. Poisonous. Toxic to cats, dogs, horses, cattle, pigs, sheep, goats, chickens.**

This iconic weedy "wildflower" is found mostly on the west side in the PNW, all along the coast from Alaska to California, eastward to the Rockies, and in the north-eastern US. It thrives in disturbed conditions, including meadows, woodland edges, clearcuts, and roadsides, and is invasive in some areas, competing with native vegetation. It can also be fatal to animals grazing it. Purple foxglove is still sold as an ornamental and is the source of many cultivars and hybrids in the nursery trade.

A typical biennial, *Digitalis purpurea* begins as a basal rosette of leaves in its first season. These are long-stalked, oval in outline, light green, and conspicuously fuzzy, with rounded teeth along the margins. The basal leaves overwinter, remaining more or less evergreen. The following spring, a single, erect flowering stem shoots up. The cauline leaves, alternate to whorled, are gradually reduced in size up the stem. The inflorescence is a long, one-sided raceme of showy flowers. The floral corolla is a tube composed of 5 irregular, fused lobes, the lowest one being the longest and visibly spotted through the middle of the flower interior. The flowers give way to many small seed capsules, each containing many tiny, dark seeds. A single plant can produce as many as 2 million seeds, easily dispersed by wind, water, animals, and human activity.

Admittedly attractive in bloom, the plant may charm gardeners, but it has a short season of appeal and looks terrible at other times when the thick, fuzzy leaves go mushy and the spent flowers turn brown, and it is potentially invasive in wild lands as well as aggressive in the garden. For those who love the height and the tubular flowers, there are many other *Digitalis* species worth trying, some perennial and most better-behaved than this one.

Purple foxglove has a fairly limited fibrous root system and is easily removed by hand or by hoe. The leaves are toxic, so wear gloves for protection when working with a large patch. Burning has been tried unsuccessfully for larger patches; the plants did not burn hot enough to kill the seeds, and the toxic smoke injured workers.

# Kickxia elatine

## TWINING TOADFLAX, SHARPLEAF CANCERWORT, SHARP POINT FLUELLIN

Non-native annual, to 32 in. Flowers yellow, white, purple, to 0.6 in.; late spring–midsummer. Leaves alternate, to 1.3 in. Unpalatable.

*Kickxia elatine* (syn. *Linaria elatine, Antirrhinum elatine*) is introduced in much of eastern North America and along the west coast from BC to California. This diminutive European native enjoys moist, sandy soils with minimal competition from larger plants and is often found on the edges of agricultural fields and in gardens. The plant was previously placed in *Linaria* (toadflax) and *Antirrhinum* (snapdragon), both genera familiar to gardeners. The genus name honors Belgian botanist Jean Kickx.

Twining toadflax is a delicate, fuzzy annual with slender, trailing, multi-branched stems. The leaves are variable, from oval to arrowhead-shaped. The flowers resemble those of its relatives, toadflax and snapdragons; they are bilaterally symmetric, with a 2-lobed upper lip and 3-lobed lower lip.

Harmless and cute as it looks, *Kickxia elatine* can self-seed with enthusiasm and become a nuisance. Pull or hoe, and follow with mulch to prevent seedlings.

# Linaria dalmatica

## DALMATIAN TOADFLAX, BASTARD TOADFLAX

Non-native perennial, to 5 ft. Flowers yellow, to 2 in.; summer. Leaves alternate, to 2 in. Toxic to cattle. Noxious in BC, WA, OR, CA.

*Linaria dalmatica* (syn. *L. genistifolia* subsp. *dalmatica*) is a European native that has become a widespread weed in many countries. It's been present in North America since the late 1800s, introduced as an ornamental and escaping cultivation to become widely naturalized. It can be seen throughout much of the US, excluding the Southeast, and in much of southern Canada. In the PNW, it is common from BC to California, in fields and vacant lots, on roadsides and woodland edges. It is listed as noxious or invasive in parts of Canada and in several US states. Often forming expansive stands, the species displaces native vegetation as well as desirable forage plants.

Growing from a robust taproot that can go 5 ft. deep into the ground, the plant spreads by horizontal roots that may extend 10 ft. from the mother plant. Stems are erect, branching at the top, with narrow, light green, waxy leaves that are sessile to clasping. The snapdragon-like flowers, borne in long racemes, are bilabiate and spurred. A single plant may produce up to 500,000 small seeds, carried in small round capsules. Most fall near the mother plant; others are dispersed by wind, water, and vehicle tires.

Small invasions are easily removed by hand if found early enough. Pull and dig when the soil is moist. Repeat annually for several years for established populations. Herbicides are often used for large infestations.

# Linaria vulgaris

## YELLOW TOADFLAX, GREATER BUTTER-AND-EGGS

**Non-native perennial, to 2.5 ft. Flowers yellow, 5-lobed, to 1 in.; midsummer–autumn. Leaves alternate, to 4 in. Parts medicinal with caution. Noxious in BC, WA, OR.**

*Linaria vulgaris* was introduced from Europe into North America in the 1600s as an ornamental and a dye plant. It has since spread throughout most of the continent and is listed as a noxious weed in several Canadian provinces and western US states. It can be seen, often in large swaths, along roadsides, in abandoned fields, vacant lots, rangeland, farmland, and meadows. An aggressive spreader, it forms colonies and crowds out native vegetation, agricultural crops, and desired pasture plants. It looks very similar to *L. dalmatica* but is generally shorter, with linear leaves (vs. the more heart-shaped, clasping leaves of Dalmatian toadflax).

At maturity, yellow toadflax has a taproot to 3 ft. deep. Creeping horizontal rhizomes may extend up to 10 ft. from the mother plant, sprouting new vertical shoots along the way. The multiple, erect, usually unbranched stems are clothed with numerous narrow, waxy, sessile leaves. The whole plant is malodorous.

Flowers are borne in terminal racemes to 6 in. long. Each bilabiate flower has a pronounced straight spur to 0.5 in. and a raised lower lip with orange fuzz. The flowers are followed by cylindrical seed capsules to 0.4 in. long, bearing many small seeds. A single plant may produce 20,000 or more seeds in a season, and these may last in the soil for a decade.

Established populations can be very difficult to eradicate, due to vegetative regeneration of even very small pieces of stem or rhizome. Mowing and burning are ineffective, due to persistence of underground plant parts. Some populations have also developed herbicide resistance. Smaller infestations can be dug out when the soil is moist. Take care to excavate the taproots and rhizomes; this can be a very labor-intensive process. Mulch heavily and monitor for resproutings and new seedlings.

# *Plantago coronopus*

## BUCKHORN PLANTAIN, CUTLEAF PLANTAIN

Non-native annual or biennial, to 12 in. Flowers green, brown, to 0.04 in.; spring–summer. Leaves basal, to 10 in. Parts edible/medicinal.

Buckhorn plantain, a Eurasian plant of sandy coastal areas, is found along the west coast from BC to California, as well as in Texas and a few northeastern states. It invades agricultural land, orchards, pastures, grasslands, riparian areas, beaches, and salt marshes, spreading by seed and forming dense mats that exclude native vegetation. It may gain an advantage in dispersal when it contaminates grass seed.

Plants grow from a stout taproot. The leaves are all basal, lanceolate in outline, hairy, and usually pinnately divided or coarsely toothed. The flower stems are leafless and mostly decumbent. The inflorescence, as for other *Plantago* species, is a long, narrow, terminal spike of many densely clustered, tiny greenish flowers, with conspicuous white anthers.

Small invasions can be pulled, hoed, or dug out, with care taken to remove the taproot. Larger patches can be suppressed with thick mulch.

# Plantago lanceolata

## ENGLISH PLANTAIN, LANCELEAF PLANTAIN

**Non-native annual, biennial, or perennial, to 2 ft. Flowers green, brown, to 0.1 in.; spring–late summer. Leaves basal, to 15 in. Parts edible/medicinal.**

This is one of the most common and recognizable garden weeds—make a garden and it will come. It's widely distributed in the PNW and across North America. The species is native to Eurasia, introduced over other continents and assorted islands. In the PNW, it's common on roadsides, driveways, cropland margins, and in yards, vacant lots, and fields. *Plantago* species have long been used medicinally and are still propagated deliberately for that purpose. This species has also been planted as forage for cattle and sheep and as a functional groundcover. In some areas it can be competitive with native vegetation and with crop plants; it is a listed noxious weed in several states.

English plantain has a taproot and a modest volume of fibrous roots. From a thick, woody crown grows a rosette of long, narrow leaves. The leaves are distinctive, each with 3–7 prominent longitudinal veins. In spring to late summer, one to several leafless flowering stems arise. At their tops are narrow cylindrical spikes 0.5–3 in. long, covered densely with tiny florets that appear gray-green before they open. They open sequentially, in a spiral beginning at the bottom of each spike. As they open, relatively conspicuous white anthers on long filaments become visible. Many tiny, mucilaginous seeds are produced, dispersed by wind or by sticking to animals and people.

The plants are very easily removed by pulling and hoeing when the soil is moist. Mulch to prevent further seeding.

# *Plantago major*

## BROADLEAF PLANTAIN, COMMON PLANTAIN

Non-native perennial, to 20 in. Flowers green, brown, to 0.13 in.; spring–summer. Leaves basal, to 7 in. Parts edible/medicinal with caution. Toxic to horses.

This European weed is common in many countries and present over most of North America. It's a low-growing perennial of roadsides, agricultural land, gardens, urban lots, and gravel driveways, tolerating compacted soils and wet or dry conditions.

*Plantago major* grows from shallow, fibrous roots, with a semi-woody base. All leaves are basal and ground-hugging, broadly elliptic or rounded, sometimes sparsely hairy when young but at maturity hairless and leathery, with 5–7 prominent parallel veins. The margins are entire and wavy, or irregularly toothed. The leaves have thick stalks, with concave grooves along their entire length. The plants bloom intermittently, typically with several flowering stems that bloom in succession. The flowering stems are leafless, with the inflorescence a narrow, cylindrical spike to 10 in. long occupying the upper two-thirds.

Tiny flowers are densely clustered along the upright rachis, green with protruding white stamens. Flowers give way to seed capsules that ripen from green to purple or brown. Seed production is prolific, with estimates reaching over 10,000 seeds for a plant in a year. The seeds can be viable for decades.

Broadleaf plantain is a frequent lawn weed, escaping mower blades by hugging the ground. Younger plants are easily pulled or hoed when the soil is moist, but the tough root crowns of mature plants, which require digging out, are more of a project. Cover with thick mulch to eventually suppress the plants.

# Veronica arvensis

## CORN SPEEDWELL, FIELD SPEEDWELL

**Non-native annual, to 8 in. Flowers blue, violet, white, 4-petaled, to 0.13 in.; late spring–autumn. Leaves opposite, alternate, to 0.5 in. Parts medicinal.**

Corn speedwell is a very widespread weed over most of North America, most common along the west coast and in the eastern half of the US. It's a diminutive inhabitant of gardens, lawns, roadsides, field edges, vacant lots, and many places with disturbed ground and sparse vegetation. At least a dozen similar, small non-native *Veronica* species occur in the PNW, as well as several natives.

With a slender taproot and shallow fibrous roots, the plant sends up one to a few slender stems. The stems are hairy, erect to prostrate or sprawling, and ascending, sometimes multi-branched below, the prostrate stems sometimes rooting at the nodes.

Lower leaves are opposite, short-stalked, and rounded, with rounded teeth. Higher on the stem the leaves are alternate, more sessile, and more elliptic, with entire margins. Flowers are borne singly in the axils of some upper leaves and in terminal racemes. Each is stalked and subtended by a leaf-like bract. The flowers have 4 lobes, the upper 3 larger than the lowest one. Each flower lasts less than a day; they are followed by heart-shaped seed capsules. A single plant may produce thousands of seeds.

One can't help but be charmed by the lovely blue flowers of this belly-plant (one that requires lying on the ground to fully appreciate), and you may be loath to kill it at first bloom. However, later in the season, as the lower leaves are turning brown and there are more seed capsules than flowers . . . the charm fades just a bit. These plants are easy enough to remove at any stage, by pulling or hoeing when the soil is moist. Mulch and replant with something larger.

# Veronica chamaedrys

## GERMANDER SPEEDWELL, BIRD-EYE SPEEDWELL

Non-native annual or perennial, to 14 in. Flowers blue, violet, 4-petaled, to 0.5 in.; late spring–early summer. Leaves opposite, to 0.6 in. Parts medicinal.

Germander speedwell is a European weed widely introduced in northeastern North America and along the west coast from BC to northern California. It is very common in western Oregon particularly and is found in scattered areas of western Washington. This small weed inhabits meadows, lawns, gardens, and roadsides.

*Veronica chamaedrys* grows from a slender rhizome, with semi-erect, slightly fuzzy stems. The stems can also creep along the ground, rooting at the nodes. The leaves somewhat resemble those of the mint germander (thus the common name): they are oval and their margins may be entire or with shallow, somewhat scalloped teeth.

Loose racemes of long-stalked flowers are borne in the leaf axils. Like other *Veronica* species, the corolla has 4 lobes and is somewhat bilaterally symmetric. The flowers are usually a striking, vibrant true-blue with a white center and dark central vein. Individual flowers last only a day, fading to purplish as they wither the next day.

This is one of the veronicas that cause little trouble for home gardens, though plants could be a nuisance for fastidious gardeners or keepers of commercial turf. Pull and dig, removing the rhizomes, be prepared to repeat this, and mulch when possible.

# Veronica persica

## PERSIAN SPEEDWELL, BIRD-EYE SPEEDWELL

Non-native annual, to 20 in. Flowers blue, 4-petaled, to 0.25 in.; early–midspring. Leaves opposite, alternate, to 0.75 in. Parts medicinal.

Persian speedwell is a Eurasian weed found over much of North America, including the west coast from BC to California. It inhabits a variety of disturbed sites, including agricultural fields, orchards, vacant lots, roadsides, lawns, gardens, and commercially landscaped properties. It seems to be particularly at home hiding under the grass of lawns. Note: the common name "bird-eye speedwell" is shared with *Veronica chamaedrys*.

This low-growing, unobtrusive, taprooted annual is often seen just "winking" from lawn grass when in sky-blue bloom. The slender, hairy, sprawling stems may be branched at the low end or unbranched; they are prostrate and often root at the nodes. The short-petiolate leaves are oval to elliptic, with shallow, rounded marginal teeth. Primarily opposite, the leaves become alternate on the upper stems. The flowers are borne on stalks, singly in the upper leaf axils and in terminal racemes. They are somewhat bilaterally symmetric, with 4 irregular lobes, the uppermost petal being distinctly larger, the lowest narrowest and often paler, and each etched with a series of darker parallel lines.

*Veronica persica* matures quickly and blooms and sets seed, as many as 6,500 per plant, for several months. Seeds can persist in the soil for decades. These abundant small seeds can be a pest for growers of small grain or grass seed crops. In those contexts, tillage and various herbicides have been used successfully.

This weed is unlikely to cause much trouble for the home gardener. Pull when it's crowded among other plants you want to keep, or hoe when possible.

# *Veronica serpyllifolia*

## THYMELEAF SPEEDWELL

Perennial, both native and introduced, to 12 in. Flowers blue, white, 4-petaled, to 0.25 in.; midspring–midsummer. Leaves opposite, to 0.75 in.

*Veronica serpyllifolia* is found in much of the western US, including coastal BC and Alaska, as well as in northeastern North America. It's one of several small, weedy *Veronica* species commonly found in lawns and gardens. It can be differentiated from the other species by its strictly terminal racemes, never bearing either single flowers or racemes in leaf axils. In the PNW, its preferred habitats are disturbed, moist ground, often with light shade; besides lawns and gardens, it is found in meadows and parks and on the shores of streams and lakes.

Thymeleaf speedwell grows from a fibrous root system with branching rhizomes. A single plant produces several slender stems, mostly unbranched except for occasional prostrate, lower branches. The stems initially trail on the ground but become more semi-erect in bloom. Stems and leaves are slightly fuzzy. The leaves are oval to elliptical, the lower ones short-stalked and the upper ones more sessile. Their margins are entire to slightly toothed.

The small, bilaterally symmetric flowers are lovely, pale blue to white with darker blue veining. Typical for the genus, there are 4 petals, with the upper one being largest. The flowers are borne on short stalks in loose terminal clusters up to 7 in. long. The seeds are tiny and are dispersed by the wind and various animals. In addition to seeding, the plant multiplies vegetatively via rhizomes and stolons.

*Veronica serpyllifolia* can form small, matted colonies but is not generally a troublesome weed. It can be sweet when in bloom but a bother for fastidious gardeners or when it's in the way of other small plants. It can also be a nuisance in lawn maintenance, particularly in commercial turf. Remove it by pulling or digging when the soil is moist, being careful to remove the rhizomes, and follow with mulch. Some repeated pulling may be necessary.

# Fallopia convolvulus

## BLACK BINDWEED, CLIMBING BINDWEED, IVY BINDWEED

Non-native annual vine, to 5 ft. Flowers white, 5-lobed, to 0.2 in.; midspring–autumn. Leaves alternate, to 2.5 in. Parts edible with caution.

*Fallopia convolvulus* (syn. *Polygonum convolvulus*) is a widespread weed found over most of North America in farmland, gardens, vacant lots, and roadsides. It's an important agricultural pest worldwide, competing with wheat and other grain crops, reducing yields, and

contaminating seed products. Note: Bindweed is in an unrelated genus (*Convolvulus*), to which this invasive vine bears a resemblance.

Black bindweed grows from long, slender, multi-branched fibrous roots that can reach 30 in. deep into the soil. The slender, weak stems are branched at the base and clamber and twine on other plants or trail along the ground. The leaves are arrowhead-shaped to oval or heart-shaped, on long, slender petioles, borne at wide intervals along the stems. Typical of the buckwheat family, an ocrea occurs where the petiole joins the stem. Plants bear loose, axillary and terminal spikes of 2–6 flowers each. The tiny flowers consist of petal-like sepals, reddish-green to white. Flowers are followed by profuse seed set, with estimates ranging to 30,000 per plant. The seeds are dispersed by wind, water, farm machinery, and human activity and can remain viable in the soil for years.

Farmers combatting large invasions have used repeated tillage and herbicides, such efforts being hampered by the long growing season for this species and its persistent regeneration, with a large and lasting seed bank. For small invasions, early detection and prompt removal before flowering and seed set are key. Pull and dig when soil is moist, retrieving as much of the root mass as possible. Follow with heavy mulch to prevent subsequent seedlings.

# *Persicaria lapathifolia*

## PALE SMARTWEED, NODDING SMARTWEED

Native and non-native annual, to 5 ft. Flowers white, pink, 4- or 5-lobed, to 0.13 in.; late spring–autumn. Leaves to 8 in. Parts edible/medicinal with caution.

*Persicaria lapathifolia* (syn. *Polygonum lapathifolium*) is by far the largest of the smartweeds. It is generally considered invasive/non-native in Canada and native throughout the US (though there may be European strains). Whatever its nativity, it is a plant that can show up uninvited in gardens and other moist, disturbed soil, often near wetlands.

Growing from shallow, fibrous roots, the stems of pale smartweed are tall, erect, and multi-branched. The leaves are long and narrow, on short stalks, with woolly surfaces and minute hairs along the margins and ocreas at the petiole bases. The inflorescence is a usually terminal but occasionally axillary cluster of several dense, nodding, spike-like racemes, to 6 in. long. The tiny flowers never fully open but appear as if in bud. Seed production per plant varies; estimates range as high as 19,000, and large colonies can form.

Pale smartweed is a weed of many crops in many regions of the world, where herbicides are often used to control it. In the home garden, it is usually easily vanquished by pulling, hoeing, and digging, best done when the soil is moist and well before seed formation. Follow with mulch, replant, and monitor.

# *Persicaria maculosa*

## SPOTTED LADY'S-THUMB, SMARTWEED

Non-native annual, to 3 ft. Flowers white, pink, 4- or 5-lobed, to 0.12 in.; spring–autumn. Leaves alternate, to 4 in. Parts edible/medicinal with caution.

*Persicaria maculosa* (syn. *Polygonum persicaria*) is widespread throughout North America and in many other countries. This European weed inhabits moist ground on streambanks, waste places, roadsides, farmland, gardens, wetlands, meadows, and drainage ditches. It is a significant nuisance weed of many crops.

Growing from shallow fibrous roots, the stems can be branched or not, reddish or green, erect or sprawling, hairless (usually) to slightly fuzzy. Stems can sometimes root at the nodes, which are marked by swollen joints, typical for the family. The leaves are elliptic to lanceolate or narrowly oval, from 0.3 in. to 1 in. wide, usually with a triangular or V-shaped purple blotch in the middle. Leaves lower on the stem narrow to thick petioles; leaves higher on the stem are stalkless. Typical for the family, a brownish to off-white ocrea wraps around the stem at the base of each petiole. It originates at a joint just below the petiole, extending upward to as much as 0.5 in.

along the stem and petiole. It may have distinct longitudinal veins and has a few short, fine bristles at the edge.

The tiny flowers are borne in erect, dense, comparatively thick, spike-like racemes, the terminal ones to 2 in. long. There are also often smaller spikes in the upper leaf axils. A distinguishing feature of this species, helping to separate it from other smartweeds, is that flowers in a single raceme may vary in color: most often they are greenish-white to pink (sometimes red or purple). Individual flowers are stalked; they seldom fully open but look like little buds. Each plant may produce as many as 1,500 small seeds. These are dispersed by water, soil movement, animals, or machines.

Large infestations are effectively combatted in agricultural situations by tillage or cultivation. Limited invasions in home gardens are easily eradicated by pulling and hoeing. Mulch well and replant with more desirable species.

# Polygonum aviculare

PROSTRATE KNOTWEED, COMMON KNOTWEED, DOORWEED

Non-native annual or perennial, prostrate. Flowers white, pink, 5-lobed, to 0.1 in.; midsummer–autumn. Leaves alternate, to 1.2 in. Parts edible/medicinal with caution.

Prostrate knotweed, one of the most common weeds worldwide, is widespread throughout North America. In the PNW, it is often found on poor, dry, or hard-packed soils, on roadsides, sidewalks, driveways, and agricultural fields. The plant often colonizes bare soil and may form dense mats, to 48 in. across, preventing other plants from germinating and growing.

*Polygonum aviculare* grows from a mass of very fine, fibrous roots and a taproot that can reach down several inches in looser soils. Its long stems are multi-branched, typically prostrate and spreading, occasionally semi-erect; they do not root at the nodes but can cover the ground densely, sometimes in layers. The nodes appear jointed, with silvery ocreas sheathing them. The blue-green leaves are generally lanceolate to oval. The tiny flowers are borne in small axillary clusters of 2–6. The corollas are apetalous and mostly closed, so that the flowers look like little buds. A single plant can produce as many as 6,000 seeds in a season, and these can persist in the environment for decades. They are easily dispersed by animals, water, and human activity.

Agricultural weed managers recommend pre- and post-emergent herbicides for large areas of prostrate knotweed but allow that herbicide resistance can be an issue. Small patches can be eliminated by pulling and digging, preferably when the soil is moist; take care to remove the taproots. As this weed typically thrives in poor soil, practices that improve soil health may be useful in combatting its return. Follow up with mulch to prevent germination from the seed bank, and monitor for recurrences.

# Rumex acetosella

## SHEEP SORREL, RED SORREL, SOUR DOCK

Non-native perennial, to 18 in. Flowers red, green, to 0.08 in.; late spring–summer. Leaves basal to 3 in., cauline alternate. Parts edible/medicinal with caution. Toxic to cattle, sheep.

This weedy *Rumex* is found across much of North America in moist meadows, pastures, lawns, woodlands, and wetland margins. It can form dense colonies, displacing natives, and it is often one of the first species to colonize land left bare by fire or other disturbance.

Growing from a shallow taproot and numerous slender, horizontally creeping rhizomes, plants send up one or several thin, erect stems, unbranched below the inflorescences. The leaves are linear to ovate. Lower leaves are long-stalked and hastate; the scant cauline leaves are progressively smaller, more linear, short-stalked to sessile, and may lack basal lobes.

Sheep sorrel is dioecious. The inflorescence is a slender, erect panicle of many tiny flowers, reddish for the females, yellow-green for the males. The female flowers give way to small red achenes. A single plant may produce up to 1,600 long-lived seeds, which are dispersed by wind, water, and animals.

The graceful, crimson panicles are attractive in flower and fruit, like upright strands of tiny red beads, at least when they're in a weedy meadow and not in your garden! Control of large populations is complicated by sheep sorrel's rhizomatous spread and many viable seeds. Burning, grazing, and mowing are often ineffective. Repeated tillage or hand cultivation (for smaller patches) can eventually suppress plants. For smaller patches, pull, hoe, or dig when the soil is moist, removing as much of the roots and rhizomes as possible. Mulch thickly, and watch for resprouts and seedlings.

# *Rumex crispus*

## CURLY DOCK

Non-native perennial, to 5 ft. Flowers green, brown, 6-lobed, to 0.25 in.; midsummer–autumn. Leaves basal to 12 in., cauline alternate. Parts edible/medicinal with caution. Toxic to horses, cattle, sheep, chickens. Noxious in BC.

This robust weed is common worldwide and over much of North America on moist ground in fields, pastures, roadsides, gardens, and farmland. With extravagant seed production, the plant can be invasive and compete with native vegetation, crop plants, or more desirable forage. If consumed in quantity, it can be toxic to livestock, due to high oxalate content.

Curly dock grows from a stout, forked, yellowish taproot that can extend a few feet deep into the soil. The basal leaves are oblong to lanceolate, to 2 in. wide, sharply pointed at the tips, and crinkly, with wavy margins. The leaf stalks are nearly as long as the blades, which are rounded or wedge-shaped at their bases. There is a brown ocrea at the base of each petiole. Cauline leaves are progressively smaller, more lanceolate to linear, with shorter stalks. The plants bear large, erect, terminal panicles of tiny flowers arranged in whorls; the whorls are often crowded toward the panicle branch tips but may be more widely spaced lower in the inflorescence. The flowers turn from greenish to pinkish and ultimately dark red-brown, remaining attached to the plant after seed set. A single plant may produce as many as 40,000 seeds in a year.

Small invasions caught early can be pulled or dug up, with as much of the root as possible. This becomes impossible as the mature taproot extends downward, but the plants can usually be killed by cutting the root with a shovel or other sharp implement to at least 4 in. below the soil. Follow with thick mulch and monitor.

# Rumex obtusifolius

## BITTER DOCK

Non-native perennial, to 4 ft. Flowers green, brown, 6-lobed, to 0.25 in.; midspring–autumn. Leaves basal to 10 in., cauline alternate. Parts edible with caution. Toxic to cattle, sheep.

Bitter dock is one of about 16 *Rumex* species present in the PNW, nine of which are introduced. This European species is found throughout North America, often on moist, disturbed ground in vacant lots, roadsides, riparian zones, woodland edges, pastures, and agricultural land. The weed can be invasive, displacing native plants and crops and reducing the forage value of grasslands.

*Rumex obtusifolius* grows from a thick, branched taproot as deep as several feet; it has no rhizomes or stolons. The stems are unbranched except in the terminal inflorescence. Basal leaves are large, to 5 in. wide and 10 in. long, with stalks that may be as long as the blade; they are obovate, with a heart-shaped base. The margins may be entire or have irregular, shallow scalloping. Cauline leaves are progressively smaller upward on the stem, more lanceolate, and with shorter stalks. At the petiole bases are ocreas, which often wither away at maturity. The terminal inflorescence is a vertical, branched panicle of many tiny flowers, in a series of whorls. A single plant can produce as many as 60,000 seeds in a season; seeds are dispersed by wind, water, or animals and remain viable for decades.

Seedlings and young plants can be pulled or dug out. Take care to remove all the taproot; as the root expands, this becomes more difficult. The plants can be killed by cutting the root to at least 4 in. below soil level. Mulch well and monitor for subsequent seedlings. Larger patches may be exhausted over time by repeated rototilling.

# Portulaca oleracea

PURSLANE

Non-native annual, to 12 in. Flowers yellow, 5-petaled, to 0.4 in.; midsummer–autumn. Leaves alternate, subopposite, to 2 in. Parts edible. Toxic to horses.

This very common weed is found worldwide. Throughout the US and much of Canada, it inhabits gardens, yards, driveways, beaches, riparian areas, fields, and farmland. It's an agricultural pest, affecting many food crops.

Purslane grows from a robust, lateral, fibrous root system and a thick taproot to 4 in. long. Several prostrate, well-branched, reddish stems radiate from a central point. Stems and leaves are hairless, shiny, and fleshy. The leaves are sessile, spatulate to oval, alternate to nearly opposite, and somewhat crowded at branch tips. Flowers bloom in both axillary and small terminal clusters. A single plant may produce as many as 240,000 seeds, which can remain viable for decades. With this extravagant output, a handful of plants overlooked in a season can quickly result in their offspring colonizing the site with dense mats that prevent the establishment of other plants.

Many foragers extol the edible and nutritional virtues of purslane. If that is not your bag, or if the plants are interfering with your horticultural vision, a small invasion is easy enough to pull up or grub out with a hoe when the soil is moist. Stem fragments left behind are particularly resistant to drying (due to their succulence) and can revive and reroot quickly. Leave uprooted plants to dry on an unwatered area, or bag and remove them. When purslane has shown up close to plants you don't want to disturb by hoeing, a heavy layer of mulch may be enough to block light and suppress it.

# Lysimachia arvensis

## SCARLET PIMPERNEL, POOR MAN'S WEATHER GLASS

---

Non-native annual, to 16 in. Flowers orange, 5-petaled, to 0.5 in.; early summer. Leaves opposite, to 1 in. Parts edible/medicinal with caution. Toxic to cats, dogs, horses, cattle, sheep, chickens.

---

*Lysimachia arvensis* (syn. *Anagallis arvensis*), a Eurasian weed, is found in scattered sites from BC to California and throughout much of North America. This tiny weed, often mixed in with larger weeds and grasses, frequents woodland edges, roadsides, wetland margins, beaches, fields, pastures, agricultural land, and lawns. The plant is potentially toxic when consumed by humans, domestic animals, or livestock.

The stems are square in cross section, prostrate to upward-reaching, slender, and branched. The oval leaves are sessile and clasp the stem slightly. The flowers are borne singly or in pairs, on long, thin pedicels in the leaf axils. The 5 petals are joined at the base, and there is usually a small, delicate bit of crimson at the base of each petal. Flowers are followed by small, spherical seed capsules, which remain attached to their long stalks. Notes on common names: most of our "scarlet" pimpernels are distinctly salmon-colored, and the flowers may not open on cool, cloudy days (hence the alternative common name).

*Lysimachia arvensis* has caused problems in some countries and is not welcome in places where livestock graze. But it's so small and charming, and so infrequent a visitor in our region, that it seems not to be a cause for alarm in the average garden. With only a slight fibrous root system and no vegetative reproduction, it's easy enough to dispatch with a hoe or by pulling. If you like the look but wish for something a little more substantial and never weedy, you might want to find *L. monelli*, a slightly larger perennial, which comes in both salmon and deep blue and is available in nurseries.

# *Lysimachia nummularia*

## CREEPING JENNY, MONEYWORT

Non-native perennial, to 4 in. Flowers yellow, 5-petaled, to 1 in.; midsummer. Leaves opposite, to 1.5 in. Parts edible/medicinal.

Creeping Jenny was introduced to the US as an ornamental, possibly in the early 1700s, and has escaped cultivation in scattered areas from BC to California and throughout the eastern US and Canada. The species invades moist ground around lakes, roadsides, gardens, moist meadows and woodlands, wetlands, and farmland. As a garden plant, it is an attractive but very aggressive groundcover, covering large areas rapidly.

The plant grows from slender, fibrous roots, with prostrate, hairless, branched stems that creep to a length of 2–3 ft., rooting at the nodes, forming mats. The leaves are round to oval, short-stalked and semi-evergreen; their coin-like size and shape inspired the common name "moneywort." The straight species has bright lime-green foliage, but a popular gold-leaved cultivar is available (and as rambunctious). Bright yellow flowers bloom singly in the leaf axils. The plant self-sows rarely, and most reproduction is vegetative.

Many of the control methods that have been tried with this species are futile or counterproductive: mowing facilitates scattering of stem pieces that will root and sprout; pulling breaks off roots that resprout; flooding only made it happy and reduced competition from other plants. Thorough digging is recommended; take care to remove all root and stem pieces. Herbicide has been used successfully. Very heavy mulching over many months may be an effective strategy. The best control is abstention: refrain from planting this species, or confine it within concrete barriers or in a container.

# Lysimachia punctata
## WHORLED LOOSESTRIFE, SPOTTED LOOSESTRIFE, YELLOW LOOSESTRIFE

Non-native perennial, to 4 ft. Flowers yellow, 5-petaled, to 1 in.; mid–late summer. Leaves whorled, to 3 in.

*Lysimachia punctata* is a widely sold ornamental that has escaped cultivation at scattered locations from BC to Oregon and in Montana, a few midwestern states, and much of the northeastern US and eastern Canada. Like its more aggressive relatives, this species prefers moist soil and spreads by self-seeding and by enthusiastic rhizomatous spread. In riparian areas, drainage ditches, or wetland margins, it can form large stands that crowd out native flora or horticultural plants.

The stems of whorled loosestrife are tall, erect, and unbranched. Stems and foliage are fuzzy. The leaves are broadly lanceolate to oval and arranged in whorls of 3 (most often). The bright yellow, cup-shaped flowers are stalked and borne in small whorls in the leaf axils along most of the length of the stem.

This is an unquestionably attractive plant, often planted in gardens. Gardeners who love it would do well to anticipate rhizomatous conquest of garden space and use containment (grow in a pot, surround with concrete, or use rhizome barriers). With a large unwanted population, mowing can forestall seed production but will not kill it and may encourage vegetative proliferation. In established populations, its roots and rhizomes can be challenging to remove. Dig out as much as possible, and monitor for resprouting. A thick layer of wood mulch may help to suppress it, but removal of rhizomes that invade desired garden plants can be difficult.

# Lysimachia terrestris

BOG LOOSESTRIFE, SWAMP CANDLE

Non-native perennial, to 3 ft. Flowers yellow, 5-petaled, to 0.75 in.; midsummer. Leaves opposite, to 4 in.

This robust wetland species, native to eastern North America, came to the PNW as a weed of cranberry bogs and is now found in scattered sites along the coast from BC to Oregon, as well as in Idaho. It spreads rapidly by rhizomes in marshes and bogs and in wet soils on the margins of lakes and streams.

The stems are erect, leafy, hairless, round in cross section, and unbranched or sparingly branched below the terminal inflorescences. The lower central stem bears small scale-like leaves, but otherwise the leaves are elliptic, to 0.75 in. wide, sessile to short-stalked.

The bright yellow flowers are starlike, with red circles at the centers of their corollas formed by pairs of dots at the base of each petal. They are borne on short, slender stalks in spike-like racemes to 12 in. long at the tops of central stems. Shorter spikes sometimes rise from upper leaf axils and from lateral stems. Reddish-brown, segmented, oval bulblets to 0.5 in. long may form in upper leaf axils late in the bloom season.

This showy weed can spread very rapidly in wetland conditions, via seeds, bulblets, and rhizomes, potentially wearing out its welcome. The gardener charmed by bog loosestrife is well advised to prevent its seeds and bulblets from escaping into the landscape by cutting it back after bloom and by containing its rhizomatous exuberance. If you've had enough, pull and dig, being careful to retrieve all the rhizomes.

# Lysimachia vulgaris
## GARDEN YELLOW LOOSESTRIFE

Non-native perennial, to 6 ft. Flowers yellow, 5-petaled, to 0.5 in.; midsummer. Leaves opposite, whorled, to 4.5 in. Parts edible/medicinal. Noxious in WA, OR.

*Lysimachia vulgaris* is a showy garden plant that has escaped cultivation at scattered sites from BC to Oregon and Montana, as well as being widespread through much of northeastern North America. It invades wet woodlands and moist ground around wetlands, lake margins, and riparian areas. With aggressive vegetative growth and self-seeding, it forms dense stands that crowd out native vegetation, clog and degrade the quality of waterways, and have negative impacts on aquatic wildlife, including salmon. It can even outcompete the notorious (and unrelated) *Lythrum salicaria* (purple loosestrife). *Lysimachia punctata*, its popular garden-plant cousin, differs from *L. vulgaris* in being shorter (to 4 ft.), with flowers borne all along the stem, not just near the top.

From a mass of rhizomes as long as 15 ft., garden yellow loosestrife sends up erect stems that begin unbranched but become more branched later in the season. Stems and leaves are hairy, the leaves broadly lanceolate to oval, short-stalked to sessile, in whorls of 3 (sometimes 2 or 4). The yellow flowers are borne in long racemes at the tops of stems and from the upper leaf axils.

An established patch of garden yellow loosestrife can form a dense underground mat of rhizomes that is difficult to dig out. Bag all plant material, as rhizome fragments left behind can sprout. Cutting or mowing is not effective in eradicating the plant, but cutting to the ground at bloom time will forestall seed production. As with other aggressive wetland invaders, herbicide can be problematic and may require permits and specific wetland-safe formulations. Any strategy employed with *Lysimachia vulgaris* will likely require repeated efforts and continued monitoring.

# Ceratocephala testiculata

## HORNSEED BUTTERCUP, BUR BUTTERCUP

Non-native annual, to 3 in. Flowers yellow, 2- to 5-petaled, to 0.3 in.; spring. Leaves basal, to 1.6 in. Poisonous. Toxic to sheep, livestock.

*Ceratocephala testiculata* (syn. *Ranunculus testiculatus*) is found in much of southern Canada and most of the continental US, with the exception of the Southeast. Preferring dry sites, this tiny Eurasian weed occurs primarily on the east side of the Cascades in the PNW. It invades prairies, cropland, rangeland, pastures, lawns, gardens, roadsides, and various ecologically disturbed or barren sites, forming mats on land left bare by misuse. It displaces natives in natural areas and is often a weed of cereal crops. It is toxic to livestock, particularly sheep, which can be killed by ingesting as little as a pound of the plant.

Growing from a small taproot, the plant produces a rosette of small basal leaves, which are divided into many short, narrow segments. The leaves and leafless flowering stems are covered with fine, woolly-white hairs. Flowers, borne singly, have 2–5 petals, unusual for the buttercup family. The 5 sepals are green, oval, fuzzy, and nearly as long as the petals, which quickly wither and fade.

Hornseed buttercup spreads solely by its seeds, which are hooked so that they can catch rides on animals, people, or tires. Dig, hoe, or pull before it sets seed, then mulch. The plant is not a strong competitor in healthy plant communities, so competitive plantings will discourage it. For larger infestations, mowing or cutting very low early in the season is effective, as is burning where practicable.

# Clematis vitalba

## TRAVELER'S JOY, OLD MAN'S BEARD

Non-native perennial vine, to 60 ft. Flowers white, 4-lobed, to 0.75 in.; summer. Leaves opposite, 5 leaflets, each to 2.5 in. Poisonous. Toxic to chickens. Noxious in WA, OR, CA.

*Clematis vitalba* is a robust, woody vine invading woodlands, riparian zones, parks, and vacant lots in scattered locations in the westside PNW from BC to Oregon. It grows rapidly, damaging structures, shading out native flora, and weighing down trees, making them vulnerable to windfall and creating hazards to humans in woodlands.

The deciduous leaves are pinnately compound, with 5 leaflets connected by petioles. Leaf margins are variable, from entire to shallowly lobed or serrated. The fragrant, frilly-looking flowers are borne in terminal and axillary clusters of up to 20. The seedheads are composed of masses of feathery styles, which aid in wind dispersal. A single plant may produce up to 100,000 seeds annually. Seedheads persist through winter, even after the leaves have fallen. In addition to self-sowing, *Clematis vitalba* reproduces by rooting at the nodes.

If discovered early enough, traveler's joy is easy to pull or dig up. Or you can yank it out, using a weed wrench. Wear gloves, because the plant is toxic and can cause skin reactions. Large infestations are best attacked in winter or spring, when the soil is moist and less damage will be done to surrounding vegetation and wildlife. Do not attempt to pull down large mats that have invaded the crowns of trees: the masses of vine attached to branches come crashing down and may cause injury. Loppers and saws may be needed. Large vines can be cut at the base and the stump treated with herbicide. Repeated cutting to the ground or mowing can at least keep the plant from spreading but will not kill it.

Gardeners who are charmed by this vine aesthetically might try *Clematis ligusticifolia*, a similar-looking but less aggressive native species.

# Ficaria verna

## LESSER CELANDINE, FIG BUTTERCUP

**Non-native perennial, to 16 in. Flowers yellow, 7- to 13-petaled, to 1 in.; early spring. Leaves basal to 3 in., cauline alternate. Parts edible/medicinal with caution. Toxic to cattle. Noxious in WA, OR.**

*Ficaria verna* (syn. *Ranunculus ficaria*), introduced as an ornamental, has been present in the US as a garden escape since at least the mid-1800s. It is now distributed over much of North America, listed as invasive or noxious in several states. In the PNW, it's found more commonly on the west side, as it prefers moist and/or shady conditions. It invades wetlands, moist woodlands, lawns, and streambanks, often forming broad, dense monocultures that crowd out natives and are extremely difficult to eradicate. It is moderately toxic to humans and cattle.

Growing from thick, tuberous and fibrous roots, *Ficaria verna* produces a ground-hugging mass of handsome basal leaves. The leaves are hairless, deep green above but lighter beneath, and triangular to cordate, with margins that may be entire, wavy, or have rounded teeth. Basal and lower cauline leaves are long-stalked; higher on the stem, the leaves are smaller and have shorter petioles. Higher leaves may also be nearly opposite.

Flowers are borne singly on long stalks at tops of stems. Two of the 5 subspecies produce aerial bulblets in the leaf axils; these can detach and take root in soil, producing new plants. Reproducing by fragmented tuberous root segments, bulblets, and seed, *Ficaria verna* can spread aggressively and is further dispersed by flooding events and by human activities that result in movement of soil and plant parts.

This exceedingly invasive noxious weed is attractive, and several cultivars are available in the nursery trade. Gardeners who like the look might find some of these less aggressive than the species. An even better choice is *Caltha palustris*, a native that looks very similar in leaf and flower and grows in similar conditions.

Land managers coping with large expanses of *Ficaria verna* report that even with herbicides, the battle can last for years. Mowing only facilitates its spread. Small patches can be attacked by digging; take care to remove all roots and bulblets. Bag and remove all plant material, don't compost it. Long-term mulching to a depth of at least 6 in. with continued monitoring may be effective for larger patches.

# Ranunculus acris

## TALL BUTTERCUP, MEADOW BUTTERCUP

Non-native perennial, to 3 ft. Flowers yellow, 5- to 7-petaled, to 1 in.; late spring–summer. Leaves basal to 3 in., cauline alternate. Poisonous. Toxic to horses, cattle, goats.

This European weed is widely distributed across North America, particularly in the northern US and southern Canada. It can be seen on moist, disturbed ground in pastures, meadows, lawns, woodlands, and roadsides. It is toxic to grazers and can be invasive but happily is short-lived, spreading only by seed.

From a cluster of slender, fibrous roots, the plant's root crown typically sends up several stems, which are hollow and upright, hairy throughout, and multi-branched toward the top. The basal leaves are long-stalked and palmately lobed, with 3 deeply incised main lobes that are again each divided into smaller segments with pointed tips. Stem leaves are progressively smaller and simpler. Individual flowers, borne in small terminal clusters, are long-stalked, with fuzzy, reflexed sepals and glossy petals. Seedheads are typical for the genus, little round clusters of pointy seeds that stick easily to passing animals, people, or vehicle tires, or may be dispersed by birds or wind. A single plant may produce hundreds of seeds in a season.

The very word "buttercup" strikes rage and despair into the hearts of gardeners suffering from *Ranunculus repens* trauma. But fear not: compared to that seemingly inexorable monster of vegetative spread, *R. acris* is comparatively benign. Just yank it out, but wear gloves to protect against possible skin irritation. Pull or dig early in the season, when the ground is moist, or mow larger populations very low before they bloom. In the garden, follow with mulch and replant.

# *Ranunculus repens*

## CREEPING BUTTERCUP

Non-native perennial, to 1 ft. Flowers yellow, 5- to 10-petaled, to 1.3 in.; midspring–autumn. Leaves basal to 4 in., cauline alternate. Poisonous. Toxic to horses, cattle, goats. Noxious in BC.

Creeping buttercup is found over most of North America and throughout the PNW, especially on the wetter west side. This aggressive weed invades wet ground in meadows, fields, riparian zones, farmland, wetlands, drainage ditches, yards, and gardens, crowding out natives and desirable garden or crop plants. It is toxic to grazing animals. At least in the western PNW, it is sometimes confused with the unrelated *Geum macrophyllum*, a widespread, rambunctious native, which also has compound, coarsely toothed leaves and yellow flowers.

The leaves of *Ranunculus repens* are dark green with small pale patches. The leaves and stems are hairy. Basal leaves are long-stalked and compound, with 3 leaflets, the central one short-stalked and the others sessile. The leaflets may be shallowly incised or deeply cut into lobes, the margins toothed to doubly dentate. Higher on the stem, the leaves are reduced in size, stalkless, and simpler in shape. Long, branching stolons rise from lower leaf axils. The flowers are very bright yellow, with a satiny gloss, with typically 5 but sometimes as many as 10 petals. The plants reproduce via seed and by stolons, above or below ground, rooting at the nodes. One plant may spread vegetatively over 40 sq. ft. in a year. Seeds develop in clusters composed of many beaked achenes on a spherical head, beginning green and maturing to brown. A plant may produce 150 seeds in a season, and these can remain viable for decades.

Mowing has little effect in discouraging the robust vegetative growth of creeping buttercup, as its growing points are all at ground level. Be alert for new seedlings, and intervene before the stolons get ahead of you. Dig out with a fork or other sharp tool, preferably when the soil is wet, being sure to remove all the stolons and fibrous roots. Be prepared to work diligently, frequently, and repeatedly. This plant forms such impenetrable mats and grows so rapidly that many people resort to herbicides when practicable; as the plant often grows near wetlands, state regulations may apply.

# Potentilla recta

SULPHUR CINQUEFOIL, ROUGH-FRUITED CINQUEFOIL, ERECT CINQUEFOIL

Non-native perennial, to 3 ft. Flowers yellow, 5-petaled, to 0.75 in.; midspring–midsummer. Leaves alternate, leaflets to 3.5 in. Parts edible/medicinal. Noxious in BC, WA, OR, CA.

*Potentilla recta* is a Eurasian weed present in the PNW since the 1930s and now found over most of the US and southern Canada. It invades lawns, vacant lots, railroad margins, roadsides, fields, and woodland edges, forming broad stands that crowd out natives in natural areas and competing with more desirable forage in pastures.

The plant grows from fibrous roots and a woody root crown that may produce several stems, some of which can eventually break off from the mother plant and persist separately. The stems are hairy, branched, and leafy. Upper stem leaves particularly may be held close to the stem, with upward-pointing petioles. Lower leaves have up to 9 palmately arranged leaflets, the higher ones as few as 3 or 5. The leaflets are narrow and sessile, with prominent pinnate venation and deeply serrated margins. Leaves and stems are slightly raspy to the touch, like fine Velcro. The upper leaf surfaces are green or grayish-green and relatively hairless; the undersides are paler and hairy.

Flowers are borne in flat-topped terminal clusters. Individual flowers are larger than many other cinquefoils, and paler yellow, often close to cream. The petals are shallowly cleft into two lobes, making a heart-like shape. A single plant may produce as many as 1,600 seeds yearly, and these can remain viable for 3 years.

Digging and pulling can be effective in removing small populations, if done when the soil is moist and the root crown can be removed. Chopping with a hoe below the root crown can also work. Mowing is ineffective, as the root crowns will resprout.

# Galium aparine

## BEDSTRAW, CLEAVERS

Native annual, to 3 ft. Flowers white, 4-petaled, to 0.08 in.; mid–late spring. Leaves whorled, to 1.5 in. Parts edible/medicinal with caution. Noxious in BC.

*Galium aparine* is a circumboreal species, native to both North America and Eurasia and present in most countries worldwide. It can be found throughout the PNW in woodlands, moist meadows, yards, gardens, agricultural land, and waste ground. Bedstraw is one of the weedy native species most familiar to gardeners, as it seems to materialize wherever gardens are planted. It is unattractive as a garden visitor but has historically been used in cheesemaking, dye work, and medicinal applications.

The plant grows from very shallow, fibrous roots, with a weak, squarish, sparingly branched, scrambling and reclining stem. The linear leaves occur in widely spaced whorls of 8 (occasionally 6 or 7). Stiff, downward-pointing hairs on leaves and stems assist in adhering to other plants for support. The tiny flowers are borne in small axillary clusters. A plant may produce as many as 400 small, tan, bur-like seeds; these are easily dispersed by wind and particularly by sticking to things, including clothing and the feathers or fur of animals.

*Galium aparine* is a serious problem for grain agriculture, where frequent cultivation is one effective means of controlling it. For home gardens, small invasions are easily removed by pulling or scraping with a hoe. Where desirable and safe, burning can control it by killing most of the seeds. Mulch and competitive plantings will help to prevent subsequent sprouts.

# Galium odoratum

## SWEET WOODRUFF, FRAGRANT BEDSTRAW

Non-native perennial, to 20 in. Flowers white, 4-petaled, to 0.25 in.; late spring–early summer. Leaves whorled, to 2 in. Parts edible/medicinal with caution.

*Galium odoratum* (syn. *Asperula odorata*) is a European species long used as an ornamental and medicinal herb. It's a popular shade garden groundcover, and whether it's viewed as reliable or inexorable is somewhat subjective. About 10 native *Galium* species, five of them weedy, are present in the PNW; *G. odoratum* is the only widely planted one. It is present as a garden escape in scattered locations from BC to Oregon, along the US east coast, and in eastern Canada. It prefers moist, cool, and shady conditions. In the PNW, it is semi-evergreen in milder places and is mostly found on the west side, on woodland edges.

Sweet woodruff is low-growing, with trailing stems clothed in glossy, deep green, elliptic leaves, mostly in whorls of 8, sometimes 6 or 10. The small white flowers bloom in terminal clusters. Foliage and flowers are sweet-scented. The plant reproduces by seed but spreads mostly by vigorous rhizomatous growth.

*Galium odoratum* looks innocent but can be a tough customer to control. Regularly chopping around the circumference of a patch you intend to keep can prevent the rhizomes from annexing more of your garden. Entirely unwelcome invasions can be conquered by pulling, digging, and chopping when the soil is moist, taking care to remove rhizomes, and likely repeating this. Mulch heavily to discourage the return of remaining rhizomes or seedlings.

# Galium verum

## LADY'S BEDSTRAW, YELLOW SPRING BEDSTRAW

Non-native perennial, to 3 ft. Flowers yellow, 4-petaled, to 0.13 in.; midsummer–autumn. Leaves whorled, to 1 in. Parts edible/medicinal.

*Galium verum* is an attractive garden escape of Eurasian origin that has become a widespread weed through most of the northern US and southern Canada, scrambling along open fields and roadsides. Lady's bedstraw is so named because it was used as a mattress stuffing in the Middle Ages; the coumarin scent of the foliage was valued as a flea deterrent. It was also used traditionally in cheesemaking and is still used in dye work.

The leaves are arranged in whorls of 8–12, and clusters of bright yellow flowers arise from the upper axils. Lady's bedstraw spreads via rhizomes and self-seeding, and the long stems will root where they contact the soil. It can form broad colonies in suitable habitat.

Smaller invasions are easily dislodged by hand and hoe, particularly when the soil is moist, and ideally before seed is shed. Mulch to discourage further germination.

# *Sherardia arvensis*

## BLUE FIELD-MADDER

Non-native annual, to 10 in. Flowers lilac, pink, blue, 4-petaled, to 0.2 in.; late spring–midsummer. Leaves in whorls, to 0.4 in. Unpalatable.

Blue field-madder is a little weed found in scattered locations along the west coast, in Idaho and Arizona, and in several southern to southeastern states. It inhabits moderately moist meadows, pastures, riparian zones, grasslands, commercial turf, residential lawns, and woodlands.

*Sherardia arvensis* grows from slender, fleshy, reddish roots that have been used to make dye. The slender stem is prostrate to ascending and either unbranched or well branched from the base; it's square in cross section and may be hairy or scabrous. The leaves resemble those of its familiar relatives, the *Galiums* (bedstraws and sweet woodruff, among others). They are short, linear to elliptical, sharply pointed on the ends, hairy on the upper sides and scabrous below, held in whorls of 4–6. Plants bear mostly terminal clusters of 2–3 tiny flowers, each subtended by several bracts. The lilac-pink to blue flowers are funnel-shaped with a tube that opens out to 4 spreading, pointed petals.

This is not likely to be your worst horticultural problem but is probably not what you want in a purely native setting or a fastidiously groomed rock garden. When it's not closely surrounded by desired plants (including lawn grass), blue field-madder is easy enough to scrape away or grub out with a hoe. Where that isn't workable, pulling is easy when the soil is moist. (If you have a whole lot of roots, you can make a pinkish dye!) Or ignore it and consider it a cute belly-plant that enlivens the boring lawn, or a living mulch or groundcover in the non-native garden.

# *Verbascum blattaria*

## MOTH MULLEIN

**Non-native biennial, to 5 ft. Flowers yellow, white, 5-petaled, to 1 in.; midspring–autumn. Leaves basal to 6 in., cauline alternate. Unpalatable.**

Moth mullein is a pretty European weed present across most of North America. It is common in sunny, often dry areas of the PNW, including meadows, agricultural fields, vacant lots, roadsides, and gravel streambanks.

Growing from fibrous roots and a stout taproot, *Verbascum blattaria* produces a basal rosette of leaves in its first year. In its second year, it sends up a single, tall, usually unbranched or little-branched flowering stem. The basal and lower cauline leaves are short-stalked and often lobed, with scalloped or toothed margins. Higher on the stem, the leaves are reduced in size and more triangular. Unlike *V. thapsus*, its larger, fuzzy cousin, moth mullein is mostly hairless.

The flowers, borne on short stalks in long terminal racemes, may be yellow or white; the petal bases are often tinged purple, and the purple stamens have orange anthers. Flowers are followed by small, spherical seed capsules, each containing many tiny seeds. There may be over 1,000 capsules on a single plant, so many thousands of seeds are produced, and these can remain viable in the soil for decades.

*Verbascum blattaria* spreads entirely by seed. While at first encounter it may charm the gardener, it can quickly take over. It's easy enough to uproot when discovered in small numbers. Pull younger plants when the soil is moist, or grub out with a hoe, cutting below the crown of the plant. For larger patches, mow close to the ground before plants bloom.

# *Verbascum thapsus*

## WOOLLY MULLEIN, COMMON MULLEIN

Non-native biennial, to 7 ft. Flowers yellow, 5-petaled, to 0.75 in.; summer. Leaves basal to 16 in., cauline alternate. Parts medicinal with caution.

Woolly mullein has been present in the US since the 1700s and is such a familiar sight throughout most of the US and southern Canada that many people think it's native. It's often seen on sunny sites on disturbed ground, including roadsides and logged or burned-over ground, abandoned farmland, meadows, and in open woods.

This biennial grows from a stout, deep taproot with fibrous lateral roots, producing a basal rosette of large,

felted leaves in the first year, followed by a solitary, sturdy flowering stem in the second. The flowering stem is erect and unbranched (or sparingly branched near the base), except when the stem is severed by cutting or grazing. It can then branch generously, sometimes in amusing Seussian ways. The stem and leaves are all densely woolly, giving the plant a whitish or grayish-green color. Basal leaves are long-petiolate; leaves higher on the stem are progressively smaller and more sessile. Leaf margins are smooth to wavy.

Woolly mullein's flower spikes are up to 2 ft. long. Individual flowers last only one day; they have 5 petals, in a slightly irregular (not fully radially symmetric) corolla. Seeds are tiny and carried in many small, spherical capsules. Seed production estimates average 150,000 per plant, with branched plants producing even more. The seeds may remain viable for decades. While the leaves wither away, the central stem often persists through winter, along with the seed capsules. The seeds are dispersed, usually for short distances, by wind, heavy rains, or animal activity. Movement of soil by human activity may be the only means of long-distance dispersal.

Many are inclined to keep the quirky-looking mullein in the garden when it shows up, as it does. But know that you may pay for this entertainment later, and deadhead thoroughly. Unwanted plants are easy to remove by pulling or hoeing when the soil is moist. Plants severed below the root crown don't resprout.

# Hyoscyamus niger

## BLACK HENBANE

Non-native annual or biennial, to 5 ft. Flowers yellow-green, 5-lobed, to 1.75 in.; mid–late summer. Leaves alternate, to 8 in. Poisonous. Toxic to horses, chickens. Noxious in BC, WA, CA.

This European species, grown as an ornamental, has escaped cultivation across the southern half of Canada from Alberta to Quebec and much of the US, with the exception of several southern states. It's a prolific self-seeder, invading roadsides, vacant lots, pastures, and residential areas. It is profoundly toxic to humans and to livestock, but animal poisoning is rare because of its strong, unpleasant odor. Humans, being less bright, become seriously poisoned when we use parts of the plant for hallucinogenic effects.

Growing from a taproot, black henbane can bloom and die in its first year, or form a leaf rosette and bloom the second year. Stems are tall, thick, upright, and branched. Leaves and stems are covered with soft, sticky hairs. The leaves are broad and sessile, with coarsely toothed or shallowly lobed margins. Borne in leafy terminal racemes, the flowers are funnel-shaped and greenish- or brownish-yellow, with purple centers and veining. They are followed by capsules that release thousands of small, long-lived seeds.

This short-lived and non-rhizomatous plant is fairly easy to remove, but wear gloves and protective clothing to avoid rashes. Pull, hoe, or dig it out, including the taproot. Larger patches can be mowed well before bloom. Any mature capsules should be bagged and removed or burned. Replanting the area with more competitive, desired plants can help to avoid future infestations.

# Physalis longifolia

## LONGLEAF GROUNDCHERRY, WILD TOMATILLO

Non-native perennial, to 3 ft. Flowers yellow-green, 5-lobed, to 0.6 in.; midsummer–autumn. Leaves alternate, to 5 in. Parts edible. Toxic to horses, cattle, chickens. Noxious in CA.

This weedy cousin of tomatillos is found across most of North America; in the PNW, it occurs primarily on the east side. It can form large colonies by spreading rhizomes, invading farm fields, vacant lots, dry meadows, and woodlands.

The plant is usually rigid and erect at first but may become sprawling when weighed down by fruit late in the season. The branched stems are green to purple, angled and grooved, and somewhat pubescent. The leaves are lanceolate to oval, up to 3 in. wide, on petioles to 1.5 in. wide; they are usually smooth-margined but may have irregular, blunt, or wavy teeth. The stalked, pendent flowers, borne singly in the axils, are funnel-shaped and light yellow, with 5 rounded, purplish-brown splotches around the center inside. The color scheme can be striking, with 5 stamens often having purple filaments and pale yellow anthers. Like the related Chinese lanterns familiar to many gardeners, the calyx of longleaf groundcherry becomes inflated and papery at maturity, enclosing the developing fruit, which is green maturing to yellow, to 0.5 in. wide. The fruit is edible but much smaller than that of *Physalis* species grown commonly for green salsa.

Uninvited longleaf groundcherry is rambunctiously rhizomatous, unlike the familiar garden tomatillo. With thick, deep, and long rhizomes, it can take over. The best time to intervene is when the plant is young and easiest when the soil is moist. Pull and dig out all rhizomes; if they have had time to wander in the garden, shallow cultivation with hand tools can be used to bring them to the surface. Mulch well, and monitor for new resprouts and seedlings.

# Solanum dulcamara

## BITTERSWEET NIGHTSHADE

Non-native perennial, to 20 ft. Flowers blue, purple, 5-lobed, to 0.5 in.; early summer–autumn. Leaves alternate, to 4 in. Poisonous. Toxic to cats, dogs, horses, cattle, pigs, sheep, goats, chickens. Noxious in BC.

This Eurasian cousin of potatoes and tomatoes is present in the PNW and across most of North America, often in partly shady, moist sites, including woodland edges, wetlands, gardens, parks, riparian areas, vacant lots, and roadsides. It can be invasive, forming dense thickets and displacing natives. Bittersweet nightshade spreads vegetatively by climbing, suckering, rooting of prostrate stems at the node, and sprouting of stem and root fragments. It also reproduces by seed, often with the help of birds that disperse the berries.

All plant parts are mildly to very toxic to people, pets, and livestock. Note: bittersweet nightshade is often mistakenly called "deadly nightshade." That is the common name of *Atropa belladonna*, which is more profoundly toxic and has black berries, distinct from the red ones of bittersweet nightshade.

*Solanum dulcamara* is shrubby and somewhat woody at its base, growing more vine-like and herbaceous upward as it climbs or scrambles over other plants, sometimes as high as 30 ft. into trees. The herbaceous upper stems are deciduous, dying back in winter. The leaves are dark green to purple, stalked, and malodorous. Some leaves are simple and oval to somewhat heart-shaped; others have a pair of smaller, ear-like lobes or leaflets closer to the petiole.

The inflorescence is a branched cluster of up to 25 star-shaped, blue to purple (occasionally white) flowers. Each flower has a corolla with 5 pointed lobes and a 5-lobed calyx with pointed, reflexed sepals. Five bright yellow stamens are fused into a cone shape in the center. Flowers are followed by clusters of egg-shaped berries about 0.4 in. in diameter, ripening from green to orange to red.

Wear gloves as a precaution when handling this plant. Young plants can be pulled, but avoid breaking stems or rhizomes, as these can resprout. Dig out more established plants, along with their roots, and remove any fruit from the site. Follow with mulch, replant, and monitor for resprouting. For larger patches, use a mower or weed whacker to take down the plants several times throughout the growing season; this can eventually exhaust the roots and cause them to die. Another approach recommended by land managers for large patches is to cut plants to the ground and cover closely with geotextile or plastic for at least 2 years; this may not be the best option for home gardeners. Try a very thick layer of woody mulch for the same period.

# Solanum nigrum

## BLACK NIGHTSHADE

Non-native annual or perennial, to 4 ft. Flowers white, 5-lobed, to 0.4 in.; midsummer–autumn. Leaves alternate, to 3 in. Poisonous. Toxic to cats, dogs, horses, cattle, pigs, sheep, goats, chickens. Noxious in BC.

This ubiquitous European weed is present throughout North America and seems guaranteed to show up out of nowhere wherever a garden is planted. It invades roadsides, vacant lots, fields, agricultural land, and yards. It contaminates some crops and, with the sole exception of fully ripe fruit, is toxic to humans or animals consuming it.

Growing from a shallow taproot and fibrous roots, the plant is sparsely hairy or hairless and either slender and erect or multi-branched and bushy. The leaves are stalked, oval to deltoid, to 2 in. wide, with margins smooth or wavy or with a few shallow teeth. The inflorescences are clusters of up to 8 flowers on peduncles to 0.75 in. long, attached intermittently along the stem or opposite the leaves. The individual flowers in turn are stalked, on pedicels to 0.4 in. In the center of each flower, the bright yellow anthers huddle in a cone around the pistil. Flowers are followed by berries about 0.3 in. in diameter, beginning green and ripening to black. A single plant can produce as many as 5,000 seeds, which are dispersed by animals, human activity, or water, and may be viable for several years.

Black nightshade can be removed by pulling, digging, shallow manual cultivation, or mowing, prior to blooming and seed formation. This may need to be repeated for a few years to exhaust the seed bank and eradicate the weed from the site.

# Solanum physalifolium

## HAIRY NIGHTSHADE, HOE NIGHTSHADE

Non-native annual, to 3 ft. Flowers white, 5-lobed, to 0.5 in.; midsummer–autumn. Leaves alternate, to 3 in. Poisonous. Toxic to cats, dogs, horses, cattle, pigs, sheep, goats, chickens. Noxious in BC.

*Solanum physalifolium* (syn. *Solanum sarrachoides*) is widespread in the western half of the US, invading fields, gardens, rangeland, and agricultural land. It is a particular nuisance in potato farming, harboring pests and diseases of potatoes and competing with the crop. Hairy nightshade is toxic if consumed by animals or humans.

The plant is bushy, well branched, and noticeably hairy all over. The leaves are stalked, oval to triangular, to 2 in. wide, with margins either smooth or with irregular, shallowly indented teeth. They may feel sticky, with hairs along the underside midveins and sometimes over the entire surfaces, above and below. The white to very pale blue flowers are borne in stalked clusters of up to 8. The petal bases are purplish-green, and the insides of the petals are sometimes flecked in pale purple. The fruit are round berries to 0.3 in. in diameter, maturing from green to yellow, purplish or pale brown, each covered about halfway with an expanded calyx. A single plant may produce several hundred to a few thousand seeds.

Hairy nightshade may be confused with black nightshade, except for these traits: the calyx of *Solanum nigrum* does not expand and retains its small, distinct, triangular sepals, which tend to reflex away from the fruit. Black nightshade berries are black; those of hairy nightshade never are. And black nightshade is hardly hairy, if at all.

Control considerations for hairy nightshade in home gardens are the same as for black nightshade: pull or dig when the soil is moist, or for larger patches, mow. Mulch and monitor, and be prepared to repeat if a seed bank has developed.

# Solanum rostratum

## BUFFALO BUR, HORNED NIGHTSHADE

**Non-native annual, to 3 ft. Flowers yellow, 5-lobed, to 1 in.; midspring–autumn. Leaves alternate, to 6 in. Toxic to horses, cattle, pigs, sheep, goats, chickens. Noxious in BC, WA, OR.**

*Solanum rostratum* is one member of a huge genus (perhaps 2,000 species), including edible tomatoes and potatoes and many (often toxic) weeds. Native to the midwestern US, this species is widely distributed throughout North America and other parts of the world. It is found on disturbed, often dry ground, in vacant lots, roadsides, fields, farmland, and yards. It is aggressive in rangeland and pastures, displacing forage plants, and is toxic if grazed by livestock. However, it's rarely eaten: its many sharp spines can cause injury. The plant often finds its way into our region as a contaminant in purchased seeds.

All vegetative plant parts are hairy and covered in straight, sharp, yellow spines to 0.5 in. long. The stems are tall and well branched. The leaves are deeply cut into 5–7 irregular, pinnately arranged, prickly lobes. The plants bear racemes of up to 15 showy, circular (like the related garden plant, petunia), bright yellow flowers. These are followed by berries enclosed in spiny calyces. A single plant can produce as many as 8,500 seeds.

Buffalo bur is fairly easy to control by repeated cutting or mowing to prevent blooming and seed production. Wear good gloves and protective clothing to guard against the spines, and pull, hoe, or dig out smaller invasions. Follow with mulch and install desirable, competitive plantings.

# *Urtica dioica*

## STINGING NETTLE

Perennial, both native and introduced, to 8 ft. Flowers white, 4-lobed, to 0.05 in.; midspring–autumn. Leaves opposite, to 6 in. Parts edible/medicinal with caution. Toxic to cats, dogs, horses.

Stinging nettle is native to several continents and introduced in others, inhabiting a broad range of habitats. It is present over much of North America, in both native and introduced forms. In the PNW, it is most often a plant of moist woodland edges and yards, vacant lots, grasslands, riparian understory, wetland edges, and farmland. With its opposite, dentate leaves, *Urtica dioica* is often mistaken for a mint, and to make matters worse, a group of mint family species share the "nettle" name.

Stinging nettle grows from a network of fibrous roots and light-colored, stringy rhizomes. The foliage can be largely hairless or fuzzy but always with the stinging hairs that give the plant its common name. The leaves are stalked and lanceolate to oval, with serrated margins. The many tiny, apetalous flowers are borne in thread-like, drooping axillary and terminal spikes.

The plant spreads aggressively by rhizomes, which can extend the diameter of a patch by several feet in a season. The seeds are dispersed by wind and water; they also attach themselves to fur, feathers, or clothing and are eaten and excreted by various animals. Stinging nettle can form large monocultural patches. The slightest contact with the leaves, even through clothing, can cause a painful burning, stinging sensation that may last for hours.

*Urtica dioica* has a long history of use for fiber, for medicinal applications, and particularly for food (carefully harvested and then cooked). Seed is still sold online for medicinal and food gardening. For those so inclined, one means of reducing its biomass might be harvesting.

Wear protective clothing (lots!) to work with it. It can be controlled by pulling very young plants, digging out with as much rhizome as possible when they are more established, or repeatedly cutting (carefully) to the ground.

# *Valerianella locusta*

## CORN SALAD, LAMB'S LETTUCE, MÂCHE

Non-native annual, to 15 in. Flowers blue, white, 5-lobed, to 0.07 in.; late spring. Leaves basal to 2.75 in., cauline opposite. Parts edible.

*Valerianella locusta* is a Eurasian species grown as a salad vegetable for centuries in Europe and increasingly in the US. It has escaped cultivation and is a common weed in lawns and gardens from BC to California, eastward to Montana and Utah, and in much of eastern North America.

Corn salad grows from a thin, deep taproot and shallow fibrous roots, sending up multiple erect, slender, weak stems. These may be unbranched or sparingly branched and opposite, like the stem leaves. Stems and foliage are hairless to sparsely fuzzy and light green. The basal and lower stem leaves are spatulate or oblanceolate and stalked; higher on the stem, they are lanceolate and sessile.

The tiny, funnel-shaped flowers, borne in small, round, dense terminal clusters, are very pale blue to white. A single plant may produce 700 seeds in a season.

Corn salad is so small and delicate that it's unlikely to cause much distress, but if you're not interested in eating it (or eating as much as you have), it could be a minor nuisance if it swamps other seedlings or rock garden ornamentals. Pull or hoe when plants are young, digging out the taproots if later in the season. Mulch, and plant other things.

# *Viola riviniana*

## DOG VIOLET, WOOD VIOLET

Non-native perennial, to 6 in. Flowers blue, violet, 5-petaled, to 1 in.; late spring. Leaves basal to 2 in., cauline alternate. Parts edible.

*Viola riviniana* is found as a garden escape from BC to California. On the PNW west side, it's ubiquitous in lawns, gardens, nursery containers, woodland edges, and vacant lots. This Eurasian species has often been misidentified, and sold by nurseries, as the eastern North American native *V. labradorica*, particularly in its dark-leaved form; however, true *V. labradorica* does not grow wild in the west.

Dog violet grows from fibrous roots, beginning with a basal rosette of heart-shaped, long-stalked leaves, followed by short, leafy flowering stems. The plant sends out stolons, which root readily and produce more plants. The bilaterally symmetric flowers are blue to pinkish-violet, with upturned, pale lavender to white spurs. Flowers are followed by seed capsules that open and shoot seeds out explosively. Seeds are also dispersed by ants.

This violet can cover ground with astonishing speed, forming mats in gardens and in containers. The stolons and roots are thin but tenacious. Pull, taking care to remove roots and root crowns. Less established plants can be grubbed out with a hoe; more robust ones can be dug. Mulch well and be vigilant. They will be back!

# Tribulus terrestris

## PUNCTURE VINE, CALTROP

Non-native annual, mat to 6 ft. Flowers yellow, 5-petaled, to 0.4 in.; summer. Leaves opposite, to 3 in., leaflets to 0.25 in. Parts edible/medicinal with caution. Toxic to horses, sheep, goats. Noxious in BC, WA, OR, CA.

You might guess that the genus name of this scourge of a plant translates loosely from the Latin for "tribulation." You'd be wrong, but not by much. It derives in fact from *tribolos*, the Greek word for a nasty three-spiked weapon, the caltrop (from which the entire family takes its common name). Puncture vine is widely hated for its wicked, spiky seeds, which can pierce shoes, tires, and flesh. A widespread weed of dry places throughout North America, it's mostly on the east side in the PNW. It enjoys sandy soils in pastures, agricultural land, and roadsides. The plant is a hazard for farmworkers and toxic to livestock, though they rarely graze it. It is a nuisance weed for several important agricultural crops worldwide.

Rising from a woody taproot and root system to 6 ft. deep, the long stems of puncture vine are multi-branched and ground-hugging and can form broad mats. The stems are clothed in small, pinnately compound, hairy leaves, each bearing 3–7 pairs of opposite leaflets. The small, bright yellow flowers are borne singly in leaf axils. The plant is actually pretty and would not inspire the animosity it does if it did not then produce seedpods that are woody burrs with sharp, rigid spines. Seed production has been assessed at up to 100,000 per plant.

The prime objective of control is to stop seed production and dispersal. Gloves and protective clothing are a must if seeds are present. Pull or hoe before roots reach down, or moisten the soil and dig out any taproots. For large infestations with many seeds on the

ground, people have devised rollers covered with sticky material; when rolled across the ground, these collect many of the spiky seeds. The seeds can germinate throughout the growing season and will last in the soil for several years, so repeated monitoring, pulling, and digging will be necessary until the seed bank is depleted. Bag and dispose of all roots and seeds, and mulch well.

# *Zygophyllum fabago*

BEAN-CAPER

Non-native perennial, to 30 in. Flowers white, yellow, orange 5-petaled, to 2.5 in.; mid–late summer. Leaves opposite, to 1.5 in., leaflets to 1 in. Parts edible. Noxious in BC, WA, OR, CA.

This invasive Eurasian species is scattered in a few places across North America. It is drought-tolerant and highly competitive in dry, rocky, or gravelly areas, spreading by seed and rhizomes. It can form dense colonies, crowding out natives and displacing usable forage plants on rangeland.

Plants grow to 3 ft. in diameter from a stout taproot and thick, woody crown, sending up fleshy, multi-branched, prostrate to ascending stems. The compound leaves are waxy and fleshy, with 2 oval leaflets connected in a Y shape and a small, distinct stipule between the petiole bases. The stalked, axillary flowers are borne singly or in pairs. The petals of the small, cup-shaped flowers have white to yellowish petals marked with dark orange. With the corolla mostly closed, 10 orange stamens protrude well beyond the petals. Flowers are followed by oblong, ribbed seed capsules to 1.5 in. long.

Young plants are easily removed by pulling, grubbing out with a hoe, or digging. Take care to remove all roots and rhizomes. As the root system matures, manual and mechanical control becomes more difficult, and resprouting of rhizome fragments is a recurring problem. Range managers coping with large colonies use herbicide.

FORBS/HERBS AND VINES

# Grasses and Grass-like Plants

These herbaceous plants (or graminoids, as they are sometimes loosely termed) are annual or perennial monocots with narrow leaves, parallel veins, and small, generally non-showy flowers. They include plants from the true grass family (Poaceae), the sedge family (Cyperaceae), and the rush family (Juncaceae). Because the flowers of these plants are tiny, we describe inflorescences rather than individual flowers.

A few herbaceous dicots have grass-like leaves, and many monocots in non-graminoid groups (the lilies, irises, and their kin) look very grass-like when not in bloom. For ID in those cases, pay careful attention to inflorescences when present, and the presence or absence of ligules or sheaths. Many herbaceous dicots have the word "grass" in their common names—don't be fooled!

Foxtail barley (*Hordeum jubatum*), at Seep Lakes Wildlife Management Area near Othello, WA.

# Cyperus esculentus

## YELLOW NUTSEDGE, YELLOW NUT-GRASS

**Native perennial, to 3 ft. Inflorescence yellow, tan, brown; midsummer. Leaves to 8 in. Parts edible/ medicinal. Noxious in BC, WA, OR, CA.**

*Cyperus esculentus* is a native sedge widely distributed throughout North America and across the PNW. It has proven so aggressive that it's a problem for both agriculture and conservation and is a listed noxious weed in several jurisdictions. It invades moist sites near streams and irrigation ditches, on cropland, and in gardens, forming dense stands that crowd out other natives, compete with crop plants, and contaminate crop seed yields.

Yellow nutsedge forms a basal bulb on the culm underground, and rhizomes grow out from the bulb, producing new shoots and terminating in tubers under the soil. The stems are erect and triangular in cross section. The leaves are mostly basal, light green, and glossy, tapering to a point. The terminal inflorescence consists of an umbel of stalked cylindrical, bottlebrush clusters of straw-colored spikelets, each to 0.75 in. long.

The plant is difficult to eradicate once established and is considered one of the worst weeds in California. It reproduces via seeds, rhizomes, and tubers. The tubers detach and stay behind when plants are pulled up. Wind, water, and agricultural activities help to move seeds and tubers around. Efforts to control the weed in agricultural or conservation settings have employed multiple chemical and mechanical methods, including carefully timed, repeated tillage, which is problematic and may be impossible in home gardens.

Small invasions in home gardens require thorough digging out and removal of underground propagules, plus vigilance and prompt action to remove seedlings and prevent both bloom and maturation of tubers.

# *Juncus effusus*

COMMON RUSH, SOFT RUSH, PASTURE RUSH

Perennial, both native and introduced, to 5 ft. Inflorescence green, brown, to 6 in.; mid–late summer. Leaves very short or absent. Parts edible/medicinal with caution.

*Juncus effusus* is native to several continents, thus embracing several non-native subspecies in addition to the one that is native to the western US, *J. effusus* subsp. *pacificus*. Perhaps because it is an attractive horticultural plant, no doubt introduced from several sources, we have widespread escaped non-native populations, including the aggressive European *J. effusus* subsp. *effusus*. Gardeners may also be familiar with the popular *J. effusus* 'Spiralis', a very entertaining twisty thing hailing from Japan.

Common rush invades moist wetland edges, including freshwater ponds and streams, brackish coastal tidal flats, meadows, pastures, irrigation ditches, and gardens. The species tolerates both inundation and periods of drought. It spreads by rhizomes as well as by a prodigious number of seeds, which are dispersed by wind, water, and animals.

The rhizomes, short and stout with fibrous roots, give rise to tall, erect, finely grooved stems. The stems are unbranched, deep green and almost satiny in texture, round and hollow, and mostly leafless. Any leaf blades are short, in papery brown sheaths around the bases of stems. The inflorescence of numerous small, stalked clusters of tiny florets mature from green to tan to brown. They are borne in a compound umbel attached to the side of the stem, in an array 0.75–4 in. across. Above it is a bract that looks very much like a continuation of the stem, for 4–12 in. at the top of the plant.

This plant can be an attractive ornamental, but it is also given to just showing up and can be a pushy uninvited guest. Small seedlings are easily dislodged from moist soil by hand or by hoe. A method that has worked on larger scales and that may be most amenable to the home garden is repeated cutting to the ground, with the goal of eventually exhausting the rhizomes and preventing seed set. Those attempting to remove larger established populations have found that mowing, grazing, disking, and burning were all ineffective. Herbicide use near wetlands is tightly regulated and requires a licensed professional. Contact your noxious weed agency for guidance.

# *Aegilops cylindrica*

## JOINTED GOAT GRASS

Non-native annual, to 3 ft. Inflorescence green, red, to 4 in.; midspring–midsummer. Leaves alternate, to 5 in. Unpalatable. Noxious in BC, WA, OR, CA.

Jointed goat grass is a European species found in BC, Mexico, and in nearly every US state. It is particularly problematic in the west, where it is a listed noxious weed in several jurisdictions. In the PNW, it is found in all wheat-growing areas, predominantly on the east side. In addition to being a serious agricultural pest in wheat fields, it can be found in pastures and on roadsides and rangeland.

The culms are tall, upright, and hollow, branching at the base. The leaves, attached along the culm, are hairy and flat, about 0.5 in. wide. The narrow terminal spikes are sometimes reddish at maturity, drying to wheat color. They bear cone-shaped spikelets alternating along a zigzag-patterned rachis. At maturity, the spikes break apart into sections or "joints" (thus the common name). A single plant may bear up to 100 spikes, producing up to 3,000 seeds. Dispersal is facilitated by the spikes sticking to animals or machinery.

In large agricultural invasions, the weed has been effectively combatted with tillage, burning, and herbicides. Mowing can be effective in preventing seed production but if timed incorrectly can stimulate additional vegetative growth from tillers or aid in dispersal of spikelets. For small invasions, pull or hoe before seedhead emergence in spring, pulling and destroying as much of the roots as possible. Because of the species' extravagant output of fairly long-lived seed, this may need to be repeated several times at later dates. Mulch to prevent subsequent germinations.

# *Agropyron cristatum*

## CRESTED WHEATGRASS, FAIRWAY CRESTED WHEATGRASS

Non-native perennial, to 3 ft. Inflorescence yellow-green, tan, to 4 in.; mid–late summer. Leaves alternate, to 5 in. Parts edible.

Crested wheatgrass is a Eurasian species planted in North America since the early 1900s as forage and for erosion control. It has escaped cultivation and now dominates millions of acres in the northern US and southern Canada, particularly on rangeland in cool, arid regions. Spreading via copious seed and vegetative reproduction, it's a rapid grower that can quickly dominate a site. Invading natural areas including woodlands and prairies, it outcompetes native vegetation.

This robust plant has roots that can reach down as deep as 8 ft. at maturity, plus multiple rhizomes and stolons. The leaves are about 0.25 in. wide, mostly flat and hairless, with upper sides rough to the touch. The terminal inflorescence is a spike to 4 in. long, turning tan at maturity. The spikelets are very uniformly spaced, alternating on opposite sides of the rachis, giving an effect similar to the tines of a comb. This distinctive appearance somewhat resembles that of *Eremopyrum triticeum* (annual false wheatgrass), a less common weed in our region.

The key to controlling crested wheatgrass is early intervention: once the roots go deep, most methods of organic control, such as burning and mowing, will be futile, and in large-scale invasions, herbicide is often used. For a small invasion caught early, pull and dig. Later, regular mowing and cutting will forestall seed set and, if pursued vigorously in combination with heavy mulch, may in time be successful in exhausting the plants.

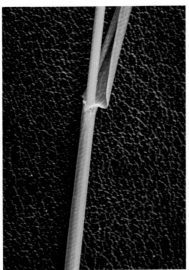

# Agrostis gigantea

## REDTOP, BLACK BENT

Non-native perennial, to 40 in. Inflorescence red-purple, to 10 in.; midsummer–autumn. Leaves alternate, to 8 in. Unpalatable.

This grass, which began its career in North America as an agricultural crop, has escaped cultivation and is now found over much of the continent, in fields and vacant lots, roadsides and the margins of agricultural land, wetlands, and open woods.

 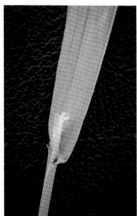

With rhizomes and roots that can go as deep as 4 ft., the plant sends up multiple stems from its base, forming loose clumps and spreading via rhizomes and stolons, sometimes forming large colonies. The stems are unbranched, sometimes prostrate and rooting at the nodes. The leaves are flat, smooth, and up to 0.3 in. wide. The inflorescence is an open panical, dark purple to red (sometimes greener in shade), oval in outline to pyramid-shaped, with the branches initially close together and the spikelets pressed against the panicle branches but spreading out during the bloom period.

Redtop spreads vegetatively and by self-seeding. It is difficult to control once established, due to its very deep roots and rhizomatous spread. In large-scale management efforts, standard mechanical means of removal have proven labor-intensive and largely unsuccessful, as any portions of rhizome left behind will resprout; thus, herbicides are often used. The plants can be slowed down and seed set prevented by frequent, very low mowing or grazing, but this will not kill them. For small invasions, if intercepted before roots reach their full potential, digging may be successful. Otherwise, repeated cutting or mowing combined with heavy mulch may eventually be a winning strategy.

# *Alopecurus pratensis*

FIELD MEADOW-FOXTAIL, MEADOW FOXTAIL

**Non-native perennial, to 3 ft. Inflorescence green, brown, to 4 in.; early spring. Leaves alternate, to 10 in. Unpalatable. Toxic to horses.**

Field meadow-foxtail is introduced throughout most of North America, with the exception of some of the southernmost states. It prefers moist to wet areas and invades meadows, roadsides, riparian areas, wetland edges, grasslands, and agricultural land. It tolerates periods of inundation.

The grass tends to form clumps, spreading out when lower nodes of the culms root in the soil and produce stolons. The inflorescence is a soft-looking, narrow terminal panicle to 4 in. long, beginning green and maturing to brown. The mostly cauline leaves are on the lower portion of the culm.

*Alopecurus pratensis* has competitive advantages in blooming earlier than some other grasses and producing large numbers of seeds. Spreading by seeds, stolons, and rhizomes, the species can form dense patches that crowd out all other species. On cropland, agricultural activities can help to move seeds and rhizomes around. The seeds can contaminate grass seed and straw bales, which then provide additional means of dispersal.

Large invasions in agricultural settings have been combatted with early-season grazing and herbicides. In the home garden, pulling and digging, preferably when soil is moist and before seed set, can be effective. Mulch heavily to dissuade new germinations.

# *Anthoxanthum odoratum*

## SWEET VERNALGRASS

**Non-native perennial, to 2 ft. Inflorescence yellow-green, tan, to 3.5 in.; early–midspring. Leaves mostly basal, to 8 in. Parts edible/medicinal with caution.**

Sweet vernalgrass is a European weed present in the US since the 1700s. It is now widely distributed in much of North America, including Alaska, with the exception of the interior regions of Canada and the US. In the PNW, it's present from BC to California. In Washington and Oregon, it is found mostly west of the Cascades. This perennial bunchgrass can be found in meadows, agricultural fields, forest openings, coastal bluffs, roadsides, and lawns. The species may displace native vegetation when it forms dense stands in natural areas.

The plant grows in tufted clumps with tall, hollow stems. The leaves are relatively narrow (to 0.25 in. wide) and flat. Roots and foliage have a sweet smell due to the presence of coumarins, compounds that in larger concentrations make some plants toxic to livestock. The inflorescence is a tight, spike-like panicle.

*Anthoxanthum odoratum* produces large quantities of seed, estimated by some researchers at several thousand per plant. The seeds may remain viable in the soil for years. Seeds are dispersed by wind and by being consumed by or sticking to the surfaces of animals.

Sweet vernalgrass spreads by seed, so the secret to success is to catch it before it self-sows. Pull or hoe when the soil is moist; follow with mulch and/or competitive plantings.

# *Arundo donax*

GIANT REED, ELEPHANT GRASS

Non-native perennial, to 20 ft. Inflorescence green, brown, to 2 ft.; late summer–autumn. Leaves alternate, to 3.5 ft. Parts edible/medicinal. Noxious in BC, OR, CA.

*Arundo donax* is a robust Asian species found in the PNW and across much of the southern half of the US, from California to the east coast. Attempts were made to cultivate it as a potential biofuel crop in Oregon, but these were abandoned. Giant reed is an environmental problem, invading waterways, altering stream channels and site hydrology, and contributing to structural damage. It is both flood-resistant and a water-guzzler, consuming available moisture to the detriment of native vegetation. It displaces native flora and causes problems for wildlife, spreading aggressively by rhizomes to form dense stands. Nevertheless, this aesthetically appealing grass can still be seen in ornamental plantings in private and public gardens, and it remains available in the nursery trade.

Giant reed grows rapidly from a large, deep root mass with fleshy lateral rhizomes. The tall, erect culms are hollow and up to 1.5 in. in diameter. In the first year of growth, they remain unbranched, branching in the second year. The leaves are deciduous, up to 3 in. wide at their bases, borne alternately and 2-ranked at nodes of varying length to 12 in. The plume-like inflorescence is a very rare occurrence in the PNW. In bloom (when it happens), this plant resembles a couple of other giant grasses (such as *Cortaderia selloana*), but *Arundo donax* is more a wetland-dweller. Throughout North America, it is believed not to produce viable seed, so that all reproduction (apart from intentional planting) occurs when rhizome fragments break loose and form new plants, particularly under flood conditions.

Elimination of small populations can be done manually, though due to the sheer size of mature root masses, it's labor-intensive. All roots and rhizomes must be removed. Very small plants can be pulled, while more mature ones must be dug out when the soil is moist. It's recommended that any plant parts be burned on the site, to prevent inadvertent dispersal to other locations. Larger projects typically involve herbicide applications, often in combination with mechanical methods that involve cutting, chainsaws, and large machines, including tractors, chippers, and backhoes.

# Avena fatua

## WILD OAT

**Non-native annual, to 5 ft. Inflorescence yellow; midspring–autumn. Leaves to 18 in. Parts edible/medicinal. Noxious in BC.**

Wild oat is found in much of western North America, as a weed in grain fields, on roadsides, and in waste places. It has been used for animal forage and human food but is less desirable than *Avena sativa* (common oat), its close cousin.

Growing from fibrous roots, the hollow culms are very tall and erect at maturity. The leaves are rough to the touch, about 0.5 in. wide. The inflorescence is an open panicle to 16 in. long and 8 in. wide, with well-separated, pendent spikelets and awns to 1.5 in.

long. It looks very similar to *Avena sativa*, but that species has a denser inflorescence with shorter awns.

As an agricultural pest, *Avena fatua* has been subject to a variety of management strategies. When plants are very young, pull, hoe, and dig. Once plants have matured, the dense roots and prolific seeding may thwart mechanical approaches. Solarization, composting, and burning have all proven successful. Follow with mulch to prevent subsequent germination.

# *Brachypodium sylvaticum*
## FALSE BROME

**Non-native perennial, to 3 ft. Inflorescence yellow-green, to 8 in.; midsummer. Leaves to 14 in. Noxious in BC, WA, OR, CA.**

This Eurasian bunchgrass was introduced as a prospective forage plant in the early 1900s in Oregon. Escaping cultivation, it is now found from BC to California and is widespread in Oregon, particularly in the Willamette Valley. It invades woodlands, prairies, roadsides, commercial timber property, and riparian zones. False brome is short-lived and non-rhizomatous but spreads rapidly by seeds, which are efficiently dispersed by wildlife and by sticking to the tires of logging trucks and other machinery. Plants grow in robust tufts, and in mature populations the bunches spread out to meet each other, forming solid mats to 18 in. thick, suppressing other vegetation, and impacting woodland and grassland natives.

The upright stems of false brome are hairy below, and the leaf sheaths are fully open. The grass grows in dense clumps of narrow, bright green to chartreuse leaves, sparsely hairy and fringed with minute hairs around the margins. The leaves are flat and lax, curving downward gracefully, typically evergreen, sometimes turning whitish in winter. The inflorescences are upright or nodding, very narrow, sparse racemes. Long, straight awns (to 0.7 in.) project from the ends of the spikelets.

Land managers have found combinations of repeated annual mowing or intensive grazing, often with herbicide follow-up, to be effective in combatting larger populations. Because the species produces persistent seed banks, continued monitoring is recommended. Small invasions can be pulled, hoed, or dug out, ideally before bloom, followed by mulch.

# *Bromus briziformis*

## RATTLESNAKE BROME

Non-native annual, to 2 ft. Inflorescence green, tan, to 5 in.; late spring–midsummer. Leaves to 5 in.

This Asian species is widely distributed on several continents, sometimes having been introduced as an ornamental. It is found over much of western North America, as well as in the northeastern US and Ontario, invading vacant lots, roadsides, and overgrazed pastures. The specific epithet refers to the resemblance of the inflorescence to those of the genus *Briza*; the common name likens the spikelets to the rattles of rattlesnakes.

The culms of rattlesnake brome are mostly hairless, hollow, and erect. The closed sheaths are covered with soft hair, and the very short ligules are hairy. The narrow leaves (to 0.2 in. wide) are pubescent to hairless on both sides. The inflorescences are one-sided, nodding panicles, each composed of a few to several delicate, lax branches, each bearing a single feather-shaped spikelet to 1 in. long.

This species is not the terror that several of its *Bromus* kin are and does not appear on any invasive lists. With its shallow fibrous roots and modest size, *B. briziformis* should be a "breeze" to control. Pull, hoe, or dig when the soil is moist. Follow with mulch and competitive planting.

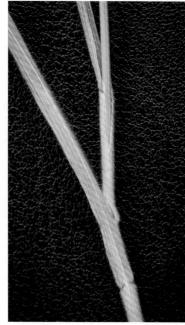

# *Bromus inermis*

## SMOOTH BROME

Non-native perennial, to 4 ft. Inflorescence green, purple, to 8 in.; mid–late summer. Leaves alternate, to 15 in. Unpalatable.

This invasive grass is present throughout North America. Introduced for soil retention, livestock forage, and hay, it has escaped cultivation and invaded roadsides, fields, woodlands, native prairies, and farm margins. With robust rhizomes, it forms dense sod, excluding other vegetation and resisting attempts to control it.

Smooth brome grows from long, creeping rhizomes and roots as deep as 4.5 ft. The leaves are flat, hairless, to 0.4 in. wide, blue-gray-green on top, green beneath. The flowering panicle is erect at first, then drooping, with several stiff branches, each bearing several spikelets that are purplish-brown at maturity. Awns are very short or absent (thus *inermis*, "unarmed"). When the grass blooms, bright yellow anthers protrude and dangle from the spikelets. A single plant may produce as many as 10,000 seeds in a season; plants also reproduce by sprouting from the horizontal rhizomes.

For small invasions and seedlings, pull, hoe, and dig out the plants. As the roots and rhizomes extend, this becomes more challenging. For larger invasions, land managers report success with mowing or burning repeatedly several times over the season, annually. Herbicide is often part of an integrated strategy. In the home garden, mulch well, install competitive plantings, and monitor.

 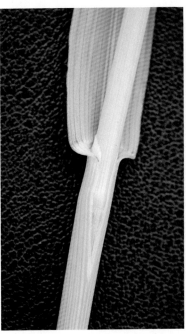 

# *Bromus rubens*

## RED BROME, FOXTAIL CHESS, FOXTAIL BROME

**Non-native annual, to 16 in. Inflorescence red-purple, to 4 in.; early summer. Leaves to 6 in.**

*Bromus rubens* (syn. *B. madritensis* subsp. *rubens*) was accidentally introduced to western North America sometime in the 1800s and quickly spread through overgrazed rangeland. This European weed is now found from eastern Washington to southern California, where it is rapidly spreading in desert areas, and eastward to Idaho, Utah, and Arizona. It invades roadsides, agricultural fields, open woodland, rangeland, and other disturbed areas.

*Bromus rubens* is a tufted bunchgrass growing on a shallow root system. The culms and leaves are finely pubescent. The leaves are narrow and flat. The inflorescence is a more or less oval, purplish panicle, to 2 in.

wide at the top. Long spikelets are crowded on short panicle branches. The awns are straight and reddish, to 0.75 in. long. The sharp awns can cause injury to domestic and wild animals when they become embedded in eyes, noses, throats, etc.

Red brome has fairly short-lived seed and limited dispersal, so eradication is deemed relatively simple and practicable. Pull, hoe, and dig before bloom, to ensure reduction of seed set; this task is facilitated by the shallowness of the roots. The species does poorly in shade and under pressure of competition from other plants, so replant and mulch to reduce subsequent emergence.

# *Bromus tectorum*

## CHEATGRASS

Non-native annual, to 3 ft. Inflorescence green, purple, tan, to 8 in.; midspring–midsummer. Leaves to 6 in. Parts edible/medicinal with caution. Noxious in CA.

Cheatgrass is a Eurasian native now found in much of the world, including almost all North America, where it has been widespread since the early 1900s. It infests millions of acres in the western US and is present in the PNW on both sides of the Cascades, though it's more prevalent on the east side. The weed invades deserts, grasslands, dry prairies, roadsides, vacant lots, rangeland, and farmland. It competes with native vegetation; it provides poor forage and may be harmful to grazing animals. It is one of several species known as foxtails, due to long, stiff awns that are particularly hazardous to dogs.

Cheatgrass can germinate in spring and then bloom, or germinate in fall and overwinter as a flattened leaf rosette, blooming the following spring and summer. Its fibrous roots spread rapidly and, although fairly shallow, can extend several feet horizontally. The plant is multi-stemmed, with flat, twisting leaves densely covered in soft hair. Leaves are bright green when young, purplish at maturity, drying to tan or brown. The terminal inflorescence is a branched, slender, one-sided panicle, with numerous pendent spikelets bearing straight awns to 0.75 in. long. Seed production is prolific, reaching 5,000 seeds for larger, less crowded plants. Seed is dispersed by wind and water, by sticking to animals, people, or vehicles, and by seed-eating birds, rodents, and insects. A major vector of dispersal is through contamination of other crops grown for seed.

As the species reproduces only by seed, early detection and prevention of seed set is important. Frequent repeated mowing is effective, but the plant can regrow and set seed after a single mowing. Herbicides are commonly used for larger invasions. Pulling, sometimes repeatedly, can be effective for small patches. Follow with dense competitive planting or mulch.

# Cenchrus longispinus

LONGSPINE SANDBUR

---

Non-native annual, to 30 in. Inflorescence yellow, tan, to 3 in.; midsummer–autumn. Leaves to 8 in. Parts edible. Noxious in BC, WA, CA.

---

This weedy grass from the eastern half of North America has spread to BC and nearly every state. It prospers on sandy soils and in dry regions. In the PNW, it is an eastside plant, invading open, disturbed areas with sandy soils, including roadsides, riparian areas, cropland, and rangeland. Its spiny burs cause problems: they can injure animals and humans, contaminate fruit and alfalfa crops, and get caught up in wool, diminishing its value.

Growing from shallow, fibrous roots a few inches deep, this species grows in clumps, sending up multiple solid, branched stems, which are flattened in cross section and may be erect, spreading, or prostrate. The stems sometimes root at the nodes when contacting soil, so that dense mats may form. The leaves are about 0.25 in. wide, with a rough upper surface.

The terminal inflorescences are cylindrical spikes to about 0.75 in. wide, partially enclosed in sheathing leaves. Each spike is composed of a wavy or zigzag rachis bearing 5–10 yellowish-green burs enclosed in spiny bracts, turning tan in maturity; they look remarkably like tiny medieval maces. There may be up to 50 burs to a spike, over 5,000 burs per plant. With typically 2 seeds per bur, a single plant may produce as many as 10,000 seeds. The burs are dispersed by floating in water or by sticking to animals, people, or machinery.

Protective clothing is essential for working with this wickedly armed plant. Agricultural infestations are prevented by careful hygiene (avoiding dissemination of seeds by machinery or feet) and combatted with repeated tillage and/or herbicide. Increased soil fertility and water reduces longspine sandbur's competitive advantage in dry or poor soils. Small invasions of seedlings can be dug up or pulled (wear gloves!). Competitive planting and heavy mulch will help to prevent more invasions.

# Cortaderia selloana

## PAMPAS GRASS

Non-native perennial, to 13 ft. Inflorescence white, pink, to 3 ft.; late spring–midsummer. Leaves to 6 ft. Unpalatable. Noxious in WA.

*Cortaderia selloana* is a popular, widely planted ornamental that has escaped gardens all along the west coast and in several southern states. Its close cousin and lookalike is the somewhat smaller, less erect *C. jubata* (jubatagrass), which is limited to the west coast. Both species have invaded dunes, wetlands, riparian areas, clearcuts, fields, and roadsides, particularly near the coast. Pampas grass is huge at maturity, difficult and labor-intensive to remove. It displaces native and other vegetation and is a problem weed in forestry plantings.

Growing from a mass of dense fibrous roots and short rhizomes, pampas grass makes an imposing clump of long, narrow, evergreen leaves with very sharp, minutely serrated margins. Flowering culms are stiff and rise above the leaves, each bearing a long, plume-like, whitish to pinkish inflorescence.

This species is gynodioecious. A female plant sets seed only if pollinated by a nearby bisexual plant. When pollination does occur, a single plant may produce 100,000 or more seeds, which are small and lightweight, and can be carried long distances by wind. Fragmented roots can also sprout and start new plants.

In preparing to do battle with pampas grass, wear gloves and other protective gear, because the knife-like leaf edges can do damage. Cut and bag any inflorescences to prevent seeding. Pull or use a hoe to grub out smaller seedlings. Shovels, mattocks, chainsaws, and weed whackers may be handy for removing more mature plants. On large clumps, it is necessary to remove the entire crown and the upper parts of the roots. For complete removal, where possible, machinery like excavators or backhoes may be necessary.

# Cynodon dactylon

### BERMUDA GRASS, DEVILGRASS

Non-native perennial, to 3 ft. Inflorescence green, purple, to 3 in.; midsummer–autumn. Leaves alternate, to 6 in. Unpalatable. Toxic to horses.

Known as one of the world's most invasive grasses, this African species is introduced throughout warmer regions worldwide and has been listed as invasive in as many as 80 countries, particularly as an agricultural pest. It was introduced to the US in the mid-1800s as a pasture grass and is also now widely used as turf. Scattered over much of the US and BC, it is less common in our cooler regions. Invading lawns, pastures, and other disturbed sites, it is rarely found in natural areas.

Most strains of Bermuda grass in the US are infertile, so most reproduction is vegetative rather than by seeds. The plant grows from a robust system of rapidly proliferating stolons and rhizomes, which may be shallow or up to 3 ft. deep. These produce a dense turf that spreads aggressively. Fragments can be dispersed by animals, machines, or water and take root to produce new populations.

Early in the growing season, Bermuda grass sends out multiple mostly prostrate stems with many short, flat, narrow, gray-green, spiky-looking leaves. The leaf sheaths are open, and the distinctive ligules are fringes of straight, white hairs. The erect flowering stems bear terminal inflorescences, each composed of 4–7 narrow, finger-like, one-sided spikes, arranged in umbel-like arrays.

Land managers facing large invasions recommend IPM strategies combining multiple mechanical means (clipping, tilling, shading) with herbicide, repeated over several years. Grazing is ineffective, and burning has worked only under limited conditions. Small invasions can be effectively combatted, particularly if caught early. Pull, hoe, and dig to remove small plants, including stolons and rhizomes. Shallow cultivation with sharp hand tools can be helpful. Simply uprooting the rhizomes and stolons in hot, dry weather can contribute to killing them by desiccation. Bermuda grass needs strong sunlight and is intolerant of shade, so shade mats, replanting with taller plants, and thick mulches can all be helpful in suppressing the weed.

# Dactylis glomerata

ORCHARD GRASS, COCK'S FOOT

Non-native perennial, to 4 ft. Inflorescence yellow, to 8 in.; late spring–early summer. Leaves to 10 in. Unpalatable.

Orchard grass is present throughout North America and common in the PNW, mostly in dryish habitat in meadows, logged land, woodland edges, roadsides, and farmland. It was widely introduced as forage for livestock and also accidentally dispersed in baled hay and straw. With wide ecological tolerance, the species has spread aggressively and competes with native vegetation.

*Dactylis glomerata* grows from extensive fibrous roots but produces no stolons and usually no rhizomes. The culms are hollow and erect, the leaves strongly keeled and mostly hairless with closed sheaths, to 0.5 in. wide.

The panicles have a characteristic shape that inspired the common name "cock's foot." The erect panicle, typically all in one plane, is roughly triangular in shape with a series of branches alternating and decreasing in length upward, bearing clusters of spikelets that are more compressed at the top. Seeds are dispersed by wind, birds, and human activity.

Orchard grass is easy to remove decisively by pulling or hoeing when young, or later cutting below the root crown, ideally before seed formation. Remove any inflorescences from the site.

# Digitaria sanguinalis

## HAIRY CRABGRASS

Non-native annual, to 3 ft. Inflorescence green, purple, brown, to 10 in.; midsummer–autumn. Leaves alternate, to 10 in. Parts edible with caution.

*Digitaria sanguinalis* is a common weed worldwide and throughout the US, a frequent invader of lawns, gardens, waste places, meadows, and disturbed wetlands and a nuisance for growers of food crops and ornamentals. Distinguishing among the approximately 200 species in *Digitaria* may require magnification and specialized knowledge. Happily, only three or four species occur on the west coast, and in the PNW hairy crabgrass is by far the most common.

With relatively shallow, fibrous roots, the plant produces several culms. These are hollow and hairless, multi-branched, prostrate or sprawling, and rooting at the lower nodes. The leaf sheaths are open and hairy, the ligules membranous. The leaf blades are flat and usually hairy, to 0.6 in. wide. The inflorescence is an erect panicle of 7–10 slender, finger-like spikes. Each spike bears spikelets in 2 rows along a flattened rachis; these turn purple and eventually brown as they mature. A single plant can produce more than 150,000 seeds in a season, and plants have been found to produce flowers and seeds even when mowed to a height of under an inch.

Due to the resulting prodigious and long-lasting seed bank, hairy crabgrass cannot be eliminated in a single year following a large invasion. Continued efforts must be aimed at stopping seed production for several years. For larger patches, burning can be effective where practicable. Heavy mulch for a couple of seasons will knock back the population. Smaller invasions can be pulled, hoed, or dug out, preferably before seed set and when the soil is moist. Follow with thick mulch and monitor for new seedlings.

# *Echinochloa crus-galli*

## BARNYARD GRASS

Non-native annual, to 6 ft. Inflorescence green, purple, to 10 in.; midsummer–autumn. Leaves alternate, to 24 in. Parts edible/medicinal with caution. Toxic to livestock.

Barnyard grass is a Eurasian weed found throughout most of the US and the southern half of Canada. It is particularly associated with rice agriculture worldwide but also invades any wet places in warm-temperate regions. It's found in farm fields, irrigation ditches, landscaped turf, orchards, grasslands, woodlands, and riparian areas. In addition to competing with desired plants, it can accumulate nitrates, making it toxic to livestock.

*Echinochloa crus-galli* sends up multiple culms from the crown. They are erect to decumbent, hairless, usually branched near the base. The leaf sheaths are open, mostly hairless, and often purplish near the base; absence of a ligule is an unusual feature helpful in identifying this grass. The blades are flat and lax, to 1 in. wide. The inflorescence consists of terminal, multi-branched panicles. Upper branches of the panicle are contracted and erect; those lower down in the inflorescence spread downward more. Spikelets are crowded along one side of each branch. The panicle as a whole may be erect or drooping.

Those managing large invasions in agricultural contexts report success with shallow tillage, but this is often not practicable or desirable for the home garden. Small invasions can be pulled, hoed, or dug easily. Heavy mulch may suppress patches of barnyard grass when not close to water.

# Elymus repens
## QUACKGRASS

Non-native perennial, to 4 ft. Inflorescence green, brown, to 6 in.; summer. Leaves to 12 in. Parts edible/medicinal with caution. Noxious in BC, CA.

*Elymus repens* (syn. *Agropyron repens, Elytrigia repens*) is a familiar nuisance for gardeners and keepers of lawns. It's also a common agricultural weed throughout cool temperate regions worldwide, causing crop losses, contamination of seed and grain crops, and problems for ornamental nurseries. Quackgrass invades pastures, gardens, roadsides, urban areas, agricultural land, wetland margins, and open woods.

This Eurasian species is very widespread along the west coast from Alaska to California, across much of the western US, and in northeastern North America.

This grass grows in clumps, with each crown sending up multiple erect to decumbent stems. Its yellowish-white rhizomes are long, tough, and wiry, extending as far as 8 in. deep and 24 in. horizontally. A plant may send out over 100 distinct, branched rhizomes, with hundreds of potential buds for new plants. It can spread at a rate of 10 ft. annually.

The culms are light green to whitish and hollow at maturity. Leaf sheaths and blades may be hairless or slightly hairy. The leaves are flat, to about 0.5 in. wide, constricted to a point at their tips, and have auricles at the junction between blade and sheath. The leaves may be somewhat hairy or waxy, green to glaucous. Quackgrass blooms are slender, stiff, erect terminal spikes resembling those of wheat. They may be awnless, or have awns to 0.6 in. long. Viable seeds are produced, but most reproduction is vegetative, from rhizome buds and from any severed pieces of rhizome.

Agricultural and environmental land managers have reported success with repeated cultivation, burning, and herbicide. These strategies have often been used in combination and with repeat and monitoring. For the home gardener, quackgrass can be a challenge when it insinuates its rhizomes into lawn or desirable garden plants. Pull, hoe, and dig to remove as many of the rhizomes as possible. Follow with heavy mulch, and monitor for recurrences.

# Eragrostis curvula

## WEEPING LOVEGRASS

---

Non-native perennial, to 6 ft. Inflorescence green, tan, to 16 in.; late spring–midsummer. Leaves to 26 in. Parts edible.

---

Weeping lovegrass is an African species planted in North America in the past for erosion control, livestock forage, and ornamental landscaping. It escaped cultivation and is widespread throughout the US, particularly in the southern half and on both coasts, including scattered sites in the PNW. It invades roadsides and other disturbed ground, woodland edges, pastures, and prairies.

This is an erect bunchgrass, growing in clumps from basal crowns that can spread to 15 in. wide. It forms an extensive mat of rapidly growing roots, reaching downward into the soil 6 ft. or more and spreading laterally as far as 10 ft. The roots branch freely and can fill in all available ground between plants. The leaves are very narrow and often rolled inward. The inflorescence is greenish, turning yellow-tan at maturity. The panicle is open with well-spaced branches becoming progressively shorter upward along the rachis, to 6 in. at the widest point, forming an elongated triangular outline. A single plant may produce up to 1,000 seeds in a season.

Small infestations can be controlled by diligent and repeated pulling, grubbing, hoeing, and digging. This is best done when the soil is moist to facilitate removal of root systems. Plants with inflorescences should be bagged and removed to prevent seeding. Repeated efforts throughout the growing season may be required for several seasons. Larger infestations can be controlled with frequent low mowing and mulching.

# Holcus lanatus

VELVET GRASS

Non-native perennial, to 40 in. Inflorescence gray, purple, whitish, to 6 in.; midspring–midsummer. Leaves to 8 in.

Velvet grass may be the most easily identifiable grass in our region, with its soft, gray, velvety leaves. It was probably introduced to North America as forage grass seed, taking hold by the mid-1700s. It's now common over much of the continent, with the exception of northern Canada and some of the drier regions of the US midlands. It's a listed noxious weed in several eastern states.

In the PNW, *Holcus lanatus* is particularly common on the west side from Alaska to California and eastward along the Columbia River Gorge. It invades agricultural land, parks, open woodlands, meadows, roadsides, lawns, and vacant lots. It's a troublesome contaminant of many grass seed crops.

The plant grows in tufts from deep fibrous roots, and after its first year also develops long stolons and spreads vegetatively. The leaves are narrow (to 0.4 in.), soft to the touch, very flexible, and covered with fine hairs. The inflorescence is a long, slender, erect, spike-like panicle.

The gray-purplish panicle is compressed initially, opening out with more spreading branches and turning whitish later in the season. A single plant may produce as many as 200,000 or more seeds in a season, and the seeds may be viable in the soil for up to 10 years. They are dispersed by wind, by human activities, and via ingestion and excretion by animals. The species can rapidly cover bare ground, forming dense populations that suppress native seedlings.

As so often happens with successful weeds, many of the methods used to control *Holcus lanatus* have only facilitated its spread in some situations, including tillage, mowing, and grazing. Herbicides, prolonged flooding, reduced irrigation, and burning have all been used in large infestations. Small invasions in the home garden are easy to combat by pulling; take care to remove all roots, and follow with mulch.

# Hordeum jubatum
## FOXTAIL BARLEY

Native perennial, to 2.5 ft. Inflorescence green, purple, tan, to 4 in.; midsummer. Leaves alternate, to 6 in. Parts edible with caution.

A native present throughout North America, including Greenland, with the exception of the southeastern corner of the US (Florida to Louisiana), foxtail barley is a common weed of disturbed soils, grasslands, montane woodlands, wetland edges, riparian areas, and saline or alkaline sites. Though native, it can be overabundant, and it is problematic in other ways. Keep grazing animals and pets away from this grass once it has begun to bloom: its long, sharp awns can enter any point on an animal's body and wreak havoc, including infections, fatal lung perforation, etc.

Foxtail barley grows in clumps from fibrous roots with no rhizomes. The stems are hairless to pubescent, with open sheaths having soft hairs along the margins. The narrow leaves are grayish-green and rough to the touch. The plant blooms with graceful, nodding terminal spikes bristling with long awns to 3 in., green to purplish, maturing to tan and becoming brittle. The ripening seeds are each attached to multiple awns and are barbed, facilitating dispersal by wind or by sticking to animals, people, and vehicles.

Agricultural land managers recommend frequent cultivation for suppression of large invasions, but this is not ideal for garden soils and not practicable for most gardens. The weed takes advantage of low, wet places, so monitor for and correct these conditions. For small invasions, pull or dig when the soil is moist, mulch well, and replace with competitive plantings.

# Panicum miliaceum

## PROSO MILLET

**Non-native annual, to 3 ft. Inflorescence green, brown, tan, to 10 in.; midsummer–autumn. Leaves alternate, to 12 in. Parts edible/medicinal. Toxic to horses, sheep.**

Proso millet has been a food crop in its Eurasian home for thousands of years and is now introduced in many countries. In North America, it has been grown for human food but is now more often fed to livestock and poultry and sold as bird seed. It has escaped in scattered sites across most of the US and southern Canada, showing up as a weed on agricultural land, roadsides, and in residential areas where bird feeders are a source of dispersal.

Proso millet has a shallow, fibrous root system, with erect stems sometimes branched at the base. The light green culms may be hairy or hairless and are leafy for most of their length. The leaf sheaths are open, pale green, and covered with long hairs. The ligule is membranous and fringed with short, straight hairs. The leaves are widest, to 0.75 in., near their bases; their margins are rough to the touch, with minute teeth. The erect or drooping, crowded terminal panicles are partially enclosed in the uppermost leaf sheaths. The inflorescence of erect or drooping, crowded terminal panicles begins light green, maturing to reddish-brown or tan, and as the oval florets develop into seeds, these appear on the panicle branches like little beads on tassels.

This distinctive grass should be recognizable fairly early, though some related and similar-looking grasses are sold as ornamentals. It's a very frequent volunteer from bird feeders. Pull seedlings, or grub them out with a hoe. Dig up mature plants, preferably before seed set; this is easiest when the soil is moist. Mulch well to discourage new seedlings.

# *Phalaris arundinacea*

## REED CANARY GRASS

Perennial, both native and introduced, to 6 ft. Inflorescence white, green, purple, to 6 in.; midsummer. Leaves alternate, to 12 in. Unpalatable. Toxic to horses, cattle, sheep, chickens. Noxious in WA, OR.

This wetland grass is native to both Europe and North America, and both European and North American forms are widely distributed across much of our continent, except for the southernmost US states. The species invades riparian areas, meadows, wetlands, and irrigation ditches. It chokes waterways, clogging ditches and impeding fish movement. Forming dense rhizomatous mats, reed canary grass crowds out native species and is a significant threat to wetland ecosystems. It spreads by seeds, rhizomes, and rooting of fragments.

The tall, hollow stems are up to 0.5 in. in diameter. The leaves are flat, hairless, rough to the touch, and about 0.6 in. wide, meeting the stems at 45° angles. The sheaths are open, and the ligules are about 0.4 in. long. Compact panicles as long as 6 in. are held well above the leaves. Many gardeners are more familiar with the very recognizable cultivars of *Phalaris arundinacea* var. *picta*. They are shorter (3–4 ft.) than the straight species and are valued horticulturally for their longitudinal white-striped variegation, sometimes tinged pale pink.

The robust rhizomatous growth of *Phalaris arundinacea* makes it very difficult to eradicate. Small patches and young seedlings can be pulled or dug; take care to remove all the roots. Heavy mulch may eventually exhaust plants, if the population is not too close to water. Herbicides are used for large infestations, but these require permits if the stand is near water and often several treatments are required to prevent recurrence.

# *Poa annua*

## ANNUAL BLUEGRASS, LOW SPEAR GRASS

Non-native annual, to 11 in. Inflorescence white, to 3 in.; early spring–midsummer. Leaves to 5 in. Unpalatable.

*Poa annua* is a little plant with outsized impact as one of the most problematic agricultural weeds in several countries. Introduced throughout North America and across the PNW, it invades woodlands, riparian areas, roadsides, vacant lots, lawns, gardens, golf courses, and agricultural fields. It has a particular affinity for highly disturbed sites, including gravel driveways and sidewalk cracks.

The root system is very shallow, only about an inch into the soil. The leaves are about 0.2 in. wide, smooth, soft, hairless, and pale green. The blades are typically folded longitudinally and end in a prow-shaped tip. The culms are hollow and can root at the nodes, forming mats. The inflorescence consists of a few awnless spikelets, on very delicate, spreading branches, in an open, triangular panicle. *Poa annua* matures and becomes reproductive within 6 weeks, and a single plant may produce over 2,000 seeds, which can remain viable in the soil for as long as 6 years.

Owing to this reproductive exuberance and to its broad ecological tolerance, larger invasions of *Poa annua* can be surprisingly challenging to control. For most home gardens, however, it can be effectively managed through pulling and hoeing, followed by competitive plantings or mulch.

# *Poa bulbosa*

## BULBOUS BLUEGRASS

Non-native perennial, to 2 ft. Inflorescence green, purple, to 5 in.; early spring. Leaves to 6 in.

*Poa bulbosa*, a European species, was initially introduced to the west for turf, pasture forage, and erosion control. It was disappointing for most purposes but escaped cultivation and is now widely distributed through much of western North America, as well as in scattered areas in the Midwest and eastern US. It is a short-lived perennial, but its bulbs and bulblets give it staying power.

A single plant may have a few erect culms rising from bulbous bases. The sheaths are open almost to their bases, and the ligules are membranous and short, to 0.13 in. The narrow blades (to 0.25 in. wide) are flat or slightly rolled, and rough to the touch. The plume-like panicles of the inflorescence may be open and spreading or compressed and narrow. The florets are often replaced with elongated purple bulbils, to 0.6 in.; these take the place of developing seeds. The bulbils are attached to long, narrow, bract-like lemmas, giving the inflorescence a tufted or fringed appearance. Although the species primarily reproduces by seed in its European native range, in North America it more often reproduces vegetatively: the bulbils drop off into the soil and develop into new plants after about 2 years. The species expands its territory when these bulbils are spread around as contaminants in seed crops or hay, or carried about by the birds and rodents that are attracted to them.

Because of the supply of bulbils that can accumulate in the soil, permanent eradication of *Poa bulbosa* does not happen immediately. Tillage has been somewhat effective in control of large populations but is not practical for most home gardens and not beneficial for soil. Burning and mowing are ineffective. Spring grazing has to be repeated for several years. For the small home garden, diligent pulling and digging, heavy mulch, and frequent monitoring may be the best options.

# Poa pratensis

## KENTUCKY BLUEGRASS

Perennial, both native and introduced, to 3 ft. Inflorescence green, purple, to 5 in.; early summer. Leaves to 16 in. Unpalatable.

This long-lived, sod-forming grass, native to Europe and Asia (at least) as well as to parts of North America, is common worldwide. It's present across much of North America but less common in the southern US. It is included in some grass seed mixes and is planted as turf on golf courses, ski slopes, and other recreational sites, as well as being used for livestock forage. With a preference for cool-temperate climates and moist, disturbed ground, it can become a problem in natural areas, competing aggressively with native species.

*Poa pratensis* grows from shallow fibrous roots and slender rhizomes, spreading both vegetatively and by seed. The culms are hollow and hairless and produce many mostly basal leaves. Leaves are folded at the point of attachment, otherwise flat and very narrow, with conspicuously prow-shaped tips. The inflorescence is an open panicle with a few well-separated, slightly upward-reaching, slender branches alternating along the rachis. These decrease in length and number of spikelets upward, so that the outline of the inflorescence is strongly pyramidal.

Mowing is mostly ineffective in controlling Kentucky bluegrass, as it can stimulate vegetative growth. Burning has been helpful in suppressing large stands. Land managers recommend pre-emergent herbicides, but herbicide resistance can be an issue. For small invasions in home gardens, the modest size of the plant and shallow underground portions should make it amenable to pulling and digging. Take care to remove all rhizomes and tillers, and follow with mulch and monitoring.

# *Schedonorus arundinaceus*

## TALL FESCUE

Non-native perennial, to 4 ft. Inflorescence red-purple, to 12 in.; late spring–early summer. Leaves to 28 in. Toxic to horses, cattle, sheep.

*Schedonorus arundinaceus* (syn. *Festuca arundinacea*, *Lolium arundinaceum*) was introduced to the US in the early 1800s as pasture and lawn grass. It continued to be used as forage and sometimes for highway plantings. Tall fescue escaped cultivation and is widely distributed through much of North America, in pastures and meadows, on farmland and woodland edges. Spreading vegetatively and by seed, it can be invasive, forming dense stands that are difficult to remove. The grass is frequently infected with an endophytic fungus, causing significant harm to livestock and wild animals.

The fibrous roots can penetrate several feet deep in moist soils. Arising from tufts of many basal leaves, the culms are mostly hairless, sturdy, unbranched, and hollow. The leaf sheaths are open, and there are prominent auricles with fine, short hairs along their margins. The leaf blades are flat, up to 0.4 in. wide. Each plant sends up as many as 30 flowering stems. The inflorescence is a long, narrow panicle with slender, well-separated branches.

Large populations can be very challenging to eradicate. Agencies coping with tall fescue advocate combinations of tillage, burning, herbicide, and replanting. For home gardeners, eradication of small infestations is not impossible but may be labor-intensive. Pulling is difficult much past seedling stage, due to the overall toughness of roots, stems, and leaves. Dig up and remove as much of the root portion as possible, and follow with thick mulch, replanting, and monitoring.

# Secale cereale

## CEREAL RYE, FERAL RYE, COMMON RYE

Non-native annual, to 6 ft. Inflorescence yellow, to 6 in.; early–midsummer. Leaves alternate, to 8 in. Parts edible. Noxious in WA.

Cereal rye has been an important food crop in its Eurasian native range for centuries. It has been grown in North America at least since the 1800s, has escaped cultivation, and is present as a weed over most of the continent. It is potentially invasive and competitive with native plants and cultivated crops. Note: plants can carry ergot, a very toxic fungal pathogen hazardous to animals or humans consuming it.

Plants grow in tufts from fibrous roots that can extend downward as deep as 5 ft. The leaf sheaths are open, with prominent auricles. The blades are flat, blue-green, to 0.4 in. wide. The slender, unbranched, flat terminal spikes of closely spaced, sessile spikelets with long, slender awns give the inflorescence a bristly appearance.

Pull, hoe, or dig small invasions. Larger patches can be mowed closely before bloom, or smothered with thick mulch.

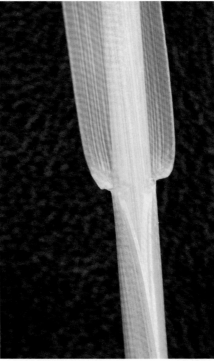

# Setaria viridis

## GREEN BRISTLEGRASS, GREEN FOXTAIL

Non-native annual, to 4 ft. Inflorescence green, purple, to 4 in.; early summer–autumn. Leaves alternate, to 12 in. Parts edible with caution. Toxic to horses. Noxious in BC.

This Eurasian grass is a common weed on several continents, including most of North America. It's a nuisance for several food crops and ubiquitous on a variety of sites with exposed, disturbed ground: parking lots, lawns, gardens, roadsides, and riparian zones.

From shallow fibrous roots, the plant sends up erect to nearly prostrate stems, often branching at the base. The leaf sheaths wrap loosely around the stems and are open, often purplish near the base, and hairless except for short, fine hairs along the margins. The ligule is a ring of fine white hairs. The blades are flat, hairless, and narrow, to 0.3 in. wide.

The inflorescence is a narrow, cylindric, spike-like panicle with very short side branches. It bristles with sharp awns that are hazardous to livestock when grazed or consumed in hay. *Setaria viridis* spreads by prolific self-seeding, with estimates ranging to as many as 13,000 seeds per plant. Seeds can remain viable for several years and are dispersed by animals, water, and human activity.

Control in an established population requires preventing bloom and diminishing the seed bank over several years. The plants can be effectively suppressed by mowing or cutting. Small invasions can be pulled, hoed, or dug out. Follow with mulch, and monitor for new seedlings.

# Sorghum halepense

## JOHNSONGRASS

Non-native perennial, to 7 ft. Inflorescence green, purple, brown, to 16 in.; midsummer–autumn. Leaves alternate, to 30 in. Parts edible. Toxic to horses, cattle, sheep, goats, chickens. Noxious in BC, WA, OR, CA.

This weedy perennial grass of Mediterranean origin is present and considered invasive in many countries around the world, particularly in warmer regions. It can form dense colonies that crowd out natives in natural areas and compete with important food crops. Though good forage when healthy, when stressed it accumulates toxins and becomes hazardous to livestock. It is present over much of North America and occurs in scattered locations in the PNW but does not establish persistent populations here. It can be found on disturbed sites, including agricultural land, roadsides, riparian zones, irrigation ditches, orchards, and fields.

Johnsongrass has a fibrous root system that can extend several feet deep into the soil and a network of thick, fleshy, fast-growing rhizomes with many buds. A single plant may produce 200 ft. or more of rhizomes in a month. The plant forms densely leafy clumps, sending up tall, unbranched, solid stems with prominent, swollen nodes. The leaf sheaths are open, with fringed, membranous ligules. Blades are hairless, flat, to 1 in. wide, with conspicuous white midveins. The large, spreading, pyramidal panicles of the inflorescence begin green and mature to deep purple to reddish-brown. Seed production per plant has been estimated at over 20,000, and these can remain viable for as long as 20 years.

With prolific seed production, deep roots, aggressive rhizomatous growth, and the ability to produce new plants quickly from small rhizome fragments, Johnsongrass is a formidable opponent. Agencies combatting it recommend a variety of strategies for large invasions, including burning, monthly tillage, plowing, monthly mowing, and herbicide, with the admonition that these must be done repeatedly and are best used in combination. Herbicide resistance has been documented, and dormant buds on underground rhizomes can survive herbicide application. Small invasions, if intercepted early, can be pulled, hoed, or dug out; be sure to remove all aerial portions and rhizomes in upper zones of the soil.

# Taeniatherum caput-medusae

MEDUSAHEAD

Non-native annual, to 2 ft. Inflorescence green, gold, brown, to 2 in.; early summer. Leaves to 12 in. Noxious in BC, WA, OR, CA.

Medusahead is an aggressive Eurasian grass present in North America since the early 1800s and now found from BC to California, eastward to Montana and Nevada, and in the northeastern US. The species invades rangeland and other ecologically damaged sites, competing with native flora and desirable forage plants.

One or more culms rise from shallow fibrous roots. The leaf sheaths are open, sometimes softly hairy, with distinct auricles and membranous ligules. Leaf blades are generally short and very narrow, mostly hairless, and evenly distributed along the stems. The inflorescence is a short, bristly spike with many small barbs and needle-like awns as long as 4 in., borne singly at the ends of stems. As the spikes mature and then dry, they change from green to gold or light brown, and may twist and bend.

Managers working with medusahead invasions on rangeland have found tillage to be effective, though it must be done multiple times during the growing season because new seedlings can emerge intermittently. Grazing is effective when plants are young, less so when they mature and become less palatable to livestock. Mowing can effectively stop the spread of this grass when done after flowering has begun but before seed set. Small patches are easily removed by pulling or hoeing, before seeds develop. Follow with mulch, and replace with desirable plants as soon as possible.

# Tripidium ravennae

## RAVENNAGRASS

Non-native perennial, to 12 ft. Inflorescence silvery purplish-brown, to 2 ft.; late summer. Leaves mostly basal, to 6 ft. Noxious in WA, OR, CA.

*Tripidium ravennae* (syn. *Saccharum ravennae*), a Eurasian/African species, has figured in North American horticulture for the past century; it is sold in a few nurseries and promoted for ornamental planting by public gardens and state extensions. The species spreads only by seeds, not vegetatively, but is capable of forming broad, dense monocultural stands that compete aggressively with native flora in riparian zones and wetland edges, particularly along the Columbia River. It is problematic in some other countries and, besides the PNW, is a listed noxious weed in several states in the Southwest and along the east coast.

Ravennagrass looks very similar to the pampas grasses (*Cortaderia*) and in some places is called "hardy pampas grass." It can be distinguished handily from the *Cortaderia* species by its leaf blades, the bases of which are densely covered with hair that conceals the ligules and adjacent upper leaf surfaces.

Ravennagrass produces a broad basal clump to 5 ft. in diameter. The stems are bamboo cane–like, hairy, and often reddish. The leaves are stiff and sharp-edged, to 1 in. wide, and grayish-green with a white central vein; they are sometimes tinged with light pink, then silver, then reddish in fall. A few much shorter leaves are scattered along the flowering stems. The plant blooms with multiple tall plume-like panicles to 6 in. wide, held high above the basal leaves. Its thousands of tiny seeds are easily dispersed by wind and water.

This grass has sharp-edged leaves and potentially irritating hairs, so wear thick gloves and protective clothing when working with it. The main focus of ravennagrass control is stopping seed production. Remove plumes before they set seed; this may need to be done several times a year to prevent reblooming and seeding. Small plants can be pulled, the sooner the better; digging out an established plant may be labor-intensive. Herbicides are an option when dealing with large, established patches.

# *Ventenata dubia*

VENTENATA, WIREGRASS

Non-native annual, to 30 in. Inflorescence yellow, to 15 in.; midsummer. Leaves to 4.5 in. Noxious in BC, WA, OR.

*Ventenata dubia* (syn. *Avena dubia*), a Eurasian species, has been present in the western US since at least the early 1950s. In the past 20 years, it has rapidly expanded its range in the PNW and is now found from BC to California and east through Idaho and Montana, as well as a few northeastern states. This delicate, fast-growing grass crowds out native and non-native grasses on pastures and rangeland; it is particularly a problem for agriculture, contaminating grain crops and grasses grown for hay.

Growing from very shallow fibrous roots, the slim, hollow stems are branched from the base and usually around 18 in. tall but sometimes taller. Culms typically have a very fine pubescence, and in spring the nodes are reddish-black. The leaves are concentrated on the lower stems, with open sheaths and long (to 0.3 in.), membranous ligules with the upper portion fringed. The leaves are very narrow, beginning flat but then becoming rolled inward, so that they appear even narrower. They are hairless, smooth on the upper surface and rough on the underside. The inflorescence is an open, spreading, well-branched panicle that is pyramidal in outline. It has two kinds of awns, some short and straight, the others long (to 0.6 in.) and twisted; the latter are often broken away at maturity.

Control is primarily focused on preventing seed production. The plants are easily pulled or hoed, ideally when the soil is moist and before seed set. In larger patches, repeated mowing is effective but must be done before the beginning of bloom and then multiple times during the season to prevent seed production. Mulch well to discourage subsequent volunteers, and replant with more desirable species.

# Aquatics

A quatic plants grow in fresh or salt water, rooted at the edges or underwater, with most of their foliage either submerged, extended just above the water, or floating. Control of aquatics can be very challenging technically and is often subject to regulations, when the plants grow in or on the margins of natural bodies of water (ponds, lakes, or streams, as opposed to human-made ponds or "water features"). Permits may be required. Some of these regulations concern permissible herbicide formulations and the need for a licensed applicator. Others have bearing on manual or mechanical methods that could impact fish habitat (most importantly) or shoreline stability. These regulations may vary enormously among different jurisdictions. We are therefore not discussing control measures for this group of plants. We urge you to contact your local weed agency for help with identification and for guidance as to what, if anything, private citizens can or should do.

Yellow floatingheart (*Nymphoides peltata*) forms a dense mat on the surface of a small private pond near Custer, WA.

# Sagittaria platyphylla

## DELTA ARROWHEAD, CHILENSIS

Non-native perennial, to 5 ft. Flowers white, 3-petaled, to 1.2 in.; summer. Leaves basal, to 7 in. Parts edible. Noxious in OR.

Delta arrowhead is native to much of the Southeast and Midwest but is present as an introduced species in a few sites in the PNW. It is probably a horticultural escape here, as it is widely sold as an aquarium or pond plant. *Sagittaria platyphylla* inhabits mudflats and shallow, slow-moving water of ponds, streams, and freshwater wetlands, forming dense stands that compete with native vegetation and impact wildlife habitat. It could be confused with *S. latifolia*, an iconic PNW native found in much of the US and southern Canada, but that species has strongly arrowhead-shaped leaves.

Growing from creeping stolons in mud or underwater, delta arrowhead produces two kinds of leaves. Leaves found entirely underwater are sessile on the substrate and strap-like, to 10 in. long and 2 in. wide.

Above water or floating on it are large, ovate/oblanceolate leaves on stalks that are long (to 30 in.) and triangular in cross section. The tall, leafless, erect flowering stems bear racemes composed of whorls of flowers. Male flowers are slightly larger and positioned above the female flowers. Each flower has 3 green sepals and 3 white (sometimes pinkish) petals. These are followed by the seedpods, in rounded clusters of 3 fleshy green, one-seeded fruits resembling somewhat flattened berries, each to 0.5 in. in diameter. A single plant may produce thousands or even 100,000+ seeds in a season. Seeds are dispersed by waterfowl and other animals, water, and soil movement. Plants spread by this prolific seed production as well as vegetatively, via stoloniferous expansion, tubers, or stolon fragments.

# *Butomus umbellatus*

## FLOWERING RUSH

Non-native perennial, to 5 ft. Flowers pink, white, 6-petaled, to 1 in.; midsummer–autumn. Leaves basal, to 40 in. Parts edible. Noxious in BC, WA, OR, CA.

Flowering rush is unrelated to the true rushes (Juncaceae) of the previous chapter. It doesn't look much like a rush when in bloom but, like many rushes, grows in wetlands. It's found on the margins of freshwater wetlands in the PNW and Idaho, as well as in several northern and northeastern states and eastern Canada. It is a listed noxious weed in several jurisdictions and a weed of concern, especially in wetland conservation. While not yet widespread in the PNW, our mild climate and many rivers provide plenty of potential habitat.

From the long, fleshy rhizomes arise long, sword-shaped leaves that can be submerged, floating, or rise above the water. The tall, leafless flowering stems bear terminal umbellate inflorescences with 20–25 showy flowers on long, thin pedicels. Each flower has 3 outer tepals that are a bit shorter and narrower than the inner ones. The tepals may be accented with purple veining, and the pistils are deep pink.

This markedly showy species was originally introduced as a garden ornamental. Some sub-groups of *Butomus umbellatus* do not reproduce by seed; others spread by abundant self-sowing. All spread rhizomatously, and broken-off pieces of rhizome can form new plants as well. In addition to seeds and rhizomes, there are bulbils borne at the base of the pedicels and at the roots. The leathery seedpods float, and the plant gets help when moved around by animals like muskrats, as well as by hitchhiking on the undersides of boats. Plants can tolerate deep water levels (to 9 ft.), and fluctuations in water levels in wetlands confer an advantage and help it to spread. The species is still available in the nursery trade, and so it gets some help from gardeners who can't resist it or who underestimate its tenacity.

Flowering rush displaces native aquatic vegetation, and dense rhizomatous colonies can impact boat traffic in rivers. Control is difficult due to its multiple means of reproduction and dispersal. State agencies coping with large infestations are experimenting with herbicides, but their use near wetlands is limited by environmental restrictions. In the home garden, small populations can be dug up. Be sure to remove all bulbils as well as seedpods and pieces of rhizome. Gardeners who aim to keep the plant should keep it contained and deadheaded, and be careful about any potential propagules, particularly near moving water.

# Schoenoplectus mucronatus

## RICEFIELD BULRUSH, BOG BULRUSH

Non-native perennial, to 3 ft. Inflorescence brown, yellow, spikelets to 0.5 in.; midsummer. Leaves to 6 in. Parts edible/medicinal. Noxious in WA.

*Schoenoplectus mucronatus* (syn. *Schoenoplectiella mucronata*) is a Eurasian/African species that has become a problematic weed, particularly for rice agriculture, in over 40 countries. In North America, it's found in a handful of sites in southwest Washington and Oregon, several counties in California, and several midwestern and northeastern US states. A wetland dweller, ricefield bulrush invades pond margins, marshes, drainage ditches—and rice fields.

The plant has very short, hard rhizomes and stolons attached to tubers. It grows in tufts of tall, narrow stems that are sharply triangular in cross section. Each bears 1–2 leaves that are reduced to bladeless sheaths without ligules. The inflorescence is a spherical, spiky-looking head of up to 20 sessile, brownish to straw-colored spikelets, each to 0.5 in. long. A narrow bract to 4 in. long rises above the head, sometimes vertically but usually at an angle; it resembles a leaf or continuation of the stem. Plants reproduce by self-seeding and by sprouting from tubers and stolons.

# Myriophyllum aquaticum

PARROT'S FEATHER

Non-native perennial, to 16 ft. Flowers white, 4-lobed, to 0.02 in.; early–midsummer. Leaves whorled, to 2 in. Noxious in BC, WA, OR, CA.

This South American species, present in the US at least since the early 1900s, is used as an ornamental in aquariums and pond gardens but has escaped cultivation, invading freshwater canals, ponds, and slow-moving streams across most of North America. It forms dense mats that shade out native plants, impede water flow, degrade salmon habitat, and interfere with recreational activities.

The long, branched stems, arising from long rhizomes on muddy underwater substrates, bear feathery, pinnately divided leaves in whorls of 4–6. Each leaf has up to 37 thread-like divisions. The plant remains entirely submerged until it blooms, at which time emergent stems may grow to 12 in. above the water's surface. These above-water stems are bright green, stiff, and erect, resembling miniature conifers. Tiny flowers are borne in the leaf axils. The species is dioecious, but in North America, only female plants are present. They are apetalous with feathery stigmas. Parrot's feather on this continent reproduces vegetatively by rhizomes, adventitious roots at stem nodes, and stem or rhizome fragments. Plant fragments are easily dispersed in water, sometimes hitching rides on boat hulls.

*Myriophyllum aquaticum* is distinguished from most *Myriophyllum* species in the PNW by the appearance of its emergent stems and by having only female flowers.

# Myriophyllum spicatum

## EURASIAN WATER-MILFOIL, SPIKE WATER-MILFOIL

Non-native perennial, to 20 ft. Flowers white, 4-lobed, tiny; midspring–autumn. Leaves whorled, to 1.5 in. Parts edible with caution. Noxious in WA, OR, CA.

Eurasian water-milfoil is one of at least 10 *Myriophyllum* species present in the PNW, most of them native. It has been present in US waters at least since the early 1900s. It is used as an ornamental in aquariums and pond gardens but has escaped cultivation and is now present in lakes, ponds, and slow-moving streams over most of North America. It grows aggressively, forming dense mats that shade out native vegetation, degrade wildlife and fish habitat, inhibit water movement, and impede water-based recreation. Seeds and vegetative fragments are dispersed by aquarium dumping, waterfowl, boat hulls, and flooding.

Eurasian milfoil grows, mostly submersed, from spreading rhizomes with thin, whitish roots in bottom sediments. Its reddish stems branch freely close to the top; they may be unbranched or few-branched toward the bottom. The well-spaced leaves are attached in whorls of 4 (sometimes 5) along the stem. Each leaf is oval to elliptic in outline and pinnately dissected into 5–12 pairs of thread-like segments. Plants are monoecious; they sometimes flower twice during the bloom season. The inflorescence extends above the water surface, with reddish terminal spikes to 4 in. long. The tiny male and female flowers are apetalous. The purplish male flowers are higher on the spike; the females below them are whitish. Female flowers are followed by small 4-parted seedpods, each containing 4 seeds. Each plant may produce about 100 seeds in a season, but most of the plant's reproduction is vegetative, via rhizomatous spread and rooting of stem fragments.

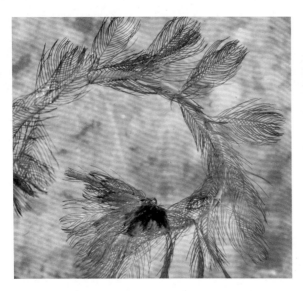

# Egeria densa

## BRAZILIAN WATERWEED, BRAZILIAN ELODEA

Non-native perennial, to 20 ft. Flowers white, 3-petaled, to 0.75 in.; midsummer–autumn. Leaves whorled, opposite, to 1 in. Noxious in BC, WA, OR, CA.

This aggressive aquatic weed from South America was introduced as an aquarium plant and has been present as an escape in bodies of water at least since the late 1800s. It is found in water up to 20 ft. deep in ponds, lakes, ditches, and slow-moving streams along the west coast from BC to California, as well as across much of the southern US. It forms dense stands that can cover hundreds of acres, competing with native vegetation, degrading water quality and fish habitat, restricting water movement, contributing to multiple ecological changes, and impeding water recreation. The plant is easily confused with an aquatic native to our region, *Elodea canadensis*, but that has shorter leaves in whorls of 3.

*Egeria densa* is mostly completely submersed but can form dense floating mats on the water surface. The very long stems are sparingly branched and root at the nodes. They are clothed in many small, soft, light green, linear, strap-shaped leaves with minute marginal serration. They are opposite or in whorls of 3 low on the stem and in whorls of 4–6 higher up. The distances between whorls are very short high on the stems, giving the plants a somewhat bushy look. One to several small but showy flowers rise from nodes on long pedicels, each with 9 conspicuous, bright yellow to orange stamens. All plants in the US are male, so no seeds are produced, but vegetative expansion is very rapid and prolific, with sprouting from stem nodes and from stem fragments.

# Nymphoides peltata
## YELLOW FLOATINGHEART

Non-native perennial, to 6 ft. Flowers yellow, 5-lobed, to 1.5 in.; midsummer–autumn. Leaves alternate, to 6 in. Parts edible/medicinal. Noxious in BC, WA, OR, CA.

This Eurasian species is sold as an ornamental and has escaped cultivation widely along the west coast from BC to California, as well as in several southern, midwestern, and northeastern states. It is found rooted on the bottoms of and floating in shallow ponds, slow-moving streams, and reservoirs, crowding out native aquatic plants and forming dense masses that block waterways. It is sometimes confused with another showy, bright yellow, floating plant, the native *Nuphar polysepala*, but the leaves and flowers of the latter are quite different in shape.

Yellow floatingheart has creeping rhizomes on substrates below bodies of water and stout, branched stolons to 9 ft. long. The leaves float on the water surface at the ends of petioles as long as 12 ft., rising from the stolon nodes. They are rounded to heart-shaped with wavy, shallowly scalloped margins; their undersides are purplish, upper surfaces deep green, sometimes with purple mottling. The flowers, borne singly or in small clusters of up to 5, are held just above the water on long upright stalks; their bright yellow petals are rimmed with fine fringe. They are followed by seed capsules to 1 in. long, each containing numerous seeds. The species reproduces by seed and vegetatively by sprouting of rhizomes, stolons, and any severed fragments of these.

# *Nymphaea odorata*

FRAGRANT WATER LILY

Non-native perennial, to 9 ft. Flowers white, pink, 20- to 30-petaled, to 7.5 in.; early summer–autumn. Leaves to 10 in. Parts edible/medicinal with caution. Noxious in WA, CA.

Native to eastern and central North America, this showy aquatic has escaped cultivation and invaded ponds and lakes along the west coast from BC to California. Present in the region at least since the early 1900s, it is particularly seen in Washington lakes, where people planted it in the past for ornamental effect. It grows in the soft substrates of shallow, natural bodies of water, including ponds and slow-moving streams, as well as in marshes, irrigation ditches, and canals. The plant can form dense stands, covering hundreds of acres on lakes during the growing season, obstructing water recreation, and crowding out natives. When not in bloom, it may be confused with the native aquatic *Nuphar polysepala*.

*Nymphaea odorata* grows from multi-branched, creeping rhizomes and coarse fibrous roots in bottom sediments. The rhizomes may be several feet long, floating just below the water's surface, with new plants and thread-like adventitious roots developing at the nodes. Leaves are round to heart-shaped, attached to the rhizomes by slender petioles up to 6 ft. long. The showy, solitary flowers are borne on long peduncles rising from the rhizomes. Each fragrant, white to pale pink flower has 4 green sepals, up to 100 yellow stamens, and up to 9 stigmas. They open in the morning and close in the afternoon. The flowers are followed by leathery, berry-like capsules, each containing many seeds. *Nymphaea odorata* reproduces by seed and by rhizomatous spread. Rhizome fragments may also take root and form new plants.

# Ludwigia hexapetala

## SIX-PETAL WATER PRIMROSE

**Non-native perennial, to 10 ft. Flowers yellow, 5- or 6-petaled, to 1 in.; midsummer. Leaves alternate, to 4.75 in. Noxious in WA, OR, CA.**

This South American species is found across much of North America. The plant invades wetlands, lakes, and rivers, forming mats as thick as 3 ft., impeding water flow, clogging irrigation canals, impacting aquatic animals and fish, competing with native plants, and altering shoreline ecology. Plants spread by self-seeding, by sprouting of stem fragments, and via creeping rhizomes.

Growing from rhizomes, the long stems of *Ludwigia hexapetala* float on water or sprawl across mud, rooting at the nodes both on wet soil and in water. Young leaves are rounded and form rosettes along the stems. At maturity, they are narrow, resembling those of willow, and somewhat hairy. The showy, bright yellow flowers are borne singly on upright stems rising from the leaf axils. Like other *Ludwigia* species, six-petal water primrose usually has 5 petals. (Go figure.) Both the specific epithet and this common name refer to the occasional 6-petaled plant. Flowers are followed by seed capsules to 1.25 in. long. This species looks very similar to *L. peploides*. However, in *L. hexapetala*, the flowering stems, leaves, and floral tubes are somewhat fuzzy (vs. the typically hairless *L. peploides*). Also, in *L. peploides*, mature leaves are more oval and not as long or narrow as the leaves of *L. hexapetala*.

# Ludwigia peploides

FLOATING PRIMROSE-WILLOW, CREEPING WATER PRIMROSE

Non-native perennial, to 10 ft. Flowers yellow, 5- or 6-petaled, to 1 in.; midsummer–autumn. Leaves alternate, to 3.5 in. Noxious in WA, OR.

This aquatic species is a troublesome weed in many places beyond its native territory in North America and Europe. Introduced widely as an ornamental, it has escaped cultivation and is now found from Washington to California and over much of the southern and eastern US. *Ludwigia peploides* is an aggressive invader of wetlands, ponds, streams, and irrigation ditches. It proliferates rapidly, mostly by vegetative spread, and forms dense mats over water, crowding out native aquatic and shoreline plants, altering oxygen and pH levels, and increasing sedimentation. It impacts wildlife, interferes with flood control systems, and clogs waterways.

Growing from a system of fibrous and fleshy roots, the long stems of *Ludwigia peploides* float across water or trail across muddy ground. The bright yellow flowers are held on long stalks from the upper leaf axils. The leaves are lanceolate to oval, tapering to short stalks; they are hairless, with smooth margins. The plant produces seed but reproduces mostly vegetatively, often from stem fragments that break off and root.

# Veronica anagallis-aquatica

## WATER SPEEDWELL

Non-native perennial, to 2.5 ft. Flowers blue, violet, 4-petaled, to 0.25 in.; early summer–autumn. Leaves opposite, to 4 in. Parts edible/medicinal.

*Veronica anagallis-aquatica* is a European species found over much of North America in association with wet places, including streams, irrigation ditches, wetlands, springs, and seeps. This is a short-lived perennial with fibrous roots, as well as rhizomes or stolons. The stems are slender and typically erect, the leaves opposite, sessile to clasping, and narrowly oval to elliptic, with margins that may be entire or serrated.

The long-stalked axillary and terminal racemes, each to 6 in. long, bear up to 60 flowers. Individual flowers are borne on fine upward-curving stalks to 0.3 in. long. Only a few flowers in a raceme bloom at once. The corolla is blue to violet and marked with fine lines in dark blue or purple, radiating from the center, which fades to whitish- or yellowish-green. The lobes are slightly irregular, with the lowermost of 4 petals being noticeably smaller. In fall, the blooming shoots die down and are replaced by sterile shoots with low rosettes of oval leaves.

# *Phragmites australis* subsp. *australis*

COMMON REED

---

Non-native perennial, to 15 ft. Inflorescence green, purple, to 14 in.; midsummer–autumn. Leaves alternate, to 24 in. Parts edible/medicinal. Noxious in BC, WA, OR, CA.

---

This large Eurasian subspecies was introduced accidentally in the eastern US, possibly as early as the late 1700s. It is now present in scattered areas in the PNW and widely distributed across North America, invading riparian areas, roadsides, irrigation ditches, and other moist, disturbed sites. It is extremely aggressive, displacing native plants, including the native *Phragmites australis* subsp. *americanus*. The non-native subspecies forms vast, dense monocultural stands that negatively impact aquatic ecosystems in multiple ways.

Common reed grows from an aggressive root system, with rhizomes that can grow 30 ft. in a year. The tall stems are hollow, light green early in the season, turning to tan as they dry in the fall. The leaves are smooth and flat, as wide as 2 in., and blue-green (vs. the lighter, yellowish-green leaves of subsp. *americanus*). The sheaths are firmly attached (vs. the loose sheaths of subsp. *americanus*).

The inflorescence is tall and feathery, about 6 in. across and somewhat oval to lanceolate in outline, changing from green to purple in full bloom, then aging to gold or light brown. Plants may produce as many as 2,000 seeds per inflorescence (subsp. *americanus* has fewer viable seeds).

# Spartina alterniflora

## SMOOTH CORDGRASS, SALTWATER CORDGRASS

**Non-native perennial, to 4 ft. Inflorescence yellow, to 16 in.; late summer–autumn. Leaves to 20 in. Noxious in BC, WA, OR, CA.**

*Spartina alterniflora* (syn. *Sporobolus alterniflorus*) is a profusely rhizomatous grass native to the east coasts of North and South America. It has been introduced on the west coast several times both accidentally and deliberately (e.g., for stabilization) and is present in multiple sites, thriving in the lower (saltier) intertidal zones of the Pacific, the Strait of Juan de Fuca, Puget Sound, and the brackish mouths of some rivers. This species forms dense colonies, displacing native vegetation and disrupting habitat for marine fauna including fish, birds, and invertebrates. In favorable conditions, it spreads very rapidly by seed, rhizomes, and fragments. As a grass of the intertidal, it is very unlikely to show up in the average garden.

Smooth cordgrass grows in clumps that may be closely spaced, rising at short intervals all along the underground rhizomes. The culms are erect, hairless, and hollow. The leaves are fairly narrow, to 0.6 in. wide, rolled inward at the tips. The sheaths are open, and the ligule consists of a line of fine hairs. The inflorescence is a narrow, erect, dense, spike-like panicle with several main branches that remain very close together.

# Spartina anglica

COMMON CORDGRASS, ENGLISH CORDGRASS

Non-native perennial, to 3.5 ft. Inflorescence yellow, to 16 in.; midsummer–autumn. Leaves to 18 in. Unpalatable. Noxious in BC, WA, OR, CA.

*Spartina anglica* (syn. *Sporobolus anglicus*) is a stable, though morphologically variable, hybrid of *Spartina alterniflora* and *S. maritima*. It produces at least some viable seed and spreads aggressively by rhizomes and tillers as well. In Washington, common cordgrass occurs in at least seven counties, mostly bordering on the Puget Sound and Strait of Juan de Fuca. The species was introduced to the Puget Sound region in the 1960s, in the mistaken belief that the plants were *S. ×townsendii*, a sterile hybrid of the same parent species. Like its parent *S. alterniflora*, *S. anglica* is an aggressive weed of the intertidal, forming dense mono-cultural stands that impact tidal ecosystems.

*Spartina anglica* is about half as tall as *S. alterniflora*. Like the latter species, common cordgrass has leaves that are flat or inrolled, to 0.5 in. wide, and its ligule is a fringe of hairs. Its narrow, compressed, spike-like pani-cles are similar in appearance to *S. alterniflora*.

*Spartina densiflora* and *S. patens*, both introduced, are also present (but quite rare) in the PNW. *Spartina densiflora* differs from other *Spartina* species discussed here in that it lacks rhizomes and spreads only by seed; it is found along the northern California coast and in a handful of sites in Oregon and Washington. In addition to these invaders, there are two native *Spartina* species in the PNW, *S. gracilis* and *S. pectinata*. Consult online guides or your local weed agency for help with ID.

AQUATICS

# Potamogeton crispus

## CURLY PONDWEED

Non-native perennial, to 3 ft. Flowers brown, green, 4-lobed, to 0.13 in.; mid–late summer. Leaves alternate, to 4 in. Parts edible with caution. Noxious in WA.

Curly pondweed has been present in North America at least since the mid-1800s and is now found in fresh or brackish water of marshes, lakes, ponds, and slow-moving streams across most of the US and southern Canada. It is invasive, forming dense floating mats that crowd and shade out native aquatic plants and contribute to eutrophication when they go dormant and leave masses of dead vegetation in late summer. The broad mats also restrict access to water and water-based recreation. Curly pondweed is thus listed as a noxious weed in many areas. The plant may be introduced with fish and fish eggs shipped to hatcheries and continues to be readily available in the horticultural trade, even where illegal.

Curly pondweed dwells entirely underwater except when its flower stalks rise above the water. Growing from slender rhizomes, the stems are branched and partly flattened, with reddish-green to brownish, sessile or clasping leaves. The leaves are oblong to strap-shaped with strongly curled, minutely serrated upper margins, rounded tips, and 3 prominent longitudinal veins. The minute, brownish or reddish-green flowers are borne in spikes to 1 in. long, on peduncles to 3 in.

Seeds are produced, but the majority of reproduction for this species is vegetative, via rhizomatous spread, rhizome fragments, and turions (buds that can break away and start new plants). In late summer, *Potamogeton crispus* goes into vegetative overdrive, producing turions by the thousands. These can overwinter on the bottoms of bodies of water and be dispersed by water movement. After turion production, the rest of the plant goes into dormancy. When temperatures cool, it will grow actively again and remain evergreen through the winter, even under ice.

At least 18 *Potamogeton* species occur in the PNW, so confident identification may be a challenge. *Potamogeton crispus* may appear most similar to the native *P. richardsonii*, but that species has longer, broader leaves with margins not serrated.

# Typha angustifolia
## NARROW-LEAF CATTAIL

Non-native perennial, to 12 ft. Flowers brown, tiny; midsummer. Leaves alternate, to 6 ft. Parts edible. Noxious in WA.

This species, one of three introduced *Typha* species in the PNW, is widespread across much of North America, growing in the shallow water of ditches and pond edges. Our native *T. latifolia* is easily distinguished from these invaders thanks to its inflorescence, in which the lower, pistillate (female) and upper, staminate (male) portions touch each other. Cattails often form broad colonies, reproducing vegetatively from rhizomes, as well as by prolific seed production.

Growing from shallow fibrous roots and creeping rhizomes, narrow-leaf cattail produces a clump of very erect, unbranched, pithy stems. The leaves are long, narrow (to 0.5 in. wide), and 2-ranked (growing on a single plane), sometimes twisting as a group into a loose spiral. They are deep green, flat on the inner side and convex on the outer side. The terminal inflorescence is a spike consisting of minute brownish flowers, male and female on the same stem—but separated. The staminate portion is above, to 5 in. long. It is separated from the lower, female segment by a section of bare stem to 4.75 in. long. The pistillate spike is thicker, dense, cylindrical, and dark brown, to 6 in. long. A single plant may produce as many as 250,000 very long-lived seeds in a season.

# *Nanozostera japonica*

## JAPANESE EELGRASS

Non-native perennial, to 12 in. Flowers green, tiny; midspring–autumn. Leaves alternate, to 14 in. Noxious in WA, CA.

*Nanozostera japonica* (syn. *Zostera japonica*) is an Asian eelgrass species probably introduced to the west coast of North America accidentally with imported oysters or oyster spat. Since the 1930s, the species has spread to intertidal zones from Alaska to California. The species can be found between high and low tides on mudflats or sand; it is typically higher in the intertidal zone than the native *N. marina*, which can also be distinguished by its much taller and broader blades. This non-native has changed some distributions of native eelgrass and had negative impacts on oyster production.

Japanese eelgrass is a low-growing, rhizomatous plant with very narrow (to 0.04 in. wide) leaf blades of somewhat variable length. The tips may be obtuse to retuse or mucronate. Leaf sheaths are open and overlapping, to 2 in. long, each with 2 short, membranous flaps.

The inflorescence consists of a one-sided array of very minute, green flowers without petals or sepals, along a flattened, thickened stem portion to 2.5 in. Each male flower has a single anther; each female flower has 1 style and 2 stigmas. Seeds are borne in utricles, elliptical membranous coverings to 0.1 in. long. Seeds are dispersed in water, by waterfowl consumption and deposition and by hitchhiking on boat hulls. Most colony expansions are via rhizomatous spread.

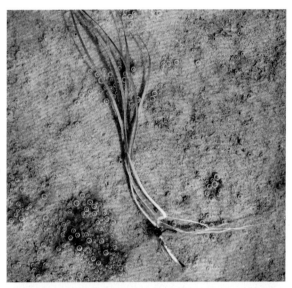

# About the Photographs

Most field guide users start with the photographs, matching characteristics of the plant in front of them with the pictures in the book. I worked hard to photograph the plants in a way that makes identification as easy and accurate as possible, while simultaneously employing the artist's tools of composition, light and shadow, and point of view. One or more key characters of the species are illustrated in each photo.

The photographs were made over a period of 25 years, although the majority were created in two intensive field seasons. I drove thousands of miles, with repeated trips across the Northwest to capture the plants in bloom. Most of the photos were made within a short walk of a road, sometimes literally standing in the roadside ditch. I was guided to locations by herbarium and iNaturalist records provided by botanists who came before me.

I worked in all kinds of weather and lighting conditions, from bright midday sun to rain. With so many plants and locations spread over such a wide area, I did not have the luxury of waiting for perfect conditions. Most of the time I used whatever light was available, modifying it with a reflector or diffuser for the close-up images. I battled wind, particularly when photographing spindly grasses. I sought vantage points that let me separate specimen from background. While all my subjects were firmly rooted, that didn't make them easy.

Surprisingly, some of the weeds were hard to find. On the other hand, over 125 of the plant photos were made in our family's garden or elsewhere on our property on the outskirts of Bellingham. The hard-to-find weeds were often ones on official noxious weeds lists because they're just starting to appear in our region. Sometimes an herbarium record I was chasing turned out to be on private property, behind a locked gate. A few times, I photographed plants just before the weed control folks showed up to dig or poison them. In other cases I had my eye on a roadside weed patch, waiting for it to be ready to photograph, only to return later and find that everything had been mowed off. That's a problem I never encountered when photographing wildflowers.

The great majority of the photographs were made with Canon digital single-lens reflex cameras. A few originated on 35mm slide film. I used a variety of lenses, from 16mm ultra wide-angle to 400mm telephoto. Three lenses were the workhorses: 24-105mm, 100mm macro, and 70-200mm. I almost always work with my camera on a tripod, both to hold the camera steady and as a compositional tool.

Once field photography was complete, I selected—from over 20,000 candidates—the best views of each species. I made my selections using Adobe® Lightroom® and did most of the post-capture processing in the develop module of the same program to adjust density, color balance, and contrast.

—*Mark Turner*

# Additional Photography

All photographs in *Weeds of the Pacific Northwest* are by Mark Turner, with the exception of the following:

**Zoya Akulova-Barlow**
*Centaurea melitensis* (foliage), page 140

**Lyle Anderson**
*Panicum miliaceum* (specimen), page 400

**Charles T. Bryson**, USDA Agricultural Research Service, Bugwood.org
*Sesbania punicea* (flower), page 71

**Gerald D. Carr**
*Abutilon theophrasti* (flower), page 312
*Halogeton glomeratus* (flower), page 108
*Halogeton glomeratus* (specimen), page 108
*Pastinaca sativa* (flower), page 119
*Xanthium spinosum* (flower), page 188

**Robert L. Carr**
*Cyclachaena xanthii folia* (foliage), page 155

**Peter M. Dziuk**, www.MinnesotaWildflowers.info
*Silene noctiflora*, page 248

**Mark Egger**
*Salvia aethiopis*, page 308

**David Giblin**
*Nymphoides peltata* (flower), page 420

**Ben Legler**
*Anchusa officinalis* (flower), page 192
*Carduus acanthoides*, page 132
*Cyclachaena xanthiifolia* (flower), page 154
*Cyclachaena xanthiifolia* (specimen), page 154
*Erechtites minimus* (foliage), page 157
*Erechtites minimus* (specimen), page 157
*Physalis longifolia*, page 364
*Poa pratensis*, page 404
*Veronica chamaedrys*, page 355

**T. Abe Lloyd**
*Panicum miliaceum* (foliage), page 400

**Mourad Louadfel**
*Raphanus raphanistrum* (foliage), page 228

**Gary McDonald**
*Centaurea melitensis* (specimen), page 140

**Leslie J. Mehrhoff**, University of Connecticut, Bugwood.org
*Tamarix ramosissima* (flower), page 96

**Barry Rice**, sarracenia.com, Bugwood.org
*Sesbania punicea* (fruit), page 71

**Clifford W. Smith**
*Delairea odorata* (flower), page 156

**Rebekah D. Wallace**, University of Georgia, Bugwood.org
*Raphanus raphanistrum* (flower), page 228

**Barbara Wilson**
*Sorghum halepense*, page 408

**Peter Zika**
*Anchusa officinalis* (specimen), page 192
*Delairea odorata* (foliage), page 156
*Ludwigia peploides*, page 423
*Pastinaca sativa* (specimen), page 119
*Schoenoplectus mucronatus*, page 416
*Spartina alterniflora*, page 426

**Jordan Zylstra**
*Centaurea melitensis* (flower), page 140

# Conversion Table for Metric Measurements

| INCHES | CENTIMETERS |
|---|---|
| 0.1 | 0.25 |
| 0.2 | 0.51 |
| 0.25 | 0.64 |
| 0.3 | 0.76 |
| 0.4 | 1.02 |
| 0.5 | 1.27 |
| 0.6 | 1.52 |
| 0.7 | 1.78 |
| 0.75 | 1.91 |
| 0.8 | 2.03 |
| 0.9 | 2.29 |
| 1 | 2.54 |
| 2 | 5.08 |
| 3 | 7.62 |
| 4 | 10.16 |
| 5 | 12.70 |
| 6 | 15.24 |
| 7 | 17.78 |
| 8 | 20.32 |
| 9 | 22.86 |
| 10 | 25.40 |
| 11 | 27.94 |

| FEET | METERS |
|---|---|
| 0.25 | 0.08 |
| 0.3 | 0.09 |
| 0.5 | 0.15 |
| 1 | 0.30 |
| 1.5 | 0.46 |
| 2 | 0.61 |
| 2.5 | 0.76 |
| 3 | 0.91 |
| 4 | 1.22 |
| 5 | 1.52 |
| 6 | 1.83 |
| 7 | 2.13 |
| 8 | 2.44 |
| 9 | 2.74 |
| 10 | 3.05 |
| 12 | 3.66 |
| 15 | 4.57 |
| 18 | 5.49 |
| 20 | 6.10 |
| 25 | 7.62 |
| 30 | 9.14 |
| 35 | 10.67 |

| FEET | METERS |
|---|---|
| 40 | 12.19 |
| 45 | 13.72 |
| 50 | 15.24 |
| 60 | 18.29 |
| 70 | 21.34 |
| 80 | 24.38 |
| 90 | 27.43 |
| 100 | 30.48 |
| 125 | 38.10 |
| 150 | 45.72 |
| 175 | 53.34 |
| 200 | 60.96 |

# Bibliography

Baldwin, Bruce G., et al. (eds.). 2012. *The Jepson Manual: Vascular Plants of California*, Second Edition. Berkeley: University of California Press.

Burrows, George E., and Ronald J. Tyrl. 2013. *Toxic Plants of North America, Second Edition*. Ames, IA: John Wiley & Sons, Inc.

Calflora Database. calflora.org.

California Department of Food and Agriculture. *Noxious Weeds*. cdfa. ca.gov/plant/ipc/encycloweedia/ encycloweedia_hp.html.

California Invasive Plant Council. cal-ipc.org.

Canadian Poisonous Plants Information System. cbif.gc.ca/eng/ species-bank/canadian-poisonous-plants-information-system/ introduction/?id=1370403266264.

Centre for Agriculture and Bioscience International. *Invasive Species Compendium*. cabi.org/isc.

Chace, Teri Dunn. 2013. *How to Eradicate Invasive Plants*. Portland, OR: Timber Press.

Chalker-Scott, Linda, Ph.D. 2020. A Tale of Two Weeders: Lessons in Managing Aggressive, Perennial Weeds. The Garden Professors Blog. gardenprofessors.com/a-tale-of-two-weeders-lessons-in-managing-aggressive-perennial-weeds/.

——. 2015. The Myth of Landscape Fabric. Washington State University Puyallup Research and Extension Center. s3.wp. wsu.edu/uploads/sites/403/2015/03/ landscape-fabric.pdf.

——. 2015. The Myth of Weed-Killing Gluten. Washington State University Puyallup Research and Extension Center. s3.wp.wsu.edu/uploads/ sites/403/2015/03/corn-gluten.pdf.

——. Wood Chip Mulch: Landscape Boon or Bane? *Master Gardener*, Summer 2007. s3.wp.wsu.edu/uploads/ sites/403/2015/03/wood-chips.pdf.

Clackamas Soil and Water Conservation District. Weedwise. weedwise. conservationdistrict.org.

Colorado State University Guide to Poisonous Plants. csuvth.colostate.edu/ poisonous_plants/.

Department of the Army. 2009. *The Complete Guide to Edible Wild Plants*. New York: Skyhorse Publishing.

Deur, Douglas. 2014. *Pacific Northwest Foraging*. Portland, OR: Timber Press.

Duke, James A. 1992. *Handbook of Edible Weeds*. Boca Raton, FL: CRC Press.

eFloras.org. efloras.org.

Facciola, Stephen. 1990. *Cornucopia: A Source Book of Edible Plants*. Vista, CA: Kampong Publications.

Flora of North America Editorial Committee, eds. 1993–. *Flora of North America North of Mexico* [onlinc]. 22+ vols. New York and Oxford. floranorthamerica.org.

Friends of the Wild Flower Garden. friendsofthewildflowergarden.org.

Gibbons, Euell. 1962. *Stalking the Wild Asparagus*. Chambersburg, PA: Allan C. Hood & Company, Inc.

Global Biodiversity Information Facility. gbif.org.

Harris, James G. and Melinda Woolf Harris. 2001. *Plant Identification Terminology: An Illustrated Glossary, Second Edition*. Spring Lake, UT: Spring Lake Publishing.

Hilty, John. Illinois Wildflowers. illinoiswildflowers.info

Hitchcock, C. Leo, and Aurthur Cronquist. 2018. *Flora of the Pacific Northwest, Second Edition*. David E. Giblin et al., eds. Seattle: University of Washington Press.

HorseDVM. *Toxic Plant Finder.* horsedvm.com/toxicfinder.php.

Invasive Species Council of BC. 2021. *Field Guide to Noxious Weeds and Other Selected Invasive Plants of British Columbia, Eleventh Edition 2021.* bcinvasives.ca/wp-content/uploads/2021/02/Field_guide_to_Noxious_Weeds_11th_2021.pdf.

Jefferson County Noxious Weed Control Board. Best Management Practices Bittersweet Nightshade (*Solanum dulcamara*). co.jefferson.wa.us/DocumentCenter/View/2946/Bittersweet-Nightshade

King County, Washington. *Noxious weeds in King County, Washington.* kingcounty.gov/services/environment/animals-and-plants/noxious-weeds.

Klinkenberg, Brian. *E-Flora BC: Electronic Atlas of the Flora of British Columbia.* ibis.geog.ubc.ca/biodiversity/eflora/index.

Kloos, Scott. 2017. *Pacific Northwest Medicinal Plants.* Portland, OR: Timber Press.

Lins, R.D. and J.B. Colquhoun. 2008., Small Broomrape Biology and Management in the Pacific Northwest. Oregon State University, August 2008. catalog.extension.oregonstate.edu/sites/catalog/files/project/pdf/em8884.pdf

Maine Department of Agriculture, Conservation and Forestry. Invasive Plants. www.maine.gov/dacf/mnap/features/invasive_plants/invasives.htm.

Michigan State University. Midwest Invasive Species Information Network. www.misin.msu.edu/

Minnesota Wildflowers, a Field Guide to the Flora of Minnesota. minnesotawildflowers.info

Montana Noxious Weed Education. Montana Noxious Weed Education Campaign. weedawareness.org

Maine Department of Agriculture, Conservation and Forestry. Invasive Plants. www.maine.gov/dacf/mnap/features/invasive_plants/invasives.htm.

Michigan State University. Midwest Invasive Species Information Network. www.misin.msu.edu/

Minnesota Wildflowers, a Field Guide to the Flora of Minnesota. minnesotawildflowers.info

Montana Noxious Weed Education. Montana Noxious Weed Education Campaign. weedawareness.org

National Park Service, University of Georgia Center for Invasive Species and Ecosystem Health, Invasive Plant Atlas of New England, and the Lady Bird Johnson Wildflower Center. *Invasive Plant Atlas of the United States.* invasiveplantatlas.org.

Oregon Department of Agriculture. *Noxious Weed Policy and Classification System 2020.* www.oregon.gov/oda/shared/Documents/Publications/Weeds/NoxiousWeedPolicyClassification.pdf.

Oregon Department of Agriculture. *Oregon Noxious Weeds.* oregon.gov/oda/programs/weeds/oregonnoxiousweeds.

Oregon State University College of Agricultural Sciences Department of Horticulture. Land-scape Plants. landscapeplants.oregonstate.edu.

Oregon State University Department of Botany and Plant Pathology. *Oregon Flora.* oregonflora.org.

Peischel, An and D. Dickinson Henry, Jr. 2006. Targeted Grazing: A Natural Approach to Vegetation Management and Landscape Enhancement. University of Idaho Rangeland Center and American Sheep Industry Association, webpages.uidaho.edu/rx-grazing/handbook.htm.

Plants For A Future. *A resource and information centre for edible and otherwise useful plants.* pfaf.org.

Portland, Oregon. *Integrated Pest Management*. portland.gov/parks/nature/integrated-pest-management.

PoultryDVM. Toxic Plant Finder. chickendvm.com/toxic.php.

Prather, Timothy, Sandra Robins, and Don Morishta. University of Idaho Extension, Moscow, Idaho. *Idaho's Noxious Weeds 5th Edition*. jeromecountyid.us/DocumentCenter/View/108/Idaho-Noxious-Weed-Guide-PDF.

Roché, Cindy Talbott, et al. 2019. *Field Guide to the Grasses of Oregon and Washington*. Corvallis: Oregon State University Press.

Texas Invasive Species Institute. texasinvasives.org.

Taylor, Ronald J. 1990. *Northwest Weeds: The Ugly and Beautiful Villains of Fields, Gardens, and Roadsides*. Missoula, MT: Mountain Press Publishing Company.

Thayer, Samuel. 2010. *Nature's Garden: A Guide to Identifying, Harvesting, and Preparing Edible Wild Plants*. Birchwood, WI: Forager's Harvest Press.

Thayer, Samuel. 2006. *The Forager's Harvest: A Guide to Identifying, Harvesting, and Preparing Edible Wild Plants*. Birchwood, WI: Forager's Harvest Press.

Turner Photographics. *Wildflowers of the Pacific Northwest*. pnwflowers.com.

United States Department of Agriculture Cooperative Extension. Invasive Species. invasive-species.extension.org.

United States Department of Agriculture Natural Resources Conservation Service. USDA Plants Database: Plant List of Accepted Nomenclature, Taxonomy, and Symbols. plants.usda.gov.

United States Forest Service. Fire Effects Information System (FEIS). www.feis-crs.org/feis.

University of Alaska Anchorage. Alaska Center for Conservation Science. accs.uaa.alaska.edu.

University of California Agriculture and Natural Resources, Statewide Integrated Pest Management Program. *Weed Photo Gallery*. ipm.ucanr.edu/PMG/weeds_intro.html.

University of California Cooperative Extension and Agricultural Experiment Station. *Weed Research and Information Center*. wric.ucdavis.edu.

University of Georgia Center for Invasive Species and Ecosystem Health. *Bugwood*. bugwood.org.

——. *EDD Maps*. eddmaps.org.

——. *Invasive and Exotic Species of North America*. invasive.org.

University of Idaho Extension. uidaho.edu/extension.

University of Illinois Library. *Plants Toxic to Animals*. guides.library.illinois.edu/plantstoxictoanimals.

University of Nebraska–Lincoln Institute of Agriculture and Natural Resources Cropwatch. *Pest of the Month*. cropwatch.unl.edu/tags/pest-month.

University of Washington Burke Museum Herbarium. *Burke Herbarium Image Collection*. biology.burke.washington.edu/herbarium/imagecollection.

US Department of Agriculture Agricultural Research Service 2011. *Plants Poisonous to Livestock in the Western States*. Agriculture Information Bulletin Number 415.

Varner, Collin. 2020. *Edible and Medicinal Flora of the West Coast*. Seattle: University of Washington Press.

Washington Department of Fish and Wildlife. 2015. *Aquatic Plants and Fish: Rules for Aquatic Plant Removal and Control*. Olympia: Washington Department of Fish and Wildlife.

Washington State Noxious Weed Control Board. nwcb.wa.gov.

——. *Noxious Weeds in Washington: Everybody's Problem, Everybody's Solution*. nwcb.wa.gov/pdfs/NoxiousWeedsBooklet_web.pdf.

Zachos, Ellen. 2013. *Backyard Foraging*. North Adams, MA: Storey Publishing.

# Glossary

**achene**. Small, dry fruit, not opening at maturity, containing a single seed; seed attached to ovary wall at a single point.

**alternate**. Arranged singly at different heights along stem.

**annual**. Plant that germinates, flowers, seeds, and dies in one year.

**anther**. Pollen-producing segment of the stamen.

**apiculate**. Having a small, sharp pin-like projection at the tip.

**armed**. Bearing prickles, thorns, or spines.

**ascending**. Curving or angling upward from the base.

**auricle**. A small, ear-like appendage or flap, at the base of a leaf or at the sheath in grasses.

**awn**. A bristle, usually at the tip of the flower parts in grasses.

**axil**. The inside angle between the leaf and the stem.

**axillary**. Pertaining to the axil. In the axil.

**barb**. A short, backward-pointing point, like that of a fishhook.

**basal**. Found at or near the base of a plant or plant part, particularly referring to leaves.

**berry**. Fleshy fruit with more than one seed within the soft tissue, lacking a central core.

**biennial**. Plant completing the life cycle in two years.

**bilabiate**. Having two lips, as in irregular flowers.

**bilateral**. Two sides mirror images of the other, as in leaves or flowers.

**bipinnate**. Twice pinnate, with the divisions again pinnately divided.

**bisexual**. A flower with both pistils and stamens; perfect.

**blade**. The expanded part of the leaf.

**bloom**. Waxy or chalky substance coating an entity such as a leaf or fruit, usually giving it a whitish appearance.

**bog**. Nutrient-poor wetland that receives a majority of its water from precipitation, characterized by peat deposits, acidic water, and sphagnum moss.

**brackish**. Somewhat salty waters.

**bract**. Small leaf-like structure, usually at the base of a flower or inflorescence.

**bractlet**. Small secondary bract.

**branch**. Secondary stem, growing from main stem.

**bristle**. Large, stiff, straight hair.

**bulb**. An underground bud containing fleshy leaves, like an onion.

**bulbil**. A small bulb, attached to a larger bulb or growing from a leaf axil or within an inflorescence.

**bulblet**. A small bulb.

**calyx (calyces)**. Whorl of sepals, the lowest or outermost part enclosing the rest of the flower. Often green or tan.

**capsule**. Dry, many-seeded fruit, opening at maturity.

**catkin**. Flexible, compact cluster of unisexual flowers without petals or stalks.

**cauline**. Of, on, or pertaining to the stem, as leaves attached to the stem above ground level.

**ciliate**. Edged with minute hairs.

**circumboreal**. Around the world at northern latitudes.

**compound leaf.** A leaf divided into two or more separate leaflets.

**corolla.** Collective term for petals of the flower.

**crown.** Persistent base of an herbaceous perennial; in grasses, the point from which the leaves and culms emerge.

**culm.** Jointed flowering stem of grasses.

**deciduous.** Falling off at the end of the growing season or sooner, often referring to plants that are leafless part of the year.

**decumbent.** Lying on the ground with the tips pointing upward.

**decussate.** Each successive pair of opposite leaves at right angles to the lower pair.

**dentate.** Toothed along the edge, with the teeth pointing outward rather than forward.

**dioecious.** A species in which male and female flowers are borne on different plants.

**discoid.** In the Asteraceae, flowers of a head all tubular, bisexual or female.

**entire.** Without teeth, notches, or divisions, as in the smooth margins of some leaves.

**evergreen.** Remaining green through the dormant season and persistent for more than two seasons.

**filament.** The stalk of the stamen that holds the anther.

**floret.** Small individual flower in a larger flowerhead, as in sunflowers.

**fruit.** A ripened ovary and associated parts containing the seeds.

**glabrous.** Smooth, hairless.

**gland.** Secreting structure, emits a sticky substance, sessile on the outer layer or on end of hair.

**glaucous.** Covered with a whitish or bluish waxy coating or bloom.

**gynodioecious.** A species in which some plants have only female flowers and others have only bisexual flowers.

**hair.** Thin to thick threadlike growth on outer surface.

**hastate.** Narrowly triangular, spearhead-shaped.

**head.** Dense collection of sessile or nearly sessile flowers making up an inflorescence.

**hermaphroditic.** A flower with both pistils and stamens; bisexual; perfect.

**hip.** Enlarged, leathery structure containing several achenes, as in roses.

**hybrid.** Plant created when two different species interbreed.

**inflorescence.** The arrangement of the flowers, or cluster of flowers, on a plant.

**invasive.** Characteristic indicative of an organism's ability to move into new territory, displacing and replacing some of the former inhabitants.

**involucre.** Whorl of bracts below a flower or flower cluster.

**lanceolate.** Lance-shaped, much longer than wide, with the widest point below the middle.

**lateral.** On or at the side.

**lemma.** Lower of the two bracts enclosing a grass flower.

**ligule.** The joint in grasses where one piece of stem emerges from the one below, marking the transition from sheath to leaf blade.

**linear.** Narrow with parallel sides, line-like.

**lip.** Upper or lower section of an unequal corolla or calyx.

**lobe.** A projecting segment of an organ. The free parts of a flower tube.

**lyrate.** Wavy, lyre-shaped.

**margin.** Edge, as of a leaf blade.

**monoecious.** Having male and female floral parts on the same plant.

**mucronate.** Ending abruptly in a pin-like point.

**native.** Growing in place without human aid or as a result of human activity.

**node**. Point on a stem where one or more leaves originate.

**nut**. Dry fruit containing a single seed.

**nutlet**. A small nut.

**obcordate**. Heart-shaped, with the narrow end at the base.

**oblanceolate**. Lanceolate but blunted at the tip.

**oblong**. Longer than wide, rounded.

**obovate**. Somewhat blunted at the tip.

**obtuse**. Somewhat blunted.

**ocrea**. A brownish, papery sheath of fused stipules wrapping around the stem, primarily in the buckwheat family.

**odd-pinnate**. Having pairs of opposite leaflets and one terminal leaflet.

**opposite**. Arranged in pairs at same level, and on opposite sides, often said of leaves on the stem.

**oval**. Longer than wide, both ends similar in shape; a squashed circle.

**ovary**. Structure that contains ovules and eggs, develops into a fruit after fertilization.

**panicle**. A branched, spreading inflorescence with flowers opening from the bottom upward.

**pappus**. The modified calyx of the Asteraceae, including awns or bristles at the tip of the seed.

**pedicel**. Stem of a single flower in an inflorescence, or of a grass spikelet.

**peduncle**. Main stalk of an inflorescence.

**perennial**. Plant living longer than two years.

**perfoliate**. Appearing as if the stem pierces the leaf.

**persistent**. Remaining attached, not falling off plant for some time.

**petal**. Member of the corolla, often colored, serving to attract pollinators.

**petiolate**. Stalked.

**petiole**. Stem or stalk of a leaf.

**pinnate**. A compound leaf with leaflets arranged on opposite sides of the axis.

**pinnatifid**. Pinnately divided or lobed halfway or more to the midrib of a leaf.

**pistil**. Female reproductive organ in angiosperms, typically made up of an ovary, style, and stigma.

**pod**. Dry fruit that splits into two or more parts to release the seeds.

**pollen**. Collective term for pollen grains, which are microspores containing the male gametophyte.

**polygamodioecious**. A species in which some plants have both bisexual and male flowers, and others have bisexual and female flowers.

**prickle**. A small, sharp outgrowth of epidermis or bark, usually slender.

**propagule**. A structure, such as a seed or spore, which gives rise to a new plant.

**prostrate**. Lying flat on the ground.

**pubescent**. Covered in soft hairs.

**raceme**. An unbranched, elongated inflorescence with flowers opening from the bottom upward.

**rachis**. Main axis of a structure, such as a compound leaf or inflorescence.

**radial**. Structures coming from a central point, like the spokes of a wheel.

**ray flower**. In the Asteraceae, flower with petals fused into a short tube with a single elongated strap-like petal.

**reflexed**. Bent or curved downward, backward, or outward.

**retuse**. Blunted with a notch.

**rhizome**. A horizontal, underground stem.

**riparian**. Pertaining to the environment adjacent to streams.

**root**. Portion of plant axis lacking nodes and leaves, usually underground; anchors plant and absorbs nutrients and water.

**rosette**. Cluster of leaves at ground level, usually in a circle.

**runner**. Stolon; elongated stem creeping along the ground.

**sagittate**. Arrowhead-shaped.

**samara**. Dry, winged fruit, not opening at maturity, as in maples.

**scabrous**. Slightly rough to the touch.

**scalloped**. Pattern of rounded teeth along a margin.

**scrub**. Shrub-dominated vegetation type.

**seed**. Structure formed by the maturation of a fertilized ovule in seed plants, typically consisting of a plant embryo, endosperm, and seed coat.

**sepal**. Part of the calyx, usually green and leaf-like.

**serrated**. Toothed along the edge, saw-like, with sharp teeth pointing forward.

**sessile**. Attached directly, without a supporting stalk, as a leaf without a petiole.

**sheath**. Tubular covering, as in the leaf base of a grass surrounding the stem.

**shrub**. Perennial woody plant, typically with several stems arising from the ground or shortly aboveground.

**shrub steppe**. Steppe vegetation, dominated with grasses but with a significant shrub component.

**silicle**. A short, broad silique.

**silique**. The dry seedpod of the Brassicaceae, usually more than twice as long as wide, with the two halves separating to release the seeds.

**simple**. Composed of one part, undivided.

**spathe**. Sheath-like bract.

**spatulate**. Spoon- or spatula-shaped.

**spike**. An unbranched, elongated inflorescence with flowers maturing from the bottom upward.

**spikelet**. A small or secondary spike; the ultimate flower cluster of grasses and sedges.

**spine**. Stiff, sharp-pointed outgrowth; a modified leaf or stipule.

**spreading**. Held outward from point of attachment.

**stamen**. Male reproductive structure, usually composed of the filament and anther.

**stem**. The central support of a plant bearing nodes, leaves, and buds, usually aboveground.

**stipule**. Small wing-like, leaf-like structure.

**stolon**. Runner; elongated stem creeping along the ground, often rooting at the nodes when contacting the ground.

**subtend**. Below and close to, often appearing to support or enfold, as a bract below an inflorescence.

**teeth**. Alternating projections and indentations on the margin.

**tendril**. Slender twining or coiling structure, used for support.

**tepal**. Perianth not differentiated into sepals or petals.

**terminal**. At the tip or end.

**thorn**. Stiff, pointed, woody modified stem, often used as general term for similar-appearing structures.

**throat**. The expanded opening of flowers with fused sepals or petals.

**tiller**. Basal or underground shoot that is more or less erect, usually referring to grasses.

**toothed**. Having teeth.

**tree**. Perennial woody plant, usually with a single trunk or stem.

**tube**. Fused sepals or petals forming a cylindrical structure.

**tuber**. Thickened portion of a rhizome bearing nodes and buds.

**tuft**. Cluster of short-stemmed leaves and flowers growing from a common point.

**twig**. The terminal, outer portion of a stem or branch, constituting one to several years of growth.

**umbel**. A flat-topped or convex inflorescence with the pedicels coming from a common point, like the ribs of an umbrella.

**umbellate**. In umbels; umbel-like.

**unarmed**. Lacking spines, thorns, or prickles.

**vegetative**. Nonfloral parts of a plant; reproduction by means other than seeds.

**vein**. Vessels by which water and nutrients are transported.

**vernal**. Pertaining to spring.

**vine**. Trailing or climbing plant whose stem requires external support.

**whorled**. A ring of three or more similar structures originating from a node or common point.

**wing**. Thin, flat extension of a surface or edge.

# Index

# About the Authors

**Mark Turner** has more than 30 years of experience photographing garden and native plants for books and magazines. He brings the eye of an artist together with the mind of a botanist to create clear, high-content photographs that enable viewers to learn about and understand the characteristics of the plants he photographs. Mark is a board member of the Washington Native Plant Society and maintains the Pacific Northwest Wildflowers website. He is also a well-regarded speaker on the garden club and native plant circuit and gives workshops on both plants and photography.

After an earlier education in arts and sciences, **Sami Gray** returned to academia to pursue graduate work in botany at Oregon State University. She has worked as a botany research assistant (field and office), collected native seeds, operated a small native plant nursery and landscaping business, and taught workshops on native plants, as well as blogging and providing education on plant-related topics online. Sami is the creator and principal administrator of PNW Plant Geeks, a Facebook group for advanced gardeners and plant professionals.